EDUCATING FAITH

EDUCATING FAITH

An Approach to Christian Formation

Joyce E. Bellous

TALL PINE PRESS
Edmonton, Alberta

Educating Faith
Copyright © 2006 Joyce E. Bellous
All rights reserved.

3rd Edition published 2015 by Tall Pine Press
94 - 11215 Jasper Avenue, Edmonton, AB T5K 0L5, Canada
Web: www.tallpinepress.com   E-mail: tallpinepress@gmail.com

First published by Clements, Toronto, ON, 2006.

Unless otherwisenoted, all Scripture quotations are from the Holy
Bible, New International Version. Copyright © 1973, 1979, 1984 by
the International Bible Society. Inclusive language edition 1995, 1996.
Used by permission of Hodder & Stoughton, a member of the Hodder
Headline Group. All rights reserved.

Library and Archives Canada Cataloguing in Publication Data

Bellous, Joyce Edith, 1948-
    Educating faith : an approach to Christian formation /
Joyce E. Bellous.

Includes bibliographical references and index.
ISBN 978-0-9810149-2-0

    1. Faith development. 2. Spiritual formation. I. Title.

BT771.3.B44 2006   234'.23   C2005-905068-3

CONTENTS

PREFACE

This book is for people interested in religious education. As I was writing, I had three groups in mind that make up my audience. The first group is teachers. Unlike other subjects, educational theory and practice is comfortable in secular and religious worlds because good teaching is a human problem, not just a religious one. While I teach from a Christian point of view, I believe every educator wants to get better at helping people learn. Good theory and effective practice cross-fertilize secular and religious classrooms since an art of learning is needed in both places. This book discusses theories that shaped and distorted education; teachers recognize these theories and have an interest in thinking about them. I wrote with that sort of dialogue in mind, even though my main interest is with Christian spiritual formation.

A second group I had in mind are students required to read this book. I know it can be frustrating to read assigned books you are not sure will benefit you except by fulfilling course requirements. This book might surprise you. I wanted it to speak directly to personal experience. As you read, I invite you to consider your own spiritual identity and its potential to provide you with resources for the rest of your life. Read with a question in mind, one that bothers you about spirituality or about faith. See what insights you get.

A third group of readers are practitioners in the church—pastors and teachers. In church, there are two primary learning goals—

one is to become a member and the other is learning how to be a member once you are one. Both learning goals need an education in faith. My bias is that, while it is essential to develop personal faith in a healthy way, good education is given less than adequate attention from church leaders. I think church life could improve its potential to live up to God's offer of salvation though Jesus Christ if people took education seriously. I say this because faith must be learned (or formed) even though it is a free gift.

This book is a way of thinking about education that welcomes personal involvement in faith formation so that, even as leaders, you enhance your maturity at the same time as you help others. Educational change is always like that: we are drawn to those who know how to be what they teach others to become. Observing a leader's maturity is contagious; wisdom is compellingly attractive. It is the best advertisement for an education in faith.

While it is about religious education, this book exchanges the term religious education for another one I believe is timely. I use the expression faith education not religious education. The shift is important in a variety of settings, for different reasons. I make a substitution because of the perspective I take on teaching religion—I focus on its products—faith and the worldview that frames personal faith. Before we start to teach them, learners have a personal worldview that is under construction (although they may think it is fully formed or finished). Teachers want learners to be aware of the worldview that shapes their experience and was shaped by it. Faith education is precisely what it says: teachers enable learners to realize what they put faith in and help them assess whether that is where they want to continue putting faith.

As I observe his approach, this is what Jesus did. Following him, I want people to be aware of the faith they hold and that holds them. Faith education encourages people to be reflective and attentive as they exercise faith everyday. It also aims to enhance membership in a religious tradition but does so by helping people reflect on the worldviews they have already constructed out of their personal experience—worldviews they inevitably bring to church or to class. If it is effective, education focuses effort on enhancing every learner's faith, particularly by helping them to observe and understand it.

In addition, faith education describes best practice for those who teach religion in settings outside the church. For a long time, religious educators quibbled over whether they teach people about religion or teach them to be religious. Controversy fails to capture the influence teachers have over learners whether or not they try to reproduce their own perspectives in the young. It also fails to acknowledge resistance learners exercise in refusing to emulate them, even when teachers (covertly or overtly) expect them to do so. Learners are different from their teachers—experientially, culturally and in terms of their needs.

For example, I am dismayed when teachers or professors think their goal is to rid the young of religious naiveté (without discovering first whether they are naïve) and do so by harassing simple belief. Faith education approaches simple belief with a different intention: it aims to help people mature in faith by realizing they do not abandon Christianity or Christ in growing up. Rather, it is by following Jesus that people gain courage to leave behind inadequate understandings of what being his disciple means. In short, faith education involves a movement from naiveté to critical reflection on simple faith, but goes beyond being distant from and critical of it to a second naiveté, in which people come to know faith in a new way. That is, first we believe, then we see what we believe and finally we realize our need for belief because we are limited, frail, mortal humanity.

I make two further claims about the approach in this book. Faith education is spiritual education plus Christian (or other religious) education that focuses on becoming a fully articulate member of a given faith community. Education in a religious community works best when it is built on a particular foundation. That foundation, spiritual education, can be taught in daycare centres, home-schools, school classrooms, or church communities. My second claim is related to the first: spiritual education is necessary for those who hope to raise a generation capable of meeting the demands of modern living. The spiritual dimension was disregarded by modern culture, even in church; religious and secular communities are impoverished due to its neglect. As I consider what I propose in this book, I realize Western Christianity infuses every word I say. Yet I claim that all religious educators want to be effective in teaching people to reflect on their worldviews so as to hold them more responsibly; faith education is a way to accomplish that aim. But Christianity influences my views so deeply I can't be certain faith education applies to different religious traditions without hearing from other people, so I welcome that exchange.

Although this book describes faith education for adults, the first two chapters begin with children's education and the young are referred to throughout for two reasons. The first is that children's well-being indicates a society's overall health. If they are well cared for, it is because society sees and carries out its social responsibility for generating a good future for all members regardless of their capacity to contribute directly at the time. The second reason is that adults are never far away from childhood questions and seldom surpass the depth of insight children have about God. Adults retain spiritual understanding they had when we were young, which needs to be mature rather than thrown away. Spiritual education reconciles but does not reject what we learned as children. I do not say this to convey that adults are more important than children, but to say childhood and adulthood are linked and cannot be divorced, as I will show in chapter two.

In the first chapter, I summarize human spirituality as a starting point for explaining faith education and outline human spirituality by describing its formation. Then I explain spirituality by pointing out how its central practice, spiritual conversation, actually works. A developed capacity to converse about what matters to them is something children are good at, if given an opportunity. If we listen, we learn from children how to teach them. They need teachers to provide an environment in which it is possible to say what they think about themselves, their worries, hopes and fears as well as what they think about God. Adults need this kind of environment as well. Spiritual conversation prepares people for Christian education by allowing people to ask and pursue their own real questions.

The second chapter argues for saving the spiritual environment. If we want to engage in spiritual conversation, it is only safe to do so in an environment that welcomes inquiry. There are five activities outlined in this chapter that help create the environment for spirituality to thrive: including, attending, embracing, releasing and remaining. As an activity, including is hospitality offered to unique and common attributes of every child in a group. Attending justly distributes attention so that children can establish themselves meaningfully with other people. Embracing refers to appropriate ministrations of presence so that children learn to be relational. Releasing refers to the timely regard for enabling children to learn on their own so they experience the satisfaction of being productive and come to see that spirituality needs work. The fifth activity of remaining refers to the faithful constancy of 'being there', of dependable availability, as well as to integrity—staying faithful to one's own identity and the process of its growth and maturity. To remain faithful is to become wise. By carrying out these five activities—including, attending, embracing, releasing, remaining— adults create an environment that fosters spiritual growth and they also grow towards human maturity.

The fifth activity, remaining in the right way and for the right reason, is central to a life of faith. These five activities culminate in a capacity to be authentic and faithful—to remain, so that our children and communities benefit from strength offered through participation that can be counted on. All the following chapters in the book, three to ten, explore and explain what it takes for someone to learn how to remain faithful. It is only when we have the courage to remain faithful that we flourish as adults. But our culture does not know how to be authentic and faithful at the same time, so the book addresses the complexity implied in this dual human task.

To explain being faithful, the third chapter begins by outlining aspects of faith and by contrasting it with terms such as religion and spirituality. The chapter proposes that faith is a universal attitude. Since exercising faith is part of what it means to be human, the chapter argues that every one has a concept for God, regardless of their religious upbringing. In order for us to mature, our concepts must grow up. Addressing our God concepts through faith education encourages us to grow up because God concepts have a unique position in the mythology of mental life. God concepts are transitional objects that cannot be made to disappear but are intimately linked to self-perceptions; as a consequence, concepts of God fundamentally influence self-concepts. Chapter three proposes that mature people reconcile their worldviews with communal concepts for God through personal lifelong learning. While remaining authentically vital, personal worldviews benefit from communal, formal ideas of God. The chapter establishes essential conditions for securing links between personal and formal concepts of God.

While faith is universal, the outcome of faith produces a worldview in which God concepts and self-concepts are in relationship. Chapter four presents a troubling aspect of that relationship by asking whether we can love God and ourselves at the same time. As faith is formed during childhood, we inevitably get an image of ourselves along with concepts of God and the world. The value we place on self-image is referred to as self-esteem. The term is useful for the purposes of this book because it has been employed historically in Christian literature to name a tendency that has not always been admired or seen as something people should pursue. In the chapter, I recount a history of the idea of self-esteem to reveal the struggle believers have when they try to think christianly about themselves. The tension within self-esteem complicates our attempts to love ourselves. Yet the freedom to regard ourselves compassionately is foundational to being mature. The aim of faith education rests on getting a fresh look at ourselves so we can learn to pay attention to what we are doing and becoming without hating ourselves or harming other people. This chapter explains an art of self-regard that is capable of sustaining a healthy sense of self, as groundwork for understanding other people.

Chapter five summarizes faith education up to this point by stating its central purpose and describing its four main aims. As already mentioned, it is a design for personal lifelong learning and focuses attention on providing an environment in which learners gain knowledge and understanding about God, other people and themselves by beginning with self-understanding. Self-understanding is secured through the practice of self-observation. The chapter situates a call for self-observation in a social context that disdained spirituality and focused instead on other apparently pressing global concerns. Atheistic Existentialism is one of those global phenomena that eclipsed spirituality and religion, in particular during the twentieth century. In the West, atheism was presented as the most worthy worldview for reasonable people to adopt. This chapter counters that prejudice and asserts that the natural history of God is reproduced in every life whether or not a child experiences a religious tradition. The chapter summarizes the formation of God concepts in children and argues for the freedom to be religious and spiritual as a fundamental human right.

On the basis of one to five, chapters six through nine identify problems believers engage as they grow up into the fullness of God. I use the word in a specific way: problems are complex, many-sided issues that are not solved so much as they solve us by explaining us to ourselves and to other people. These problems cannot be avoided in life; they are addressed effectively or ineffectively—faced or ignored—but if we ignore them, they wreck our lives. As we engage these human problems intelligently, they help us gain wisdom. The problems discussed in this book are the following: overcoming cultural disenchantment with maturity, linking faith with reason, addressing inevitable opposition to personal happiness, and learning empathy. To link reason and faith adequately, face opposition wisely and exercise empathy fully provides a believer with courage to grow up into the fullness of Christ.

To establish the need for faith education, chapter six counters a cultural tendency to prize youth and disdain maturity by revealing a twentieth century prejudice against God. This chapter discusses the influence of Sigmund Freud, who persuaded the twentieth century that growing up only takes place if we reject God. I continually meet people (secular and religious) whose views on religion are utterly Freudian, if they only knew it. His influence is impossible to overestimate. This book addresses his influence so we can move forward in helping people grow up wisely, but he was not entirely wrong in his criticism of religion and of education. He said education must be moved by reality. In this I believe he is right, but his view of reality omits everything that makes belief in God credible. He was biased against religion for reasons from his personal history—his is a story of disappointment. Yet in his rejection of God, he was unable to eradicate a human need for ritual. He discovered an important truth about ritual. He saw ritual behaviour as the human attempt to solve a dilemma by carrying out a specific action, or actions, repetitiously.

As a consequence of his insight, he generalized about ritual and criticized religious ritual, calling it empty repetition, yet he relied on ritual to the end of his days. In examining his polemic against religious education, he helps us see what can go wrong with religion—bad religion hurts people—but he also reveals the weakness of his own assertions. He did not perceive the sacred in religious ritual. Christian faith invests ritual with Presence because God shows up in it. It is a human response to a need for God. Ritual is a request made in faith; God answers a cry for help. Understanding the relationship between faithful action and God's response is the heart of faith. Whether ritual is prayer, Baptism, Communion (Eucharist), or action emanating from Christian virtue, its quality and kind is learned through experience, in community. This chapter addresses the complexity of that relationship. Freud's inability to perceive God, to feel God in his being, focuses attention on human helplessness and our absolute need for God's willingness to be present. Chapter six argues that a Christian concept of reality unites spiritual and material aspects of experience and provides an education for reality that includes both dimensions. Faith education secures the faithful in their encounters with God and in their longing for consolation and protection—two needs Freud never outgrew. In describing faith education, this chapter establishes a relationship between reality and ritual that allows faith to grow up.

Chapter seven outlines the tension inherent between thinking rationally and believing faithfully. Faith education proceeds on the following model: establish memory (naiveté, simple faith), build reason (critical distance from simple faith) and nurture insight (second naiveté). The transmission of faith through education is not a detriment to rationality, as Freud thought, but is necessary for the future of reason. Without a foundation in memory, reason has nowhere to erect its building materials. A mind without memory is inconceivable; a mind without trained memory is a cluttered parking lot—not a solid, stable foundation on which reason may be built. Freud incited the West to dismiss its foundation in memory and to emphasize reason alone. The chapter proposes that religious memory is as good as any other foundation and has advantages, *contra* Freud and much of what passed as educational wisdom in the twentieth century. The chapter argues that memory plus reason produces insight: The marriage of memory and reason requires personal spiritual work, i.e., self-observation of a particular kind that produces the offspring of insight. Through an art of self-observation, incorporating reason at the right time, we are able to make faithful use of ordinary experience and let our concept of God grow up.

Chapter eight pursues the idea of exercising freedom as we learn to grow up in faith. The chapter describes the problem of opposition that challenges faith's capacity to enjoy freedom in Christ. Opposition is broader than the idea of conflict but is linked to it. In order to grow up, the faithful must find adequate ways to face opposition and the suffering that comes along with it. Opposition is understood as an event or action that threatens personal happiness. The chapter outlines the tension between opposition and freedom by describing two types of freedom: liberation as a one-time event and practices of freedom that are learned after someone is liberated or saved. These two types of freedom are exemplified in scripture. Freedom in both senses is secured through facing opposition of various kinds. To explain opposition fully, the agonistic culture of biblical eras provides a framework for thinking that informs our current struggles as well. Life inevitably presents us with opposition. Opposition threatens to undo us. Yet without opposition there is no growth. The chapter aims to elaborate and relieve the tensions between opposition and insight. In establishing that relationship, examples from David and Jesus show us how opposition is useful for producing insight for life.

Chapter nine summarizes the central role of empathy as the fruit of faith education by describing conceptual and practical relationships among empathy, anxiety and guilt. Empathy is a mature response to the problem of opposition, enabling renewal and providing resources for maturity by permitting us to face problems that are inescapable in human experience. Empathy offers healing for guilt and anxiety. It is an outcome of faith education that moves lifelong learning in a healthy direction. The chapter establishes that skill in empathy begins with an infant's adeptness at affect attunement with its mother (usually) and a child's know-how for perspective-taking with other people. The book comes full circle— from childhood and back again to show that what we learn when we are young is reconciled by maturity. The chapter proposes that empathy can be learned by facing the problem of opposition and that scripture provides us with superb models for empathy, most poignantly through the example of Christ. Jesus faced opposition continuously. His witness and testimony shape our responses to life and to suffering by letting us see how empathy works and by helping us realize that, in sending Christ, God empathizes with us.

In conclusion, chapter ten emphasizes the role of the heart in the life of faith. A theme in all the chapters positions the heart as the central location for personal lifelong learning. The heart, from a biblical perspective, unites willing, thinking, feeling and acting so that a faithful person is able to do what he or she longs to do for love of God. The final chapter outlines theological reflection based on the work of French sociologist Pierre Bourdieu and argues for theological reflection that links personal faith to communal faith. The chapter suggests that, in order for the faithful to learn what is implied in growing up, theological reflection must increase in vitality in churches and seminaries as a primary way for addressing the problems of living. Leaders must be able to teach people how to reframe their worldviews using theological ideas to produce insight that enables them to mature in the faith. Critically informed theological reflection is invaluable in the project of growing up.

I want to thank people who helped me along the way. Dorothy Pinnock read a draft and made helpful comments that I have applied to all my writing. Dr Lois Tupper's compassionate and kind support was balanced with sharp insight and intelligent questions that improved the text, in particular by forcing me to say what I meant by the word faith. Stuart Harsevoort carefully read the manuscript and made useful comments. Karen Elliott and I enjoyed many conversations that helped shape my perspective as I wrote. I want to thank Buff Cox for her encouragement and wisdom; she was central to getting me through to the end of the project.

Finally, the book itself is dedicated to my husband, Ken—a life-long love, for life-long learning.

Other conversations over the years influenced the book and for these I am grateful. My greatest concern in writing was to enable believers to get a fresh glimpse of faith's power to transform experience into maturity and faithfulness. I continue to be impressed by the human longing for faithfulness, sometimes potently portrayed in popular films made by people who may have no insight into a Christian cure for diseases associated with anxiety and guilt. As human beings, we long to be with people we can count on for support and permanent affection. We long for safe houses where we are loved despite ourselves. If we learn to be faithful to one great love, the love of God, we can bring what we learn through this relationship to life in general. Of this I am comfortably certain. But faithfulness is hard work. My prayer is that this book will offer power and hope to those who long to love God more than any other love, and love their brothers and sisters with affection and kindness, as they learn to love themselves compassionately.

1

SPIRITUALITY AND SPIRITUAL EDUCATION

"We have much to say about this, but it is hard to explain because you are slow to learn. In fact, though by this time you ought to be teachers, you need someone to teach you the elementary truths of God's word all over again. You need milk, not solid food! Anyone who lives on milk, being still an infant, is not acquainted with the teaching about righteousness" (Hebrews 5:11-13).

"Therefore, I urge you, brothers and sisters, in view of God's mercy, to offer your bodies as living sacrifices, holy and pleasing to God—this is your spiritual act of worship. Do not conform any longer to the pattern of this world, but be transformed by the renewing of your mind. Then you will be able to test and approve what God's will is— his good, pleasing and perfect will" (Romans 12:1-2).

RECOVERING THE WAY IT IS

Maggie wanted to talk about God. I have been a Christian for a long time and am slowly learning she is not unusual. Maggie (not her real name) and I talked together for a half hour in a restaurant she runs. She told me she has cancer and conveyed how much each day means to her.

1

While she spoke easily about God, she had no interest in Church. She tried them all, as she put it. What can we learn from Maggie? She is spiritual but not religious. She represents many people who believe in God. They are aware they are spiritual, but do not connect spirituality with going to church. I argue in this book that we need to build Christian education on a spiritual foundation so we can invite people like Maggie into faith community. The spiritual education I will present can be taught in any place that we are trying to prepare people to meet the relational demands of modern living. In my own experience, I teach spiritual education to diverse groups of learners from seminary students to teachers of Daycare. I suggest that if Christian education were to develop on a spiritual foundation in churches Maggie visited, when she discovered she was sick she could have counted on a community of believers committed to standing by her as her friends in the same local church.

In this chapter, I introduce spiritual education and outline how spirituality forms in every person. Though I describe the human spirit using Western Christian perspectives, I believe becoming spiritual is a universal human reality. I begin with children's experience because the care we offer the young is a good indicator of the overall health of our communities and culture. Spirituality deals with personal experience accumulated and organized meaningfully from childhood. In response to the way we become spiritual, I argue that an adequate education reconciles with and does not reject what we learned when we were young. I define spirituality as *a sense of felt connection* that, under favourable conditions, permits and sustains human communication so that the capacity to talk together eventually develops into genuine dialogue, with the right sort of practice. Dialogue with God, inwardly with ourselves and outwardly with other people is a sign of Christian maturity, as well as the means for its achievement. My aim overall is to show that faith maturity is attractive and meets the deepest human longing we have, which is a need for meaning. I believe we need to feel our connection with God, ourselves, other people and the world if we are to enjoy lives that are meaningful.

Human spirituality is a framework for thinking about making life meaningful. As mentioned, I define it as *a sense of felt connection* that arises multi-dimensionally from birth. The dimensions of its formation are biological, cultural, sociological, neurological and psychological. These formative dimensions of the human spirit cohere in the psychological processes of object-relating. The central activity of object-relating is the making of meaning; spirituality is at the core of what it means to be a particular human being. Under favourable conditions, human spirituality expresses itself relationally and conversationally, and if it finds ways to flourish, strengthens personal identity. Whether or not conditions are favourable, the outcome of spiritual experience is the formation of a personal worldview each of us has by early adolescence. If the spirituality of children is neglected, they form an impoverished worldview, one that will not sustain them through the crises of ordinary living. In particular, they will not feel well-connected to God, the world, other people or themselves if their spiritual needs are unmet.

Spiritual poverty—an inadequate *sense of felt connection*—occurs because arriving at a worldview is not simply a personal project. Environments in which spirituality flourishes or fails matter a great deal. A spiritual environment is created and sustained in families of origin and the family is nested within larger social, cultural, gendered, racial and economic frameworks. In this century, culture, as one example, is more than a national issue; worldviews are shaped by what we experience globally, not merely nationally or in the family. It is common wisdom in the West that children should be kept from religious education until they are old enough to choose a faith for themselves. Public schools do not teach religion in North America, as they do elsewhere. The idea that religious education is not for children was proposed by Sigmund Freud, along with others, such as Emile Durkheim. They gave us bad advice but were widely influential. For example, Freud's influence was immense. From about 1920 onward, his views on religion attracted a following greater than any other thinker until he set the cultural agenda, creating a climate of opinion that was central to the imagination of that age, especially in North America.[1] Underlying the belief that children must wait and choose their religion is a serious error about how spirituality forms in the young and informs their perceptions of the world. Children are spiritual beings and begin to organize a spiritual world the moment they are born into social life.

Everyone needs an education in faith since every person is spiritual, whether or not there is comfort with religion or church, as Maggie's case demonstrates. If Christian education can learn to begin with spiritual education, it is possible to imagine a social world in which a fuller range of human experience enjoys freedom of expression, and further, to imagine solutions to a problem modern reformers such as Freud and Durkheim foresaw and tried to solve by excluding religious education from childhood. Durkheim, for example, was moved by a desire to hold the social world together so that young people would not resort to suicide. He saw religion as a divisive social influence and wanted moral education to be based on commitment to society as a whole. He did not foresee the intractability of human reliance on God. Freud made a similar mistake. His refusal to admit human need for God shaped a twentieth century determination to reject religious education. Both reformers chose science as their gods, so it is odd that science itself might be coming full circle to persuade us that belief in God is not something humanity can do without, for examples, as genetic research implies.

Despite his negative effects on religious education, Freud deserves a central place in the twentieth century given the stock of knowledge he added to our understanding of the human condition. Along with other modern reformers, he perceived social and personal problems that arose after the end of social unity provided by the Medieval Church. Many reformers (e.g., Hegel and his contemporaries) saw the fragmentation of the social world as debilitating for individuals and society. Modern reformers made various proposals for gluing together the social bits leftover in the aftermath of religion's social dominance. Freud's proposal was to grow up by rejecting God altogether. He disdained religious education of any kind because it prolonged a delusion that God is capable of offering protection and consolation. I believe we must reintroduce Christian religious education as a twenty-first century phenomena in public discourse so that this century can be more humane than was the previous one.

4

I make the case because everyone has spiritual needs. The human spirit is alive and well, living in human hearts, waiting for expression. It is an agency of communication that gets or fails to get support from its environment as it tries to comprehend its reliance on God. A human spirit awaits an education that will allow faith to survive and thrive. While spirituality and Christian education are not the same, they work together: Spiritual education develops faith—which is also the heart of what it means to be mature Christian believers.

THE HUMAN SPIRIT

Children provide evidence of what their spirituality is like. In conversation, they demonstrate readiness to use religious language to express their own spiritual insights. In one conversation, for example, Katie (age 6), told Rebecca Nye (a Cambridge University researcher into children's spirituality) that she recently became the owner of a Bible, but said she had never been inside a church. Rebecca asked her what she thought about God, and Katie replied: "I don't know yet, because I haven't read it very long."
Rebecca: "Did you know about God before you got your Bible?"
Katie: "No, not at all."
Rebecca noted that Katie had little coherent understanding of formal religion. However, early in the conversation she told Rebecca, when discussing a picture of a starry sky that: "You [i.e., Rebecca] couldn't even reach that high; no one can, except God."[2]
At another point in the conversation, when asked, "What sort of things could somebody know about themselves that nobody else could know," Katie replied: "God knows everything." And in another moment, reflecting on how we know things, the little girl identified her moral knowledge of when she's being good or bad as God-given. Katie also decided that other kinds of knowledge are beyond human understanding and may be special knowledge available to God, such as the mystery of "like...um...how we get alive."[3] In conversation with Rebecca, Katie conveyed knowledge of God and theological insight. When given opportunity, she revealed that she had been thinking about God. Nye asserts that, like Katie, most children in her research expressed some developed religious conceptualizations

they could employ in the task of making meaning, although she also points out that children are reluctant to stay with religious dialogue for very long.[4]

As they develop, children ask spiritual questions, whether or not their families adhere to a religious tradition. In asking their questions they unveil needs that are characteristic of all human beings, regardless of age or situation. Do we answer their questions? Research on church-based Christian education suggests that teachers neither hear nor satisfy the small voices that want to know how the world began, how it will end, and what their own lives signify. As well as asking important questions, children show that they care about each other and if given opportunity, demonstrate their capacity for empathy and inquiry, which are central to spiritual education.

I suggest that spiritual education is pre-requisite to Christian education. If we understood human spirituality we would be more effective in helping people love God and live faithful lives. Spiritual questions surface as we listen to people speak about their ultimate concerns. Exploring relationships between a human spirit and the Holy Spirit uncovers spirituality as the groundwork for an education in Christian faith. In relating the human spirit to the Holy Spirit, I make two claims about spiritual education:

• Every human being has a spiritual dimension that requires an education in faith.

• Christianity relies on human spirituality and situates the human spirit within a world of other spiritual realities.

The second claim proposes that religious and secular worldviews hold assumptions about the spiritual world. In the case of materialism, its worldview humiliates and silences spirituality because it assumes its unimportance, making it hard to live out the implications of being a spiritual person if materialism shapes the environment. In contrast to materialism, Christianity insists that we are spiritual creatures made in the image of God.

If we want to love God, we will seek to understand spiritual needs and motivation. To help in that search, believers can access social science research on spirituality and realize that research strengthens biblical insight. Christianity implies relatedness between human experience and environmental (cosmological) contexts that shape

6

the comprehension of spirituality. There is a Christian spiritual cosmology, not spelled out in the New Testament, but implicit in its pages. In what follows, I situate the human spirit within a New Testament cosmology and summarize five dimensions of spirituality: biological, cultural, social, neurological and psychological. Then I will demonstrate and describe how to have spiritual conversations. My aim is to say that human spirituality grounds education if we want to achieve best practice. I begin by situating spirituality in the New Testament to say Christian education is incomplete without a spiritual foundation.

The Human Spirit and the Holy Spirit

In the New Testament (NRSV) there are 338 references to the word spirit or spirits. Terms describing the human spirit, which also apply to the Holy Spirit, are life, wind, energy, receptivity, movement, action, presence and feeling. Functions of spirit are also named that cohere around its capacity as an agent of communication. The spirit indwells (Rom. 8:11), bears witness (Rom. 8:16), intercedes (Rom. 8:26), advocates (John 15:26), directs (Acts 11:12), prays (Eph. 6:18), interprets (1Cor. 2:13), reveals (1Tim 3:16), yearns (James 4:5), speaks (Rev. 2:11), strengthens (Rom 8:26), guides (Gal. 5:25), unifies (1Cor. 6:17), comforts (Acts 9:31), confirms truth (Rom. 9:1) and conveys Presence (Col. 2:5). Romans 8:27 says that God who searches our hearts knows the mind of the Spirit; the Spirit intercedes for the saints in accordance with God's will. The Holy Spirit connects humanity with God and is the agent of communication within the Holy Trinity.

In their capacity for communication, the human spirit and Holy Spirit are in significant relationship to one another and establish a link described in parental terms. The human spirit is an aspect of what it means to be a person and has a Father. Jesus distinguishes between those whose Father is the devil and those whose Father is God. (Matt. 10:20) In Christian cosmology, the human spirit is not simply good or neutral; it is connected to a Father. The outcome of that connection is evidenced through the life a person leads so that spirituality implies and shapes morality. In spirituality research, a link is also made between spirituality and morality. Our sense of connection to others as well as a feeling of obligation for the way we treat them are directed by spiritual experience and the assumptions and beliefs derived though that experience.

Christian cosmology, an interpretation of the universe as a whole, describes a spiritual kingdom that includes the following participants: the human spirit, the Holy Spirit[5], unclean spirits, demons, Your Father (the devil), Abba, Father (God), spirits of the prophets, spirits of the dead, foul spirits, elemental spirits of the world or the spirit of the world. It would seem that every person has a spirit but people can become unspiritual (1Cor. 2:14) i.e., dull to spiritual urgings. The spiritual kingdom is inhabited by angels (Heb. 1:14), messengers of God, and demons, unclean or evil spirits led by Satan. Christians are encouraged to stand against devilish schemes and recognize that our enemies are not human but spiritual. As scripture says: "For our struggle is not against flesh and blood, but against the rulers, against the authorities, against the spiritual forces of evil in the heavenly realms" (Eph. 6:12). The spiritual kingdom is multi-layered and scripture affirms the human spirit's strength to resist the enemy due to the power and Presence of God. As James 4:8b says: "Resist the devil, and he will flee from you. Come near to God and God will come near to you."

People are influenced spiritually by their interpretation of a cosmological order of things. Christian cosmology differs from secular and materialistic views, as well as from other religious perspectives. This is important to realize. Children need to see a big picture of the world so the full range of personal experience can find meaning within its range. They need to see how the world began and how it will end. They want to name their fears and know they are safe. They need a comprehensive story that enfolds them into its meaningful wholeness. This is not to say the Story we share with children explains every possible experience that life brings; it is to say they need to be embraced by a Story that affirms their significance to God and each other and that is large enough to nurture their trust in God, themselves and the world. Describing a cosmology of the human spirit from a Christian perspective is part of that Story and it resonates with social science research into the human spirit as well.

Dimensions of the Human Spirit

At the outset, I noted that spirituality is formed through biological, cultural, sociological, neurological and psychological processes. It is my belief that object relations theories unify these dimensions. At the heart of spiritual experience is gaze behaviour between mother and child that initiates the inter-subjective experience of infants, introducing them to the personal, spiritual and material worlds they inhabit for the rest of their lives. I will sketch below theory associated with five dimensions of spirituality's formation in childhood. In general,

- Biological dimensions of spirituality are an issue of human survival
- Culture transmits spiritual data to children through what are called memes
- Spirituality is shaped by a sociological need to fit into an environment and distinguish ourselves from it and there are patterned behaviours characteristic of spiritual experience
- Many researchers believe the brain is hard-wired for religion; particular genes are dedicated to enabling human beings to experience self-transcendence which is essential for realizing a connection to God, other people, the world and ourselves
- Object relations are at the heart of spirituality and are psychological in nature

I will expand on these dimensions but two points must be kept in mind. The research is active; new information continually finds its way into popular culture; secondly, while each dimension is discussed separately, they operate conjointly in people's experience.

The biological dimension forms a basis for spiritual awareness in that biology implies human beings are deeply connected. Long-term survival depends on acknowledging connections that make life bearable. Alister Hardy, a committed Darwinist, proposed the hypothesis that religious experience has evolved though the

9

process of natural selection because it has survival value to the individual.[6] What he called religious experience, researchers now call spirituality—i.e., a form of awareness, transcending everyday awareness, potentially present in all human beings, which has a positive function to enable individuals to survive in their natural environment. It is expressed as a feeling of absolute dependence which is not simply an emotion; it is more like a perception that there is 'Something There.' Spirituality forms at birth in part because we are hard-wired for it genetically and in part because we are born in bodies, cared for by other people. Spiritual awareness is expressed differently in various cultures, but is universal and implies a core assumption that all of life is connected: humanity is a team whether or not we play together well.

Culturally, on one theory, the spiritual is transmitted *via* memes, i.e., units of information that are passed on through the culture we inherit by a process of imitation. We imitate what we see other people doing and by doing so, we learn to be human in a particular way. Meme theory relies to some extent on gene theory and proposes an evolutionary connection between culture and biology. Richard Dawkins (1976) asserted the possibility of passing on memes that lead people to act in certain ways; to him, human culture can be seen as an inheritance system, analogous to the genetic system, but different from it. I want to be clear that memes are a theory; they are conceptually possible rather than literal entities, although as Dawkins notes in regard to the influence of his idea, meme theory is a successful meme itself.[7] Memes explain an observable tendency people have to learn certain patterns from one another and to change these patterns when they learn something different due to an introduction of new memes into the cultural system so that social learning is the mechanism of cultural inheritance.[8] We do not learn to be human as isolated individuals, but by trial and error.

On this view, "culture, like any other learned behaviour, provides a means of achieving the normal evolutionary goals of survival, reproduction and successful parenting [and to] the extent that environments tend to remain the same through time, [finds it] appropriate to act in similar ways"[9] over time. Even though the term meme is problematic, it is a useful shorthand way of saying that

10

culture is an evolutionary system involving inherited 'know-how' that depends on the existence of *a sense of felt connection* as the bedrock for all social learning. I suggest it is the active presence of *a sense of felt connection* that makes survival, reproduction and successful parenting possible. Memes are replicated among human beings by means of *a sense of felt connection* that is necessary for that transmission to be successful. Sociological, neurological and psychological dimensions of spiritual formation support the idea that human survival depends in part on spirituality.

But meme theory also points to a problem in Western spirituality. Hay and Nye explored the idea of memes (1998) and suggest that a cultural tendency in Western modernity stressed an individualistic meme at the expense of communal memes. Their argument is based on William Durham's book, *CoEvolution,* an interpretation of Dawkin's meme theory. Hay and Nye pointed out that a disposition for relational consciousness (what I call *a sense of felt connection*) can be assumed to have remained stable for most of history, due to its biological role in human survival. While gene-based natural selection occurs through consequences, (i.e., fit genes survive and replicate themselves), cultural selections operate differently. Meme imitation may be based on the consequences of specific behaviour as it becomes evident, but that is not the only way that meme replication happens.

As an example, say we make a decision to let gambling proliferate legally because we think its monetary proceeds (whether in terms of taxes or job creation) will benefit society. We wait to find out whether we were right based on the consequences of deciding to let gambling proliferate. Under certain conditions, the process could be like natural selection, but only if we were mechanical entities and not human. Unlike natural selection, cultural selection is influenced by social power. Small groups can impose their will on a mass of people even by non-violent means. For example, by broadly advertising their view and transmitting memes that are self-referential (in terms of the group's own good only), that small group may promote gambling by suggesting it's in society's best interest or at least that it's inevitable in human society (e.g., people will gamble whether it is legal or not, so we might as well legalize it.) In terms of meme theory, if an activity is made public and seen as generally acceptable, it gathers strength as a meme even if it is harmful to humanity as a whole. This is the point Hay and Nye make about meme theory generally.

They conclude by asserting that "relational consciousness," richly present in young children as their research shows, is "obscured, overlaid, or even repressed by socially constructed processes which contradict it."[10] They identify a meme that has overlaid relational consciousness as "modern individualist philosophy".[11] That is, individualism itself silences the processes that inform and strengthen human spirituality. Their point is important. In the chapter on the problem of opposition, I describe a worldview typical of strong group cultures (Douglas 1982) that have preserved the communal meme. Further, in his recent book, *The God Gene*, Dean Hamer traces Jewish experience as a unique example of collaboration between genes and memes (nature and nurture) that has allowed Jews to remain genetically as well as culturally consistent for centuries despite the Diaspora.[12] While Jewish experience (he also mentions Arabs in his analysis) is unique, strong group cultures (who do not prize individualistic memes) constitute a large percentage of the world's population. As a result, not only is radical individualism harmful to spirituality, it is a minority view historically and globally, yet it retains strong cultural impact as a modern Western meme.

Cultural insights into the human spirit are also informed by sociological research. For example, in Durkheim's study on suicide (1973;1979), his theory of *anomie* can be understood as a consequence of the absence of *a sense of felt connection*, i.e., impaired religious consciousness. His concern was with young people that felt no connection to society and killed themselves as a result. In response to this presenting problem, he proposed the end of religious education as a solution. He wanted moral education to hold appeal for non-religious as well as religious people; he sought a moral education capable of strengthening bonds of attachment people felt for society, bonds that would provide courage to choose life over suicide. He thought religion got in the way of loyalty to these social bonds because they couldn't hold those who chose not to be religious. Yet it is possible to see Nazism as an outcome of

12

his prescription for social cohesion based on absolute loyalty to the social bonds that came to have totalizing effects on German culture. The benefits spirituality offers to the problem of securing satisfying attachment to the social world inhere in its capacity to address two human longings simultaneously: a need to fit within one's group and a need to differentiate from it, a point central to spiritual education as I understand it.

Durkheim's prescription to terminate religious education was based on a perceived need to secure bonds of social attachment that did not require religious commitment. His view shaped education in North America although it did not hold sway in Britain where religious education continues to be required in what North Americans call public school. Yet Durkheim's solution raises a tension within spirituality research itself so that understanding his objection to religious education is necessary to establish what is meant by spiritual education. Research into spirituality divides over this point (see Figure 1). There are those who sever religion and

Figure 1

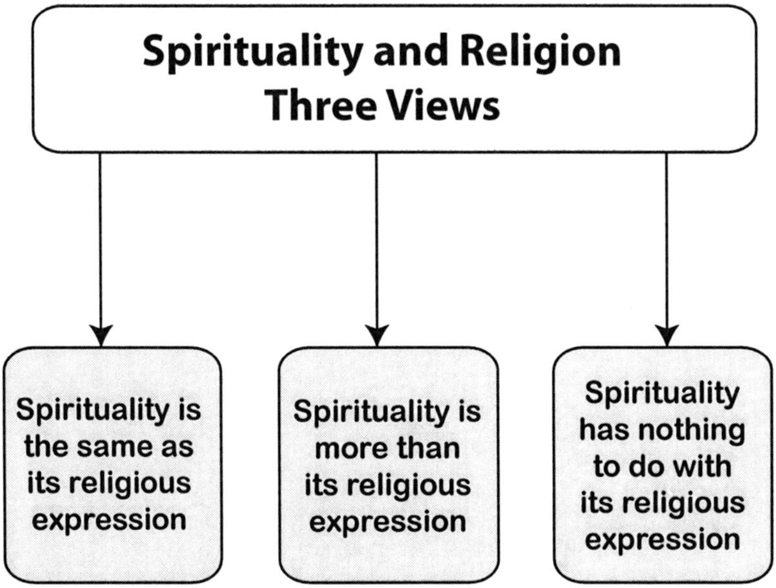

**Spirituality and Religion
Three Views**

Spirituality is the same as its religious expression

Spirituality is more than its religious expression

Spirituality has nothing to do with its religious expression

spirituality, albeit for different reasons.[13] There are those who assume spirituality and religion are the same.[14] A third group conceives spirituality on one hand as more than its religious expression, yet on the other as having intimate and important links to religion. The third group find an origin in William James's *Varieties of Religious Experience*. Following James, I take the view that spirituality is more than its religious expression, although it is most often expressed in religious language. If Christian education built its foundation on spiritual education, believers could perceive connection to humanity as a whole and also realize their uniqueness as Christians. Faith education acknowledges that human spirituality is present in those that have no religious background, as evidenced by Katie's story. But there is a strong caveat in proposing that spirituality is more than its religious expression. It is essential to note that since even non-religious spirituality uses God language, whenever and wherever religion is oppressed, suppressed or disdained, spirituality is threatened because it is a fragile aspect of the human condition, very sensitive to its environment, easily humiliated and silenced. Therefore, religious freedom is paramount to the vitality of human spirituality. In part this point is sociological, as I hope to show.

A sociological feeling of fit with one's environment is required for spirituality to thrive. Spirituality is conveyed through identifiable, observable patterns of behaviour that are common to it. Hay and Nye analyzed these patterns and their description is worth reading. Through Nye's research, they identified common patterns that are observable in the following tendencies:[15]

- Contexts: Childhood relations with God, others, the world and the self
- Conditions: expressed in language, play and games
- Processes: qualities of attentiveness that mark spiritual awareness
- Strategies: implicit as well as explicit used for expressing spirituality
- Consequences: states of being, outcomes when children are talking about ultimate concerns

14

Their research agrees that spirituality is more than its religious expression since they propose that even without formal religious education, children are aware of and able to converse about their perceptions of God.

They observed in children's expression of relational consciousness, an unusual level of consciousness or perceptiveness, relative to other passages of conversation spoken by that child. Relational consciousness (*a sense of felt connection*) is observed in conversations that convey how the child *related* to things, other people, the self, God. They see children's spirituality as a distinctive property of mental activity, profound and intricate enough to be termed consciousness and remarkable for its broad, relational inter- and intra-personal domain. Consciousness for them refers to something more than being alert and mentally attentive; it is like meta-cognition in that children are aware of the remarkable nature of their own mental activity in certain contexts, which Hay and Nye see as an apparently objective insight into children's subjective responses to an event or person, for example, that which fosters a new dimension of understanding, meaning, and experience. Relational consciousness is objective awareness of oneself as a subject of this depth of experience. It is an awareness important for encouraging children to perceive the world in relational terms.

For Hay and Nye, relational is not a term applied in a narrow sense; it is a capacity for connection that makes possible all aesthetic, scientific and religious experience. Spirituality grounds moral sensibility since it is a sense of connection to others and to the world. Awareness of connection is enhanced in that it is unusual when compared to other sections of children's conversation. Based on research they believe spiritual awareness is an identifiable sociological phenomenon:

- Spiritual awareness is intense
- It is a sense of being objectively aware of oneself as subject
- An aware of one's awareness, and of a reality that
- Is a feeling of objective presence; a perception that there is 'Something There'

15

felt connection
to self, others, the divine

- Experienced as a direct apprehension of that reality
- It is felt by those who have religious affiliations and those who have none
- Spiritual awareness is far-sighted, lifted above the myopia of individual concerns

In their view, spirituality links human beings to one another and grounds moral obligations that are necessary for holding the social world together. Yet there is also a limit to sociological descriptions of children's spirituality. Every child organizes relational consciousness in an authentic way so that a 'Spiritual Signature' shows up.[16] The uniqueness of this signature offers evidence of genetics and psychology, which address in spirituality the dual human longings to belong and to be unique that typify the struggle to differentiate from and fit in social community.

So far this analysis of the human spirit suggests a tension in spirituality due to nurture in the form of memes and sociology as opposed to the influence of nature. Meme theory and sociology emphasize a communal aspect of spirituality, though personal signatures were noted. Neurological theory, on the other hand, supports the presence in everyone of a predisposition for spirituality by asserting that it results from nature (while acknowledging the role of nurture in meme theory). Some genetic research addresses the tension by using gene theory to explain why we believe in God and meme theory to explain why we express belief in cultural ways (Hamer 2004), arguing for evidence that belief has a genetic[17] and religion a cultural source. The recent technological freedom to observe what happens as people engage in activity has permitted researchers to study an active brain as people pray, as far as brain functioning is concerned. The specific recorded feature of human spirituality that Christian and agnostic geneticists observe is a feature called self-transcendence.[18] They measure self-transcendence as a marker for spirituality; it has three characteristics:

- Self-forgetfulness: a normal focus on the self is replaced by focusing on others
- Transpersonal Identification: a perception of a connection to the world at large

16

• Mysticism: a perception of connection to supernatural entity, the 'Something There'

In analyzing these aspects of self-transcendence, spirituality as *a sense of felt connection* provides a unifying theme, distinguished in each case by its object of connection: first the object is other people; second, the object is the world as a whole; third, it is the supernatural. It is significant to note that Hay and Nye include a child's relation to the self as part of relational consciousness, as is also implied by spirituality as 'a sense of felt connection.' The relation to self is implicit in this view of self-transcendence, not directly named.

Genetic research supports other dimensional claims that spirituality offers evolutionary advantage by providing people with a sense of purpose, courage and a will to overcome hardship and loss. Due to its strengthening effects, spirituality contributes to survival and therefore its own replication in the genes of offspring. Hamer, for one, claims to have identified genes that are responsible for self-transcendence and make it possible. It is essential to point out that he, and other researchers like him, only identify the human side of spiritual experience and make no claim to prove God's existence or to exhaustively explain the spiritual relation between humanity and God. Yet they offer evidence for the potential of spirituality in every human being and show that monoamines (a particular gene group) play a key role in consciousness by linking objects and experience to emotions and values.[19] That is, genetic researchers provide evidence for other claims that spirituality is *a sense of felt connection* that grounds moral sensibility and is good for humanity as a whole. Although the title is misleading, Hamer's book, *The God Gene,* is worth reading since it lays important groundwork for understanding how genes influence human development. In summary, he asserts that genes are responsible for spirituality and memes are responsible for religion.

In terms of a fifth dimension of spirituality's formation in childhood, American psychoanalyst Ana-Maria Rizzuto studied Freud's object relations theory to show how object relating establishes *a sense of felt connection,* though she does not describe spirituality in this way. Freud wanted to know how people come to possess actual belief in the existence of God.[20] His theory of object relations answered the question from a psychological perspective. In general, object relations theories explain our need for others, since they are "theories about our relations to the 'objects'—people and things—to which we are attached and which give meaning to our lives."[21] In writing about object relations, Rizzuto's aim was to demonstrate how object relations theories illuminate the formation of God concepts. She asserted that religious education must negotiate the mental mythologies each person develops; my view is that we do that best through spiritual education. Her expression, 'God concept' represents a union of ideas, feelings and images that each person associates with God. These images, feelings and ideas are acquired early in life.[22] She asserts that everyone constructs a concept for God so there is no such thing as a human being without a God concept and she proposes that, in the course of development, each individual produces an idiosyncratic, highly personalized concept derived from object relations, evolving self-representations, and environmental systems of belief; and further, once formed, a God concept "cannot be made to disappear; it can only be repressed, transformed or used."[23]

Other research posits that God concepts form in a space carved out between mother and infant in their mutual relationship. The "early stage in this development is made possible by the mother's special capacity for making adaptation to the needs of her infant, thus allowing the infant the illusion that what the infant creates really exists."[24] God concepts form in a space between infant and mother that is its own reality; in that space, these meanings contribute to a child's sense of being real and living in a real world. This space of experiencing is located between two elements necessary for normal functioning: an inner psychic or soul reality—which we tend to situate in the mind, head, belly, heart or some other physical part of the body as a simple way to express its identity and explain its function—and also an external reality, the people and objects outside the psychophysical entity we call a human being. Experiencing takes place in the 'space' between the mother and child,[25] a place with the potential to house healthy illusions or unhealthy ones.

Rizzuto was interested in children's subjective experience, i.e., illusions, threads of fabric (images, feelings, ideas) woven together during the process of elaborating a concept for God. Her research is evidence for a correlation between a children's experience of parents and their view of God. It is as though God is ultimate parent viewed as highly capable of meeting needs, being loving, providing consolation and protection, or else as entirely incapable of providing these resources. Rizzuto is clear: God concepts remain entwined in a complex way with one's experience of parents, as Freud's case reveals[26] but the construction of a God concept is made with more elements than parental relations alone. Parents, teachers, significant others, as well as salient things (e.g., church buildings, television programs) are influential in constructing a child's expectation that God is dependable, good and kind, or not, even if the child has no formal religious training. To her, God concepts may be repressed or transformed but cannot go away, so that we *learn* through experience whether or not it is wise to trust God. And we learn this lesson by being with other people and through the experiences of object relating.

To sum up, the five dimensions that form spirituality are persuasive of the view that all human beings are spiritual and have spiritual needs that must be accounted for by education. As examples, people need to make meaning, celebrate, mark significant moments, bear witness to truths learned about life, tell their story, grieve, mourn, lament, connect with the past, make significant journeys, express themselves symbolically, seek purpose, ask ultimate questions, survive, flourish, experience longing and enjoy some satisfaction, relax, cope with life circumstances, be seen, be heard, have a name, be part of a larger community, organize experience meaningfully and maintain human dignity.[27] Spiritual need is satisfied in communities that permit people to talk about their ultimate concerns, raise authentic questions and persist in being what they are, given the pressure faced whenever we try to be ourselves while being with other people who are significant to us. A central educational activity that supports human spirituality and meets spiritual need is an engagement in spiritual conversations like those with Maggie and Katie. But what is educationally significant about spiritual conversation? How does it differ from other ways of talking together?

SPIRITUAL CONVERSATIONS

Jesus engaged in spiritual conversation of the sort I will explain. If we consider his encounters with Nicodemus, a Samaritan woman and Peter, to name a few, we can identify aspects of the way spiritual conversation works. Nicodemus, for example, came to Jesus with a vague inquiry, not really a question, but it was personally important, even if it seemed like a test. In response, Jesus raised the issue of being born again. Nicodemus reacted with incredulity. They were not on the same page about a second spiritual birth but their conversation opened up the possibility for a Jewish religious ruler to realize there might be something missing in his worldview. We are not told the outcome of the conversation in this passage (John 3:1-21) but we know that Nicodemus offered support for Jesus later on (John 7:50) and came to get the body after the crucifixion (John 19:39). During their initial conversation, something happened to spark an intimate connection between them, which Nicodemus followed up on later, at considerable personal risk.

With the Samaritan woman, Jesus initiated a conversation and during it, revealed to her his identity as the Messiah, which he had not yet revealed to his disciples. The two of them spoke about issues of ultimate concern. As a result, the woman returned to her village to tell people that he might be the Messiah. Her connection to Jesus, established and sustained by the conversation, enabled her to have the courage to name her own past and overcome shame that silenced and isolated her, if we take the point that she came to the village well at midday as an indication of her social status, or its lack (John 4: 1-42). A third example, a conversation with Peter, is also interesting. Jesus began by asking all the disciples a question: "Who do the crowds say that I am?" Peter responded with the insight that he was God's Messiah (Luke 9:18-20). Peter and the other disciples do not appear to have fully comprehended this flash of insight but a gap opened in their religious worldview to let Jesus demonstrate his identity through the transfiguration (Luke 9: 21-35).

In general, spiritual conversation allows two people (or more) to tell each other the truth as they understand it. Speaking the truth is central to a life of faith (Ephesians 4:25). Telling the truth is not the same as telling Truth. Our spiritual hoard of illusions is not occupied by Truth so much as it is a gathering place for meanings we accumulate through experience and over time. The disciples had a certain meaning for the word Messiah. Jesus did not always conform to their expectations of what a Messiah would accomplish. Yet in conversation, if we genuinely engage, we tell the truth in the sense that we give others our true and best reasons for believing or doing something and let them into the storehouse of meanings contained in our view of the world. Human understanding is made possible through talking together truthfully because through conversation we share actual meanings we use to construct our view of the world and to make sense of it. In popular culture, we have come to think the mere presence of an illusion in our worldview is evidence that it is 'my truth'. We have mistaken meaningful illusions for what is real. Illusions form the foundation of personal worldviews but it takes spiritual work to find out whether or not they convey what is real and therefore True.

When spiritual conversation encounters Christian education something good takes place. In talking together people convey to each other personal meanings for ideas, values, feelings and beliefs and set illusions beside Truth revealed in Jesus Christ. During conversation carried out in Christian community, deep calls to deep: hearts become acquainted with the Heart of God. With trust and friendship, conversation allows meanings we attach to words, values, feelings and beliefs to be transformed in the light of scripture. Our questions surface and we put them on the table without fearing rejection or disdain. One heart talks with others: speaking to people and communing with God in spiritual conversation lets us to move closer to Jesus Christ, with the help of the Holy Spirit, and illusions are revised by coming in touch with God who lives above our little human concepts.

In spiritual conversation two voices communicate. Spiritual conversation is public and private; internal and external. It is essential to understand the role inner conversation plays in revising meaning, which spiritual conversation makes possible. Internal conversation has a particular, important spiritual quality. For example, think of internal conversations you have when you are trying to work something out. As you wrestle with something or someone, you start an internal conversation that relies on aspects of real experience as a guide; e.g., you imagine a talk you might have if the other person was present. Notice the conversation: while it seems real and satisfying, it is imaginary. You invent yourself and the other: motives, words, outcomes. Yet you rely on real encounters you had with the person and your knowledge and observations of them. Your conversation is based on real experience or it wouldn't satisfy you. You don't simply invent the other (illusions are not delusions) but neither are you entirely accurate in portraying them. Accuracy fails because the only way to know others is to have a conversation in which you let them speak for themselves.

You need the other to know the other. All else is illusion in a sense referred to earlier in describing the contents of a child's mental mythology. In general, spiritual conversation relies on illusions that populate a spiritual space created by object-relating; a space filled with embodied concepts or transitional objects, as psychologists call them. The conversation with Katie is one example. She told Rebecca her illusions about God, illusions that are integrated thoughts/feelings/images. In a spiritual conversation, these illusions emerge because the environment is perceived as safe and receptive. Spiritual conversations are informed by illusions (not delusions) that have taken up residence in a spiritual space between inner and outer worlds of experience. The following is another example of spiritual conversation.

At one church, I took a turn once a month in the nursery. One Sunday I had a chance to converse with Alan (not his real name). Alan was 8 years old and lived with his mother and younger sister. His mother was a single parent. When I arrived Alan was already playing, as was his sister. When it came time for church, I asked Alan if he was going to the service. He said no but would go to Sunday School. His class met in the same large room the nursery used. During the worship service there were only two children in the nursery, Alan and his little sister, Janie. They began fighting over a toy. I walked over and sat down. He gave the toy to Janie without being asked and sat down beside me. At this point, his class had started and his sister went to her class. We had the following conversation:

> J: Alan are you going over to your class now?
> A: No. I don't want to go.
> J: You don't want to go? I thought you were going to your class. Alan, are you comfortable going to your class?
> A: What?
> J: John, is there someone in your class you don't like being with? Alan I am sorry, I called you John. I do that sometimes, don't I?
> A: Yup.
> J: Alan I know it is really frustrating when someone calls you by the wrong name. I am really sorry. I will try hard not to do that again. What if you do something like...what if you shake your finger at me and say: You called me by the wrong name! What if you do that, then I will remember.
>
> A: No, what if I do this? [He tilted his head back but I didn't understand what he meant]
> J: If you do what?
> A: Roll my eyes like this. [We both laughed]
> J: Oh I see. Okay, roll your eyes and I'll try to remember.
> J: Alan, is there someone in your class that makes you uncomfortable?
> A: Yes.
> J: Is it John? [There was persistent tension between John and Alan as long as I had been in the church. John was the only son of another single, female parent.]
> A: Yes. John makes me uncomfortable. He bugs me.
> J: How does he do that?
> A: He just says stuff and does stuff to me. He always does stuff to me. Janie always gets what I want. She always takes what I want.
> J: So John makes you feel uncomfortable by saying and doing things to you.
> A: I work at school. That's where I work. I like to work there. Here I like to stay with the babies. I like to be with the babies.

I had to think for a moment. I didn't want to force Alan to go to the class because I observed that he is bothered by the other kids. John was a strong leader; if John opposed him, Alan would have little honour in the group of males that made up the class.

> J: Well, last weekend I went somewhere and some people there made me uncomfortable.
> A: Someone made you uncomfortable, how did they do that?
> J: Well, this other women walked in the room and I was sitting down already. She stopped and looked at me and then didn't sit beside me. I felt embarrassed.
> A: Well, she didn't have to sit beside you. People don't have to sit beside you; they can sit anywhere they like. Why didn't she sit beside you?
> J: I don't really know. But I think it was because I looked so different from everybody else. I wasn't dressed the same. I didn't look like her, so she didn't want to sit with me.

> A: People aren't all the same. It's okay that people are not all the same. What would happen if everybody was the same? [Alan laughed when he said this.] If everybody was the same they would all have to be born of the same mom and dad. [We both laughed at this.]J: Yeah and if everybody was the same, we would all have to live in the same house. [More laughter]

Alan and I talked for quite a while. We had a hilarious time imagining things that people would have to do if we were all the same: live in the same house; eat the same food; go to the bathroom at the same time; say all the same things at the same time; ride the same bus at the same time. It was fun. At one point Alan began to imagine things I wasn't comfortable with: imagine if people were all cut up in pieces they would all have to be in the same pieces. I simply offered another possibility and refused to follow his lead in that direction. In playing the game we were playing, I was able to 'discipline' Alan by not following a lead that I could not in good conscience follow. That's when I used the bathroom example and we laughed over everyone flushing at the same time. This reference went some way in his direction, but didn't violate my own values. I didn't have to correct him overtly. I wanted to be true to myself as well as open to Alan. At this point someone brought a baby to the nursery:

> J: Alan, are you going to your class?
> A: No. I want to stay here with the babies; I always stay with the babies at church and I like it. I like to work hard at school but I like to stay with the babies here.

Alan's concept of work and his skill at empathy surprised me. These aspects of our conversation would help direct me in the future if I were his teacher. The point of spiritual conversation is to suggest a direction for personal and collaborative inquiry. Alan's idea that work is not what he does at church is shared by many people who merely attend church on Sunday mornings. His notion of spiritual work needed to grow up, but spiritual conversation permits education to be more than a lecture—than me telling him what to think.

Alan and I were not arguing; we were playing. In play, illusions in his worldview become evident. I was not simply trying to make him go to class; I wanted to understand him. A bond exists between us that matters to us both. I suggest we all need someone to know us well enough to 'get' what really matters to us. In spiritual conversation, someone recognizes our value and welcomes our voice, permitting us to speak authentically by making space for conversation to take place when two people want to converse. Recall that illusions are the basis for all science, art and religion; illusion is not delusion. It is the same in conversing with God: if our illusions are to grow up, God must speak to us.

SPACE FOR THE SPIRITUAL

In spiritual conversation, inner values and insights are heard and recognized by another. The audible conversation is fed by an inner one—like the internal type described above. Inner talk is populated by illusions we have accumulated through experience that form a worldview, i.e., the way we see the world as a whole. For the non-

25

religious and religious, a worldview is a personal response to the whole nature of things. It is systematic and reflective (though I do not say True), binding a person to certain inner ideals. In short, spirituality bridges objective and subjective experience (Figure 2) as an intermediate link between personal and material worlds, built from birth. In the space between inner and outer reality, illusions form and meaning is created. This third site is a relation—neither the self nor the world but influenced by both realities. It is the genesis of spiritual life; in it, object-relating leaves its traces. Spirituality is a mid-point reality between subjective and objective realities; e.g., what Martin Buber calls a relation, which he thought of as a spiritual connection. As he put it, "In the beginning is the relation—as a category of being, as readiness, as a form that reaches out to be filled..."[28] He identified a spiritual link between self and object by using childhood as an actual and metaphorical ground for describing subject/object relations, i.e., for his theory of object relating, although he did not use that term.

As a consequence of object relating, illusions form as a child experiences the self and the world; these illusions or transitional phenomena influence ongoing perceptions of everything. This intermediate space houses illusions and is an area of experiencing, "to which inner reality and external life both contribute," and which, in turn, acts back on one's perception and understanding

Figure 2

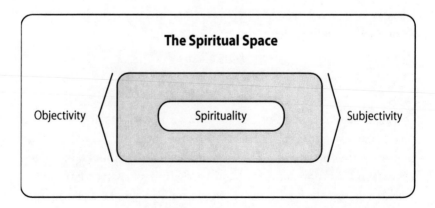

The Spiritual Space

Objectivity   Spirituality   Subjectivity

of outer and inner reality....[acting as] a stronghold created by the "perpetual human task of keeping inner and outer reality separate yet interrelated."[29] Spirituality integrates experience, forming embodied concepts people live by. Embodied, emotionally laden concepts (illusions) may shift their shape with changes in experience or be maintained as fortresses against change. Reflecting on new experience is spiritual work that can be repressed and its repression is strongly influenced by culture. When spirituality is repressed it may be substituted by attachment to food, sex, money and power as some examples, in our vain attempts to satisfy spiritual needs.

I want to be clear about what I mean by illusion since the word has cultural connotations that are misleading for my purposes. Illusions that populate the spiritual space are not false concepts. Illusion is not delusion. As mentioned, all art, science and religion depend on illusion; it is the bedrock of learning, since all learning is organizing experience. It is in the intermediate space between subjective and objective worlds that this organization happens. In making meaning from personal experience, we organize illusions into a worldview. Illusions are neither true nor false necessarily; they are idiosyncratic, useful organizing principles for ordinary living. They are not simply personal. Illusions are also culturally transmitted and are reinforced daily by dominant social and cultural beliefs.

Throughout life, we are called upon to test the organization of illusions (worldviews) that we use to make sense of the world. Illusions that flourish in the intermediate space between self and the world are called transitional phenomena, transitional objects of perception. They (feeling, image, idea) are the stuff of thinking; they are experience-rich and assumption-laden. These rich, laden illusions influence perception in terms of one's relation to God, other people, the world and the self, for example, in the value we attribute to other people's lives, to sex, money, food and power or to ideas about our own potential, possible success and well-being. In this spiritual space a worldview forms that gives meaning, direction and purpose to life (or fails to do so); it includes insights, values, beliefs, attitudes, emotions and behavioral dispositions.

People are more than material realities. (Figure 3) In addition to meaning we make of experience, spirituality is a dimension of identity formation that helps us sense how we are related to more than material realities and motivates us to work towards healthy community the moment we recognize our own humanity in others and sense that losses of humanity for them are losses of humanity for us and a loss of meaning for the whole world. Human beings experience something in them "that expresses and carries the continuity of living personhood...a sense of a 'real me' that lies behind the accumulation of events that constitutes each life from beginning to end, an entity that has been called a soul."[30] For spirituality to flourish, cultures must honour its expression.

In the West, spirituality is disdained. Particularly in North America, children learn early that if they talk freely about their spiritual experience, they will be ridiculed, humiliated and laughed at, even by adults. The fear of humiliation oppresses spirituality. Spiritual education is hospitable to a child's imagination. It welcomes conversation about what really matters. In contrast, spirituality research conveys that children want to talk about the following concerns:

- What is the world like?
- What happened at the beginning? What will happen at the end?
- How did rocks and trees come to be?
- What will I be able to do in the world?

Figure 3

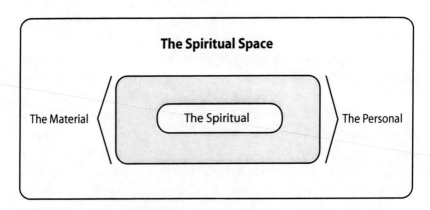

28

Shaped as we are by genes, memes and biology, we learn to tell a story based on illusions that inhabit a spiritual space that links us to the world and its objects. Spiritual work includes learning to hear the story we are telling ourselves and other people about the meaning we have made of life and allows us to ask ourselves whether it is the story we want to continue telling. If we encourage spirituality in children we let them sense their personal experience so they can hear that story eventually and realize

- What they think, feel, imagine
- The role imagination plays in forming thought-life
- The way they think about God, themselves, others, the future

Children need to relax with people that matter to them in order to consider the spiritual side of their experience. For spirituality to be vital we must give attention to spiritual needs.

If we listen to their ways of constructing meaning, i.e., the stories they tell, such as those told by Katie and Alan, we enhance their self-understanding. Spirituality as *a sense of felt connection* is strengthened between people, initially mother and child through gaze behavior; and on its basis, a child comes into being as a person. Children are material bodies, spiritual beings, personal identities and social players. To connect Christian education with spirituality we utilize spiritual conversation built on religious understanding, practices, texts, tradition, culture, stories, rituals, buildings and personnel in a particular tradition. Religion and spirituality are not the same but they overlap: religion is public and corporate; spirituality is its private and personal side. Spiritual identity derives from a cosmos that is held together by God. Our *felt* connection to God grounds moral obligation; spirituality is also a *felt* connection to neighbors and to the world; public religious experience depends on that sense of felt connection.

Christian education's best practice is informed spiritually and welcomes learners' insight and questions so they come to know God more fully, even as they are fully known. These questions are generated by current conceptions of what God is like and who Jesus is *to them*. As a result, learners immerse themselves in Biblical narratives and let illusions about life, God, themselves and other people mature through exposure to scripture. In what follows, I offer some suggestions as to questions that help us invite children into spiritual conversation.

SPIRITUAL QUESTIONS

As was the case with Katie and Rebecca, children respond to story, art and events in ways that open the door to their spiritual perception of the world. Teachers can access these insights by providing an environment in which it is safe and acceptable to raise spiritual questions such as those that follow:

- What is the character of this universe in which we dwell?
- What do you long for? Where and when is it?
- How is God involved in what is happening to you?
- Why do people hurt each other?
- Why do people help each other?
- Why do you hurt people?
- Why do you help people?
- Why do you hurt yourself?
- Why do you help yourself?
- Why do people hurt the Earth?
- Why do people help the Earth?
- What is beautiful to you?
- What terrifies you?
- What is Jesus like?
- What is prayer and how does it work?
- What is your body for?
- How do you experience meeting death?
- What makes an ordinary day pleasant for you?
- Draw a picture of God.
- Draw a picture of your family.
- How do you imagine Heaven?
- How do you imagine Hell?
- What are your favourite objects? Why do they matter to you?
- Where are your favourite places?
- Where are your frightening places?
- Describe a happy time or experience in your life.
- Draw a happy time or experience in your life.

- What does it mean to be a Spiritual person?
- What does it mean to be a religious person?
- What does it mean to be a good person?
- What helps people get along with each other?
- Who is your spiritual hero?
- What is this person like?
- What do you not want to be like?
- What do you hope will happen when you grow up?

In teaching children, we invite them to consider their views on these questions by offering an opportunity to respond linguistically or non-linguistically.[31] Spiritual conversation also emerges from casual conversation if a teacher is sensitive and attentive to statements children make about what really matters to them.

Responding non-linguistically, children draw pictures of families, God, Jesus, the Church, its members and then explain meanings they attach to the images. They may also use thinking maps to help convey what they already imagine.[32] Instead of drawing, mapping or organizing their thoughts visually, children can be invited to tell stories about these aspects of their lives. If teachers engage with these questions, it is my experience (and others I consult with about spiritual education) that children's insights are profound and surprising; even children who are two or three years old provide superb insights about God. Children can also be invited to complete ideas such as the following:

- Once, when I thought about God...
- I feel closest to God when...

Again, their insights are significant and provide opportunity for spiritual conversation so teachers can learn about the worldviews children construct out of everyday events.

In spiritual conversations, a teacher is not trying to correct the content children present, particularly if a question asks for the child's own experience primarily. Rather the teacher and child need to hear these answers so they come to understand each other better. As a teacher leads a session, the ideas/thoughts/feelings each child brings are expanded by exposure to scripture. However, non-linguistic representation is an opportunity to expand children's ideas by working collaboratively with a group. Together, ideas about

God are built on scripture and group insight. In this case, each child's view is not under correction but the whole group works toward understanding something more fully. The point here is to demonstrate to the child that their illusions, the concepts in their mental mythology about God, are not wrong so much as they are partial—we have part of the picture of God, not the whole picture; we need scripture and other people who also know God to help us complete that picture, as much as is possible this side of heaven. The awareness that human knowledge is partial is an important building block for a child's future: we must all realize knowing God is lifelong learning, accomplished personally and communally.

Adults also are invited into spiritual conversation and can be engaged by focusing on the questions listed above. In addition, the following scenario is useful for inviting adults into conversation about what matters to them. As they engage the scenario, they explore worldviews they constructed when they were young, and perhaps remain essentially unaware of, even though they are strongly influenced by them. In a group, I would first ask someone to read the scenario aloud and after the reading would ask them the question: *How would you console John?*

SCENARIO

John grew up in a Christian home. He had two sisters. John's parents were very involved in the local church. His father attended meetings most evenings. When John got his first bike, he asked his father to help him learn to ride it. He and his father were just going out the door, hand in hand, when a couple from the church stopped by. They wanted to talk. John's father let go of his hand and welcomed the couple with a friendly handshake. He invited them into the house.

As his father let go of his hand, John asked: "What about my bike?" in a voice loud enough for the couple to hear. His father told him to go to his room. Later that night he got all three children together and said that it was their Christian duty to help people in need. He was angrier than the children had ever seen him and he said he never wanted a child of his to be so selfish again.

Since the scenario doesn't explain everything about the role of its characters, those who respond to the question of how they might console John begin to express the way they perceive the world and why they might do so. During conversation, adults may recall and name events that have shaped the way they think and what they assume about the world, God, the Church, parents, parenting, as well as insights about themselves, whether or not they are still believers.   *I tend to resolve issues.*

It is important to realize offering the scenario to adults is educational, not psychological practice. While people remember emotionally-charged events (recall that illusions are feeling-laden), the emphasis is on becoming aware of assumptions and beliefs about those events and engaging in a conversation that helps people see what tends to happen if they live according to assumptions and beliefs they took on when they were young. As one outcome of the task, they can ask themselves whether they want to continue holding these assumptions or trade them in for something that is more consistent with values they now hold. Christian spiritual conversation aims at educating faith and encouraging faith maturity. In a non-judgmental environment, insights are gathered and questions asked that lead to learning and incite curiosity about scripture and the Christian faith—or at least to an explanation of why learners find Christianity or the Church so painful—an insight that may come to them for the first time.

Spiritual conversation builds toward the rich potential of dialogue, described by Paulo Freire in his important book, *Pedagogy of the Oppressed*. The worldview we formed when we were young influences our willingness and ability to dialogue. Dialogue is an encounter between people, mediated by the world they share, in order to understand the world together. It is life-giving, not the consumption and exchange of deposits of knowledge; neither is it hostile, polemical argument between people. To Freire, dialogue is an act of creation that cannot exist separately from love for God, others and the world. If I do not love the world, life, and other people, I cannot enter into dialogue. Dialogue cannot exist without humility; I cannot dialogue if I am elitist. It is an engagement in the common task of learning and acting. I cannot dialogue if I always project ignorance onto others and never

stop to listen

perceive my own or if I think of myself as a special, exclusive case. I must recognize myself in others. I cannot dialogue if I am afraid that my way of seeing the world will be displaced by another's view. In dialogue, I recognize my need for other people. Self-sufficiency is incompatible with dialogue.

Dialogue produces an encounter; it arises from attentiveness between two people in that both see the other as a real person with a past, present and future. In dialogue each person realizes that the other has existential problems that affect their understanding of the world. In dialogue, trust develops along with listening so that those involved gain a genuine concern for each other's welfare. Dialogue takes account of both parties as a bodily presence and requires an intense faith in people and in the power to make, remake, learn and unlearn, create and re-create our understanding of the world we try to speak about it together.

A dialogic person sees that knowledge is always partial and people are damaged in their humanity but is challenged by those insights and understands that a basic commitment in dialogue is to try to perceive and express each other's meaning. The goal of effective dialogue is not a mere human accomplishment; God gives the outcome. Founding itself on love, humility and faith, it builds relationships that nurture mutual trust; trusting others strengthens the trust we have in ourselves. Dialogue requires hope—can't exist without hopefulness; hope is rooted in our awareness of our incompleteness (our knowing only in part). Hopelessness is empty silence. Hope moves us beyond our illusions to search for what is worthy and expects something to come from our efforts.[33] Spiritual conversation is a humble beginning for dialogue, accessible to small children and adults. But before conversation becomes dialogue, our faith must grow up. Dialogue and immaturity are incompatible. In the next chapter I will explore the sort of environment that would make it possible for faith to grow up and for spiritual conversation to become genuine dialogue.

In summary, spirituality is an aspect of human experience that is inevitable because we are human; we are formed and limited by that reality. Spirituality is a process constructed biologically, culturally, sociologically, neurologically and psychologically. The product of spirituality is a personal worldview that operates over time to shape the way we see the world. It is a product that influences and directs other dimensions of life, motivating the story we tell ourselves about the world. Spirituality is *a sense of felt connection*: in embryo we are connected to our mothers and cut off from them as the umbilical cord is severed. It is as if that *sense of felt connection* is a metaphysical umbilical cord: we keep hold of one end and hope to connect the other end to something, someone we deem worthy of that attachment.

It is popular in secular contexts to talk about human spirituality. For example, in *Time Magazine*, October 25, 2004, a questionnaire to measure self-transcendence[34] was included in an article that also claims everyone is spiritual.[35] When I have used the questionnaire informally, I notice that some who see themselves as religious do not get a high score. I wonder whether its secular language fails to describe the sense of connection religious people feel towards God. The questionnaire tries so hard to avoid God language it may not capture the essence of religious experience, at least for those who see its language as an obstacle to expressing what they feel religiously.

It is fortunate that so many people are curious about spirituality. If churches were concerned about spiritual needs, they might link spirituality to Christian education more effectively. If we did this well, fewer people would have Maggie's resistance to being in church. More people would find a satisfying story to help address their deepest needs, one of which is to be in community with people who stand by them throughout life. In the next chapter I describe five activities that effective teachers practice in order to create the learning environment that welcomes spiritual expression and enables spiritual conversations to flourish.

2

SAVING A SPIRITUAL ENVIRONMENT

"Knowledge has two extremes which meet. One is the pure natural ignorance of the infant at birth. The other is reached by great minds which have passed through the entire range of human knowledge, only to find that they know nothing of the truth, and have come back to the same ignorance from which they started. This latter state is a wise ignorance which knows itself. Those who stand between these two extremes have put their natural ignorance behind them, but have not yet attained wise ignorance. They have a smattering of knowledge, and imagine that they understand almost everything. They are profoundly misguided, and can do great damage."[1]

HOPING FOR HEALTH

I f human spirituality is a fact of life and has characteristics named in the previous chapter, then the way we teach Christianity should be spiritually informed. In this chapter I suggest that in order for people to develop their capacity for genuine dialogue with others and God, they require help from an environment that encourages spirituality to survive and flourish. A healthy spiritual environment is created in the way adults carry out activities that shape and sustain that context. When children are raised in spiritually satisfying environments, their capacity to put faith in God, other people, and themselves is given its most promising foundation. In a healthy environment, spiritual conversation is not only possible, it is well practiced. Yet in my experience as a professor of Christian education, students report that spiritual conversations like those described in chapter one seldom take place in church. Why is that? Does life inside church echo secular values of public life? There are two main patterns that affect whether or not we are Christian *and* spiritual. The first is that secularism alters Christian culture when allowed to do so. The second pattern occurs if Christian culture privileges one way of being spiritual at the expense of other ways, so that its fullest Christian expression is excluded. I explore the second pattern in this chapter, and the first pattern, the hegemony of secularism, is addressed in chapters that follow.

When groups focus on one way of being spiritual, its religious practices dominate church culture. As a result, there is a way to be Anglican or Pentecostal that people see as a telltale identity sign. Educational practices echo the dominant personality, conveyed to members and expected from them, to the exclusion of opportunities to express difference. Children are especially at risk. Their spiritual personalities are affected adversely by a dominant practice, if they differ from it. Since they are dependent, they can't leave even though they feel like misfits. The issue raised here is essentially sociological: people need to feel they fit in an environment in order to sense that they belong to it, so that their faith can take root and grow.

In contrast to cultures that privilege one way of being religious, spiritual education, as the groundwork for Christian education, welcomes diversity. In its overall program, people are able to integrate and differentiate themselves within a community and recognize themselves, rather than feel estranged. Faith communities support spiritual personalities of members by letting diversity flourish within the legitimate broad strokes of the faith tradition. They take spiritual education seriously. Spirituality itself encourages inclusion since its sociology reveals a need for people to feel they fit in the environment in order to have courage to express spiritual needs and ask their own real questions.

38

SAVING A SPIRITUAL ENVIRONMENT

While spiritual education implies a method and content, it refers mostly to the way teachers teach, i.e., the way they know what to do in classrooms. To describe spiritual education more fully, I focus on its third aspect: knowing what to do in the classroom. As teachers focus attention on how to develop a classroom environment, they make it either possible or impossible for everyone in a group to feel they fit in. When I talk about environment, I am referring to complex, cumulative effects of social interactions that leave an impression on a dominant way of being; "environment is anything and everything—biological, physical, and intellectual—that [people don't] inherit as DNA."[2] Teachers shape classroom environments; to be effective, they work to ensure that the spiritual environment is healthy for every child through five activities that I want to spell out in this chapter.

The five activities are including, attending, embracing, releasing, and remaining. Including refers to the hospitality offered to personal differences so that each child shows up in the environmental landscape. With including, I introduce a framework for thinking about diversity based on spiritual personalities.

In brief, attending refers to just distributions of attention so that children establish their own being meaningfully. Embracing refers to appropriate ministrations of presence so that children learn to be relational. Releasing refers to the timely regard for enabling children to learn on their own so they experience the satisfaction of being productive and come to see that their spiritual lives need work.

Finally, the activity of remaining refers to the faithful constancy of 'being there', of dependable availability, as well as to integrity—staying faithful to one's own identity and the process of its growth to maturity. Without remaining, there is no wisdom. It is a mature activity expressed through a ministry of Presence—of showing up and being there for others and to ourselves. I will describe these five activities in this chapter but the theme of remaining underlies all the chapters that follow. I hope to show its centrality for creating Christian communities that are capable of meeting deep human needs. Remaining permits spirituality to flourish by encouraging spiritual conversation and dialogue and by staying present to lifelong implications of those conversations. By carrying out these five

activities—including, attending, embracing, releasing, remaining—
adults create an environment that fosters spiritual growth, and grow
toward human maturity themselves.

INCLUDING: A FOUNDATION FOR SHOWING UP

As I taught a university class on *Children and Spirituality,*
I noticed two students in particular. As part of the course, I
introduced two quite different teaching methods: PromiseLand
and Godly Play. Jenny (not her real name) is a Christian in her
twenties who grew up in the United Church of Canada, a composite
of Methodist, Presbyterian and Congregational churches that
joined to form a uniquely Canadian church. She had a positive
response to *PromiseLand*[3] and a negative reaction to *Godly Play.*[4]
She was immediately engaged as the *PromiseLand* lesson began
and she quickly moved to the front of the group during the singing,
dancing, music and action. She was comfortable in the small group
experience that followed this high energy introduction and spoke
freely when her turn came. The entire session caught and sustained
her attention. She felt no reservation about participating fully.

David (not his real name) is a Christian who grew up as a
Canadian Baptist, also in his twenties. He was quite reserved during
the *PromiseLand* experience. He described feeling interested in
observing the dancing, singing and excitement of others but did
not want to participate. He remained at the back of the room and
watched those who were comfortable being involved. He did not
want to be drawn into the action. Yet he was very much at ease with
Godly Play, enjoying its quiet wondering approach to the story as
well as the freedom to be left alone to think at his own pace. Jenny
on the other hand, commented that she kept wondering when *Godly
Play* would start to be fun.

The class discussed the implications of these different approaches
in light of our hope to create inclusive educational programs for
children. The question that arose is whether these two approaches
could become inclusive of all the spiritual personalities present. I
won't pursue that question except to say that research would be
helpful. These two anecdotes do not constitute research into the

question of inclusion, although they are instructive. As I result of my own curiosity, I asked Pastor Denise Peltomaki,[5] who presented *PromiseLand* to my group, and Jerome Berryman, author of *Godly Play*, whether their approaches could be inclusive. Both thought they could include all children in their purview.

In considering the resistance of my two students, I asked all the students in the class to complete a spiritual personality assessment written by Corinne Ware, adapted from the work of Urban T. Holmes. In filling out the self-assessment, Jenny and David identified very different spiritual personalities. David thought his spiritual personality was congruent with *Godly Play*, which he felt explained his comfort with it and his discomfort with *PromiseLand*. When Jenny evaluated her spiritual personality, and compared herself with her own church community, she realized for the first time the extent to which she did not fit in her church's worshipping culture. She observed that she, and others like her, chose to teach Sunday School rather than stay in the worship service. She now wondered if their choice was motivated by the discomfort of not fitting with the dominant way of being spiritual conveyed through worship. Yet she chose to teach as an adolescent. Children do not have her choice. As she reflected on her childhood, she recalled struggling to appease adults that did not perceive her need for fun as something they were obliged to take seriously.

As a consequence of these observations, I adapted a map that includes four spiritual personalities characteristic of Western Christianity, broadly understood. I suggest that teachers need to attend to the diversity represented by the map if they wish to include all learners in the heart of what it means to be a spiritual person. Being inclusive is not an easy task and requires careful planning aimed at formulating an overall pattern for the kinds of learners we want to encourage and sustain through programs we devise for spiritual education. At the heart of spiritual education is a commitment to be inclusive, even if the aim has complex requirements for the way we teach the young. Inclusion compels teachers to find ways to build an environment that welcomes all the children present, in terms of their spiritual personality.

Yet inclusion is only the beginning of creating learning communities that support and sustain children in their quest for spiritual meaning. There are some assumptions teachers share if they hope to offer spiritual education. These assumptions include the ideas that:

- Every human being has spiritual, personal and material needs
- The spiritual aspect of human being is acquired through ordinary human processes organized around object-relating
- Every human being desires meaning, love and work
- The self is a meaning-making activity
- A personal worldview is an outcome of spiritual work

These assumptions establish groundwork for spiritual education that acknowledges the role of meaning-making as the central activity of human life. Meaning-making is spiritual activity that influences life's other aspects, e.g., approaches to relational labor (effort expended to initiate and maintain connections to other people) and to productive labor (effort expended through using abilities to get resources to live on).

On the basis of these assumptions, the aim for the activity of including is to provide each child with a meaningful fit in the environment. Every human being needs to be recognized as having a place in the community into which they are born; children cannot flourish unless they fit to a satisfying degree, so that their presence and person is visible to others. A feeling of fit is essential for spiritual growth but is this feeling of fit bestowed (completed action due to one's place in a society, i.e., granted by others) or a task (ongoing learning in which one tries to fit and succeeds or fails but keeps working at it, i.e., personal effort)? Is a feeling of fit a given, a task, or both? If it is a task, whose work is it?

To ask if a feeling of fit is a given or a task is to raise the question of spiritual work. Recall from the last chapter that 8-year-old Alan had already decided he worked at school but not at church. It seems he had no intention to work at being a spiritually mature Christian. Why did he think that way? How did it happen? I think Alan represents many children and adults who do not think of Christian maturity as spiritual work. Yet what sort of work is it?

I suggest that spiritual work is both communal and personal in the sense that human beings must learn to individuate themselves from and integrate themselves within a community of belief and practice (something we do not do all by ourselves). The nature of spiritual work is precisely to accomplish both at the same time. That is, the feeling of fit in community is granted by others who love me—because God loves them and me—and it is something I work at through personal effort. A feeling of fit in an environment is not the same as being coterminous with it. In order to show up, feeling I fit does not erase my freedom to differentiate myself from an environment at the same time that I feel at home in it. The making of personal and communal meaning always includes integration and differentiation. In this way, the core assumption that the self is a meaning-making activity in collaboration with others is realized as central to personal spiritual work.

The list of spiritual personalities reveals that people differ from one another even though they locate themselves in the broad, historical picture of Christianity, hence they do spiritual work somewhat differently from one another. Authenticity depends on realizing we are not the same as other people and have permission to be different, while still being included. Yet if a religious setting privileges only one way, the idea of a self engaged in meaning-making activity is undermined. In addition to personality differences, meaning derived through object-relating (core spiritual experience) does not remain constant over a life time, unless individuals shut down, get stuck and are stymied. When things are going well, meaning accumulates and people grow in Christian understanding. Feeling stuck is a sign that something is wrong. Inclusive environments are conducive to levering stymied people out of the sticky mire, whether they are stuck intellectually, practically or emotionally.

In summary, a diverse Christian spiritual education provides an environment in which fully-orbed spirituality is possible and encouraged, so that every person is challenged to grow in areas they might not perceive as important. That is, effective spiritual education allows everyone to show up and be represented in the environment and also to learn to appreciate that other people express their spiritual personality in ways that differ from them.

to understand their own spirituality

In general, spiritual education asks whether teachers are creating healthy environments to foster spiritual growth by awakening learners to the spiritual work of making meaning as a central aspect of the development of personality.

SPIRITUAL DIVERSITY

Every community is built on a place to stand, a room in which to abide, a home culture to which its participants return for refreshment and strength needed for everyday life. Against a tendency to privilege one way of being, teachers have a duty to provide spiritual education for children, established and maintained through five activities named earlier: including, attending, embracing, releasing and remaining. A teacher's duty to carry out these activities is due to the spiritual needs of every human being. The more I research into children's spirituality, the more its complexity and breadth strike me. It is powerful to realize that the spiritual life of children may be ignored or disdained during a day at school, in North America and elsewhere. Even when Religious Education is compulsory, as it is in Britain, there is no guarantee that spiritual needs of children are met in classroom culture. When one considers, as I have, that object relations are at the heart of spirituality, and further, spiritual aspects of existence bridge personal and material worlds, subjective and objective experience, it is appalling to fail to encourage children to be spiritual. Not to mature spiritually is not to grow up at all.

In the previous chapter, spirituality was defined as *a sense of felt connection*, which is intended to be descriptive of all relationships, not just the human connection to God. Yet it is compatible with a definition employed by Corinne Ware that spirituality refers to activities and attitudes that characterize attempts to connect with Deity. As a consequence, she outlines modes of worship and prayer that are used as the means to make that connection.[6] She argues for the importance of access to a full range of spiritual experiences if one wants to be holistic and to prevent the aberrations that are possible if one type is emphasized at the expense of all the others.

Ware relies on the life of Christ as exemplar for the four spiritual personalities she outlines. In her view Jesus expressed himself in

[handwritten margin note: spiritual needs for adults are not always met]

all the ways she names. He expressed connection to God through his mind (thinking), heart (feeling), being (receptivity) and doing (activity), which constitute the four aspects of spiritual personality. She suggests that if Jesus displayed all four types in his interactions with the world, his followers ought to aspire to the balance implied in doing so, which Christian communities and traditions generally fail to do. To support her assertion that we tend to privilege one way to connect with God, we often find the breadth of Jesus' behavior hard to encompass in our own understanding. Perhaps we feel at home with Jesus as storyteller or logician, but less so, or ignorant of, his action of cleansing the temple with whips to make his Father's House accessible as a House of Prayer (John 2: 13-25) or with the receptive, contemplative aspect of his own prayer life.

Based on the breadth of Jesus' example, and the diversity within Christian tradition as a whole, I adapted and expanded four spiritual types. The four personalities or types represent a focus on:

- Words: content and the congruence between them; its aim is to stretch personal experience; action is typically speaking: e.g., Jesus in the Sermon on the Mount (Matt. 5-7)
- Music: with evangelism as its aim along with personal renewal; again, action tends towards speaking, witnessing; Jesus sending out the twelve disciples (Luke 9: 1-9)
- Silence and hearing, connecting with, spending time with God so as to enjoy union with God: Jesus in prayer by himself, in quiet, solitary places (John 6: 14-15)
- Action as theologically astute prayer; vision, single-minded crusading to regenerate society: Jesus preaching the Seven Woes (Luke 6: 17-26)

The division between words and witness (types one and two) on the one hand versus impressions and action (types three and four) on the other, conveys two broad cultural approaches to spirituality. The first way is oral, rational, sequential, orderly and concrete; it is a manner that engages an environment actively. The second way is intuitive, tacit, far-ranging and perceiving connections among diverse phenomena, abstract, mystical, receptive to and motivated by that environment but less articulate about that environment than types one and two. In the first two types, it is essential that religious meanings be explained and expressed; in the second two, it is important that religious meanings be experienced and acted out. If we think of the styles as a circle divided into four equal parts, a line may be drawn down the middle that distinguishes one side by sound and the other by silence. When we are trying to fit into a culture or trying to help others fit, we need to become aware of irritations with a primary orientation to sound on one hand, or silence on the other. Jenny was comfortable with sound; David sought silence. Feeling irritated itself may be a sign that we are out of sync with an environment; irritation can lead to anger and withdrawal, but doesn't need to if we come to understand and value our differences.

In addition to outlining four types of spiritual personality, Ware identifies two aspects of experience already mentioned that are necessary to spiritual health. The first is the need to integrate into a community; the second is a need to individuate oneself within that community. Integration (effectively fitting into the whole) and individuation (distinguishing oneself from the whole) constitute the work of creative community living—whether it is one we were born into or one we chose. Ware is clear that individuation is not separation: we do not become ourselves by abandoning community; living reclusively is an aberration not a healthy sign of spiritual life. To enjoy spiritual experience corporately, we hold in tension an outer form with an inner meaning—a collaboration that reconciles past and present experience.[7] For her, individuating is not leaving; it is a process of becoming aware of authentic individuality. In differentiation, we become uniquely and courageously ourselves and realize innate capacities and gifts that help us stand out.[8] The processes of individuation and integration are interactive:

> We cannot integrate the potentially enriching experiences of others into our own self-understanding unless we first have a self; to gain a self, we must first relate to and then differentiate from community. It is a continuously enriching circular movement of interaction and definition. Once one is able to accommodate to new configurations of self, the personality remains open to alterations and enrichment.[9]

46

Individuation and integration are learned together over time in a community that enables people to believe and belong and also understands that believing or belonging may weaken at any given point unless the community members converse together about what really matters to them.

In order be oneself and also fit in, a spiritually sensitive person asks what significant other people are letting them do or are keeping them from doing. In that awareness they consciously decide whether these activities and habits are ones they want to continue with or drop. Becoming spiritually educated requires that we learn to observe ourselves. In self-observation, we notice ourselves and what happens if we remain the same or alter our ways of being. One step in this iterative process is to ask ourselves two questions: What sort of person do I want to be? What is it like to be in my presence? If we ask the second question, we need other people to give us their responses to it. The second question implies that we are in community. We need other people to provide us with insight to help us sense our own identity. Yet the choice implied in the first question (what sort of person I want to be) remains central even after we hear from others; individuation recognizes and chooses personal identity, inherited or acquired—individuation requires choice. But it would be a mistake to think that all choice is free choice; to speak of choice as entirely free is to forget the environment in which we dwell. We have personalities, given and learned, that have to be taken into account as we try to live well with others who have personalities of their own, even though we share Christian commitment.

FOUR SPIRITUAL TYPES

In order to perceive and understand our differences, in what follows I rely on a variety of sources as well as my own experience to outline four spiritual types. The types use religious language taken from the Judeo-Christian tradition. If Christian spiritual environments are to be inclusive of legitimate diversity within our historic tradition, there should be opportunities for children and adults to experience four ways of being Christian as they learn to be people of faith. The four types include the spiritual personalities that follow.

Head Spirituality (Speculative, Kataphatic, Cognitive; Expressive, God as Revealed)

This is a cognitive, thinking approach to spiritual experience based on the significance of words. It is thought plus concreteness. Kataphatic means affirmative and is a tendency to think of God as revealed, knowable, concretely available. God is represented anthropomorphically, i.e., as Personality with personal attributes. This personality prizes what can be seen, touched, vividly imagined. Scripture is highly valued. Words and accuracy are important.

This perspective focuses on God the Father and affirms theological reflection that gets the right words right—or at least expressed more correctly. As a result, exemplars of this personality produce scholarship and rigorous theological commentary on the meaning of the faith. The spoken word is central, as is the written meaning of words. Living rightly and ethical imperatives also matter. The transformational goal is personal understanding.

The extreme and distorted form of head spirituality (aberration) devolves into rationalism, mere cognitivism or conceptual moralism: all that matters is having the right idea, word or meaning. The extreme of this personality is expressed in relentlessly pointing out that everyone who does not agree with their view is incorrect. Emotion is not relevant to what one considers to be true.

Emotion is unreliable so that this extreme fails to recognize the role that thinking and feeling play together in mental activity and is mistaken with respect to how thinking itself works. However the contribution of this personality is core to Christian faith and the development of religious understanding.

Heart Spirituality (Affective, Kataphatic, Heartfelt)

With heart spirituality, emotion is central. Like head spirituality, the concrete expression of God is highly prized; music and oral witness play central roles. It is emotion plus concreteness. This personality values what is deeply felt as good in itself and, "far from being an indolent substitute for scholarship, entails...hard

Is formal theological education about thin

work."[10] This personality values the hard emotional work of personal renewal and a free expression of feeling, embodied as well as oral. God is here, now, immanent, relational; the satisfying lover of the soul. Intellectualism is suspect. Evangelism matters, but rather than rational argumentation, it focuses on flashes of insight, personal testimony, words of knowledge got directly from God. Its transformation goal is personal renewal. This personality offers the Christian community a clear witness to Christianity's message and power. *verbal ?*

Its extreme forms (aberrations) are Pietism, Enthusiasm and Emotionalism. Tension between head and heart spiritualities were typical of the eighteenth century; for example, Kant abhorred Enthusiasm and insisted on pure reason as a compass for thinking as a rational human being, so that the division between head and heart is a fulcrum of modernity. To its discredit, extreme forms of heart spirituality fail to notice how unresolved pain, suffering and loss may drive their spiritual agenda. Emotional responses may be under-analyzed, not held accountable for their influence on spiritual hunches, so that hard emotional work is not done. Heart spirituality is highly contagious, but unbridled leadership may lead a group toward harm. If extreme forms of head spirituality tend to isolate adherents due to their abrasive correctness (ignoring indelible ambiguities in scripture) extreme forms of heart spirituality tend to unite disenchanted followers under a common emotional cause— which may persist regardless of its enduring worth within the Christian community.

Mystic Spirituality (Affective, Apophatic, Mysterious; 'Impressive'; God as Spirit)

For both head and heart spiritual personalities, the need and freedom to express one's way of being spiritual is paramount. Both types tend to create a talking culture when they dominate a religious community. The other two spiritual personalities (three and four) are unified by habits born of silence. Mystic personality withdraws from speaking about spiritual meaning due to a perception that using words always falls short of capturing rich experience.

While head and heart spiritualities (one and two) are expressive and active; mystic spiritual personalities are passive and receptive, waiting to hear God speak, not quick to speak for God. Apophatic means negative and refers to conceiving God in non-concretized ways, as mystery. Mystery is elusive, more felt than spoken. It is above being captured in words and is unavailable for complete revelation until heaven. In type three, to explain fully is to lose something precious. Mystic spirituality combines emotion, solitude, the music of the spheres. It focuses on the Beauty of God's own self, as conveyed from Heart to heart. It pays attention to the Unseen. The transformational goal is to enjoy union with God. Imagination is nourished by felt manifestations of God's presence, by impressions of God being present. This personality offers Christian community devotional works that enlarge the boundaries of spiritual experience.

The extremes of this personality draw one toward Reclusivity and Quietism. The practitioner withdraws from trying to express outwardly what is perceived inwardly. The inexpressive aspect dominates the need to communicate orally; communion with other ordinary people is abandoned. For example, Gnosticism is an extreme form of inward knowing that denies value to the material world and abuses the body through ascetic practice. Christianity does not disdain the body or dismiss the pleasure of being human as this personality may come to do. Yet without its mystical warmth to deepen and broaden spiritual experience, we are left with cold, hard ideas that cannot sustain us in the crises of life and do not explain the strange, supernatural encounters people have with spiritual realities, and with God, even when they say they are atheists.

Kingdom Spirituality (Speculative, Apophatic, Concrete)

The inability to express itself fully to other people links Kingdom spirituality to its Mystic neighbour. The speculative and concrete aspect of this quadrant drives an individual to change the world, rather than only to pray for it, as a Mystic might.

If the transformational goal for the third personality is union with God, the transformational goal in the fourth is to change conditions in the world that cause harm. The focus for this group is visionary justice. People with this personality are single-minded, thoughtful, thought-provoking prophets. They are driven by concrete conditions in the world to be witnesses of God's justice. They are motivated by a union with the world's deepest needs; addressing them is an unswerving mission. If mystic spirituality is lived out in quietness and isolation, this spiritual personality is moved by an isolating need to save the world single-handedly, often without the help of others who are judged to be too blind to see what needs to be done or too cowardly to try to accomplish it.

Hence, its aberration is Encratism and Practical Moralism. Its extreme expression alienates other people at the same time that it calls them to join in world-saving mission. Without the skill of words, of talking, this personality cannot easily draw others toward its goals. The world must be saved at all cost: no time to think or talk; action alone justifies the claim to being a follower of the radical Jesus. Even its moderate exercise tends to alienate others since there is little that softens this personality. The alienation of others is in part caused by an inability to articulate what needs to be done and offer reasons for doing it. Even its moderate expression is ruled by passionate impatience. This personality insults and ridicules others who appear less committed and can become activism for its own sake, harshly judging people who fail to see needs and act quickly enough to ameliorate them. But if this personality is motivated by compassion (their own or another person's love for them) and if it is infused with humility, one life can and does change the world for God's sake.

These four personalities can explain experience and behaviour that up to now has made no sense. In my own encounters with, for example, type four individuals, once I understood that alienating others was a sign of impatient passion and stopped taking these judgments personally, I was able to come alongside significant change-agents to support their challenges to social injustice, which without their irrepressible effort, seem impossible to stop or alter. The point of articulating these spiritual personalities is three-fold, to help:

51

- Self-identify by offering explanatory frameworks for self-knowledge
- Notice differences in children characteristic of the four types to encourage their authenticity
- Paint a broad picture for personality to create and sustain the development of these ways of being spiritual so that each type has a moderating effect on the excesses of the others

When teachers include all children, they provide an environment that encompasses scholarly disciplines, for example, by analyzing important words of faith; they sense insightful emotional work and help people learn through feeling; they value participation in music and dance (among the most ancient and enduring of all spiritual practices); they encourage the silent language of inner impressions based on God's willingness to commune with people; and they actively engage with the world so as to improve it, in God's name. The educational activity of including is effective when it combines with the other activities inherent in saving a spiritual environment mentioned earlier, namely attending, embracing, releasing and remaining. For example, the focus on attending makes it possible to be inclusive of spiritual differences first of all by giving them recognition.

ATTENDING: A FOUNDATION FOR BEING AND MEANING

The activity of attending takes its starting point in object-relating gaze behaviour between mother and child, which was introduced in chapter one. While spirituality is formed biologically, culturally, sociologically and neurologically, object-relating (its psychological dimension) is the heart of spirituality as far as I am concerned. Ana-Maria Rizzuto studied the theory of object relations that Freud discovered when he asked how people come to possess actual belief in the existence of God.[11] The theory of object relations answers his question. Object relations theories are shaped by what can be observed so it is passing strange that Freud eliminated mothers from his proposal for how God concepts form. Rizzuto addressed the omission of mothers, as did John Bowlby (1988) in what he calls attachment theory. In response to this omission, I focus on the mother/child relation in this chapter.

In general, object relations theories explain our need for other people and tend to have as a central conviction that personality development occurs in the context of interactions between other people and the environment, rather than through internal processes of maturation alone. Object relations theories describe our spiritual work and require a spiritual education, which is missing in many schools and church cultures. Robert Kegan focuses on the complexity of modern life as a new source for its need?[12] In Kegan's view, complexity in the demands of living create opportunity for what I call spiritual education. To him, we have not caught up with requirements of modern (not to mention post-modern) life.[13] He does not discuss spiritual education *per se* but his emphasis on meaning-making through object-relating is central to understanding how spirituality works. Kegan provides a good basis for understanding why we need a spiritual education.

To him, object-relating is of intrinsic human interest: ego activity *is* object-relating and begins at birth.[14] He organizes psychological development and educational transformation around object relations. His interpretation of object relations is fundamental to understanding the role of spirituality *per se* in the human project of growing up because he thinks the essence of humanity is the making of meaning. As mentioned in chapter one, object-relations theories assume that all learning is organizing experience. What an organism does, to put the point generally, is to organize and "what a human organism organizes is meaning."[15] In making this claim about the formation of personality, Kegan re-interprets Piaget's analysis of human development. Kegan's analysis reveals an omission in developmentalism that matters to researchers of children's spirituality. For a long time, they suspected children were capable of empathy and insight Piaget seemed to deny was possible. While being faithful to Piaget's stages, Kegan focuses not on developmental plateaus but on the process of moving from one plateau (stage) to another. As a result, he emphasizes the activity of meaning-making in the process of growing up and thinks stages (plateaus) do not offer a framework for thinking about human growth, even though he seems uncritical of Piaget's plateaus themselves.[16] In exploring human development, Kegan thinks Piaget described the achievement of meaning-made, not the dynamic self engaged in the struggle "to make meaning, to have meaning, to protect meaning, to enhance meaning, to lose meaning and to lose the 'self' along the way."[17] This dynamism of the self in motion is an ebb and flow of loss and recovery with respect to meaning attached to the various illusions we hold in our mental mythology. The heart's hard spiritual work is to move through loss to recovery so that meaning is re-organized sufficiently and life can be sustained hopefully.

While I suggest that object-relating is the heart of spiritual processes, the psychological is not detached from the biological. Meaning-making is both, since the spiritual work of making meaning is also a survival activity. We know that well-fed, warm, disease-free infants may die if unable to attach themselves to other meaning-makers, if not allowed to 'mean'. Religious experience evolved through a process of natural selection because it has survival value to the individual, as established in the previous chapter. The biological survival function of spirituality is conveyed through a feeling of absolute dependence, which is "not simply an emotion, but something more like a perception."[18] Spiritual experience is emotion and motion in a specific sense: it is the movement of finding, losing, recovering, losing and finding again those objects that we layer with meaning, then organize and re-organize into a personal worldview.

In forming personal worldviews, spirituality mediates object and subject, personal and material worlds. Spirituality is the mediation within ourselves and with objects in the world until we come into being as an object ourselves and move through meaning-making to become a fully formed self, capable of meeting the demands of modern living.

Spirituality is object-relating. The term object relations can convey a cold interpretation of the connection between human beings but its etymology defies this association. Object signifies motion at its root. As an example, we use the word 'eject' to signify motion, e.g., when we eject DVDs from video players. The root (ject) refers to the activity of throwing; the word object "speaks to that which some motion has made separate or distinct from, or to the motion itself."[19] Object-relating has to do with the movement implied between people and things in the world that some motion has made separate or distinct, i.e., object relations are "our relations to that which has been thrown from us, or the experience of this throwing itself."[20] Emotion and motion are in iterative relation: motion initiates emotion; emotion instigates and signifies motion.

Object-relating refers to the motion of a self through life such that an experience of being embedded in the world's objects is replaced, hence lost, through a process of differentiating the self from these objects. As a self that makes meaning, even though we lose meaning when we are separated from these objects, we are in motion and recover meaning if we are able to do so. This is an evolutionary process in which we move forward in making meaning about significant objects. For example, following Piaget, an infant is embedded in impulses and emerges from these impulses by differentiating himself from them. In this way, the self becomes its own object, distinct from a mother that was previously indistinguishable from his own being, from the infant's perspective. Object relations emerge out of a continual process of loss and recovery, of differentiation and integration, of losing one's center and coming back home, where home is not the same as it was when we were young, but is still recognizable.

The early dynamics of the formation of a self through meaning-making based on object relations includes moving through stages of consciousness, according to Kegan, to a level of consciousness, at which point the self is organized as a system:

- Sensori-motor: embedded in reflexes, then reflexes show up to the child as perceptions
  - Mother shows up as separate, lose-able; infant expresses separation anxiety
- Pre-operational: embedded in perceptions, then perceptions show up as the concrete
  - Self emerges as an object
- Concrete-operational: embedded in the concrete, then concrete shows up as thought

- Self emerges as a role

• Formal-operational: embedded in thought, then thought shows up as organization

- Self emerges as a system

The self as a system is formed around eleven or twelve years old and lasts into adulthood;[21] it is a meaning system constructed through relational experience.

The movement of meaning-making is necessarily relational—an adult attends to an infant and attunes herself to one who depends on that gaze in order to come into being and make meaning. Attending creates an environment for spirituality to flourish because it provides children with resources of attention, a commodity just like money that may be more important than money for the future opportunities of the young. Attention is "one of the great generic currencies of social life," a distinct social phenomenon that can be analyzed to establish the value of a human life.[22] The more attention children are skilled at getting, the more value they have. Those unable to secure other people's attention are impoverished by their lack of skill; their poverty goes very deep—creating an expectation they will neither be heard nor seen: they believe they are invisible, no one cares for them, or they see themselves as someone that can be trampled upon.

Attention that counts in creating and sustaining human value is focused on a person rather than behaviour. For example, even as limits are set on children, if they feel recognized and have a sense that adults understand how they interpret their experience (whether or not adults interpret behaviour in the same way), they can find limit-setting tolerable and even feel relieved at being 'caught'; but if a child does not feel recognized, he or she resents limit-setting as a violation of identity, which is what it is.[23] In addition to recognizing people rather than emphasizing behaviour, parents and teachers must be drawn to and stay with a child if attention is to have full effect in paying out value to one who is a focus of attention. We attend easily to those with the requisite skill to draw our attention to them and who are talented at recruiting us to pay attention freely. These children receive attention from peers and adults, seemingly without effort, so they are never perceived as attention-seeking. If children have to work hard to get attention, they are spotted as attention-seekers and given a negative label.

Attention-getting bestows recognition; attention-keeping conveys that value is secure and permanent. In his analysis of attention-getting, keeping and giving, Derber asserts that Western culture is addicted.[24] We are so driven to seek attention no one is left to give it. The modern self carries a unique distress: "Each person... has received the burdensome gift of an overgrown self. We enjoy the positive, attractive features of this self-orientation, but...fail to appreciate how much it costs us as well."[25] Adults are not exempt from an insatiable desire for attention and only give generously on the strength of their commitment to bless the young.

Giving attention is significant in terms of human survival and meaning-making. If attention-getting establishes personal currency, Kegan points out that "survival and development depend on our capacity to recruit the invested attention of others to us."[26] People have to be recruited to draw close and stay by an infant if that child is to survive. An infant's capacity "to hold the mother with a recognizing eye is as fundamental to...development as is the prehensile capacity to hold a physical object."[27] Infants learn to grasp physical objects and human objects in order to achieve their own maintenance—to remain alive in the world. While we do not like to think of people as objects, the capacity to get and keep attention is an exercise in which infants are trying to recognize and be recognized. Whether the object grasped is a thing or a person, the infant aims to accomplish a similar end: to make meaning with these objects, which are the transitional objects of ordinary life. The term transitional implies motion—we grow up with respect to our perception of these objects and a sense of self that develops over time through experiencing them, which evolves into the meaning they hold for us.

Meaning-making is a social and survival activity because an infant's meaning-making depends on someone who recognizes and collaborates with the child. The experience of getting and giving attention informs children about recruitability. Some children have the misfortune to be raised by parents that are incapable of being recruited by them and do not provide attention for their young, even though physically present. Some children learn to recruit, others do not. The greatest inequality in a classroom is not class, race or gender but an unequal capability students have to recruit the interest and attention of other people *in them*.[28] An ability to recruit is learned; teachers can influence children's ability to recruit, which in turn influences children's capacity to organize experience meaningfully.

From birth to death we are involved in making meaning and throughout a normal life we are in motion-organized relationships with objects of experience. Multi-dimensional aspects of spirituality (biology, culture, sociology, neurology and psychology) convey the process of this evolutionary motion. The process refers, in my view, to spirituality itself. The product of human spirituality is a worldview each individual constructs as a consequence of the process. Included in a worldview is a notion of the self; part of our spiritual work is learning how to regard ourselves in a healthy manner. Self-concepts, God-concepts and concepts of other people intertwine during meaning-making, a relationship I pursue in chapter four.

With respect to a spiritual environment, teachers attend to inequality in a classroom by paying attention. Children carry an inability to recruit in their very being—by seeming invisible or by being demanding. In either case, the child is unsatisfied by attention that allows for meaning-making and cannot relax with other people. A lack of skill to recruit attention is a powerful determinant of future thriving.[29] Some children need help with learning to recruit attention. They may have learned to be irritating out of desperation or learned to disappear as a way to relieve their disappointment. A teacher's role in spiritual education is to distribute attention justly; they work intentionally at attending, which includes the following:

- Holding on, being held
- Looking at, looking with, looking for
- Touching, welcoming touch
- Speaking to, speaking with
- Listening to, listening with

The responsibility to attend to every child fairly cannot be overemphasized. Attending unites with the other activities inherent in creating a spiritually healthy environment to foster the care children need to grow up well. These spiritually informed activities go beyond giving attention and include a commitment to embrace the young in a parent's or teacher's own being.

EMBRACING: A FOUNDATION
FOR RELATIONAL LABOUR

Attending is a response to two human longings: a yearning for inclusion and a yearning for distinctness.[30] The same is true for the activity of embracing. If the primary metaphor for attending is a humanizing gaze between mother and child, embracing, appropriate ministrations of presence, is conveyed through the metaphor of healthy holding on,[31] in which a caregiver un-anxiously holds an anxious child. It is not simply the gesture of holding, which also characterizes attending, embracing is the ability and willingness to hold on in the right way, at the right time, for the right length of time, and for the right reasons; its appropriateness lays the groundwork for healthy separation[32] since holding "on without constraining may be the first requirement of care."[33]

Embracing is a way of being present to another so that the attention we pay *is to them*. We respond to a person not a problem: As Kegan put it, to respond to the problem is not to trust the child. The ability to be present to others when they are anxious, to acknowledge anxiety without becoming too anxious oneself or immediately trying to relieve it, is understood to be a feature of competent, professional psychological help.[34] Embracing is an act of presence required of teachers that hope to educate learners eventually not to need them. It is only by embracing the person behind a presenting problem that it is possible not to be needed at some point in the future, which might be why some adults refuse to embrace children and instead constrain them; they do not hold children, they hold them back.

Consider the following example as a model for embracing in the best sense. A young mother goes for coffee at a neighbor's house.

They each have a child roughly the same age. We observe the interaction between one mother and child. The child sits on her mother's lap while the two women converse. Then the child looks at the other child playing. She gets down with a hand on her mother's lap and leans toward an enticing game. She watches, and moves close to the play, toys and a partner her size. Then she climbs back on the lap. Her mother welcomes her but now as she sits on her perch her whole attention is on the game played by the other child. She gets down, joins the play. The pattern of closeness and distance continues until her dependence on her mother is distracted by the fun of playing with another child. Being near and moving away is a game the young learn, under favorable conditions, as they begin to learn independence. I suggest even in romantic love a pattern repeats itself: nearness, distance, then nearness again. Intimacy is built through moving forward and coming back home.

The mother is doing many things at once: conversing, drinking coffee, watching a clock, donating her lap to a child. The activity of embracing is built on self-donation—a mother's lap to a child's need for it. A mother gives herself to a child's need, yet has time for friendship. Mother and child relax in their availability to one another. Availability depends on economics. If mother is destitute she is unavailable; if she is emotionally pre-occupied, she is not present. Is her availability a sacrifice of her being for the child's greater good? Is the child somehow more important than she is? If we answer yes to the second question, how could an inferior person have significance for the child? What would she teach a child? Would she not, in part, teach the child that she is inferior, and that the child is superior—a debilitating and damaging message for any child to get? I say rather that mother and child are equally valuable, even economically. Availability is an offering to a child, expressive of a mother's value. Embracing is a form of self-donation in which both parties enjoy value, although needs differ, in this case, particularly with respect to their urgency. Self-donation is a giving, losing and regaining of self and it structures the parental relationship.

Tension in self-donation arises as one tries to give oneself without losing oneself entirely. If mothers appear to get lost for a time, due to a child's urgent, foundational needs, self-donation requires them to regain themselves. We cannot donate what we have lost. Regaining self implies *not* getting lost but temporarily and willingly giving priority to another's need. Self-donation is conscious, intelligent action, not enslavement. Slavery has two forms: it carries out action in the interests of others that slaves have no interest in; interests include a need for material resources to live on and recognition for values held as ultimate concerns. I suggest it is in this mother's personal and social interest to care for her child. A second form of slavery fails at self-mastery. People are slaves to whatever has mastered them, including their own insatiable desires. Is this mother capable of self-mastery in the act of self-donation? This question is more complex.

On its own, self-donation is not an offense against one's interests and does not signal a lack of self-mastery. But due to current sociological patterns, self-mastery is an issue for a young mother. At present, adolescent girls seem unwilling and unable to gain mastery over skills in the way boys are adept at doing (Fels 2004), for example, by joining a debating team, playing video games or mastering a skateboard in front of friends that give attention and approval for their skill. Self-mastery is a sociological puzzle for many young girls and has a relationship with the human capacity for industry.[35] If self-donation is healthy, it is based on a successful history with self-mastery so that there is a well-defined self to return to when donating oneself to others diminishes as a consuming task. If there is no self underlying an act of self-donation—a self that is capable of differentiation—giving oneself away to another's need, even temporarily, can de-generate into slavery. If this young mother is to care for her child, it is imperative that she be industrious in doing so, since caring for a household is hard emotional, intellectual and physical work, when done well, and she needs to be seen as skillful. The danger in maternal self-donation is the absence of social value for her availability and the poverty of support for its success.

I do not give the example of this mother to say that all women should continuously stay home with children, although being with one's children is a human good. Rather, I suggest embracing begins with a child's need; they are helpless and dependent on the goodwill of caregivers. While embracing begins by focusing on a child's needs, it raises the question of what sort of selves we need to be so we are able and willing to donate ourselves without a fundamental loss of self. From a Christian perspective, Jesus gave himself without losing himself (John 10:17-18). His resistance to Satan in the desert was his refusal to being enslaved to someone else's interests (Matt 4:1-11). Yet in self-donation there is a loss of some kind that cannot be evaded. To put oneself at the disposal of another's need is to turn our attention from our own, which may be quite pressing in its own right. While it may be argued that looking after one's own children is a way of giving attention to ourselves, e.g., to convey that we own excess wealth, how does self-donating apply to embracing other people's children, in whom we have no self-interest?

Caring for other people's children points us toward a most basic aspect of self-donation: it is "the will to give ourselves to others and 'welcome' them, to readjust our identities to make space for them, [and this act of turning our attention to them] is prior to any judgment... except that of identifying them in their humanity."[36] In building an understanding of self-donation, Volf asserts that embracing cannot take place until truth has been said and justice done. Embracing is not slavery if it refuses to let injustice go unchecked. If the tendency for girls not to gain mastery (as a basis for self-mastery) is a social fact, then it is a problem that must be ameliorated by healthy spiritual communities that value all their members. As Volf notes, "even if the will to embrace is indiscriminate, the embrace itself is conditional"; it is always also a struggle against "deception, injustice, and violence."[37]

The will to embrace rests on justice and equality. Genuine caring for others distinguishes legitimate from illegitimate demands by assessing the source and nature of other people's need for us. With respect to caring for one another in a Christian community, our embrace of others is not commanded by rules, regulations or universal laws[38] so much as it is a response to love. Filled by the Holy Spirit, early Christians embraced one another, gave and received basic necessities of life, held all things in common in Jerusalem (Acts 2) (not necessarily elsewhere); this embrace was the result not of neglect, abuse or violence, not even of manipulation, but an outcome of love. God's love for individuals was enjoyed corporately.

Embracing is an activity in which I identify myself as one who makes room for others as an aspect of being myself and being with them, which necessarily impacts self-identity. The willingness to make space for others is at the heart of the availability of the young mother, who could be doing other things with her time, but chooses to be with her child. Those who care for other people's children choose to give others room within their very identity—an intrusion that has material and spiritual costs and benefits. Embracing is work we take on because we perceive and practice that we are free to do so and know we have value. Embracing is enacted intentionally by adults who refuse to be alienated from a spiritual environment in which they carry out the work of caring for the young, or any other work they are called to take up.

We can only adequately embrace our work and other people if we also refuse to practice our own insignificance in the environment where we carry out a ministry of Presence. If we want to show up in that environment, we must refuse invisibility—whether in a household, workplace or church. The hard work of showing up in a world of others who also want to show up in that environment (sometimes at our expense) is explored in the chapter on the problem of opposition. We learn the work of being church with other people who are also trying to do it too. As a result, our concept of work is fundamental to a spiritually healthy environment. If education aims to link spirituality and faith we need to attend to our idea of work. Learning to work is like learning to live.

RELEASING: A FOUNDATION FOR PRODUCTIVE LABOUR

If attending grounds being and meaning, embracing is relational labor that prepares the young for separation, and releasing is its educational partner. Releasing refers to a timely regard for letting students learn and work independently. Education itself, *educare* (nurture) and *educere* (leading out), signifies healthy embrace and separation—good teachers work themselves out of a job eventually by enabling students to work on their own. Learning to work is related to the recognition that comes with attention. The freedom to work is a function of recognizing and being recognized. Work shapes how we perceive ourselves and our place in the world; it is part of the process and product of spirituality. But releasing learners to work on their own benefits them only if they have requisite foundational skills implied in the task of working on their own.

Work, love and meaning are aspects of human experience that shape how we perceive ourselves and our place in the world. Learning to work is an indication of personal value and is an object, like anything else involved in object-relating; as we relate to it, we make it meaningful.

Those who learn to work effectively do so, despite bosses or teachers that grade them, because they separate some people's social power in an organization or school from the psychological power and ownership they retain over their own work.[39] Effective workers are not alienated from their labor; they perceive the complexity of modern labor but understand that refusing to feel alienated is part of the job.

In making this point, I do not underestimate the influence of harmful work environments, yet I take seriously Bourdieu's point about active complicity.[40] Modern labor requires that we learn to work *with* an environment *because we are so influenced by it*; this work is spiritual. The ability to work without becoming enslaved or feeling alienated has to do with making meaning—its sustenance, loss and recovery. When we understand how to work, the self as a system developed at eleven or twelve shows up as an object of attention that we 'have' rather than being a system that has us: if we are embedded in it, we are unable to reflect upon it. The spiritual work of meaning making takes us beyond a third level of consciousness and allows us to reflect on the system we made when we were young. As we learn to work, we let the self as a system show up as distinct from the self we are becoming. In the activity of meaning-making, the part played by releasing prepares children to gain ownership and mastery over content and skills they want to acquire so they will eventually gain mastery over themselves.

The classroom is a good place for children to learn to own their work as teachers release them to do so.[41] I think we face a general inability to own our labour but the problem is not new. Antonio

Gramsci (1891-1937) observed the same malaise. At the turn of twentieth century Italy, school reform was carried out by Gentile and Croce, two ministers of education (1921-1923). They reformed an education they saw as instruction, i.e., narrow, formal and sterile.[42] Gramsci thought they went too far in diminishing work and discipline in primary schooling; he thought it "necessary to enter a 'classical,' rational phase", with inclusive goals for learning so that all children could access education in an environment in which they fit.[43] He was motivated by a desire for working class children to enjoy a feeling of fit in their environment and noted aspects of schooling that prevented that fit from occurring. To enable all children to access learning, he thought it necessary to have two phases to schooling: a common education which instructed children in the basis skills of civil life and a creative phase that taught them to work out implications of individual talent by engaging in collaborative projects. For him, schools "should aim to insert young men and women into social activity after bringing them to a certain level of maturity, of capacity for intellectual and practical creativity, and of autonomy of orientation and initiative."[44] I would add spiritual maturity to his list of intellectual and practical skills.

Gramsci noticed aspects of learning that were taken for granted by middle class citizens, for example, the capacity to sit still long enough to absorb lessons. He saw that in "a whole series of families, especially in the intellectual strata, the children find in their family life a preparation, a prolongation and a completion of school life; they 'breathe in'...a whole quantity of notions and attitudes which facilitate the educational process properly speaking."[45] From a later perspective, Pierre Bourdieu identified modern female labour (the activity of our young mother) as a vast work of reproduction; an "economy of practices"[46] that support and sustain other forms of capital accumulation. To Bourdieu, the "social world is accumulated history;" embodied, living domestic labour takes time to accumulate but produces profits of various kinds, including the general capacities to fit in school culture.[47] Gramsci noted that this cultural capital is something that poor children live without because poverty makes parental attention a scarce commodity.

Gramsci invented creative education to erase unjust social disadvantage. Creative schools are a culmination of active schools (i.e., using Montessori methods) because they combine a first phase of discipline with a second phase of collective activity. He thought combining instruction and action would expand a child's personality and provide a solid base for moral and social conscience, i.e., the basis of civil personality. He worried about social disintegration, as did Durkheim. Gramsci thought educational foundations should come before innovation and independence to address inequalities among the children entering school. Since they offer no common grounding, Gramsci criticized Montessori-like approaches for allowing learners to pursue their own inquiry and agenda, which he thought allocated discipline to a child's personal (family) responsibility.[48] He didn't reject action-based learning *per se*; rather he abhorred its inequality. He believed Montessori-like schools were dependent for their success on middle-class experience. For the working class, empty of the requisite skills to accomplish active schooling's end goals, learning is inaccessible. Poor children were unprepared for collaborative learning. Inequality persists when dominant practices leave learners out, e.g., if differences in recruitability (attention securing) are ignored.

Gramsci's critique remains timely. If church culture is just, it is composed of people from different classes and races. In my own church I became aware that adolescents from working class families are counselled differently from those in the middle class. One young man recounted an experience of being told by his public school guidance teacher that he was not smart enough to be a math tutor, even though he loved math and was good at it. I asked him whether the counsellor used those exact words. He replied that she did. I was aggrieved. He is not the only young person in my church community counselled in how not to excel at school. When I raised the issue at youth group, most of the young people recounted similar tales. This practice is unacceptable to me as a member of their faith community. Fortunately, after conversing with several of us, this young man went back to school and made an effective complaint against his guidance counsellor. As Bell Hooks points out, class issues at church are often insufficiently perceived and addressed

(Hooks 2000). Injustice is epidemic but a faith community can be resourceful for those dis-privileged by the world's way of valuing people, i.e., by their culture's worldliness.

In churches, the issue of neglect is worsened by a general neglect of education. There is often little time to educate the young; store-bought curricula determine the agenda. The tendency for a teaching approach or written curriculum to dominate the environment is endemic, to the detriment of children who can't get with the program because they don't have the skills needed to comply with it. A primary need to address is the provision of the cultural and social capital assumed by an approach or curriculum.

Bourdieu analyzed cultural and social capital to identify embodied, objectified and institutional forms and to reveal the role of family in their accumulation.[50] In his analysis, he observed that membership in a group provides each member with connections to collectively owned capital, credentials that entitle members to various kinds of credit. These connections are not natural givens, or even social givens; they are the product of endless effort in investment strategies (e.g., domestic labour), individual or collective, conscious or unconscious; they are strategies aimed at maintaining social relationships or transforming contingent relationships (neighbours, colleagues or relatives) into relationships that imply durable obligations that are subjectively felt in gratitude, respect, friendliness or friendship.

In short, "the reproduction of social capital or social trust presupposes an unceasing effort of sociability, a continuous series of exchanges in which recognition is endlessly affirmed and reaffirmed."[51] An embodied form of social capital is knowledge that 'knows how' to arrange for its own increase and sets out to gain it. There is a practical link between a child's ability to recruit attention and his or her cultural and social capital. Bourdieu argued persuasively that owning cultural and social capital provides the bases for acquiring economic capital. Working class children have no access to family-based advantages that take time and leisure to build. Forms of capital that directly influence one's capacity to benefit from school are unevenly distributed; but this is not a new point. While I agree with his criticism of action-based approaches, it is important to see what Gramsci excluded from schooling so that a general need for spiritual education can be perceived. While we establish compensatory cultural and social capital programs at church, we must also challenge the public school system's right to exclude spiritual needs from the curriculum. The exclusion of religion from public schooling is partly a result of Gramsci's reform.

For him, there were two main aims to modern education, realized to a large extent during twentieth century in the West. Children were taught the rudiments of natural science and civility. They were taught to fit into the world of things and the world of other people. During modernity, children attended to the world as the site of objective, intractable laws that governed both natural and social worlds. They were to attend to these laws in order to participate in life and possibly influence the future development of humankind. In shifting attention to laws of the world as it really is, children were to leave behind myths and folklore to cleanse themselves of the residue of traditional, homey, conceptions of the world. Modern schools opposed the homespun wisdom of religion and family[52] and aimed to liberate children from worldviews acquired when they were young. Religious education itself was perceived as harmful.

As already mentioned, modern reformers decided that liberation was accomplished best if children reject the religion of home and family. Yet I suggest that emphasizing natural and social worlds (things, self and others) omits the spiritual bridge between personal and material worlds and fails to acknowledge that spirituality is inevitable because it is formed biologically, culturally, sociologically, neurologically and psychologically. Education that focuses on the material can't attend to spiritual aspects of meaning making that are central to personal formation. The process of growing up in community is spiritual; its end-product is a worldview that is also available for revision. Creative education should take spirituality into account if it aims to develop the human capabilities of the young. Like poor children, children are misfits in school if they are religious and the environment is not, or if they are atheists and an environment assumes positive belief in God. Spiritual education offers a positive fit for all children, whether or not they are religious, because they all have spiritual needs. To live in environments that disregard spiritual needs is to be cast aside, neglected; it is to be profoundly unhappy and to lose hope. Hope is the crowning attribute of a positive spiritual disposition and foundational to education. I suggest that to educate every child adequately, we offer creative education that affirms spirituality as a core element.

This is an argument public schools, but can Christian education become creative? Religious instruction is sometimes seen as indoctrination—an approach that precludes creativity since it forecloses on independent thought. Indoctrination is authoritarian. It transmits judgments to learners for acceptance, with emotional impact. Indoctrinated learners demonstrate an unreflective, unquestioning stance that tends to continue over time. They fail to examine the world for realities that question the accuracy of these judgments, which were passed on without giving reasons for them, so children cannot assess them independently. Yet as Gramsci pointed out, indoctrination is successful only if learners are passive recipients of data, incapable of thinking for themselves. But children are not accurately described this way; further, there is no point to education at all if children are incapable of thinking for themselves. Spiritual education is not indoctrination; it is obligated to show how judgments are arrived at and to reveal its frameworks for spiritual experience.

Education is not indoctrinating if it teaches the young to do their spiritual work. Learning to work is a spiritual activity in which children come to feel connected to their abilities and the role they will play in the future. Gramsci's creative education distinguished two types of solidarity: mechanical and organic. Mechanical solidarity is unity made possible when people are alike in terms of language, race or territory and arises among these people due to unity in which they rely on being alike and therefore feel they belong. Organic solidarity emerges through differentiation as a sentiment that holds people together when they choose to achieve a common goal or try to live together amiably due to the interdependence that their differences make necessary.[53] Organic solidarity is learned as people work together. I suggest that spiritual education is neither mechanical nor organic, but a combination of both and is the basis for learning to be ourselves in the presence of others by collaborating with them. It is mechanical, because everyone has the same spiritual needs;

it is organic because we differ in our spiritual personalities. True collaboration depends on both types of solidarity.

In collaboration, people are aware of expertise others have even if they don't carry out the same tasks. They learn to appreciate the whole enterprise and identify their role and responsibility in it. They identify what is and is not their work but a sense of connection to the whole enterprise and its purposes prevents people from being alienated. Learning requires spontaneous and autonomous effort; teachers are friendly guides, but learning is built on a developed capacity for discipline and work. The aim is to encourage a child's own learning, carried out in community—an idea alien to what Alan, in the last chapter, expected from Sunday School.

Gramsci used the example of an editing house to describe a creative process that produces effective, collaborative workers. An editing house acts as a unit in which each person is an expert in his or her own field, but each helps enhance the expertise of the whole. He thought collective action of the whole would raise the corporate level of expertise. He noted that combined activity would have to express an "unyielding struggle against habits of dilettantism, of improvisation, of 'rhetorical' solutions or those proposed for effect." [54]In collective effort, each is required to do his or her proper work well, respectfully of others and to focus on truth implicitly and explicitly expressed in the expertise each brought to the table. He thought the most skilled people would raise the level of the least skilled to accelerate the skill of the overall effort. A division of labour based on ability could secure a corporately successful end. Creativity and hard work produce innovation. In a creative school, innovation is understood in a particular way: "to discover a truth oneself, without external suggestions or assistance, is to create, even if the truth is an old one." [55] Innovation signals mastery over methods used and demonstrates that learners have entered a new phase of intellectual maturity in which they discover new truths in addition to reviving old ones.

If creative schooling helps every child to gain self-knowledge, self-mastery teaches them to work collaboratively. Any attempt (even inadvertently) to indoctrinate is overcome through the personal ownership of learning. Gramsci rejected religion because he misunderstood how worldviews form as products of ordinary experience. We do not save a spiritual environment by abandoning a religious past but by remaining with it, yet wisely so.

Following Gramsci, we need to enter a classical, spiritual phase and situate rationality within that framework. In the first phase of Christian education, learners are securely situated in scripture and tradition so that they find an identity that helps them organize experience meaningfully and acquire basic skills of the faith. Biblical literacy is essential. In addition, methods used to read scripture and interpret tradition are acquired by the young. On the foundation of spiritual education, children begin to learn faith on their own, follow out their own questions and provide leadership for each other under the friendly, resourceful guidance of a mature believing adult. What would happen in churches if spiritually formed, creative education that encompassed the full range of human experience was offered to children and youth? But of course, there is a catch. The idea of really educating the young depends on the willingness and ability of adults to embrace them in the first place. The good news is that children long for adult investment in their lives. The bad news is, too few adults are willing to embrace the young and remain faithful.

REMAINING: A FOUNDATION FOR GAINING WISE IGNORANCE

Remaining is a quintessential adult activity and refers to being faithful to one's own identity and the process of its growth and maturity. The activity of remaining refers to faithful constancy, to being there for others and being dependably available. It is mature activity expressed through a ministry of Presence—of showing up and being there for others and through being present to ourselves. In remaining, we care for the young and conserve environments where they can grow and flourish. We remain faithful to primary relationships and faith communities. It is hard now to persuade adults that remaining is a good, wise approach to life. We are busy pursuing options. The radical independence of modernity disdained remaining. Its emphasis on freedom created a context in which growing up was marked by an increasing independence—freedom of thought, freedom of association, freedom of religion, freedom to walk away as one chose. Feminist theories cautioned modernity's addiction to freedom by emphasizing human connection and noting that abandonment is a consequence of radical individuality—pointing to the human harm leaving cavalierly costs other people. But do we simply remain to benefit others? Is the notion of remaining altruistic only? I will address this question since it is central to the whole idea of being faithful. It is not attractive to be faithful unless we sense personally the benefits of remaining.

A primary tension in remaining lies between individuation and integration, i.e., the realizable potential to be part of something yet distinct from it. As noted earlier, people long to be distinct and to be included. How can they be both? The pre-modern era emphasized inclusion, modernity focused on distinctness. In theory, remaining opens up a post-modern option by suggesting it is possible to remain with and be distinct from other people: it is possible to be near to them and different from them, to be socially and emotionally integrated while being psychologically distinct. Remaining implies staying, being there, being true, constant, consistent, loyal, integrous; it is steadfast courage and perseverance. But how do we remain with others and yet be true to ourselves?

A second tension for remaining has to do with our view of human development. There is a strong assumption in developmental theory that an old way of being must die before a new way can grow up in its place. Development proceeds through loss and recovery—bearable in terms of individual development but unbearable for dependent and inter-dependent relationships. The idea that something must die before something new can live explains why so many people abandon relationships during mid-life; development appears to justify leaving. If relationships are tied to old, personally hazardous ways of being, leaving the relationship seems like the only way to secure a good future. What is the difference between leaving an old way of being by abandoning it and rethinking personal identity as an act of renewal?

Abandonment hurts children. If adults forsake a way of life by separating themselves from a primary relationship, because it is associated with unfulfilling behaviour, their loss creates a very special tension for children. Kegan is clear that remaining for one's children permits the young to move through their own developmental process. From a child's perspective, the culture in which she or he is embedded must remain in place during a period of transformation (loss and recovery) so that what was part of the child and gradually becomes no longer part, can be successfully reintegrated as an object of the child's new balance:[56] we need our environment to remain in place so we can grow up with respect to it. Remaining requires us to comprehend human growth in a different way. Growth

> is not alone a matter of separation and repudiation, of killing off the past. It is a matter of transition. Growth involves...reconciliation, the recovery, the recognition of that which before was confused with the self. This is precisely the process of meaning-making that is central to the formation of personality.[57]

If a child's environment is lost during development, that loss can be so great it is impossible to recover balance; depression may result; it is a common insight "that the underlying substrate of depression is loss" (Kegan 1982, 131). To lose a home environment (culture of embeddedness) is to lose part of oneself:

> For the culture to disappear at exactly the time when the child is experiencing a loss of herself is to leave the child with a kind of unrecoverable loss, a confirmation of her worst suspicions about the life project....The normal experiences of [meaning-making] involve recoverable loss; what we separate from we can find anew. [It is unnatural] for a culture of embeddedness to disappear through psychological withdrawal or psychical disappearance...[particularly during a] critical period roughly nine to twenty-one months of age.[58]

I want to explore the idea of remaining, so unattractive to modern individuals, by examining a tension in Kegan's own thought on the subject.

Between two books Kegan wrote on meaning-making he reflected on the problem of remaining. On the one hand, he thought of all growth as costly: "It involves the leaving behind of an old way of being in the world,[59] and further, "all transitions involve leaving a consolidated self behind before any new self can take its place."[60] In his second book, *In Over Our Heads*, largely through paying attention to feminist critique, he pointed out that: "There is no necessary *identity* between taking command of ourselves and taking leave of our connections."[61] He came to see that increasing differentiation can be a story of staying connected in a new way, of continuing to hold on to precious connections and loyalties while refashioning one's relationship to them so that one *makes them up* rather than *gets made up* by them. Increasing autonomy does not have to be a story of increasing aloneness. Deciding for myself does not have to be deciding by myself. Autonomy is self-regulating but that regulation might well be on behalf of preserving and protecting one's connections according to an internal compass or system, since abiding and journeying are contexts for transformational development. Kegan notes that the capacity to take a more differentiated position can permit us to move closer to another person.[62]

I suggest it is through remaining that we grow up, as we reflect on the system we created when we were young, and as we regard it as an object of attention. Modern reformers, such as Freud, insisted that we should abandon the worldview we got as children in order to grow up. I agree with Kegan that we should come to understand, observe and reflect on that worldview carefully so as to ask whether all of its aspects compel us equally. Authenticity is realized as a human goal by looking at our commitments rather than by leaving them. Dis-embedding oneself (growing up) involves permitting ourselves to let 'a way of seeing now be seen through,' in Kegan's own words. Remaining, properly carried out in relationship to other people, is not slavery but is a forward motion in which we allow the system we organized when we were young to shift its shape and change—changing us along with it.

Kegan's metaphor for the system we were when we were eleven or twelve is that of family religion. Until we reflect on the third level of consciousness, the system we became as adolescents, we take our worldviews to be the whole truth and the only way to see the world. When Freud said that we should grow up and reject God, it would

74

have been psychologically and communally healthier for him to say with Kegan that we should reconsider our family religion, which is not the same as Jewish, Christian or any World Religion. Our family religion is a unique blend of ritual and innovation that created the environment we called home; it is an idiosyncratic construction produced through one's interactions with that environment. It is not the Truth, neither is it absent of Truth. In the home and family there are expectations and patterns that shape our view of the world—these ways of being are our family gods. As faithful Christians, we are free to critique the family gods; the God of scripture lives above them, waiting to be known.

Freud would have done well to critique his family gods rather than reject them. He lived with a mother who was especially incapable of attending to her children's emotional pain. She offered no consolation or protection but demanded to be protected from any knowledge that would cause *her* pain or remove her from center stage.[63] He also lived with a father who was incapable of protecting him from his mother's demands. His omission of mothers from the formation of God concepts is explained largely by this experience. As an architect of twentieth century thought, he did not experience a home environment constituted by including, attending, embracing, releasing and remaining. His disappointment with and rejection of God arose from inconsolable rage at his father's ineptness at remaining the adult he needed him to be—he knew unrecoverable loss. We are compelled to understand his rejection of religious education in the twentieth century if we hope to regain ground lost to the church during those decades. Freud did not see the value of remaining. For him, it was a sign of immaturity.

But remaining is an adult activity, without which children are not safe to grow up. Previous generations understood that staying together for the children's sake was a human good. Perhaps they did not know how to integrate and differentiate themselves, to remain, yet be authentic; or, perhaps our own addiction to personal freedom prevents us from perceiving the ways they were successful at being themselves in community.

Our challenge is to see how to be with others without losing ourselves. To accomplish that aim, we need to reflect on worldviews

same for faith community

we constructed when we were young. The road ahead is paved with the evolution of meaning. Work awaits us. The chapters that follow carry on the project addressed by learning to remain in a healthy way. If we want to come out all right in the end, we are well advised to engage in spiritual education. Its whole point, explored in the following chapter, is faith maturity.

3

FAITH TO BEGIN WITH

But solid food is for the mature,
who by constant use have trained themselves to
distinguish good from evil (Hebrews 5:14).

For it is by grace you have been saved, through faith—
and this is not from yourselves, it is the gift of God—not
by works, so that no-one can boast. For we are God's
handiwork, created in Christ Jesus to do good works, which
God prepared in advance for us to do (Ephesians 2:8-10).

THE POINT OF BELIEVING

C hristianity offers eternal life. Jesus said, "Now this is eternal
life: that they may know you, the only true God and Jesus
Christ, whom you have sent" (John 17:3). From Christian
perspectives, faith education aims to reconcile belief in Jesus Christ
with human experience. It allows us to grow in knowledge—which
is more than what we have in mind—it is also what we have in our
hearts. In this chapter, I argue that every human being is compelled
to express faith whether or not they are religious, because faith is
universal. The growth of healthy Christian faith comes about as we
learn to let belief inform experience and allow experience to mature
faith. To explain the relationship between faith and experience, I will

first explore faith conceptually. After offering definitions for faith, I speculate on how it operates in the world. Finally, I connect faith to social intimacy. In healthy environments, we have faith in God and exercise that faith to satisfy spiritual needs so that Christian community is characterized by social intimacy, i.e., the willingness and ability to be near each other and yet be distinct as persons. Faith education develops personal identity in socially intimate relationships. Social intimacy is a capacity for being relationally close to others but also free to be different from them; it requires us to form reasonable trust in ourselves, others and God.

If the point of Christianity is to ground personal faith in the Living God, we must ask what faith is and how it works. If faith is influenced by experience, our work is to see to it that faith communities provide incentives for being faithful. What are some of these incentives? Hear a description of early Christians written by Athenian orator, Aristides, to the Roman Emperor Hadrian (117-138 A.D.). Aristides simply reported what he saw.

> The Christians know and trust God....They [win over] those who oppress them and make them their friends; they do good to their enemies. Their wives are absolutely pure, and their daughters modest. Their men abstain from unlawful marriage and are free from all impurity. If any of them have bondwomen or children, they persuade them to become Christians for the love they have toward them; and when they become so, they call them without distinction brothers....They love one another. They do not refuse to help the widows. They rescue the orphan from him who does him violence. He who has, gives ungrudgingly to him who has not. If they see a stranger, they take him to their dwellings and rejoice over him as over a real brother; for they do not call themselves brothers after the flesh, but after the Spirit and in God....If any one among them is poor and needy, and they do not have food to spare, they fast for two or three days, that they may supply him with necessary food. They scrupulously obey the commands of their Messiah. Every morning and every hour they thank and praise God for His loving-kindness toward them.... Because of them there flows forth all the beauty that there is in the world. But the good deeds they do, they do not proclaim in

the ears of the multitude, but they take care that no one shall perceive them. Thus they labor to become righteous....Truly, this is a new people and there is something divine in them.[1]

Early Christians were moved to love God and accrued social capital (social trust) that pervaded their communities. Christianity didn't invent faith; Christians can't be adequately human unless they exercise it. But what is faith?[2] The conceptual question invites a focus on identity. Faith shapes identity because we become like the people, things or ideas we place faith in. We are well-advised to consider the objects of faith very carefully. Trying to understand what we are becoming is the main reason for trying to understand faith. The purpose behind asking about the concept of faith is to recognize what are currently valuing is what we will likely become. I suggest that this is precisely what Jesus was doing when we urged people to pay attention to faith.

Asking conceptual questions about faith has a disadvantage I want to point out as I begin. In carrying out a conceptual analysis, faith is named; but as we describe its nature, it also names us. An inquiry about faith's nature is useful in that it clarifies and stipulates an identity for faith and provides criteria so we can perceive what faith is, but as we do this, faith can be trapped inside the inquiry and domesticated beyond recognition, since conceptual analysis ignores faith's current and historic social context. A second question is equally plausible: How does faith operate? This question follows post-modern critiques of modern prescriptions for words like faith, typical of Michel Foucault's analysis of power[3] or Jean Baudrillard's critique of social relations.[4] The second sort of inquiry is dynamic and descriptive; faith is a moving target.

Suppose we ask these questions sequentially: faith is depicted yet dynamic. But a conflict remains. As we ask the second question, we challenge the framework for faith that was established by the first question. I think this is a reasonable approach to the complexity of an idea like faith. The disdain some people have for conceptual analysis, and for those who insist there is one right way to understand faith, is that once a word is named, its meaning appears hermetically sealed. We have to be aware we also search for faith's *modus operandi*. We gather meanings about faith, and allow them to speak to one another, acknowledging they are partial. As we recognize that knowledge is partial this side of heaven, we build a collaborative meaning-making environment and open up the possibility for more voices than one to contribute to the conversation.

Being open to others is not the same as being confused; we present knowledge as open and invite others into a reflective space to dialogue further about faith—our openness does not preclude the analytical work we did first. The point I am making here is not simply theoretical. Recall the activity of including described in chapter two. I suggest we have to be intentional at every point to be inclusive of difference. In this case we are addressing a word so foundational to people's experience that those who are primarily mystical get annoyed or feel misunderstood as soon as some of us want to get clear about its meaning. Strong activists feel impatient if we spend time discussing it at all—let's just get on with living faith they may say. Those who feel faith emotionally and express their experience effectively aren't looking for more depth than they believe they already have. These are all legitimate responses. Yet I would urge Christians to consider that one of the most important elements of faith education, especially for adolescents, is the work of bringing our concepts of God to maturity. We consider our words carefully so that our God concepts can be shaped more accurately by the light of scripture and well-conceived thought. Ultimately, conflicts between different spiritual personalities are informed by social intimacy, the willingness and ability to be different but close.

WHAT IS FAITH?

If we ask what faith is and how it works, we perceive the bases for social intimacy. Faith establishes the groundwork for social intimacy to build its home. Faith builds toward intimacy because it holds confidence and vulnerability in tension. Faith opens up the possibility of hope. Intimacy likewise depends on hope. Intimacy is the developed capacity to be vulnerable and feel safe. Social intimacy adds to this definition a developed capacity for being near and different. I ask the reader to imagine that, standing behind this inquiry, is a relationship between an adult and a child. The adult longs to help the child discover and strengthen faith. The child longs for a spiritual friend. What may they hope? What might they learn together? Intimacy is not acquired apart from committed, constant, long-term relationships within a faith community; faith is insecure unless adults remain faithful. In relationship, adult and child learn to have faith and enjoy hope.

If we want to understand faith, we first ask hard questions: Why believe in God? Why believe in a Christian view of God? Depending on what happens to us, responses to this question range from rage to ridicule. This is because the possibility of believing in God is closely tied to people's experience. How could it be otherwise? From a Christian perspective, God came near to us in Christ so as to communicate what it means to believe in God. For better or worse, the marriage between faith and experience holds our attention. Experience pulls at us as we read scripture. Perspectives we gain on what it means to be people of faith are constrained *and* enlivened by what actually happens to those who believe.

What do people want to accomplish when they put faith in God? The answer to that question is the heart of everything I want to convey. Believing itself is inevitable: humanity is compelled to have faith. But what do we put faith in, and why we do so? What is happening to the faith we invest in people, things or God? Is it growing and gaining interest, or is it buried in the ground? The point of believing is faith itself. Education helps to consider faith consciously and intentionally and asks questions such as the following: What is faith like? What is it in? Has faith grown? How does a person exercise faith? What would it be like not to have faith? What would happen to us? Why do we believe in the way we do? These questions are addressed in this book, but a central question, posed throughout, concerns Christian maturity. How does faith grow up? Do we know how to examine ourselves to see how we are doing with faith? (2Cor.13:5)

Every human being requires an education in faith. Two of its aspects matter to education: the noun faith and the verb to believe. The noun and its adjective are expressed in the following sentences: Her parents' faith is Christianity. She is a faithful person. The second aspect is conveyed in the sentence: He believes in God. Under certain conditions, the second sense is an activity: faith is exercised. Faith as noun or adjective is the confidence, trust, reliance or conviction we place in someone or something. As it is exercised, faith becomes an attitude of the heart, i.e., a disposition. People that exercise faith can be counted on to act in certain ways since placing confidence in a person or thing alters thought and action with respect to that person or thing and to the world in general. Exercising faith is as changeful as is physical exercise.

Faith, then, refers to content and to a way of life. As content, faith is intellectual assent, which implies that a person holds consciously chosen statements about the world. These statements may be crass: "Look out for yourself! No one else will do it for you." This belief is a barricade to social intimacy. In general, those who give assent feel bound to act according to implications of statements they prize. I say generally because a dynamic of faith is caught in the relationship between what people say they affirm and what they actually rely on. Affirmation implies conscious intentionality. Yet there may be deep cleavages between what we say and what we count on when the going gets tough. Observing our own faithfulness (and its failures) requires noticing conscious and intentional congruity between what is said and what is done, a continuity that is more elusive than we like to admit, but it's the heart of the spiritual work of growing up.

As a consequence, there is a relationship between content and faith's exercise. When we ask what faith is, we pose a question about human experience. While faith is essential to being human—everyone exercises faith—establishing a happy continuity between what we say and actually trust, is difficult. When we ask how faith operates, we observe particular traditions. Faith may be expressed in loyalty to a tradition that is consciously chosen as a way of life. Faith as a way of life has to do with fidelity, with holding fast to one's integrity and keeping one's word; it is belief put to use. Faith's exercise implies a kind of attentiveness: we observe ourselves acting congruently with what we claim to believe. Faith as feeling is a way of loving the world. It is an attitude that opposes itself to fear and is forward-looking; mature faith makes peace with uncertainty because it is a comfortably certain grip on the picture of the world a person holds.

Another dimension of faith is specifically religious. Faith is a comfortable grip on God. Faith holds sure in God, as confident reliance on God's own Self. From Christian perspectives, faith is not superstition but relies on Christ's once-for-all sacrifice on the cross at Calvary. It is based on a belief that the faithful are related to God *via* historical events of Christ's life, death and resurrection. Faith is grounded on God's initiative from start to finish. Faith as holding sure in God opens the possibility for enjoying the resources of God's grace: forgiveness and a future. A response to God's generosity expresses itself in worship, integrity and service—of being a God-infused community, offering ourselves to those who suffer the realities of ordinary living. As such, it is a new way of hearing and seeing the world and ourselves in it. People see through eyes and hear through ears of faith, or else they perceive experience through a veil of despair. Believing is an outcome of faith: it is the action of faith—it is the energy and information that influences ordinary experience. An essential human task is to learn to use faith in the right way, whether or not people place faith in God.

Faith is never far from us. Every human being has the capacity for exercising faith. There are three parts to the activity. There is the agent of faith—the person that exercises faith. There is the object of faith—the something or someone the agent puts faith in. And there is the relation between the agent and the object. Suppose a young child exercises faith in her mother. As they go for a walk, they come to a playground. The little girl indicates that she wants to play on the slide. She climbs up the steps. As she sits at the top, her mother stands at the bottom of the slide. The mother looks steadily at her daughter and says she will catch her little girl. The child fixes her gaze on her mother's face. The little girl glances down the slide and is afraid but looks back to the familiar face and pushes away from her safe resting spot, keeping her eyes on her mother. Her mother catches her. The relation between mother and child is carried through their mutual gaze and expressed in their shared joy at success. Faith addresses fear. Faith is the opposite of giving in to fear. Faith tries things out, and failing or succeeding, goes on trying. While it may be possible to avoid slides in a playground, every human being learns to exercise faith. We put faith in our trust or mistrust of other people. This little girl is likely to put her faith in trusting others.

We learn about faith as infants. Consider an infant who plays a game of peek-a-boo with his father. The father, the game and the baby constitute an activity in which the infant is learning that his father exists even though the baby can no longer see him. As they play the game the baby learns to have faith in things unseen. Faith is active when we cannot make use of our five senses. Faith is the consequence of experimenting with trust. We put faith in something or someone with the result that we acquire certain beliefs about the world. If conditions are *favorable*, beliefs form about the world encouraging us to exercise trust rather than succumbing to fear and refusing to put faith in anything that we cannot see, smell, hear, taste or touch.

People are compelled to put faith somewhere. Some put faith in the story that life will always disappoint them. Some even put faith entirely in themselves, or more accurately, in a snapshot—an image they make into an idol. But we all inevitably exercise faith. We have faith that the sun will come up tomorrow and that the seas will stay in place. We put faith in the roof over our heads and that the weather will bring sun and rain to make our fields produce food. We put faith in other people. If we did not put faith in ordinary things we would not have enough energy to go on living. People who cannot put faith in the predictability and orderliness of the world are unwell. They become neurotic or psychotic. They are overwhelmed by anxiety and crushed by the demands of living. Faith speaks to anxiety. Faith is built into reality and confirms the wisdom of having faith in the predictable length of days and seasons, in rain falling to water the earth and in the sun shining to warm it.

In order to organize reality meaningfully, we need a story to shape our perspective. This perspective is also what we call faith. Faith is the story we tell ourselves about the world. Faith

> does not create new things but it adds a new dimension to the basic realities of life. Faith brings our fragmented personality into a meaningful whole and unifies our divided self. It is the

source of inspiration for a searching mind, the basis for a creative community and a constant incentive for an on-going renewal of life.[5]

The primary assumption then, is that every human being exercises faith. Faith cuts across secular and religious worldviews. Faith is an attitude that integrates the experience of a whole person—an entire self. In its integrative role, faith influences human action due to the way it organizes the perception of experience. If human beings want to be well, they are compelled to make sense of life. Faith fills in gaps in our experience between what we are able to touch, taste, see, hear or smell and realities that we cannot perceive or test empirically. This feature of faith is as true for scientists who study the atom as it is for those who trust an invisible God. Faith refers to a reality beyond mere seeing—a subject on which good science can only pay its humble respects.

Faith Integrates Experience

Modern science was consumed with division and order—a place for everything and everything in its place. But while modern order explained aspects of human experience, it could not account for its sum total. Human experience moves beyond our capacity for summing things up neatly. In the aftermath of modernity, our spiritual task is to disturb the order of things sufficiently to let old ideas recover a rightful place in the human landscape and allow new ideas to emerge into the light of day. Though we value the wealth modernity made, it suffered from poverty as well. An enormous loss to humankind was felt in the field of faith. Modern secular voices embarrassed the faithful into silence. Science overwhelmed the faithful and left them with little to say in a marketplace tyrannized by empirical truth. Science believed it had the last word on experience and reality.

In modern science, Reality is what is Measurable—a view now challenged by scientists themselves. For example, John Polkinghorne asserts that both theology and science are amenable to a critical realist's understanding of their unique endeavors to explain the world. He argues "both science and theology have to express their belief in the existence of unseen realities, be they confined to quarks forever hidden with nuclear matter or be it the invisible reality of the divine presence."[6] The justification for confidence in things unseen is the same in both cases: "the appeal to what is not directly perceptible makes sense of great swathes of more accessible experience."[7] Mature faith is flexible enough to integrate new knowledge within its frame of reference and keep pace with new discoveries of the human mind. It is essential for mature faith to be willing and able to shift gears, integrate new insights and revise its position.[8]

To pursue this inquiry, a prior question presents itself: how does human experience come to us? A useful image situates its integrative role and accounts for our need for faith as well. To say faith is an attitude is to say it is 'the responsive side of human consciousness' and is found in mental states such as attention, interest, expectancy, feeling, imagination and reaction.[9] Faith is more than a mental state, it is expressed in action, but as an attitude, it is "a subjective response to the power or powers that people conceive as having ultimate control over their interests and destinies"; it is an "attitude of a self toward an object in which the self genuinely believes,"[10] even if the 'object' is an object of thought, idea or a faith tradition.

When we think of religion broadly, we can describe God as the Determiner of Destiny. Religious people attune themselves to the Determiner of Destiny—at the general and personal level. Destiny refers to what is going to happen to the world, humanity in general, as well as what is going to happen to you and me. We may even agree with Immanuel Kant (1793) that while there is only one true religion, there can be several kinds of faith[11] (e.g., Hindu, Christian, Jewish, Muslim). We might suggest further that there is faith that does not depend on religious tradition, hence it is something we might call secular faith. These notions gain support from the view that spiritual needs are universal, for example, "the intuition to hope is a significant and essential aspect of what it is to be human."[12] Hope grounds faith. Regardless of particular traditions, faith integrates human experience with respect to the Determiner of Destiny—or as many young people say, it answers questions about the sense they have that there is Something There. The vagueness of their view of Ultimate Reality may be due to inexperience with a religious tradition.[13]

An archipelago is a useful image of what faith is, how it operates, and especially how it integrates experience.[14] Human experience is like an archipelago—a landform in which islands are surrounded by expanses of water so that island surfaces are seen but the root connections between islands cannot be seen, they must be imagined. As we look at islands, it is reasonable to suppose there are underwater connections. Modern science focuses on landforms; faith focuses on what lies between. Landforms can be charted and measured, their materials tested. Measuring landforms is repeatable work. Human beings cannot regard islands without making assumptions about the deep waters between them—even casual observers sense there is something there. Mature faith takes account of the landforms but also imagines, speculates upon, believes in and narrates the depths beyond sight. Faith helps make sense of the geography of human experience and orients thinking about life as a whole.[15]

All people are compelled to make sense of experience. The stories we tell orient the way we think about the world and convey how to link events together. Explanations for what holds life together shift and change over a lifetime. Faith integrates and orients the process of maturity implied in letting our mental landscape include the reality of measurable landforms and the reality of deeps that lie between them.

The Structures of Faith

If it orients thinking, how is faith built up? An analogy from Wittgenstein explains how faith might be structured and how it structures thinking. Ludwig Wittgenstein (1889-1951) was instrumental in the demise of modern confidence in religious faith, yet notes he finished a few days before he died assert faith's inherent reasonableness. It is possible to read his book, *On Certainty*, which is a collection of aphorisms, and organize an argument for faith or more precisely for believing, as the solid ground on which many reasonable people stand. It is important to realize he was writing at a time and for an audience that vigorously derided religious faith *per se.*

Wittgenstein explored the idea of what we can know for sure.[16] In doing so, he probed the structure of thinking about anything at all. In expressing his perception of problems associated with knowing, he used the following analogy to depict the structure of what we know. He began by suggesting that everyone has a world-picture, what I have been referring to as a worldview. He noticed that we do not get pictures of the world by satisfying ourselves they are correct. Neither do we keep them because we are satisfied with their correctness. The deepest layers of what we claim to know is an inherited background against which we distinguish what is true from what is false.[17] The propositions that structure our knowledge are part of a kind of mythology. An analogy for the mythology of mental life is a riverbed. Some inherited knowledge forms the bedrock of the river; it is solid and firm, virtually unchanging, functioning as channels for other propositions that are not hardened. Some propositions are fluid like the waters that flow over the river-bed, or that shift like sands that lie on the hard rock.[18]

Wittgenstein acknowledged a change of state was possible between the waters and the river-bed (some ideas that were once solid may become fluid), but distinguished between water and river-bed in the following way: "the bank of the river consists partly of hard rock, subject to no alteration or only to an imperceptible one, partly of sand, which now in one place now in another gets washed away, or deposited."[19] He later pointed out that "when we first begin to believe anything, what we believe is not a single proposition, it is a whole system of propositions,"[20] i.e., a mental system or a world-picture. Children, for example, acquire a whole narrative about the world, so to speak. That is,

> The child learns to believe a host of things. I.e. it learns to act according to these beliefs. Bit by bit there forms a system of what is believed, and in that system some things stand unshakeably fast and some are more or less liable to shift. What stands fast does so, not because it is intrinsically obvious or convincing; it is rather held fast by what lies around it.[21]

Wittgenstein pursued this line of thought. He noted that: "*Very intelligent and well educated people believe in the story of creation in the Bible, while others hold it as proven false, and the grounds of the latter are well known to the former.*"[22]

In making this point about beliefs held by reasonable people, he implied that all thinking is grounded on believing, i.e., on holding assumptions (propositions) that we seldom doubt. Thinking must rest on a solid foundation. Even for the most thoughtful, some ideas are steady and reliable like the hinges on a door that allow the door to open. As he put it: "One might say that, 'I know' expresses comfortable certainty, not certainty that is still struggling."[23] He spoke of comfortable certainty as neither hastiness nor superficiality, but as a form of life.[24] Believing orients thinking, because, as he put it: "knowledge in the end is based on acknowledgement."[25] Further, "the rules of caution," so characteristic of skeptical moderns, "only make sense if they come to an end somewhere. A doubt without an end is not even a doubt."[26] Knowledge finds its resting place; it activates us according to a way of life that makes sense, so that we make sense to other people.

What do Wittgenstein's aphorisms contribute to our discussion? Believing is built up by layering assumptions begun in infancy. His insight is linked to a Hebraic understanding of faith. The precise meaning of faith to ancient Hebrews was "Hold God."[27] What is a faithful grip on God like? Also for the Greeks, Philo in particular, faith was a kind of certainty.[28] What sort of certainty is it? Wittgenstein's expression elaborates these ancient contexts. The grip of faith holds God with comfortable certainty—it has stopped struggling. It is a form of life designed as world-pictures we get as children, reconfigured over time through personal and corporate experiences. When we ask the second question, how faith *operates*, we turn to specific narratives of faith. Faith *operates* within a particular form of life. I chose Christianity. It is an offspring of Hebrew and Greek perspectives. In Christianity, faith is material worked with and upon in an aesthetic of hearing and seeing, which influences an idea of God as the Determiner of Destiny, and proposes that God is perceived as much more.

An Aesthetics of Faith

Christianity has a unique perspective on faith and its role in religion. In addressing faith from a Christian perspective, I assume that Jesus of Nazareth, as human being, worked from an integrous center: as a consequence, his statements about a particular topic cohere in a meaningful relationship to one another. From the beginning of his ministry, he focused on faith. Jesus saw who had faith and who did not. His emphasis on the measure of faith was so pervasive that the disciples at one point asked him to increase their faith. He responded to their request by saying that if they had faith the size of a mustard seed, which is extremely small, they could move mountains. So on one hand, Jesus appeared to consider the measure of a person's faith to be central to their capacity to receive what they asked of him, on the other, a tiny amount of faith was sufficient to produce profound change. What is going on between Jesus and faith?

I suggest that in presenting faith, Jesus used *complex irony.*[29] Complex irony is a figure of speech in which what is said both is and is not meant. Its complexity comes about through a set of conditions that are social as well as personal: irony moves people to think about what is being said in light of their current conception of it. Complex irony also conveys change in a concept so the idea can keep pace with something new—usually large-scale change. Complex irony requires that we first understand simple irony. The purposes of simple irony may include humour, mockery or riddle. When irony riddles, it risks being misunderstood.[30] Complex irony riddles with a word's meaning, creating a break in our understanding of it, so that new meanings may emerge.

In simple irony, what is said is not what is meant. Something contrary to what is said is to be understood. Taken in its ordinary sense, simple irony only works if what is said is not what is meant. Suppose on a certain day a teacher is frustrated with a student's lack of progress, when the student is normally quite good. The teacher says: "You are being unusually clever today." If the statement were to be read as it stands, the teacher's meaning would not break through. If the student could not read the simple irony, he or she might think the teacher was offering praise. The student would be wrong. Further, if the teacher were trying to deceive the student, irony would not work. Irony in its simple sense only works if the hearer 'gets it', if the hearer comprehends that what is said is not what is meant. Irony requires us to think for ourselves. Like all significant communication, irony puts the burden of communication on the hearer. But complex irony lays on its hearers an additional burden. Only those who have ears to hear will make sense of complex irony.

When Jesus said that the measure of one's faith matters and also said that faith the size of a mustard seed suffices, he was using complex irony. He both meant and did not mean what he said. He aimed our focus on faith as a centrepiece of spiritual relationship with God. Our relationship with God depends on faith, specifically in Jesus, and grows more intimate with an increase of faith that comes about through each act in which faith is exercised. Faith is a complex irony. If we believe that our acts save us, we place confidence in ourselves not in God. If we wait for God and do nothing, our faith will not grow up. If we place our faith in God, and act out of believing, we move forward in faith toward maturity. Jesus' point seems to be that we must become aware of the measure of our faith, and however much we have at the start, faith must be exercised so that it can grow, hence the seed metaphor. Exercising faith matters very much. Yet it is always God and not our faith that saves us, so even a little faith can move mountains.

If we take its point, we notice that complex irony works with ambiguous terms such as faith. What makes complex irony effective is its relationship to ambiguity. Faith has more than one meaning. In addition, ambiguity is intensified under conditions of social change when social meaning is actually shifting. And not with words only, but entire social systems are under revision. Jesus was doing two things at once: he was honouring a system already in place (Judaism) and bringing about significant changes within that system through the use of complex irony. Jesus claimed that the changes were contiguous with the central and important message of the old system. The role of faith in Christian life is the core of those changes. Throughout the rest of the New Testament, early believers struggled with the meaning of faith and its application to life. For example, faith shows up 246 times in 227 verses in the New Testament (NRSV). The early inquiry about faith was grounded on the investigation Jesus began in his followers. In effect, Jesus asked the following questions: Where is your faith at this moment? What is the object of your faith? What is the measure of your faith? What is the strength of relation between the object of your faith and you? Can you see that your faith will grow as you use it? What might your faith accomplish if you put it to work? In all of this inquiry, the point for the believer is to engage in self-observation. How am I exercising faith at this moment? In whom am I placing my faith right now? What am I counting on? Self-observation is at the root of a faithful life. Educational issues regarding faith stem from self-observation. Christians do two things simultaneously: they observe themselves carefully; they keep their eyes on Jesus.

Faith as Embodied Learning

In addition to self-observation, Christian scriptures say that faith comes by hearing (Rom. 10:17). What is implied in aural/oral transmissions of the Word for a person of faith? What does it mean that faith comes by hearing, specifically, by hearing the word of Christ? I am not asking a theological question. My question is educational. In terms of the teaching/learning relation, what does hearing suggest as a way of becoming a person of faith? Through hearing, faith forms on the layers of assumption made from infancy onward that Wittgenstein described. Hearing happens communally. Personal identity forms in association with a group; identification is accomplished through oral, embodied interactions of the whole. What we hear, we hear together and the other is sometimes God. Yet hearing is utterly personal: we hear what we are able to hear at any given moment.

Hearing *per se*, interiorizing sound, constructs aspects of human identity in a unique way through the 'incorporating' function of sound. In community, learning is embodied. Embodied learning is derived from embodied talking and hearing. Learning through talking and hearing is learning "by observing and listening, by repeating [what is heard], by mastering proverbs and ways of combining and

92

recombining them, by assimilating other formulary materials, [and by participating] in a kind of *corporate retrospection....*"[31] Talking and hearing imply practice, until 'doing' forms a new member of the incorporating group.

An outcome of oral learning is a developed capacity for empathy and solidarity among its members. People draw near to hear one another. The metaphor for incorporating aspects of learning is the Incarnation of Christ. Christ exemplified the necessity of *being with* others as a way of becoming a person of faith. *Being with* engenders the empathy and solidarity that signify closeness, which is central to intimacy. As a result, members of a faith community learn to be near one another; neighborliness inheres in a community of faith, with all the reciprocal obligations that being a good neighbor imply. An oral way of learning leaves its impression on the interiority of group members. When fully formed, this impression expresses itself in the disposition to be a person of faith. Through Incarnation, Christ modeled being near and different, i.e., being human and yet divine, thus showing us the essence of social intimacy. Nearness or closeness is a by-product of incarnational learning, e.g., mentoring and apprenticeship.

But social intimacy and healthy relational intimacy in general, require that people learn more than how to be close. They need to be neighborly, yet sustain important personal differences to grow in social intimacy. Intimacy flourishes as the child of two kindly parents: neighborliness and authenticity. Hearing has the unique attribute that it is corporate—we hear together—and personal— what I hear is my own. Our understanding of faith and its personal and corporate implications unfold over time. The meaning we attach to faith in religious experience is a central differentiating aspect among the various faiths that flourish in the world. From a Christian perspective, faith comes by hearing: one must be actively engaged in thinking for oneself, observing oneself, learning through each exercise of faith and living a faithful life in the company of others. Hearing has these implications. Hearing also unites with seeing, in a special sense.

If hearing draws people close, an aesthetic of seeing allows them to stand back and get a larger view of their authentic location in the group. Seeing combined with hearing, particularly as we understand a Christian perspective of faithful seeing, links nearness to difference. Under these conditions, how does seeing work? From a Christian perspective, faith is seen but is not sight. Seeing in a perceptual and philosophical sense is more typical of Greek than Hebrew perspectives.[32] 2 Corinthians 5:7 says, "for we walk by faith, not by sight." In Hebrews 11:1 "faith is the assurance of things hoped for, the conviction of things not seen." Faith is related to hope. Hope is based on seeing what cannot yet be seen with the eyes.

Faith requires hope. Faith is aware that people are damaged in their humanity and is challenged by this insight. Faith understands that our fundamental commitment as human beings is to try to be human, even when it is hard. We try; God gives the outcome. Hope produces people we might call hopists. A hopist is neither an optimist nor a pessimist. The pessimist sees that nothing can be done; the optimist sees that everything can be done. The hopist has courage to perceive that some things can be done and sets about seeing what this might be. The hopist says to the pessimist that if something is to be done, we have to be attentive to the potential in things and not dismiss them in advance. The hopist says to the optimist that life is complex: there may be degrees of accomplishment in what we are trying to do. Faith cannot exist without hope. Hope is rooted in our awareness of our incompleteness (our knowing only in part). Hopelessness is a sorrowful form of silence. Hope moves us beyond our settled opinions to search for what is worthy. Hope amounts to expecting something good to come from our efforts. Hope delivers us from the "tyranny of the present;" from the feeling we must "grab as much as we can before all opportunity passes away for ever;" with hope we are able to live "in the light of eternity" rather than with a madly relentless drive to 'seize the day'.[33]

If faith is grounded on hope, what is seeing by faith? Seeing by faith is an aesthetic skill in the same way an artist sees a picture she will paint, realizing her vision in the final product. Faith sees like an architect designing a building with paper and pencil. Faith's seeing is like a gardener who observes her garden each year, confident that next year this or that plant will be even more beautiful. Faith sees like an interior designer who knows what a room will look like when he is done even though the rough materials clutter the room at present, or are not even purchased as yet. Seeing with the eyes of the heart is like a dress designer who takes shapeless material and sews it into garments that fit the body and soul of another woman. Faith's manner of seeing comes through practice in the company of faithful people. Faith is the capacity to see what is not yet visible and work for its realization with sustained and sustaining passion. Faith allows the materials at hand, and people close by, to be part of the fabric of the final product. Faithful seeing is the heart's intellectual work. Faithful seeing brings the intellect to bear on the problems of life.

FAITH AND REASON

It is clear from the New Testament that faith is foundational to Christian experience. In order to observe how faith operates, I assume the New Testament is a narrative that hangs together (along with the Old Testament) and reveals the learning process of first generation Christians. I take this point of view from an idea of revelation as "the record of the particularly transparent people and events through which God has graciously shown forth the divine nature."[34] Narrative is not the only model for understanding revelation. In the ancient world, revelation was understood as the flashes of insight, characteristic of Socrates, as well as the slow, deliberate inductive approach, characteristic of Aristotle's method of research. Yet the benefit narrative offers, as a way of describing revelation, is its capacity to show how people learn something new. In the records of first generation believers, we see how faith and reason play out in their attempts to apply Jesus' words to their prior understanding of God.

As experience unfolds in New Testament believers, faith moves to the center of their relationship with God. As an example, Jewish rules about male circumcision are refocused in light of Christ's emphasis on the centrality of faith.[35] As a consequence, there is a shift from an old system of rule-following based on Law, to a new one that relies on faith and reason. Obeying God remains a condition of faithfulness, but Christian attitudes and practices require people to give themselves reasons for doing one thing rather than another, e.g., to eat meat offered to idols or refrain from doing so. Each believer must make these judgments personally but they are also constrained to do so with a mature knowledge of how their decisions affect other believers and non-believers. Believers exercise conscience in light of Christ's life, death and resurrection within the context of a faith community. They assess their own behavior according to knowledge and experience they accumulate over time as disciples of Jesus. They learn to notice and respond compassionately as their behavior affects others.

God does not abandon Christians to figure things out alone. Precedent for the help God offers is found in the Old Testament narrative. When God said to Cain, "if you do not do what is right, sin is crouching at your door; its desire is to have you, but you must master it" (Gen. 4: 7b), Cain is held responsible for what he does, but with God's help. God holds us morally responsible. There are rules to govern action, but the relationship between rules and reason is dialogical. As scripture says: "being confident of this, that he who began a good work in you will carry it on to completion until the day of Christ Jesus," "so that you may be able to discern what is best… continue to work out your salvation with fear and trembling, for it is God who works in you to will and to act according to his good purpose." (Phil.1:6; 1:10; 2:12b-13) Faith relies on reason but reason depends on faith, in a relationship articulated by Kant.

Reason has two senses that are relevant at this point. The first sense inheres in the essential rationality of all people implied in the instruction to work out your own salvation in fear and trembling, with God's help. If we were not capable of thinking for ourselves, we could not be required to participate cooperatively with God in the project of building faith. Without relying on reason, which permits different choices to be made by equally faithful people, Christianity would be uniform everywhere. Yet diversity not uniformity characterizes Christian experience—differences move around a core of belief and practice. Authentic, faith-based differences exist among equally sincere believers as one of the distinguishing features of Christianity itself. The second sense of reason is found in scripture verses that demonstrate how to work out a relationship with God. The first eight chapters of Romans and the book of Hebrews are two prime examples of philosophically astute uses of reason as a way to figure out how to be people of faith, always under the guidance of the Holy Spirit and through the example of Christ.

What is reason's relationship to faith? Earlier I situated the groundwork for knowing anything at all in Wittgenstein's insight that we come to hold certain beliefs and assumptions because we grow up with other cultural members. The insight that our beliefs and assumptions are culturally given influenced the twentieth century; this insight is confirmed by experience. But the inevitability of getting our mental mythology in this manner does not give us permission to remain in our particular culturally made beds forever. If we consider the circumcision issue more fully, we see that New Testament believers made a reasoned shift to a new perspective in which a physical, cultural act (circumcision) was no longer the primary sign of righteous relationship to God. This was a significant move and not everyone made it. Those whose conscience would not allow them to break with Jewish Law were in constant tension with believers whose conscience was free to do so. To put it one way, first generation believers learned how to walk in the dark.

To unpack this metaphor, I examine Wittgenstein's insight from a perspective on reason offered by Kant. Kant argued that pure reason orients thinking about supersensible beings that we cannot perceive with our five senses, such as God. He argued on the basis of reason itself. One implication of his view is that mature believers work with faith and reason to transcend cultural/personal views about God that prevent intimacy with the God because God lives above these inadequate notions. A second implication is that mature believers must work out a relationship between personal freedom and communal responsibility on the basis of Jesus' words and example. Freedom and responsibility unite in the skill of walking in the dark.

Kant explained pure reason by describing how we orient ourselves outside at night or inside in a dark room. The word orienting refers to using a given direction to find other things, literally, to find the sunrise.[36] At night, I orient myself without the help of the light of day by fixing on the North Star (Kant called it the Pole Star). I am able to find my way even if some trickster changed all the stars and planets, reversing their east-west order, while keeping their relative relation to each other the same, (which of course would be very confusing to eyesight alone). That is, even if the world shifts, I can still find my way outside at night by keeping my eyes on one constant Star that shines above the disorder and darkness.

If I am in a dark room, I need only put my hand on one familiar object to help me find my way to the light switch. The sense of left and right (that every human being has) is used outside at night or inside a dark room to orient me spatially. By analogy, reason orients me rationally by deploying a skill similar to knowing my right hand from my left. In terms of pure reason, Kant implied that reason plus God enables a person to decide how to act, i.e., take a step here or there, eat meat offered to idols, or not. In judging how to act, I differentiate between one thing and another subjectively on the basis of my sense of reason (like using my sense of left and right). Kant was clear that rational beings learn to find their own way in the dark and do not rely on the help of other people to guide them, if they want to be mature,[37] but they do rely on God.

He described reliance on God as inherent in pure reason itself. Pure reason is an attribute of all rational people based on their humanity. By this he meant that pure reason did not depend on experience but is built into being human. To him, reason orients thinking based on reason's own need, as he put it, and reason's own need requires God. He worked out the connection between God and reason by basing his view of pure reason as he understood the human condition itself, i.e., with respect to rationality. He put forward two foundational ideas that, to him, linked pure reason to God.

First, pure reason needs a concept of the Unlimited to ground all human concepts of all limited beings, and other things.[38] We require a sense of unlimitedness in order to sense what it means to be limited. Second, reason needs to presuppose the existence of God to account for the contingency, purposiveness and order of all things in the world, which Kant "encountered everywhere in a wondrous degree".[39] He thought that without assuming an intelligent author or source for the intelligibility that stands behind our ability to use reason, we would fall into absurdity. Reason's needs (for the

Unlimited and for Intelligibility) are theoretical and practical. We need God's existence in order to make theoretical and/or practical judgments. Even if we avoid making theoretical judgments (we have no interest in being philosophers or theologians) we must make practical decisions in order to be human. Christianity stresses our need to make personal, practical judgments about how to act, so as to be faithful, but this is a developed skill quite different from standing back and self-righteously judging others. Making judgments about what cannot be perceived with the senses is just as necessary to being human as is making judgments about what we can sense, that is, e.g., in order to judge that it is unsafe to run out into the street when a truck is coming.

But believing is not the same as knowing. Kant located God's existence as a condition for the use of theoretical reason and distinguished believing from knowing. Knowing referred to absolute certainty, what we could know for sure. In contrast, believing guides practical judgment. That is, we cannot make judgments about what is good, which we must do to be fully human, unless we assume a Highest Good, i.e., God, but believing is not the same as absolute certainty. Kant was thinking of knowing something by sensing it directly as his model for knowing with certainty. Believing is not certain, i.e., based on what we sense; it is subjective. To him, rational belief, or faith, was grounded on no data other than those contained in pure reason. Knowing, i.e., what we can prove empirically, is not the same as believing. To Kant, all believing is "a holding true which is subjectively sufficient"[40] so that we can actually find our way outside at night or in a dark room. Thus it is a felt need of reason (believing) that orients thinking. To Kant, believing, or rational faith, is never transformed into knowing through the use of experience (sense data) because we cannot see God. God's existence is not proved by sight but by faith. The holding true of faith is subjective, namely a necessary need of reason and not based on experience. Reason requires God or it won't work. Reason must have an Unlimited and Good Being on which to base its judgments and as long as we are human, reason will always have this need.

But believing (holding true) is not inferior to knowing. For Kant it is a different kind of thinking. Pure reason is a compass and measure to orient ourselves with respect to God whom no one has seen. The issue for pure reason is not that believing is unreasonable, as some secular thought accuses it of being. Rather, Kant's view of reason allowed human limitation itself to show up. The real problem between faith and reason has been a refusal to admit that human beings are essentially limited. It is hubris not secularism *per se* that is the enemy of Christian faith. Kant foresaw the problem of hubris as he analyzed reason. He pointed out that reason is necessarily social, kept healthy by engaging in one's community and is necessarily linked to conscience, uniting us to duties to ourselves as well as to others. Further, it is subject to its own laws, which require certain assumptions about God's existence. He strenuously objected to all who thought human thinking could follow its own lead without limit. To him, if we forget the limits of reason, in the darkness, we become mired in enthusiasm (feelings only), superstition or even atheism. With reason as our god, a limitless capacity to understand the world or ourselves is not possible. If we set reason on the throne, forgetting its humble needs, we become uncivil libertines, recognizing no duty to one another at all:[41] "freedom in thinking finally destroys itself if it tries to proceed in independence of the laws of reason".[42]

In the twentieth century, reason took the unhappy trajectory Kant predicted. In particular, Freud set reason on the throne of his own life. His pervasive influence persuaded many others to do likewise. The role that Freud played in twentieth century is profound. It is difficult to understand what happened to religious education without investigating Freud's life. His rejection of religious education had an effect on all believers—inside and outside the Church. It is not too much to say that Kant was proved right: human reason as god is harmful to civility. If we consider carefully how faith and reason operate together, faith is not the enemy of reason, but her colleague. Faith in what we cannot see makes sense of what we can see. Kant insisted that believing is as good as it gets with respect to what cannot be seen. But our relationship with what cannot be seen by the senses sometimes flirts with atheism, magic and superstition, as Kant said it would.

Faith is Not Magic?

The necessary relationship Kant established between God's existence and the needs of pure reason help explain his view that, while there is only one religion, there may be many forms of faith, mentioned earlier. On Kant's view, God is perceived in general terms, for example as Ultimate Presence with certain essential attributes, including Unlimitedness and Goodness. From a specifically Christian perspective[43], faith takes on a character that has Jesus Christ at its center. While God is unseen, Christ was seen and touched; ordinary human beings experienced him, even if it was a long time ago. Jesus showed us that faith addresses problems of life with courage and hope. Jesus displayed astonishing power through his miracles. In his presence, people were healed and consoled. His miracles were an important sign of his identity. Christianity is powerful. Its idea of power is based on the power inherent in Jesus' life, death and resurrection, which is grounded in God. Power is one of Christianity's problems, specifically for the twentieth century, and in particular for Freud who led the rebellion against God for reasons associated with the complexities of God's power (or its lack, as he saw it).

The New Testament sets parameters around power but points to Christianity itself as a site of power. What sort of power is Christianity? The initial records of the Church, found in Acts, detail relationships that believers have with other forms of power. These forms of power include the State, social relations generally, as well as magic. In Acts, examples demonstrate the use, source and manifestations of power that continue to operate as guidelines for ministries of healing. Fundamental relationships among aspects of magic and power must be managed by the faithful, for two reasons. All social relations are relations of power: believers must understand how power is exercised in domestic, political, economic, juridical, cultural, sexual, racial, and spiritual forms if they would use reason wisely. Secondly, we all grow up in a realm of power we are compelled to address if we hope to become mature. Children live in a magical world that is hard to leave on the shelf. Faith and magic are powerful. Mature believers observe how they use power to understand more accurately why they do what they do. Post-modern critiques point out that Kant under-analyzed power in his description of an individual's use of pure reason.

The book of Acts begins with a powerful occurrence referred to as the Coming of the Holy Spirit, Acts 2. After this event, Apostles are able to heal the sick and raise the dead (Acts 3, Acts 5: 12ff, Acts 9: 32ff and Acts 20:7-12). In Acts 8: 9ff we hear of Simon the Sorcerer who witnessed power exercised by Peter and wanted this power for himself because it seemed greater than his own. In Acts 13: 6-12, a Jewish sorcerer, Elymas, was confronted by Paul. Acts 16:16-38 tells of a slave woman who had a gift for fortune telling. She was healed and the business she created for her slave masters collapsed. In Acts 19: 11-16 there is a confrontation between Apostles and some Jews who practice the art of driving out evil spirits. The thread of these accounts conveys that Christianity is powerful, identifying the source of power and its effectiveness in the person of Jesus Christ—his name, life, death and resurrection. Believers that wish to grow up into the fullness of God must reconcile faith, power and magic.

Whether or not we witness acts of spiritual power, we have all experienced domestic power through the magic years of childhood. Faith whispers to the magic of childhood and woos it to mature. Yet Christianity also compels us to keep our childlikeness so we can continue to believe in God's Magic, to use C.S. Lewis's expression, for example in his children's story, *The Lion, Witch and Wardrobe*. Spiritual power is conveyed by signs and miracles reported in scripture and throughout Christendom. Odd, isn't it: To believe and not to believe—these are in tension. Faith is complex. But by the magic years of childhood, I want to be precise. Children are magicians. In their earliest conceptions of it, the world is magical. They believe their actions and thoughts bring about events. They extend their magical system: they find human attributes in natural phenomena and see human and supra human causes for natural events and ordinary occurrences. Slowly, children learn to distinguish varieties of causes for events and are freed from imagining themselves at the center of the universe.[44] To leave behind the magic of childhood is to be liberated from the burden of carrying the whole weight of the world alone.

As Ana-Maria Rizzuto has shown,[45] during childhood, in the midst of a magical universe, every child concocts representations for God. Ideas for God are not text-based; children are not little people of the Book. On one hand, her view supports Kant's assertions about pure reason as a universal characteristic of all rational persons. On the other, her view grounds a conception of God in experience, as Kant did not. But we must note that Kant and Rizzuto are not using the word experience in exactly the same way. For Kant, experience refers to what we take in through our senses. Rizzuto uses experience in the same way as did Wittgenstein. For Rizzuto, as for Freud, life experience and care-giving personnel constitute sources for our feelings about and images for God.

Rizzuto demonstrates the wisdom of Wittgenstein's insight about the structure of thinking. For example, in gaze behavior between infants and their mothers, a social relation is worked out that influences a child's self-concept. Children require the right sort of relationship in order eventually to discover their own value.[46] In their mutual gaze behavior, children depend on appropriate responses from parents. When encounters continually go wrong, that is, they are over-loved or under-loved, children may develop a false self: self-esteem and self-concepts suffer. When children suffer, their potential to be a person of faith is impoverished as well. Self-important children believe they shape their destiny by themselves. Deprived children cannot believe the Determiner of Destiny (Ultimate Presence) takes an interest in them. Due to experience, and the child's own reasoning, a disposition toward God, other people and themselves slowly forms along one of three pathways: indulgence, deprivation or trustful faith. If they are fortunate, children learn who God is according to a faith tradition that is larger than their own household gods. When children are able to compare their personal mental constructs with formal thinking about God, they mark boundaries around power, magic and faith as well as around ideas of self and other that inhere in each tradition. While God is powerful, faith is not magic. We cannot simply want something so intensely that God is compelled to comply. Faith is risk-taking behavior that requires us to be disappointed sometimes so that we never lose a grip on our need for God.

In faith education, teachers collaborate with concepts of God that children produce on their own. They treat these concepts educationally. Faith education nurtures the child's developing reason, say for example on the basis of patterns seen in Romans and Hebrews, as two bibilical examples. If religious education fails to address their own concepts and questions, children are left to their hapless constructions—some of which produce terrified slaves, some which produce savage tyrants. Slaves and tyrants have no developed capacity for exercising social intimacy. Faith education necessarily focuses on trust and its development. The connection between faith, trust and reason emerges as a child's concepts and questions about God encounter and enjoy a sensitive and wise spiritual environment.

FAITH AND TRUST

Trust and mistrust are emotional, dispositional outcomes of a child's experience with power and faith. On the positive side, believing is a form of trust. As mentioned, under favorable conditions, children learn to put faith in the trustworthiness of other people. In contrast to the verb, faith builds upon the foundation that trust established through experience. Faith is larger than trust because it has numerous layers or dimensions. In general, from a Christian perspective, faith is a perspectival concept; it is a way of perceiving the world based on the growing trust we place in God that expresses itself in relation to the believing community and the world; it is intimacy with God due to the promise of friendship with God that enables the faithful to grow up into the fullness of God.

The developing capacity to be a person of faith is related to and enhanced by the growing skill children acquire as socially intimate human beings, i.e., by learning to be both near to others and different from them. Social trust is an ingredient in the process of learning to be socially intimate. Faith and trust[47] have important links conceptually and experientially. Personal trust is based on deliberately cultivated, face-to-face relationships with friends and family.[48] Social relations and the obligations inherent in them, are mainly responsible for the production of trust, which in turn facilitates cooperation.[49] Trust is a public good. Historically, trust was supplied through shared common traditions, a sense of community, as well as through the Church.[50] Trust is an active political accomplishment that addresses the threat of skepticism. Trust responds to skepticism through its understanding of hope. Trust provides a range of benefits that are fundamental for stable relationships, cooperation, and change. Trust shapes all aspects of human life. When trust is damaged, societies falter; if it is destroyed, societies collapse. Trust is essential for problem solving and for enjoying community. Communication based on mutual trust coordinates social and political interaction; without social trust, community is not possible.[51]

Conceptually, trust is related to confidence, as is faith; both terms include a condition of dependence and uncertainty. Faithful, trustful certainty is comfortable, not absolute; it is sure, but not cocksure. Faith as trust always relies upon a vague and partial understanding of its object. It is not passive acceptance of the unknown; rather it is a strategic decision to take a risk under the conditions of some uncertainty. Faith as trust always has non-rational and incalculable elements. Faith by itself has an element of duty: we must keep the faith as the foundation of social life. Trust has the sense of promise attached to it; if we trust someone, perhaps they will trust us in return, although this aspect must not be allowed to break down into manipulation. Some uncertainty is common to trust and faith. In this way, trust is a form of faith in which confidence vested in probable outcomes expresses a commitment to something rather than just a cognitive understanding of it. Confidence is firm trust—it is trust that has stopped worrying.

The main difference between trust and confidence is the degree of certainty we attach to our expectations. We exercise trust on the basis of making a judgment about something or someone with respect to something else: We trust the milkman to deliver milk tomorrow. We trust a new colleague to reciprocate trustworthy communications. This second sense has more personal risk involved since we could go to the store if the milkman fails us. Anything that facilitates accurate judgments about whom to trust has important social value. A combination of interdependence and freedom make trust a complex social phenomenon.[52] Regardless of how hard we try

Faith, reason, trust

to make good judgments about people and situations, trust by its very nature is a risky business.

Trust implies dependence upon something future or contingent so that a dimension of time is always involved: we trust now about something we await. Trust is more than intellectual assent; to trust is to believe, despite uncertainty. To trust is to put our weight down on an object of trust. Trust involves action—like actually sitting in a chair that we trust will hold us up. Risk is involved due to our inability to monitor the behavior of others and have complete knowledge of their motivations or the vagaries of ordinary life. Trust operates by influencing our behavior on the basis of beliefs about the likelihood that others will behave or not behave in a certain way rather than by firm and certain calculation.[53] The relationship between trust and rationality is complicated and uneven: the complexity of this relationship is nowhere more evident than in the difficulties faced by all rational attempts to build trust.[54] As we practice trust, we develop expectations. Expectations accumulate by learning what happens when we work together and carry out mutual obligations (or fail to do so). In the social world there is always ambiguity: there are always those who act with integrity according to their obligations and those who ride for free. As a consequence, trust builds slowly from the ground up and can be destroyed easily and quickly.

Faith and trust have cognitive dimensions. We hold certain assumptions about other people and the world in general, built up from childhood and through experience. Trust learns to discriminate among people and institutions by classifying them into trustworthy, distrusted and unknown categories. Trust always implies holding sure to expectations about the future.[55] Trust has an emotional dimension based upon an affective bond among those who participate in one's social world, those closest setting the groundwork for our beliefs about what we can expect from those who are more distant. Trust also implies a willingness to accept the pain of disappointment as part of life rather than as evidence that we were wrong to trust. Finally, trust has a behavioral dimension: it is undertaking a risky course of action (inaction cannot be included here—trust must express itself in action of some kind) as we place some confidence in the behavior or disposition of someone else and even ourselves.[56]

Trust and reason (in the context of what we cannot see) are connected in all their dimensions through the practice of believing. Trust is learned through experiencing others and acquires a sense of appropriateness about who and when to trust, if trust wishes to become wise. The disposition to trust wisely, to reason carefully and to hold sure faithfully are essential for the growth of intimacy, since they enable the believer to connect with other people effectively but also to make personal and discriminating choices about how to live authentically for God.

Faith and Social Intimacy

Intimacy has to do with the inner life. Erik Erikson stressed how careful balance between closeness and distance is a most critical psychological task of people emerging from adolescence as they try to develop lasting and productive relationships.[57] Maturity comes when a growing intelligence is animated by the desire not to suffer arrested development, but to keep pace with the intake of relevant experience.[58] Our interior lives are complex; life in the world is complex. If we engage with life and attempt to clarify and understand it as best we can, complexity is a source for maturity. Yet there is continual tension between experience and faith.

There are at least two sources of conflict that can shut down the progress of faith. On one hand, conflict between authoritative theology and a child's own experience, and on the other, contradictions between privileged theological ideas and a child's growing sense of morality and justice can be sources of doubt and disappointment.[59]Disappointment may produce rebellion against or rejection of a faith tradition; but the way forward is to integrate experience with the diversity inherent in all religious traditions. (Sometimes conversion to different faith is the only path forward for a particular person.) People of faith can learn to have the right closeness and distance from the dominant aspects of their religious tradition. They can search through the diversity of their own tradition to find an authentic location within it. Faith as trust "creates the possibility of a religion of search."[60]

On its quest, mature faith fills a creative function: it has unifying power to bring together isolated realities of life and cast them into a meaningful pattern. Faith as trust is a unifying perspective; giving meaning and direction to life; it reveals a goal and creates a task to be accomplished. Based on faith as trust, intimacy secures an optimum grip on the future. I agree with Harriet Lerner: intimacy is more than mere closeness. It is closeness balanced by distance to achieve optimum proximity between people that matter to us. Her point is similar to one made in the previous chapter about a mother and child as they work out nearness and separation (the child acts out a pattern of sitting on her mother's lap and then getting down to play with another child her age); in their interaction, the child begins to experiment with moving away and growing up. Intimacy is true and enduring closeness balanced by appropriate distance; it is not just intensity.

Lerner notes that some people confuse intimacy with intensity. But intimacy implies both authenticity and vulnerability: it is cool and intense, depending. With authenticity, people are safe to be themselves, to talk openly and freely declare their limits. In intimate relation, neither party is silenced; personal sacrifice is not total because the self is not betrayed; each person is strong and vulnerable, weak and competent in balanced ways. With intimacy, it is possible to define a whole and separate self as well as to establish a more connected and gratified unity among people. To be intimate is to have a relationship that does not operate at the expense of the self and does not operate at the expense of the other.[61]

A sense of optimum proximity is captured in a familiar tale of two porcupines wintering in a cave. As they seek to be close and warm yet avoid getting poked by the other's quills, the animals move backwards and forwards until they find an optimum proximity to each other—one sufficiently close for warmth and reasonably distant to be safe from each other's quills. Optimum proximity is not static. Life brings new challenges. Shifting position vis-à-vis significant people is an ongoing process. Likewise, faith as trust is an optimum grip on the future and prepares the ground for intimacy. But faith must be learned through experience, for example, by learning to be intimate in relationship.

Intimacy is operative when we stay in relationship over time. Only in long-term relationships are we called upon to navigate the delicate balance between separateness and closeness, in which we address the challenge of sustaining both without losing either when the going gets tough.[62] As with porcupines, while intimacy is a desired state of affairs, it is also threatening. Intimacy opens up the possibility of being hurt and not having important needs met by others. Neighbors, friends, colleagues and family are sites for developing social intimacy. The way we think about the world informs our capacity for social intimacy. In social intimacy, we take a long view of the earth's value in order to be neighborly.

When we experience social intimacy, we are comfortably certain that we are not alone in the universe, an awareness that becomes embodied knowledge so that we carry ourselves as those who are not alone. Intimacy involves reciprocal caring with people we recognize as being as significant as we are. In intimacy we want an understanding to exit between us, hence we cannot hide behind a façade. Intimacy implies having deep knowledge of the other.[63] As with faith, intimacy is inherently risky, especially at the beginning. Those who are intimate are open to committing themselves to and accepting others. Intimacy implies that we are moved by other people's interests as well as by our own. Intimacy recognizes that other people are deep and the surface we see does not capture their identity sufficiently. Over time, in intimacy there is no fear of being betrayed.

To be intimate with oneself is to be critically aware of ourselves through self-observation that produces self-knowledge. But we often confuse closeness and sameness.[64] Often closeness operates to reduce or eliminate the differences between people: in order to feel safe, sometimes people think they must be the same as other people, and for example, have the same opinions. But the presence of difference is the only way we learn social intimacy. It is our difference from others that helps us acquire a sense of ourselves. In social intimacy, everyone is able to recognize their personal bottom line, a price they will not pay for the sale of their integrity. A bottom line position evolves from a focus on the self, from a deeply felt awareness (which cannot be faked, pretended or borrowed) of one's own needs and the limits of one's tolerance. When we focus on being a self, through self-observation, we become less of an expert on others and more of an expert on ourselves—which is not the same as being self-absorbed.[65] A self-absorbed person is not self-observant.

Intimacy is not suffocation, i.e., feeling much too close, and it is not isolation, i.e., feeling too great a separation from other people. Intimacy implies setting reasonable limits for reciprocation and obligation.[66] Social intimacy is a place of listening, recognizing, attending, smiling, greeting, waiting, respecting, helping, trying again, and ultimately feeling safe when we turn our backs in a group because we know we are valued and safe. Social intimacy calls forth commitment. Hubert Dreyfus notes an interesting observation made by Soren Kierkegaard (1813-1855) as he witnessed the emergence of modernity. Kierkegaard saw that the public sphere was destined to become a detached world in which everyone has an opinion about and comments on all public matters without needing any first-hand experience and without having or wanting any responsibility. In observing his own the times, Kierkegaard said: "The public is not a people, a generation, one's era, not a community, an association, nor these particular persons, for all these are only what they are by virtue of what is concrete. Not a single one of those who belong to the public has an essential engagement in anything."[67] To him, commitment was essential to the vitality of social life.

The combination of effortlessly offered opinion when we have no responsibility for circumstances surrounding the subject of opinion opens up the possibility of endless reflection.

For example, we may have opinions about our political leaders but if we have no responsibility for the work they do because it is not our work, our opinions are offered in ignorance of what they must account for as they carry it out. If they do not make decisions or take action, and have no actual experience with the complexity of the situation, mildly interested individuals can look at all things from all sides and always find some new perspective. If their opinions are influential, action is postponed. In *The Present Age*, Kierkegaard offered the following motto for the press because he felt the media were at the core of his criticism about the proliferation of irresponsible and uninformed opinion: "Here men [sic] are demoralized in the shortest possible time on the largest possible scale, at the cheapest possible price."[68]

People are demoralized in at least two senses: they lose their integrity and become indifferent and idle; they lose the passion to make a difference in the world—they become calloused to their own potential to make life meaningful. While a position of endless reflection seems safe on the surface: anonymous spectators take no risks, have no fixed identity that could be threatened by disappointment, humiliation and loss,[69] endless reflection fails to use its own reason and refuses to trust. I agree with Kierkegaard; superficiality does not ground social intimacy. In social intimacy one is engrossed, engaged, identified, capable of working from the authenticity that identity signifies, yet safe to be different. In social intimacy, people learn to be near and different. But if social intimacy is to flourish in a faithful community, all its members must learn to gain mastery over themselves and over the gifts they contribute to make communal life healthy.

Mastering Social Intimacy

At the beginning of chapter three, I introduce the idea of social intimacy and propose that understanding faith education requires us to imagine a mentoring relationship between an adult and a child in which the adult longs to help a child strengthen personal faith and the child longs for a spiritual friend. When these longings are satisfied, Christian community satisfies spiritual needs. But social intimacy must be mastered through experience. In making his critique about the current circumstances of endless reflection, Dreyfus identifies seven stages of learning[70] that culminate in the mastery of a particular subject matter or skill. The model he proposes suits the project of learning social intimacy since we learn intimacy by being with others. Social intimacy is an indirectly acquired sense of how to be fully human. Dreyfus uses the term stage to refer to seven separate parts of the teaching/learning relation. He makes this point to convey that later learning is dependent upon and grows out of earlier parts of the process. The process of learning, from novice to master, includes instruction, practice and apprenticeship. He is primarily concerned to identify a process of learning based on face-to-face interactions, which is why the process accommodates to learning social intimacy. He believes that learning mastery in any domain is achieved bodily.

To him, if the body is omitted from the learning environment, people lose the ability to recognize relevance, lose their adeptness at skill acquisition, and lose a sense of the reality of people and things, all of which results in the loss of meaning. I agree with him that the apprenticeship model he proposes overcomes these losses: one learns social intimacy in the arrangement of his stages because social intimacy depends on the sort of judgment-making these aspects of learning encourage. Learning to be a person of faith and learning social intimacy take place as we acquire other skills and knowledge from dedicated, knowledgeable people who are also aware of the measure of their faith and are committed, passionate, dependable and socially intimate people. His seven stages move from inexperience to practical wisdom. At the level of practical wisdom, in stage seven, learners have acquired discernment and authenticity (their own style) as well as skill with cultural style (the way their culture does things well). As a result, personal style is situated effectively within a cultural context. As a result, learners are perceived by others to have mastered the subject. In stage seven, learners receive honor and recognition for the combination of personal and cultural style. They are perceived no longer as learners but as masters.

It is the combination of personal and cultural style that ensures that social intimacy, i.e., nearness and difference, has been understood. I will outline his seven stages in the final chapter and develop the application of faith to these stages. At this point I want to emphasis what faith education requires at the outset. In stage one the novice is inexperienced. The teacher begins by decomposing the task environment into context-free features that the beginner can recognize without the desired skill. These features are what Dreyfus refers to as domain-independent. Domain-independent features do not require learners to know anything about the subject that lies ahead.

For example, suppose grade one children come to school to learn about parallel lines. A wise teacher takes the children outside to show them the line of the curb in relation to the edge of a sidewalk, and lets the children walk along (perhaps with a piece of string between two of them) so they can see that these lines never touch each other, but remain essentially the same distance apart, beginning to end. The lines are parallel. The child learns from experience to organize a new idea based on something already known and previously experienced. The children have seen these lines before, prior to coming to school and now have a new way of thinking about them. Also they have a new way to look at the world. The children are also given rules for determining action on the basis of these domain-independent features, e.g., keep the string tight. This activity is something like a computer following a program. The novice acquires features and rules on the subject to be learned. The learner must recognize the features presented and engage in drill and practice, to become familiar with these features and their rules of use. The children practice drawing parallel lines following rules about how to hold their rulers, for example. How may we apply the stages of learning that Dreyfus identified to faith education, especially at this crucial beginning point? I suggest that spirituality provides us with domain-independent features that faith education hopes its learners will master.

As *a sense of felt connection*, the spiritual aspect fills a child's mind hoard with images, feelings and ideas. If we hope for them to master social intimacy spiritually, we begin to help them sort through the contents of their mental mythology so they organize and re-organize meaning into a worldview that secures their own identity and takes account of other people. Using insights from the four spiritual personalities, a fully orbed learning environment uses methods and aspects of all four types.

Spirituality is a dimension of personal identity formation that helps us sense how we are related to material and spiritual aspects of experience as authentic members of a faith tradition. We learn to feel a sense of obligation to treat others as neighbors, at the moment that we recognize our own humanity in them and sense that their loss of humanity is also a loss for us and for the world.

How does Dreyfus help with the project of learning faith and social intimacy? His model allows for an apprenticeship between mature and young believers. The starting point of faith is crucial if apprenticeship is to result in social intimacy. For example, children need to understand the elements of faith, which address their most basic human needs,[71] which also are common aspects of human spirituality. Human needs are addressed uniquely within specific faith traditions but must be introduced to the young in a way that connects these needs to ordinary life. As Dreyfus says, apprenticeship begins with context-independent attributes of the subject or skill to be mastered, in our case, with spiritual needs identified and met in by a community of faith.

Under favorable conditions, children learn what it means to be intimate human beings; they learn how to be people of faith. With intimacy, they are able to observe themselves while keeping their eyes on those who share the apprenticing relationship with them. They learn to use reason and experience in the right ways so that faith can mature.

In Christian traditions, they learn to perceive Christ so as to keep their eyes on Him. In order to be learned, intimacy must be incarnated—we must see it active in a person we come to know. We need other people to see what we might become.

Incarnational apprenticeship, on the Dreyfus model, allows for the development of authenticity, personal style and cultural know-how. The culture of a child is not the same as the culture of an adult. Children can be encouraged to retain the uniqueness of their perspective, at the same time as they connect with a community of faith. Children must learn to negotiate their cultural landscape with wisdom and compassion. As adults take on the task of apprenticing the young, they move the future towards its brightest and most hopeful ends.

One outcome of apprenticeship is self-esteem. In the Dreyfus model, consistent, careful attention is given to the learner by people who are experts. But what keeps the learner from losing himself or herself in the midst of these knowledgeable people? How can we learn to be true to ourselves while with significant others? And further, how do we learn to have a reasonable opinion of ourselves, one that is based on accurate self-knowledge? What role does self-esteem play in becoming faithful, intimate people? In the chapter that follows, I address the issue of self-esteem because it is central to education. Self-esteem is important in becoming a person of faith and having courage to trust that we are beloved by God, and worthwhile members of the community. We learn in community that we have a contribution to make to the Kingdom arising from the uniqueness of our personal experience with God.

4

LEARNING SELF-REGARD

They will be my people, and I will be their God. I will
give them singleness of heart and action, so that they will
always fear me for their own good and the good of their
children after them. I will make an everlasting covenant
with them: I will never stop doing good to them, and I
will inspire them to fear me, so that they will never turn
away from me. I will rejoice in doing them good in this
land with all my heart and soul (Jeremiah. 32: 38-41).

Let your words combine insight and self-awareness,
so that the peaceable divine Logos [John 1:1-18]
may not be ashamed to enshrine Himself in them
because of their brashness and lack of restraint.[1]

WHAT ABOUT ME?

Can I love God and still like myself? In the last chapter we
built faith on the assumption that it is a universal human
experience. Every human being exercises faith and wants
a supportive environment so that spiritual needs are met. In this
chapter I suggest that people also have to learn to regard themselves
in a spiritually healthy way. To support my claim, I rely on Christian
insights on self-esteem. Christianity has not been seen as favorable

117

to the concept of self-esteem. Popular culture conveys that healthy people have a high view of themselves. How do people of faith resolve the apparent conflict between Christianity and culture? I suggest a way forward is to see that faith is universal: we share similar anxieties with the rest of humanity that are addressed spiritually; faith is personal and we have resources secured through following Jesus personally. Faith is universal; following Jesus is personal.

Yet Christians find it hard to understand personal faith unless they face core assumptions. For example, in the twentieth century West, personhood was shaped by a culture of authenticity. As we speak about being personal, an inescapable subject emerges: self-esteem. Modern concern for individual authenticity, which will not go away as a human interest, compels us to consider what it means to be a person, at the same time as we try to be Christ's person. People of faith wonder about self-esteem and ask how Christians should regard themselves. In this chapter, I want to work out an approach to self-esteem that encourages us to love God, ourselves and other people. But learning the best way to think about ourselves is hard spiritual work.

In popular culture, self-esteem offers each person a positive sense of self and a feeling of being special. Are Christians called to feel special? Or, are they called to feel worthy as God's beloved? What is the relationship between feeling special and being worthy? I argue throughout that the value we place on ourselves is grounded on our confidence in God and our faith in God's absolute worth. As a result of faith, believers draw close to a loving God who declares them to be worthy of love. The value we place on ourselves is a by-product of drawing close to God. The art of self-regard comes about through acts of faith grounded on the declaration of our value to God. The art of self-regard, as I hope to show, helps us develop a reasonable view of ourselves. How does having a reasonable view of ourselves, as followers of Jesus, compare with cultural notions about self-esteem?

Self-esteem is value placed on a particular self-image that is built over time. It is the outcome of self- and social evaluation. Popular culture, in the late twentieth century, assumed that people could not have too much self-esteem because it was a form of self-protection—like a coat of many colors that conveys special status. In general, during a process of self-evaluation, self-image is personally and socially constructed. How does this view of self-esteem work for Christians? I suggest that esteem plays an important role in what I call the art of self-regard and I distinguish esteem from some of the ways the term self-esteem has been used.

The issues involved in self-evaluation are personal, social and environmental. While it is often seen that self-evaluation has personal and social influences, to understand the connections among self-esteem, esteem and self-regard, Christianity expects us to critique our environment. As I explored in chapter two, an environment strongly influences how we view and value ourselves. Jesus addressed environmental influences of his day and established the basis for an art of self-regard that takes human need for esteem seriously but draws boundaries around its pursuit. I will explain the art of self-regard by exposing the boundaries of self-love and self-hate that historically limit appropriate self-evaluation, from a Christian perspective. These boundaries are implicit in Jesus' teaching but were lost sight of in twentieth century literature. They came back into view due to a proliferation of narcissism (self-love) and its negative effects on social life. To reveal the art of self-regard, I examine self-esteem as it appears in historical writings of Thomas Kempis. To provide a basis for thinking about self-regard, I first consider scriptural guidelines for self-evaluation.

GETTING OVER OURSELVES[2]

Let's begin with a thought experiment. Suppose two young Christian women see themselves as attractive. The value one of these women places on her self-image (a mental picture of herself as attractive) encourages her to feel creative and free to use her appearance as one asset for confidently pursuing her opportunities. The other woman sees her appearance as her only asset, a source of unhappy competition among women and the sole aspect that interests men. She feels compelled to be compliant to avoid attracting unwanted conflict with other women and unwelcome attention from men. Although equally beautiful, they value themselves differently.

What place should be given to self-esteem and self-evaluation in their lives? Will self-esteem help them live faithfully the full life promised in Christ?

One response we might make to both women is to say they should forget about themselves. We might think they should get over themselves by ignoring feelings, dispositions and personal experience. We might think one is too vain and the other is too hard on herself, and leave it at that. We decide that getting over ourselves means not thinking about appearance at all—a kind of self-neglect. If we were to make that judgment, in my view, we would commit a grave, unbiblical error about self-regard. In addition, we would fail to acknowledge the role environment plays in these young women's lives, with its pervasive message that good women are sexually attractive and available, including Christians. How should Christians evaluate themselves in the present culture?

Scripture provides two principles to guide self-evaluation: Christians are to think neither too highly nor too lowly of themselves. On one hand, the Bible warns against spiritual pride (Matt 6:1-13; Rom 12:3; Phil 2: 5-8) and on the other hand, against self-depreciation, a rejection of self that renders Christ's death and resurrection a waste of his time (Matt 6:26-32; 1Pet 1:17-20; 2:24). Self-evaluation takes place by establishing two extremes: there is a middle ground in which we resist the temptation to spiritual pride *and* "the temptation to self-rejection."[3] As we move to this middle ground with Christ's help, it is essential for believers to sense their environment so as to see how they are valued in it. Emphasizing a middle ground between extremes is a pattern that is observable through the centuries in Christian literature. If we compare what has been said about self-esteem, what shifts is not the balance articulated in scripture; what changes is the cultural environment that influence self-evaluation.

Self-evaluation is confusing to work out unless we attend to the way people are affected by environment. For example, if advice appropriate to those who succumb to spiritual pride is given to those who suffer low self-esteem, they slowly slip further into self-depreciation. I want to pursue this point further as it applies to the example of the two young women mentioned earlier.

The incarnation is a theological and practical assertion that everyone is of value. Jesus taught it is unnecessary to fear that God will forget us (Matt.6: 25-27) and established a basis for the art of self-regard that takes our need for esteem seriously but draws limits around it. For example, when he initiated his disciples into ministry, he sent them out with authority to drive out evil spirits and heal every disease and sickness (Matt. 10:1); his instructions show he trusted them. They were to choose a worthy house in each town. On entering, they gave it their greeting. Depending on the household's response, they let their peace rest on it. If their message received no welcome, they let their peace return to them, shaking the dust of the place off their feet as they left. Jesus established an environment in which the disciples' worth was fundamental to their work.

Further, the New Testament recounts experiences of culturally invisible men and women and signaled their worth in unprecedented ways, when compared with the ancient world environment.[4] It is remarkable that Jesus healed and restored to community a bloated man (Luke 14:1-6), a man with a shriveled hand (Luke 6:6-11), a woman subject to bleeding (Luke 8:42b-48), a crippled woman (Luke 13:10-17) and a blind man (Luke 18:35-42). None of these people, except the blind man, asked Jesus for help. The blind man called out to Christ, "Jesus Christ, Son of David, have mercy on me." The crowds rebuked him for his impertinence and pushed him back. Jesus ordered that the man be brought forward. "What is it you want me to do for you?" Jesus asked. In that simple question, we are all empowered to approach Christ, regardless of perceived social value. All those restored were valueless to religious leaders and crowd alike, until they were made visible by Jesus, who asserted that they too were daughters and sons of Abraham. He challenged his environment to count them in.

ENVIRONMENT AND SELF-REGARD

Learning the art of self-regard requires us to consider our environment. By environment, I refer to the complex and cumulative effects of social interactions that leave their impression in a dominant way of being that shapes expectations we have for

,.,,. done

ourselves, God and other people. Environments are specific because they alter over time and are unique to a given place. The tone of an environment is particularly relevant to learning how to regard ourselves appropriately.

At the core of self-regard is the acknowledgement that we all have a basic human need for esteem. From a peronal point of view, self-value is affirmed by an environment so that people enjoy esteem, or it is dissonant and they feel invisible. From a social perspective, esteem is won or lost in games of attention-getting that establish individual currency. Esteem is not an outcome of self-evaluation only; it is a function of attention we receive from others and is "one of the great generic currencies of social life;" and since "all cultures make it possible for people to get attention" that provides esteem, it is a distinct social phenomenon that can be analyzed, like money, to establish the value of a person's life.[5] When I am with students, I notice how often they credit their confidence and vocational choices to people who recognized their giftedness. They got encouragement from an environment that freely supported them. Under favorable conditions, this is how esteem works.

All learning takes place in an environment.[6] Learning the art of self-regard is no exception. Esteem comes from feeling we fit in an environment and from getting sufficient attention. But environments are not always friendly. For example, one of my students reflected on her situation:

> As a woman and a Christian, there have been times in my own life when I have felt disempowered on account of the gap between [personal and social realities I face]. I sometimes experience the socio-cultural world of my church as androcentric and do not always feel like I 'fit' as a result. For example, it seems to me that the popular interpretation of sin as pride, wanting to be like God, self-righteousness, does not apply equally to women as to men. I experience myself differently. My failure and separation from God come about in the form of self-denial (food, sleep), lack of self-confidence, insufficient self-esteem, etc. I experience sin as an undervaluing of myself more than an attempt to be like God. An androcentric definition of sin can disempower women by contributing to their failure or inability to identify and combat

sin in their own lives.[7]

This woman finds it difficult to fit into Christian community. She acknowledges that her sin is to think too lowly of herself. People who feel they do not fit seem insecure around those who fit easily— but that judgment fails to assess the environment. Other research supports her insight that "the predominately male sin is that of pride, whereas its female equivalent is that of low self-esteem."[8] While I do not say that only men succumb to spiritual pride and only women suffer low self-esteem, it is important to see that sex, race, wealth and ethnicity influence people's ease in securing adequate attention. Christians must seriously consider the value placed on these social categories if they wish to learn the art of self-regard and enjoy communities in which all those whom God loves are free to flourish.

Environments influence our ultimate concerns, i.e., what we hunger for. As an example, the Beatitudes instruct us in the art of being happy. Beatitude refers to supreme happiness, a state of blessedness. There is no indication that the Beatitudes constitute a cumulative list[9]: Any who mourn, make peace or hunger for righteousness are blessed of God. While they are not cumulative, there is at the heart of these ways of living a link that unites them. Can one truly mourn without getting hungry for God? The Beatitudes summarize righteousness and build a framework for thinking about ultimate concerns. Within this framework, the notion of hunger is central. In learning the art of self-regard we become aware of personal, social and environmental hungers that drive self-evaluation. I agree with Derber (2000) that in the present age, self-evaluation is driven by an insatiable hunger for attention.

To understand and work out the art of self-regard, and avoid spiritual pride and self-rejection, we must see how the environment currently shapes sin in our own hearts. The sin we suffer creates hunger in our souls that must be acknowledged and addressed. The art of self-regard enables us to reflect theologically and address those sins. The art of self-regard also aims to help us sense environmental influences that shape us. The art of self-regard pays attention to a middle ground where we are worthy because God declares our worth. In contrast to hungering for attention, the art of self-regard is an act of faith. Our capacity to believe in God and enjoy salvation is influenced by faith. Hunger for attention is satisfied by communities in which we enjoy sufficient esteem. As we will see, the art of self-regard lies between extremes of thinking too highly or too lowly of ourselves and requires being sensitive to environment. To develop environmental sensitivity, we can retrieve ideas of self-esteem that contribute to learning the art of self-regard.

GLIMPSING THE TRAJECTORY OF SELF-ESTEEM

As we try to grasp the influence of the concept of self-esteem on Christianity, we can look to traditions that explored the idea. The *Philokalia* is a collection of writings from the first to the fifteenth century that provides spiritual wisdom on self-esteem. In these texts self-esteem was a sin instigated by the demon of self-esteem. In this view, self-esteem is entirely negative; it is one of the three primary debilitating passions and only one better than the catastrophic sin of pride itself. The subtlety of observation in these texts is startling. As it is described, it is impossible to think of self-esteem positively. Self-esteem darkens the intellect. It is like spiritual madness that numbs the mind so that its evil invasions go unnoticed. In this view, to become mature, one must fight against the sin of self-esteem.

Self-esteem (*kenodoxia*) has the skill of diverting all attempts to please God. Distracting us from the project of pleasing God, it dazzles us with possibilities of basking in human praise. In short, self-esteem is the sin of attributing to oneself honour and glory that belongs to God. Self-esteem drives us to take credit for our spiritual gifts rather than giving credit to their Author. Self-esteem was a sub-category of self-love. In the *Philokalia*, self-love produces "self-praise, self-satisfaction, gluttony, unchastity, self-esteem, jealousy and the crown of all these, pride."[10] As an excess of self-absorbed love, the sin of self-esteem moves us to criticize others, particularly those in positions over us, and to imagine that we could do a much better job, if only we had the chance. Once we are bitten by self-esteem, we are infected by the will to undermine those we wish to usurp: actions follow desire, often expressed in gossip and even murder.

Humility is the opposite of self-esteem. Humility consists not in self-condemnation, but through God's grace and compassion, acknowledges our utter dependence on God's willingness to forgive us and secure our future. In its absolute reliance on God, humility frees the mind from all conceit. Self-esteem on the other hand, is

> a vice that is difficult to defeat because it has many forms and appears in all our activities—in our way of speaking, in what we say, in our silences, at work, in vigils and fasts, in prayer and reading, in stillness and longsuffering....When it cannot seduce a man [sic] with extravagant clothes, it tries to tempt by means of shabby ones. When it cannot flatter him with honour, it inflates him by causing him to endure what seems to be dishonour. When it cannot persuade him to feel proud of his display of eloquence, it entices him through silence into thinking he has achieved stillness. When it cannot puff him up with the thoughts of his luxurious table, it lures him into fasting for the sake of men's praise.[11]

Yet even in the *Philokalia*, esteem itself is not the soul's enemy, any more than food is the body's enemy. It is the wrong use of esteem that troubles a Christian soul. Jesus demonstrated his appreciation for the esteem shown him by the woman who washed his feet with expensive perfume and wiped them with her hair. (Matt. 26: 6-13) She demonstrated her love for him. He was grateful and valued her act because of its meaning for him. He is our example. There is no need to deny our basic human need for esteem. It is a by-product of attention and recognition, sometimes from other people, but ultimately from God. It is a satisfying sense of well-being that provides energy to go on trying to accomplish the good works that God prepared in advance for us to do. (Eph 2:10b)

In contrast to esteem, self-esteem is pervasive and subtle, tempting us *to be seen* as godly. Jesus warned about aiming actions at getting praise from other people. He pointed out that those who perform righteous acts for human praise have their reward already. Act in secret, he said. Then our Father, who sees what is done in secret, will reward you. (Matt. 6:4) He presented "a different approach to piety, one that shifts attention from the act itself to the tone or style that accompanies it."[12] The authors of the *Philokalia* took Jesus' words seriously; moulding their lives around them, they practiced the art of resisting self-esteem. Yet self-esteem goes deeper than desiring human praise.

There is a relationship between self-esteem and self-deception. Those tempted by self-esteem no longer notice that their thinking is darkened: they take the darkness within them for light. When we deceive ourselves, we lose touch with spiritual reality. As Jesus said: *If then the light within you is darkness, how great is that darkness!* (Matt.6:23b) A tendency to lose touch with others, and with God, is at the heart of spiritual pride. Other passions that trouble the soul, self-esteem included, attack and try to overcome their opposite virtue; in the case of self-esteem, the virtue is humility. But the passion of pride darkens the soul completely and leads to utter downfall.[13] The antidote for self-esteem and pride is compassion that affirms human worth (our own and other people's) and attributes glory to God.

In all of its ancient expressions, self-esteem leaves an imprint on the lives of those it invades. The mark of self-esteem is to make divisions in nature and to treat some things as worthless;" conceit is its natural offspring.[14] Privilege and elitism are the footprints of self-esteem in the soul. Self-esteem does not permit believers to grow in virtue; they remain barren. Whether believers are beginners, midway or mature "self-esteem always tries to insinuate itself and nullifies [their] efforts to live a holy life, so that [they] waste...time in listlessness and daydreaming"[15], or perhaps in unfocused, overblown busyness.

To summarize the *Philokalia's* view, self-love was synonymous with self-esteem. Self-love was "mindless love for the body"[16] and was the cause of all the soul's problems. Attempts to eradicate self-love tended toward erasing the self and promoting human worthlessness. In a very influential move, Jean-Jacques Rousseau addressed excesses of self-love and clarified its healthy and unhealthy forms. Before we consider his analysis, I want to pick out a twelfth century influence on Rousseau and then examine Thomas Kempis's contribution to the Christian notion of self-esteem.

In the twelfth century, there emerged an emphasis in some Christian writings that valued the self in novel ways, given the environment at the time. In his book, *The Discovery of the Individual 1050-1200*, Colin Morris points out an emphasis on self-regard that is distinguished by its refusal to endure abuse simply because one is lower down on the inferior/superior social ladder. A central figure in this protest is Abelard who later became the model for Rousseau's eighteenth century assertions about the value of the individual. (Abelard and Eloise together constitute his model, although Morris makes only the briefest mention of Eloise in this book.) Quotations that follow exemplify social and personal protest against personal worthlessness. As an example, one of the voices of this twelfth century protest, Guibert, assessed his former schoolmaster and confided that:

> The love that this man had for me was a savage sort, and he showed too much severity in his undeserved beatings; and yet the great care with which he regarded me was evident in his acts. Clearly I did not deserve to be beaten, for if he had had the skill in teaching which he professed, it is certain that I was, as a boy, well able to grasp anything that he taught me correctly. But because he did not say what he meant and what he tried to express was not at all clear to himself, his talk rolled on and on ineffectively in a circle, trundling along without direction, and could not arrive at any conclusion, let alone be understood. For he was so ill-instructed that he remembered incorrectly what he had... learned late in life, and if he inadvertently let something slip out, he would maintain and defend it with blows, regarding all his own opinions as certainly true. [17]

In a similar tone, Abelard evaluated Master Anselm of Laon and recounted that:

> I came therefore to this old man, who owed his reputation to long habit rather than intelligence or memory. If anybody came knocking at his door in perplexity about some problem, he would go away still more perplexed. [Anselm of Laon] was wonderful in the eyes of his admirers, but in the sight of those who asked questions he was no one. He had a marvelous flow of words, but

its meaning was trivial and its reasoning empty. When he lit his fire, he filled his house with smoke, but produced no light.[18]

Morris points out that twelfth century psychology "was abandoning a sharp division between love of God and love of self, and was moving towards a more delicate analysis of human 'affections'.[19]

With respect to a developing psychology of human value, these men identified new aspects of self-love. In particular, they distinguished life on earth from life after death in terms of self-love and argued that, in "a sense the whole drama of the life in Christ consisted, for [Bernard of Clairvaux], in the purification of motive, or intention, and it was the basis for the classification of [love], ascending from loving oneself for the sake of oneself, to loving oneself only for the sake of God."[20] Bernard came to see that loss of self was a condition pertaining to life after death. He said: "For in a sense to lose yourself, as if you were not, and not at all to feel yourself, but to be emptied of yourself and brought almost to nothing—that belongs to our conversation in heaven, not to our human affections" [here on earth].[21] Bernard also "spoke of the individual as fulfilled, not lost, in the encounter with the eternal Word; and he was prepared to take the language of self-fulfilment to great lengths."[22]

The central premise of Morris's book is that individuality was discovered in the twelfth century because men like Abelard, Guibert and Bernard refused to prize human worthlessness—they refused self-rejection. If a person is worthless, what is the point of self-awareness and self-knowledge? Without self-knowledge, how are we to progress in the journey of faith? "Self-knowledge is, for Bernard, both the beginning and the end of the spiritual journey."[23] These twelfth century insights on self-regard were not carried along in the mainstream of Christianity but resurfaced during the modern era.

As already mentioned, in *Philokalia* writings, self-esteem was synonymous with self-love, a "mindless love for the body".[24] This theme continued in *The Imitation of Christ* by Thomas Kempis (1379-1471).[25] To him, esteeming oneself as nothing was the attitude that pleased God. He wrote,

Shall I speak unto the Lord, who am but dust and ashes? If I esteem myself to be anything more, behold, Thou standest against me, and my iniquities bear true witness, and I cannot contradict them. But if I abase myself, and reduce myself to nothing, and shrink from all self-esteem, and grind myself to the dust I am, thy grace will be favourable to me, and thy light near unto my heart; and all self-esteem, how soever little, shall be swallowed up in the valley of my nothingness, and perish forever.[26]

Kempis thought God demanded self-abasement. He counselled: "Be zealous against thyself, and suffer no pride to dwell in thee: but show thyself so humble and so lowly, that all may be able to walk over thee, and to tread thee down in the mire of the streets".[27]

But he also saw limits. It was "not lawful to cast away all things, because nature needs to be sustained."[28] He realized that reducing oneself to nothing materially led to temptation. He advised those preparing to take communion not to be anxious about confession or too scrupulous in examining themselves so they became disquieted. He advised them to quickly confess sins and cheerfully forgive others their offences.[29] He said believers could be cast down in the miry streets but not be downcast. It is a trick of psychological logic the twentieth century could not endorse. It is hard to believe that he avoided the extreme of self-hate unless we assume the environment in which he wrote so disdained humanity that his limits signal an improvement to his era's view of human value.

Modern reluctance to value self-abasement is partly due to Jean-Jacques Rousseau's (1712-1778) analysis of self-love. Rousseau is credited with educating the generation that carried out the French Revolution—a revolt against the negation of human value. Through writing, he altered the environment in which he lived. His novel *Emile* is the story of romantic love between Emile and Sophie. The model for Sophie was Heloise, who was married to Abelard in the twelfth century. *Emile* is a protest against educational environments that produced tyrants and slaves. In asserting the fundamental value of all ordinary children, Rousseau distinguished two forms of self-love; one form essential to well-being and personal authenticity and another that divided humanity into tyrants and slaves.

To Rousseau, self-love is ambiguous, referring to *amour de soi-meme* and *amour-propre*. To him, these expressions were deeply different. *Amour de soi-meme* (self-regard) is concern for one's own well-being. When self-regard is guided by reason and modified by compassion, it is a source of virtue and is related to *conatus*, an endeavour in all beings to persist in being what they are.[30] For Rousseau, self-regard is not wrong or wicked; without it, we would be in perpetual self-damnation. Self-regard includes concern for basic health and complete physical functioning. It is not malicious or cruel but involves having a sense of one's value as a competent agent in personal affairs and implies self-awareness, self-knowledge and self-credibility. [31]

Self-regard entertains no desire to dominate others but seeks after its own reasonable needs.[32] While self-regard is healthy, *amour proper* (self-supremacy) is a virus. Self-supremacy is the desire to get the better of others as a way to exert personal superiority and is congruent with a *Philokalia* perspective of self-esteem as a sin. Self-supremacy is an aggressive desire to control and dominate others. Obliterating others in the process, it sees what is good and valuable in other people's lack; it is satisfied when others have little or no value. Rousseau saw that self-supremacy created domination in some people and taught others to be slaves.

These dual aspects of self-love are in tension due to a dimension in Rousseau that is generally undervalued. The environment for self-evaluation is crucial in satisfactorily working out this tension. Rousseau saw in self-regard an ordinary human need for social recognition, without which people languish. If society is civil, the need for recognition (i.e., sufficient attention) is tempered by compassion; people are not driven to domination—they are not addicted to getting attention. Claiming esteem as our due does not automatically involve denying the same to others. With an art of self-regard, we learn to see others as sources of care and support from whom we can expect and receive recognition and to whom we readily grant it.

Rousseau's insight into self-love as self-regard is elaborated in Immanuel Kant's doctrine of virtue. Kant defined self-esteem in contrast to servility (i.e., the negation of human value). He asserted that a person "can and should value himself [sic] by a low as well as by a high standard, depending on whether he views himself as a sensible being (in terms of his animal nature) or as an intelligible being (in terms of his moral predisposition)."[33] To Kant, the animal nature was to have low esteem and the rational nature, high esteem. High self-esteem is expressed in duty. To be fully human is to be dutiful, for the sake of duty. That is, self-regard has a higher purpose. Being dutiful provides moral limits for self-aggrandisement and domination, but avoids servility.

To Kant, rational people preserve moral self-esteem and are not servile, i.e., those who speak and act as if always seeking a favour. Humanity should be aware of its sublime moral predisposition and see that "self-esteem is a duty of man to himself."[34] He discussed avarice (a cardinal sin in the *Philokalia*) and pointed out a type he rejected, which was to restrict "one's own enjoyment of the means to good living so narrowly as to leave one's own true needs unsatisfied."[35] Like Kempis, Kant saw that unsatisfied personal needs leave people vulnerable. Unaddressed vulnerability can lead to self-hate. Self-hate does not help us love other people. Kant focused on a failure to meet one's basic needs as a limit condition for self-esteem. After Kant, the environment for self-esteem shifted and a broader term, self concept revised our interpretation of self-esteem.

R. F. Baumeister contributes to the revision of self-esteem. To him, self concept is a "cognitive schema that organizes abstract and concrete memories about the self and controls the processing of self-relevant information."[36] He posits that people with low self-esteem "lack a clear, stable, consistent understanding of themselves [i.e., self-image]...so that they lack "a clear idea that the self is worthy and wonderful."[37] As a result of limited or inaccurate self-knowledge and a low view of themselves, people with low self-esteem do not manage life well because they do not understand themselves in a consistently usable fashion and do not hold firm convictions about themselves.[38]

But his research shows that high self-esteem is not an improvement. He reveals connections between high self-esteem and violence: "[p]erpetrators of violence tend to have favorable opinions of themselves...[and] violence often stems from having these favorable views of the self attacked."[39] He does not make a one-to-one relation between high self-esteem and violence. There are types of high self-esteem, two in particular that are significant. Firstly, there are those who are quietly self-confident and have an accurate appreciation of their abilities. Secondly, there are those who are conceited, haughty, arrogant, with an inflated sense of their own value, who are inaccurate about their abilities. This second group are narcissists; they are self-centered, interrupt other people in conversation, express hostility toward those who disagree with them, talk *at* rather than *with* people and do a variety of things that irritate people around them.

Narcissism is "a tendency to regard oneself as superior to others and to expect other people to treat one as special."[40] It is linked to instability of self-esteem: "narcissists tend to have a high opinion of themselves that…fluctuates from day to day in response to events".[41] By studying self-esteem we understand more about the costs and benefits of holding high opinions of ourselves. For example, narcissists refuse to suffer disappointment with respect to self-value and compel others to prop up their insupportably high view of themselves. They cannot get satisfying social esteem since others do not share this high self-evaluation. Narcissism is self-defeating: impossible to maintain, it may erupt in violence.

The end of the twentieth century is often called the "Me Generation" to refer to pervasive narcissism in Western culture—an insatiable hunger for attention that harms public life. Narcissism causes personal and social pain because it shapes the environment and endangers social life due to the emotional unavailability of one person to another.[42] We are so engrossed in seeking attention no one is left to give it. The modern self carries a unique distress: "Each person in our society has received the burdensome gift of an overgrown self. We enjoy the positive, attractive features of this self-orientation, but…fail to appreciate how much it costs us as well."[43] Ancient Christian thought developed in an environment in which esteem was scarce; our environment thinks unreasonable demands for esteem are normal. Hunger for attention drives social life, but it is not evenly distributed. It is only readily available along socially contrived lines.

In summary, self-esteem passed from sin, to self-preservation, to self-supremacy. It is important to retain ancient insights about self-esteem to enjoy the art of self-regard. Since environments shape self-evaluation, we must assess Christian communities for their capacity to shore up flagging self-regard and limit narcissism. Artful self-regard flourishes among those who evaluate themselves wisely and willingly exchange esteem. But the art of self-regard, that is inherently spiritual, also requires us to reflect on the concept for God that we all hold in the fortresses of our mental life. The art of self-regard is not an act of the will, but an attachment that encourages believers to draw close to a loving God who declares them to be worthy. Christian education must allow believers to relax in God's presence so that they can sense they are loved by God. God's kindness is meant to lead toward reasonable self-knowledge. It is hard, if not impossible, to feel secure in God's love if we are perpetually anxious about ourselves. Those tossed on the waves of narcissism and self-negation cannot relax with God and do not enjoy other people. One way forward in this struggle is to pay attention to the concept of God that we hold. In attending to how we think of God, we become able to revise our view of ourselves.

THE BIRTH AND LIFE OF THE LIVING GOD

Esteem is important in education. It is fair to say that faith education is an activity in which we get and give esteem in the form of appropriate attention to ourselves, other people and God. In releasing our capacity to give the right attention to ourselves, others and God, it is essential for us to consider how our sense of self-esteem, the value we place on the image we have of ourselves, is related to our capacity to love others and God. I want to continue the discussion of self-esteem in relation to the art of self-regard. Self-regard teaches us our value as God's beloved. To learn the art of self-regard we accept the value God bestows on us and reconsider God concepts we acquired in childhood—concepts, which, though acquired during childhood, remain with us throughout our lives and influence our attempts to live the life of faith. We grow up in faith as these concepts shift and change.

As an example of the way God concepts change over the course of a life, a young woman named Sarah (not her real name) tells the story of how her God concept shifted its shape. As an adolescent, she had an image of God that put him high up in the sky peering over the edge of clouds, watching everything she did, with an expression of disapproval that worried her. She thought God was waiting to catch her doing something she shouldn't be doing. She was convinced Jesus would return the days she lied to her parents about her whereabouts. She was sure Jesus would show up at the junior high dance (where she was not supposed to be) in a blaze of glory, and pluck her out of the middle of her friends. Or worse, Jesus would return and not pick her up because she was at the dance. She would be left behind.

When she was in High School, a girlfriend disappeared for three weeks. No one knew where June was. June's parents were frantic. Her friends were dazzled and scared, secretly admiring her adventure, in their naiveté. June returned to school one day without a word. Sarah recalled the day June stopped by in her rusty Volkswagen. June wouldn't say where she had been but conveyed an air of mystery and excitement. As Sarah stood by the car window, talking about nothing in particular, she thought to herself: I don't want to be like June. I don't want to run away. I am one way at church: I am the good Christian girl, sort of. And I am another way at school—not bad exactly, but not truthful either, always trying to deny that other church self.

Sarah spoke to God in her heart and said: *Lord, I know you see the real me. I know you see me in both places. I want to be the real me wherever I am, no matter who I am with. I am tired of being two separated selves, feeling split apart—having to struggle to remember who I am—depending on where I am. I want to be comfortable with You—all the time, everywhere.* At that moment, Sarah said, God lost the peering glare that previously pinned her to her bad behavior. She saw the expression on God's face soften while God was looking at her. God smiled. Her concept of God (image and idea) changed. Perhaps God had been smiling at her for years; it was just that she couldn't see it. Now she saw God in a new way. But she had to choose what sort of a person she wanted to be. She had to re-conceive her environment. She consciously chose to perceive her environment in a new way. She stepped back to take a wider view.

Despite the first transformation of God's expression, God retained an aspect of distant judge for Sarah until she was in her mid-twenties. She got married at twenty-one and had a son when she was twenty-three. One evening their best friends from church were over and were talking about heaven. She had never heard people talk about heaven the way they were. They spoke of heaven as if it were home. A home they longed to experience. They imagined being in God's presence and feeling safe, utterly and completely, despite their vulnerability before an all-seeing God. Sarah had no sense of being at home with God. She left the room to put her son to bed. She wept. From that night onward, she began a journey that lasted for months. She searched scripture and listened to the longing in her heart. She spoke with her pastor.

Part of that journey led to the conversion of her concept of God. God looked at her with love and acceptance. She saw that God is friendly. She knew she had been a Christian from the time she invited Jesus into heart at twelve years old. She was Christian prior to this new vision of God, and she had been baptized, but she did not know God as God longs to be known by grown ups. As we mature, God concepts need conversion when they no longer fit the situation we find ourselves in. God is larger than childhood concepts—which are unfinished until the day we see God face to face and know God as we are fully known.

The process of Sarah's maturity continues; it includes a growing awareness of her God concept, which she holds beside the God concepts of other people, scripture, Christian tradition and the witness of the Holy Spirit. In continuing to discuss self-esteem, I want to make connections between concepts the young have of themselves and concepts they have of God. An art of self-regard has implications for the way believers imagine themselves and God. Reasonable self-evaluation produces self-knowledge that is conducive to a hopeful faith in God; but believers must learn to be reasonable. There is a relationship between being reasonable and feeling worthy. At times, self-esteem has meant little more than feeling good about ourselves and, as already noted, expresses itself in narcissism. Feeling good about oneself may have nothing at all to do with being good and having self-knowledge. The art of self-regard relies on connections between getting and giving esteem, acquiring a sense of personal worth and securing a sustained, hopeful view of God.

God-concepts form as a result of interactions with the social world when we are infants. This insight about object relations is an accurate description of human experience that Freud formulated. Ana-Maria Rizzuto (1979) wrote about the theory of object relations he invented. Her aim was to show how object relations theories help us understand the way personal ideas of God form and to point out limitations in the way Freud applied his own theory. Hers is not a book on religion; rather it reveals how faith education must negotiate with the mental mythologies each person brings to church. Personal concepts of God can be barriers to learning about the Holy One conveyed to us through Jesus Christ. In reflecting on her research, we can reframe one of Jesus' warnings: *But if any of you causes one of these little ones who believe in me to sin, it would be better for you to have a large millstone hung around your neck and to be drowned in the depths of the sea. Woe to the world because of the things that cause people to sin! Such things must come, but woe to the person through whom they come!* (Matt. 18.6-7)

Reframing Jesus' warning in light of God concept theory has the following implications for faith education:

- Teachers affect the formation of personal God concepts
- God concepts continue to influence people over a life time
- God concepts can limit access to reliance upon a loving God
- Direct encounters with God concepts creates effective learning
- Human experience is both bane and blessing for faith maturity
- There is a relationship between God concepts and self-concepts

We need to reframe Christian education to take advantage of these insights so that believers are free to imagine God in ways congruent with scripture, the richness of Christian tradition, and the faithful lives of that 'crowd of witnesses', living and dead, in whose presence we continue to work out our salvation in fear and trembling. Faith education permits a God concept to grow up into the fullness conveyed by God who is Wholly Other, but neither distant nor indifferent toward us.

In short, the God concept formed in a child's heart has a reality that persists in shaping a child's perception of the world, other people and the self. God concepts have power to act as idols situated in the inner shrine of a human heart, and can become a stronghold unmoved by scripture or a faith community's formal understanding of God. As part of my own early Christian education, it was commonplace to accuse the young of placing themselves on the heart's throne. Perhaps you remember the image of an inner throne on which stubborn, selfish children placed themselves, instead of choosing to do the right thing, which was to place God on the heart's throne. That approach to a child's religiosity neglects to notice how children construct God concepts in the first place. It was Freud who showed how God concepts form. Perhaps our primary teachers can be forgiven for their lack of insight. They were unaware they could apply Freud to Sunday School.

In the inner throne analogy, there are a number of assumptions that locate a child's will as the central focus of Christian education. The first is to assume that the occupant on the heart's throne is there by conscious, intentional choice and can be removed by another conscious, intentional choice. A second assumption takes it for granted that God *might not be there*, hence the child has to put God in God's place. A third assumption presupposes a uniform concept of God, one that is unproblematic. Given the way most of us tend to think, Christian educators may assume that the concept of God they happen to hold is the same one that any reasonable person would hold. If this God concept causes a teacher no apparent trouble, it is unlikely to occur to them that a God concept could cause any one trouble. Yet none of these are accurate assumptions to make about children's experience. For this insight, we are indebted to Freud.

In contrast to focusing solely on the child's will, our greatest concern in faith education is to help children sense the concept of God that already reigns in the heart. Erroneous concepts of God are a more serious threat to Christian maturity than is self-centeredness, although perhaps the two obstacles are related. Rizzuto showed that even an apparently positive concept, e.g., that God is good, kind and loves me, may interfere with our capacity to grow up in faith. She analyzed the experience of those who domesticate God. To some, God is a homey, safe divinity of simple human characteristics who lacks the powerful dimension of transcendence.[44] The transcendent God, the God above our little concepts, is revealed through the normal crises of doubt and disbelief that accompany adolescence, and that inevitably include self-examination, soul-searching and self-revision. To get too comfortable with God is ignorance of God. If we domesticate God, we are unprepared for conflict and harsh circumstances that inevitably enter our lives. We are shocked and angry at disappointment. We may reject God. We may say: My God would not let me suffer this way! My God would not let other people suffer this way! We lose our grip on God, or at least on the way we have always perceived God to be. This was Job's experience. His suffering brought a new vision of God (Job 42:5).

Suffering plays an important role in helping our God concepts grow up. The self-examination implied in these crises draws a believer toward humility and grace, away from ignorance and arrogance. God must become a problem before God is a solution to our spiritual quest—and its destination. The significance of this point is central. It is not by casting oneself off the heart's throne that Christian maturity begins. Rather, getting a fresh and enlivened vision of God's own Self enables people to grow up in the faith. Until we revise them in light of scripture, communal knowledge, self-examination, and finally, by seeing God 'face to face', our God concepts are products of imagination. The misdirection they proffer must be addressed if we want to grow up in the faith. God must be allowed to speak for 'Himself' in order for us to know God. We must sense the role imagination plays in forming our thought-life, and the way we think about God. Thinking is powerful. Letting God speak and be heard allows old and young to come to God fully and freely. But who is this God who is speaking? What is God's tone of voice? What is the look on God's face when we incline ourselves toward God?

As the parable of the ten, five and one talents reveals, it is our concept of God that gives us courage to put our gifts to use, just as it is a concept of God that frightens us into burying them. In Matthew, Jesus encourages us to weave together our human value with God's divine value. Jesus said: "Are not two sparrows sold for a penny? Yet not one of them will fall to the ground apart from the will of your Father. And even the very hairs of your head are all numbered. So don't be afraid; you are worth more than many sparrows" (Matt 10: 29-31). He also said, "Store up for yourselves treasures in heaven, where moth and rust do not destroy, and where thieves do not break in and steal. For where your treasure is, there your heart will be also" (Matt. 6:20-21). Self-concepts and God concepts are stored in an image-hoard in our imagination, a spiritual place we sort through when trying to make sense of our lives.

Making sense of God concepts and self-concepts uncovers a reasonable middle ground between narcissism on the one hand, and self-negation on the other, which is the art of self-regard. The way to address the personal unrest that self-evaluation generates is to rest our value in God's inherent value. Jesus affirms humanity and encourages us to place a frail sense of self in the strong hands of a loving God. But what of the child who has only had experience with hands that hurt, violated or abused the child's own being? How is that child to place himself in God's care? Miraculously, through the Holy Spirit's effective intervention, and through the persistence of people who help a child see that it should not be so, these children can and do come to God. But their hearts retain the sorrow caused by harm that could have been prevented or addressed, if their early lives had enjoyed more personal safety.

So the heart is full of tension when the subject of God is raised. This is true for abused children as well as for those whose lives have been relatively peaceful. Personal God concepts must grow up if we would engage the God who lives above particular human concepts. In the aftermath of the religious authority wars of the mid-twentieth century in the West, the strongly personal God concepts people hold are post-modern equivalents of idolatry that, unless transformed, limit learning. The presence of personal God concepts helps explain a reference from the Old Testament that John emphasized. How could he explain why people rejected Jesus? John situated their disbelief by quoting Isaiah:

> Lord, who has believed our message and to whom has the arm of the Lord been revealed? For this reason they could not believe, because, as Isaiah says elsewhere: He has blinded their eyes and hardened their hearts, so they can neither see with their eyes, nor understand with their hearts, nor turn—and I would heal them (John 12:37-40).

The ambiguity between God's willingness and human blindness is echoed in a question asked by Judas (not Judas Iscariot), who said, 'But, Lord, why do you intend to show yourself to us and not to the world? Jesus replied, 'Anyone who loves me will obey my teaching. My Father will love them, and we will come to them and make our home with them. Anyone who does not love me will not obey my teaching. These words you hear are not my own; they belong to the Father who sent me' (John 14:22-24). Jesus did not answer Judas's question except to say: Invite us home. Just as Sarah learned, and is still learning, it is only by inviting God as Wholly Other to make his home in our hearts that we can grow up in faith. God is willing to converse with us about the way we conceive God.

Another source of tension as we allow God concepts to change happens in families. As Freud and Rizzuto show, our concept for God is made from experiences we have in families of origin (although not only from this source). From my own observation, when people are asked to draw a picture of their family of origin, and also a picture of God (without knowing there may be a connection) they often see remarkable similarities between the two pictures, if invited to compare them. Our images of God are formed in family life. When the young reconsider a God concept, if families do not understand what is going on, adolescents may appear to reject the family idea of what God is like. This can be unsettling for parents or siblings who have never re-thought God. Those who have got new glimpses of God may feel less awkward with a child who passionately struggles with God and self-evaluation. Parents and teachers are to lead children to the living God. We are not to insist that our concept for God must be their only option. This would be like requiring that children continue to worship the household gods.

Until we understand how these concepts form, it is difficult to make progress in establishing a healthy view of God. Since concepts of God made from experience are personal and private, and if formal understanding is to be acquired, wise teachers take account of personal, private concepts that constitute the bedrock of individual belief. Christian educators must find ways to connect the God of scripture to a personal, private God. Without these connections, learning does not produce the transformations that personal, private concepts must undergo if they are to sustain adults through the inevitable crises of ordinary life and lead them toward Christian maturity. Sarah learned to let her God concept grow up. She was fortunate. The goal of faith education is to provide the environment, a learning community, for theological reflection that lets God speak.

THE FORMATION OF GOD CONCEPTS

I use the term God concept to designate a union of ideas, feelings and images that each person associates with God, which are acquired early in life: the "first conscious God representations appear between the ages of two and three".[45] A concept of God blends feeling-charged images with intellectually rich ideas to form a concept that has cognitive as well as affective dimensions. The mixture produces what are called transitional phenomena or objects, i.e., objects as explained in chapter two. In this case, these transitional phenomena are God concepts that every human being has as a result of early experience. They are idiosyncratic, highly personalized and life-long and may be repressed or transformed over a person's life time.

Transitional phenomena are formed due to our need for other people and explain attachments we experience from infancy onwards. God is one of these attachments whether or not a person has experience with religion. As with all theory, object relations theories are limited to what can be observed during human interaction, but, while being limited, they remain a plausible way to make human experience more understandable, bearable, and open to transformation. Since it is based on observation, what is passing strange about his formulation of object relations theory is that Freud eliminated mothers from the process of formating God concepts, [46] an omission rectified by other theorists.

God concepts form in a space carved out between mother and infant in their mutual relationship. The early stage in this development is made possible by the mother's special capacity for adapting to the needs of her infant, allowing the infant to experience the illusion that what the infant creates really exists.[47] This space of experiencing is located between the inner and outer world of the child; the spiritual is like a bridge built between a person and the world.

In this space, children play with reality, inner and outer, and form transitional objects through their interactions with objects in the world (parents, siblings, things). These transitional objects constitute the mental mythology each human being lives by. The child's sense of self develops in relation to the mother's sense of the child. If a child perceives herself as wonderful and worthy in her mother's eyes, all is well, or at least, it is good enough for the child to flourish because she can relax. But if the image formed is of a bad child, if the child has not been able to fulfill expectations parents held before her birth, there is a conflict of being. The child senses that what is wrong is not what she does, but what she is. Under these conditions, a child cannot please parents (or God) except by becoming a different sort of person. The child can never relax.[48]

God concepts also form in this intermediate spiritual space between a person and the world. In this location, illusions form and meaning is created. This third place, which is neither the self nor the world, but is influenced by both, is the genesis of the spiritual aspect of human life. The spiritual is an intermediate space between the personal and the material. It is a mid-point reality between subjective and objective realities. Objects form here as a child experiences the self and the world. These objects or concepts focus a child's ongoing perceptions of everything. The intermediate space is an area of experiencing, "to which inner reality and external life both contribute," and which, in turn, acts back on a child's perception and understanding of outer and inner reality, as an unchallenged space that an individual creates in the perpetual human task of keeping inner and outer reality separate yet interrelated.[49] The spiritual aspect integrates human experience and forms embodied concepts we live by. These embodied, emotionally laden concepts shift their shape with changes in experience. Keeping up with new experience is a spiritual task. Sanity depends on interrelating yet separating material and personal realities; it is the spiritual work involved in the in-between where illusions form.

The term illusion does not signify something false. Illusion is not delusion. All art, science and religion depend on illusion for their existence. Illusion is the bedrock of learning, since all learning is organizing experience. In this intermediate space, organizing happens. These illusions are not false; they are idiosyncratic, useful organizing principles for ordinary life. Over a lifetime, we are called on to test the world and ourselves on the basis of these objects of perception.[50] They (image, feeling and idea) are the stuff of thinking; they are experience-rich and assumption-laden. God is a transitional object in the sense implied here. Transitional objects, formed in the margins between inner personal experience and outer material reality, explain the theological idea that we are made in God's image.

Human experience inevitably forms a concept for God. As an example, it was the concept Cain had for God that prevented their intimacy, just as his brother's concept allowed Abel unhindered access to the Almighty. It is striking that God met Cain in his resentment and tried to open up his experience to hope. Cain did not accept the offer; instead, he killed Abel. Cain's pattern is oft repeated. It is as if Cain could choose to reconsider his idea of God, or murder his brother. He did not hear God's offer. He sinned. It is in this sense that I do not think Christian maturity is accomplished solely by acts of the will that put God in the right place in our hearts. Rather, it is accomplished through experiencing. Spiritual maturity is a by-product of observing ourselves and seeing God in new ways, as Job testified at the end of his suffering, and as a result of it.

The psychological idea of experiencing is similar to the educational concept of experiencing described by Hegel and used later by John Dewey. In particular, Dewey described experiencing in *Art as Experience*. He was concerned to describe the artwork's effects in the intermediate space between the person and art object. Knowing art, not its material alone, is an aesthetic experience. In this intermediate space, idea and emotion are stirred: aspects of the art are felt and known. In his description, Dewey distinguished the spiritual and the ideal[51] from the material. The quality of material objects is felt and known spiritually in the margins between inner and outer reality. Experiencing takes place in the relationship between a person and her environment.

Dewey explored the relationship we have with our environment (using aesthetic experience as a model) and noted the following elements in the interrelations and separations that are necessary for mature thought to emerge, i.e., for learning to be transformational. In our relationship to an environment, he pointed out the rhythm of loss and recovery that is essential to enjoying harmony with life. We become conscious of ourselves, our concepts and the world through the rhythm of loss and recovery. Emotion is the conscious sign of a break, actual or impending, in our union with the world and our perceptions of it. The discord caused by emotion is an occasion that induces reflection. A desire to make peace with the world converts mere emotion (such as fear) into an *interest* in new objects (or new perceptions) that offer to restore harmony between our understanding of the world and ourselves.[52]

As an example, a child who is terrified of them may choose to do a class project on spiders for school. Somewhere in the depth of curiosity, fear dissolves. Harmony between the ways we think the world is, and how it seemed to be moments before, returns when our inner concepts and knowledge of outer reality are again in concert. Losing and recovering concepts in that spiritual space leads to transformational growth: concepts in the space between the personal and material shift their shape, as Hegel put it. This is the same process of loss and recovery that Job's life demonstrated as he strove to understand God. The book of Job is a narrative showing how God concepts shift and change in the light of God's actual Being, as Wholly Other.

Rizzuto explained that the process of loss and recovery is necessary for the growth and maturing of God concepts. She identified four primary God concepts she uncovered through her research. She studied patients as well as hospital personnel to arrive at her analysis, since she wanted to "extract from psychopathology what might be of benefit to normal psychology," as Freud also wanted to do.[53] Four God concepts include the following, those who:

- Have a God whose existence they do not doubt
- Wonder whether to believe in a God they are not sure exists
- Are amazed, angered, or quietly surprised to see others deeply invested in a God who does not interest them
- Struggle with a demanding, harsh God they would like to get rid of, if they were not convinced of his existence and power.[54]

The most powerful implication of this research for religious education is that all four God concepts cause people difficulty in the absence of transformational learning. Her central thesis is that "God as a transitional representation [object] needs to be recreated in each developmental crisis if it is to be found relevant for lasting belief".[55]

Further, she noted that God concepts are linked to self-concepts. There is a dynamic, sometimes dangerous link between self-concepts and God concepts. As a consequence, "the task of teaching religion to children demands exquisite attention to the experience of the child as well as to [its content]."[56] The child's creation of God is a private process that takes place in silent exchanges between parents and child. Later on, educators, ministers and other authority figures contribute to the shape of that concept. It is not simply what these people say but what they are and do that is used by children as they reshape God according to their personal needs and their learning.[57]

The learning that takes place between child and adult is affected by the complexity of two dynamics: the child's sense of self and sense of God, and the adult's sense of self and sense of God, with the outcome that "consciously, pre-consciously, or unconsciously, God, our own creation, like a piece of art, a painting, [or] a melody" will, in "reflecting what we have done [with it, will] affect our sense of ourselves."[58] Once created, our God concept, whether it is dormant or active, remains potentially available as an object in the continuous process of integration that makes up the inevitable spiritual work

145

we are called upon to carry out. God concepts can be used during religious education because they are beyond magic, in the sense that all transitional objects are never under magical control, as are some of the objects of perception we hold in our inner hoard of personal experience that we can manipulate, for example, our parents.[59] For this reason, if children have negative or frightening concepts, interventions from religious educators that take no account of what is already in play in the child's mental mythology, can produce an effect that is more than a child is able to tolerate.[60] As children age, because there is an interrelationship between God concepts and self concepts, crises in experience influence them both.

Suppose you converse with a young father whose wife and children were killed in a house fire two years previously. He is distraught. In his unrequited anger, he conveys an image of God that haunts him. God, he says, was sitting on the couch watching television, channel surfing, while my wife and children were burning in that fire! His image of God conveys rage and despair at God's apparent inaction, and intimates anger at himself for his helplessness to save them. He would have rescued them if he could. God is strong. God could, but did not. Why didn't God help? In conversing with him, his image of God is a rich expression of his sorrow. In faith education, he comes to sense that God was not on the couch during the fire. He must find a way to re-imagine God that accords with the full range of his experience and the experience of other believers, scripture and the faith tradition, if he wishes to move forward.

God must show up, as happened for Job. He needs God in order for his view of himself to improve. In the shifting of his God concept he is eventually released from his self-punitive stance and rage at his own helplessness. He comes to see God face to face, as Job did. He becomes capable of appropriate self-regard. Yet we are never cavalier about suffering. While it may be a way forward to maturity, without friends in educationally supportive environments, suffering may lead to isolation, addiction and despair.

RECOGNITION, SUFFERING AND GODLY FEAR

Three issues are relevant to appropriate self-regard: one is the acknowledgement of our need for recognition, i.e., the need for esteem that permits people to feel they fit in the environment, along with everyone else. Another is our educative response to suffering. The third is self-regard's wisdom about godly fear. Without sufficient recognition, people are invisible to others and fail to know their own worth accurately. They act (or fail to act) from an absence of value that may lead to sin. *The Philokalia* insight that esteem is not sin, any more than food is sin, unites with Kempis's, Kant's and Rousseau's insistence that human needs must be met for people to access the benefits of God's grace. Recognition is an antidote to low self-esteem. Human worth is learned in supportive environments that provide everyone with adequate recognition, for example, just as the Grecian widows (Acts 6:1-7) received when their needs were addressed. Feeling we fit in an environment informs personal identity and conveys how we are perceived and valued by others. In feeling we fit, we become aware of what we do and do not do well—we come to assess our gifts and talents accurately. We see human limitations as inevitable, without feeling invisible or isolated in them, or because of them. Sufficient communal esteem counteracts the poverty of attention.

But the art of self-regard involves more than getting adequate attention. Self-regard is learned in suffering. In developing the art of self-regard, suffering plays a central role. *The Philokalia* notes this:

9. Suffering deliberately embraced cannot free the soul totally from sin unless the soul is also tried in the fire of suffering that comes unchosen. For the soul is like a sword: if it does not go 'through fire and water' (Ps. 66:12. LXX)—that is, through suffering deliberately embraced and suffering that comes unchosen—it cannot but be shattered by the blows of fortune.

10. Trials and temptations subject to our volition are chiefly caused by health, wealth and reputation, and those beyond our control by sickness, material losses and slander. Some people are helped by these things; others are destroyed by them.

49. In addition to voluntary suffering, you must also accept that which comes against your will –I mean slander, material losses and sickness. For if you do not accept these but rebel against them, you are like someone who wants to eat his [sic] bread only with honey, never with salt. Such a man [sic] does not always have pleasure as his companion, but always has nausea as his neighbour.[61]

To accept suffering is to learn of God. To resist self-rejection while we suffer is to learn the art of self-regard, since to reject ourselves is to negate our value. To accept unchosen suffering is to realize the meaning of scriptures that say to rejoice when we suffer for Christ's sake, which is very different from suffering due to self-absorption. (Jas 1:2-4) Unchosen suffering comes in many forms, as is evident above, and also comes in the form of two life circumstances—the problems of opposition and empathy, which I will explore more fully in chapters that follow.

The art of self-regard explains how opposition from enemies and friends is balanced by empathy. Problems of opposition and empathy prevent believers from falling into the extremes of self-love and self-hate. Artful self-regard is learned by believers who face opposition wisely and practice empathy. Opposition and empathy provide an opportunity to moderate excesses and deficiencies of human worth that express themselves in the extremes of narcissism and self-rejection. This is because the art of self-regard is not caught up in an insatiable hunger for attention. It is not self-absorbed. Narcissists, in particular, are unwilling to embrace unchosen suffering. They do not welcome the role suffering plays in self-knowledge. Yet we can hope that in supportive communities, the interplay between suffering and recognition might be a cure for narcissism. After all, hubris is not new. Excesses of self-esteem are inherent in humanity. Like the parable of the Pharisee and the tax collector, "as regards his [sic] good qualities, the proud man does not want to be compared with his equals; but as regards his failings, he is quite content to be compared with those worse than himself.[62]

Those with inflated self-esteem and those with low self-esteem share a poverty of self-knowledge and resent their insufficient social recognition. An education to help believers chart their way toward an art of self-regard allows them to sense deeply what scripture reveals about God and encourages them to ask and pursue their own questions. Learners compare what is held in the heart with what is revealed in scripture, through the ever present help of God's Spirit. Self-knowledge is the result of theological reflection.

Theological reflection teaches us to learn our worth. But what keeps self-evaluation away from narcissism and negation? What stops suffering from leading to despair? A clue found in *The Philokalia* suggests that the "first step towards excellence is fear of God, the last is loving desire for Him."[63] Theologically, fear is a complex emotion characterized by ambivalence aptly expressed in John Newton's (1725-1807) well known hymn, Amazing Grace: "Twas grace that taught my heart to fear, And grace my fears relieved;..." Ancient texts insist that fearing God is the beginning of wisdom; loving God is the outcome of that initiation. How is fear related to the art of self-regard? What we understand by fearing God is only fully realized when it leads to loving desire. Awe, reverence and worship are starting points allowing the heart to open to a loving God. God is not a trifle, a toy to be played with—a domesticated deity. Yet, God is love. The art of self-regard flourishes in this tension.

In its simplest sense, fear is an apprehension of impending peril, real or imagined. In the ancient world, fear was expressed physically: an "inward disturbance is depicted by an outward manifestation" such as trembling.[64] Fear is a strong emotion due to its perception of danger, whether that danger is due to God's presence, as Wholly Other, or arises from human threats. Scripture encourages us not to fear other people (2Chr 19:7) and to fear God in the right way and for the right reasons (2Chr 19:9). God is feared so that our conduct toward other people is constrained. Fearing God restrains our treatment of others (Lev 19:14, 32; Lev 25:17). Human integrity and right conduct *depend* on fearing God (Lev 19:14, 32; Lev 25:17). God is holy. To fear God is to be aware of human limitations (Psalm 9:20). Fear of God prevents believers from judging by mere appearances (Isaiah 11:3). In general, without fear we overstep the relational boundaries that inhere in being human.

Fear is a relational concept in Christian faith, in two senses. Fear is relational in terms of our link to God and in terms of our connection to other people. Fear is the beginning of loving God, yet love finally eclipses fear (1John 4:18) after it has done its proper work. Fear is an ambivalent emotion. Its ambivalence compels people in two directions simultaneously: they are drawn to what they fear; they flee or withdraw from what they fear. When fear is godly, we flee to God and fly from Satan (Jas 4:8a). Fear cannot be separated from faith. Fear does not hamper faith; rather it convinces us that we are wholly and utterly dependent upon God. Fear emphasizes the difference between human beings and God.[65]

Fear of the Lord is learned (Psalm 34:11). It plays a central role in faith and faith education. Godly fear does not enflame our fear of people.[66] Scripture is relentless in asserting that humanity *needs* to fear God to remain in relationship (Proverbs. 9:10; 15:33; 2Chr. 19:9; Job 28:28). Fear prepares our hearts for reverence and awe of God and convinces us that our value is neither less nor more than other people's worth.

Fear is an antidote to self-supremacy and self-rejection. To have no fear is to forget our basic human need for an horizon of meaning that compels us in a certain, steady direction and holds us accountable to its standard. Philosopher Charles Taylor's (1991) idea of authenticity, derived from Rousseau's insights about self-love, supports this. Taylor described a culture of authenticity that generates an emphasis on self-determination and extreme freedom which narcissists use to justify high expectations and which those with low self-esteem deploy for self-flagellation. Both groups are pressured by socially constructed needs based on a belief in limitless human potential. They have forgotten that without a 'horizon of meaning' as the backdrop for human action there is no way to measure human worth or the value of one life choice over another, there are no moral ideals.

A moral ideal pictures what a better or higher mode of life would look like, where 'better' or 'higher' are defined not in terms of what we happen to desire or need, but they offer a standard for what we ought to desire.[67] Inherent in ideals is a notion of limit. But narcissism implies that either there is no moral ideal at work, or if there is, "it should be seen as a screen for self-indulgence."[68] Self-indulgence has no fear and expresses itself as emotional detachment in those who feel called "to sacrifice their love relationships and the care of their children, to pursue their [desires]."[69] Authenticity as a moral ideal properly understood, Taylor argues, rejects the extremes of narcissism and negation. The idea of fear is full of tension.

Authenticity, like Christianity, encourages us to connect with something deep: it is a way to be true to God, ourselves and to be reasonable with others. Jesus said: "Have salt in yourselves, and _Color_ be at peace with each other." (Mark 9:50) As we listen to the voice within—Christ in us, hope of glory—we create an environment that gives authenticity its significance and shape, in the context of a horizon of meaning that compels thought and action. No singular God concept dominates the landscape—because we remember that they are personal constructions. We do not allow our own concept of God to dominate a faith community but we let the Holy Spirit and personal experience move us toward a more complete knowledge of God and of ourselves. We relax. The human mind is dialogical.[74] Working out an art of self-regard is a conversation, not a soliloquy.

When we converse with other people, we listen and explore; we do not argue. An art of self-regard is learned through conversation. When we are authentic, we are strong enough to engage with other voices and graciously do so. Conversing with God in community, with those who love us too much to abandon us to narcissism and negation, is the path towards faith maturity. Self-regard sets its sight on a horizon of meaning that includes loving God, acknowledges human limits, respects others, acquires self-knowledge and feels worthy. Knowing ourselves as beloved by God opens the door to an authenticity that does not forget its need for esteem and does not disdain limits God set within the human heart. The art of self-regard is learned in communion. It is a project fraught with problems, for which God does not apologize, but offers Holy Companionship.

In chapters that follow, I discuss the role that several problems play in learning to grow up in the faith. If we understand our need to do our own spiritual work, we address these problems adequately. The outcome of faith education is the flourishing of intelligence. Christian maturity is marked by intelligent faith and practice grounded on

151

God's Presence and the reality of Christ's return. Intelligence is an ability to solve problems and create products that are valued within an environment.[75] Human intellectual competence entails a set of skills for problem-solving that enable people to resolve genuine problems or difficulties they encounter and, when appropriate, to create something new or at least novel (perhaps something neglected in a faith tradition), thereby laying the groundwork for the acquisition of new knowledge.[76]

Before I discuss problems the faithful face, I want to situate faith education in a larger context by describing faith in the broadest terms. Faith education is an approach to teaching Christians about their concepts of God so that they can become more reasonable and more faithful members of the tradition they take on, without losing themselves in the process. Faith education must learn to comprehend the larger environment of twentieth century western culture, if it is to liberate Christian practice for the twenty-first century.

5

THE PURPOSE OF FAITH EDUCATION

Almighty God, give us wisdom to perceive you,
Intelligence to understand you,
Diligence to seek you,
Patience to wait for you,
Vision to behold you,
A heart to meditate upon you,
A life to proclaim you;
Through Jesus Christ our Lord,
Who lives with you and the Holy Spirit,
One God now and forever.[1]

LEARNING FAITH

F aith education aims to reconcile a person's spiritual work with the ways God is presented in Christian tradition. In the previous four chapters, I explored the first phase of faith education by describing spirituality as *a sense of felt connection* that requires a healthy environment. The first phase is not focused on content but on a way of acting. Teachers and parents encourage the human spirit by including, attending, embracing, releasing and remaining; their activity promotes healthy self-regard, respect for others and love for God. In calling it the first phase, I do not suggest that we carry out spiritual education in the first few years of someone's life and move to a second Christian phase, forgetting about the first one. And I assume that the second phase of faith education could be Jewish or Muslim, as examples, while I focus on Christianity. In this chapter, I talk about the Christian or second phase of faith education, but spiritual education lies behind, and works with, everything I say about it.

I suggest that spirituality is global, most often expressed through religious language. Environments conducive to developing the human spirit must acknowledge and understand three dimensions of experience: the personal, universal and global. I have already introduced the idea that spirituality is personal (one's own inner experience) and universal (part of the human condition). I want to say more about spirituality's universal quality as I differentiate spirituality from existentialism. I then examine the global effects of religion on the formation of faith. Christianity is a global phenomenon; its reputation affects the formation of faith. I also lay out an understanding of this second educational phase by analyzing faith more fully. My purpose is to describe faith as lifelong learning and to outline what has to be accomplished in order for faith to sustain us through the vagaries of ordinary living.

THE WORK OF FAITH EDUCATION

Faith education has four aims and one central purpose. The first aim is to comprehend what it means to be a spiritual human being. The second is to practise faith through self-observation. The third aim is to reflect on personal God concepts. The fourth aim is to become members of a faith tradition. The four aims have no sequential order. They are lifelong endeavours involved in gaining mastery over faithfulness. They are aims learners pursue rather than objectives teachers hand down to them.

The central purpose of faith education is to serve the spiritual work of growing up. The four aims enable the central purpose to be realized. Faith education is an attempt to make sense of life, ourselves and other people so that we can mature. In faith education

154

believers are teachers and learners who are trying to make sense of life from the perspective of faith. Making sense of life as we grow up is personal spiritual work lived out in the context of other people. Without engaging in the practices of faith we cannot make sense of God, the world or ourselves. The practice of faith inevitably leads believers to do the hard work of self-observation, to learn about faith by being among the faithful and by acquiring insights about the relationship between our personal worldviews and our environment so that we can figure out what God requires of us. As a consequence of this spiritual work, the purpose of faith education and its four aims become integrated in the life of a believer.

If we do this work faithfully we nurture our own maturity and that of our faith community. But how does maturity happen? What is it that begins to grow up in those who are learning to be faithful? Does knowledge grow? Does wealth increase? Do spiritual gifts flourish? Does love characterize every thought and action? Is our usefulness evident? Do exemplars become famous? Which of these paths lead to maturity? Which conveys intimacy with God? I suggest that all of these outcomes may be part of maturity but they are by-products of its central focus. If believers set out to pursue any of these outcomes as goals in themselves they lose sight of the main exercise of maturity. Self-observation, and the use we make of what we see as we observe ourselves (whether we are alone with God or with others) is the key to mature faith. Self-observation, protected by God's Grace, nourishes the soul and encourages the faithful to risk growing up. We need God and other people to take that risk.

In self-observation, we ask ourselves three questions: What is God doing? What do human beings tend to do? What am I doing? We ask these questions within a faith community. Self-observation requires a context in which believers become familiar with God's Word and ways until their lives echo God's Grace. The down-side of self-observation is that we see ourselves doing things that are disappointing, confusing, embarrassing and frustrating. As we look at ourselves, we can be tempted toward self-hatred. We desperately need to know the Grace of God and to have that Grace expressed in community with other people who are equally aware that they are frail human beings. It takes courage to observe ourselves but if we do not try, we fail at the same challenges over and over again. Self-observation enourages the growth of faith. Without learning faith, we cannot appropriate Grace. For this reason, all learning is failure-driven. First we fail. Then, we observe our failure and we begin to live up to the opportunities available through God's generosity.

The practice of self-observation provides knowledge about existential themes so believers can situate themselves in human realities such as loss, fear, joy, anger, courage, conflict and loneliness. Existential themes reveal identifiable, common patterns that believers need to comprehend. Self-observation offers self-knowledge, which allows us to assess the health of our concept of God and draws us to God who knows us intimately and loves us completely. We grow up through engaging in self-observation and making commitments based upon what we observe. Commitment is intellectual and practical, based on thinking, feeling and acting. The goal of faith education is living healthy lives; thinking well is part of being well.

The three questions of self-observation nurture health: What is God doing? What do people tend to do? What am I doing? In faith education we learn to notice how we exercise faith in daily life and learn to be personal members of a particular faith tradition. Faith education works toward reconciliation between personal and communal aspects of growing up faithfully. The relationships among the four aims of faith education, and its central purpose, constitute the core inquiry of this chapter. The relationship between our freedom to grow up and the aims of faith education is one I explore because it is the work of becoming people who have the courage and insight to remain faithful despite experiences that trouble our faith.

The primary work of faith education connects people with a community of believers and involves them in scripture in a way that helps them sense the possibility of being a godly human being. The hope of educators is that once people see a godly life, they will find being Christian compellingly attractive. I trust this does not sound easy. It is simple, but if it sounds easy it may be because we do not sense what needs to happen in a life for it to become godly. Christians do not believe that human beings can become God, or that people are gods or goddesses. We believe something complex: we believe people who begin as God's children can become God's friends. Faith education prizes a pattern that moves us from children to friends. Is this not the ideal pattern we wish for our own children? We hope our relationship with them will mature into friendship, until together we come eventually to that reversal of care that writes the back pages of family life, when children care for elderly parents. With God, however, the roles never reverse. Friends of God remain in need of protection and consolation. God continually, willingly and generously consoles and protects His children/friends, though sometimes, not as they expect.

The central purpose of faith education acknowledges the tension inherent in growing up, which modernity made far more complex. The tension is well expressed by Immanuel Kant in an essay (1784) in which he summarized sentiments that drove modernity. He wrote about immaturity and maturity and described the former as the "inability to use one's own understanding without the guidance of another."[2] For him, at the end of the 1700s, maturity was thinking for oneself, on one's own. He indicted immaturity, which seemed to apply to most men and all women. He instructed modern individuals to stop relying on spiritual directors, doctors and all other experts who kept people immature, according to him, i.e., dependent on someone else. Modern man was to stand on his own two feet—a posture impossible for women unless they had neither husbands nor children and had an income of their own. Kant's prescription prevailed, at least in terms of the story modernity told about maturity. Yet, at the very height of modernity, from one of its main architects, the psychoanalytic relation was introduced into the human situation as a way of addressing the problems of growing up. Sigmund Freud invented a mythology for maturity that in many ways replaced the roles of the pre-modern experts Kant had dismissed. Freud offered help to modern individuals because he perceived difficulties in growing up that Kant underestimated.

So what is the current wisdom on the dilemma of growing up? Are we to be radically individual and think for ourselves and by ourselves (although radical individualism was not an aspect of Kant's idea of pure reason)? Or, are we to rely solely on help inherent in psychological and psychoanalytic support? What is the role of community in human maturity? I think its role is educational but

I do not imply that psychological and psychoanalytic support is inappropriate for Christians, as its practitioners or its clients. I want the faithful to consider the role that ordinary education can play in the process of growing up. Not all the challenges that plague Christian community are due to psychological distress. Many are the result of existential conditions—of being people who were raised by other people who had existential difficulties of their own. If our educational approaches actually improved our communities, we would produce less harm to each other. Our communities could be safe havens of inclusion where differences are welcome.

Faith education acknowledges tension between individuality and community and tries to help people integrate and individuate themselves in satisfying ways. The work of faith education is designed to address the excesses of modernity without losing contributions modernity made in describing the human condition. The task of weaving integration and authenticity into healthy community is complicated by three strands I want to pick out in twentieth century global culture. The first is the influence of pluralism; the second is the domination of atheism; the third is a reputation religion lost and needs to regain. I examine these strands by explaining terms that are related to one another: faith, religion, spirituality and existentialism.

PLURALISM AND THE RETURN OF RELIGIONS

In previous chapters, I say that faith is personal and universal. Faith is also global. Personal faith is influenced by what goes on globally because it is a universal aspect of human beings. For example, North American citizens live in pluralist societies. So do the citizens of Britain and Wales. It would be difficult to find places on earth where migration and technology have not reduced the distances of space and time between peoples and ways of life. We live in proximity. Everywhere we look, whether to Ireland, India, Europe or Africa, members of one faith tradition live next door to members of a different group. One political party is neighbor to another. Former Soviet Socialist countries are abodes of pluralism. Even China struggles with influences from outside its country's expensively constructed borders.

Pluralism grew during the last century but also was resisted. In the twentieth century, after World War I and before World War II, countries in Europe were carefully carved into small homogeneous lots according to a plan proposed by the American President Woodrow Wilson and other world leaders. The project failed. The notion of coherent national groups living harmoniously with their own kind has gone by the drawing board. In the 1960s the myth of a coherent cohesive nation was called into question all over the world. In the United States, African Americans (although they did not refer to themselves as such then) pointed forcefully to the exclusion of their group's differences from the dominant and privileged ethos of American civil society. They asserted that racism excluded them from benefits of civil liberty and the privileges of citizenship. Their protests revealed prejudice and exclusion at the heart of American society.

During the same period in Canada, ethnic communities (e.g., Ukrainians in Alberta) protested a political deal made between two historic groups who referred to themselves as founding members of Canadian political society. The deal between founding members was drawn up by the Bilingualism and Bicultural Commission and did not address ethnic identities other than French and English. Other ethnic groups pointed out that a definition of Canadian identity based on French and English alone rendered them second-class citizens and failed to account for sociological realities of Canadian life. In the Canadian context, these other ethnic group members uncovered prejudice and exclusion at the heart of Canadian political life. In general, the strength of pluralism is to reveal prejudice and exclusion at the heart of public life.

For a period of time in the twentieth century, political and social pluralism was less visible because two major organizing principles kept public life relatively focused. In the West, the organizing principle could be summed up as democratic secular humanism; in the East, Marxist-inspired communism directed the agenda. Atheism was part of both systems. Within their purview, religion, if allowed at all, was kept private, excluded from public life. The Cold War between East and West expressed itself in distance and distrust. In many ways these dominant organizing principles were

159

two sides of the same secular liberal coin minted in the nineteenth century. The Cold War, a dangerous game played by two world powers, caught the world's attention to the detriment of regional groups. The world's gaze was so fixed on potential fights between East and West that a nation could afford to neglect smaller wars at home.

During that time, few people spoke of the role religion played in the construction of pluralism, since pluralism became a social fact largely through migration. As the Cold War warmed up to an even temperature, many smaller national battles got attention, such as those in Canada and the United States between the dominant group and minorities.

The spiritual dimension of ordinary human life did not disappear during the Cold War but neither did it exert direct influence on world politics. Religious traditions and the life of faith remained in the wings. In the 1980s, religions re-entered center stage in world political drama as public and political concerns.[3] Prior to its return, religion was best known for a bad public image that it still has in many contexts. Religion got a bad name during modernity. Prejudice against religion and its exclusion from public life have their roots in modernity. (From a Western European point of view, modernity lasted approximately from the French Revolution in 1789 to the mid-nineteenth century, notably 1968, although the suggestion of these dates depends on one's perspective on modernity itself.)

It is fair to say that modern secular reformers did their best to eradicate religion. Their outspoken aim was to corral religion so that if it survived the twentieth century at all, and they believed it would not, it would be too weak to harm those who had the good sense to stay out of church, synagogue or temple. As an example, as mentioned, Freud attacked religion. Christians do well to heed his rage against God because he shows us so much about modern humanity and faith's resilience. Even if we could gain these insights without him, we must face the effects of his life and work on global culture.

Freud's ideas shaped the twentieth century and influenced the world against religion, most potently in North America. Karl Marx and Friedrich Nietzsche had a similar influence elsewhere.

Christians should revisit with compassion and humility these architects of modernity because they show us at our worst. We must sense how religion can go wrong if we want to be faithful. I focus on Freud because the central issue in faith education is the problem of growing up. Few people wrestled with the dilemma of growing up more thoroughly than he did. Reflecting on Freud helps us to identify how to grow up in good faith.

Those who were responsible for religious education during the last half of the twentieth century were aware of the low view religion held in the public. From behind church walls, Sunday School teachers pursued educational aims for developing a faithful perspective in the young, but once their learners left the circle of their support, they were less sure of their effectiveness. In a media-packed week, Sunday School teachers had little time to tell the Story of Jesus. The word Sunday School itself had no cultural currency. Society outside the Church gave little support to Sunday School ideas about God and the good life. The regrettable loss to present-day North American churches of the Baby Boomer generation is one example of the mismatch between secular and religious worldviews that typified the second half of the last century.

But it is not as if spiritual experiences stopped occurring. The word spiritual itself took on new significance. The spiritual dimension was diminished by the domination of materialism. But the tyranny of materialism finally drove the West to remember the human spirit. Human hunger for spiritual reality grew strong. In the twenty-first century, spirituality has vigor and religious language is used widely, though we find it in strange places. As one example, Jean Baudrillard (referred to by some as the high priest of post-modernity) used religious language and metaphor freely. What he meant to say with his religious language is far from clear.[4] This then, is the backdrop for faith education. Given our context, in order to expand what I mean by faith education, we must get a brief sketch of the differences and similarities between several related words that are currently used to describe those aspects of human experience that are more than merely material. These words are faith, religion, spirituality and existentialism.

The Spiritual Commons

Faith education intentionally responds to the foibles of modernity. Yet what is the advantage of an educational focus on faith rather than spirituality or religion? First let me describe these terms and point out relationships among them. In unpacking these words, I have no intention to express disdain for religion in favor of spirituality. I hope to show the integrous contribution that each makes to the possibility of being a faithful personal member of a religious tradition. Even if we prize aspects of the modern perspective of what it means to be human, we must move beyond modernity's refusal to take the spiritual seriously, notably, in the corporate form that spirituality frequently assumes, i.e., in religion.

Yet I ask that you heed modernity's rage against religion as you read further. Do not disregard lessons that moved modern atheism: bad religion hurts people. Freud teaches us this lesson. Given the criticism he directed against religion, those who long to love God more than any other love, ask themselves: How can I love God and gain good faith? The advantage of a focus on faith is that it is personal. We learn to be people of faith personally. Faith education lasts a lifetime. Fundamental relationships among the words faith, spirituality and religion are cooperative. Faith requires that we do our spiritual work ourselves in a context of other people. Faith is not dismissive of religion. In faith education, we gain a healthy attitude toward religion by doing our own appropriate spiritual work.

What is spiritual work? Spirituality is that aspect of the self that unites authenticity and sociality and gives meaning, direction and purpose to an individual life in the context of other people. Kevin Mott-Thorton (1998) defined spirituality so that, to him, it does not discourage particular religious traditions and would accommodate people who believe either that there is no God or that the idea of God is, at best, uninteresting. I agree with him but want to make additions to his view of spirituality to link it to the way I defined spirituality up to now as *a sense of felt connection*. To him, spirituality is that quality of being, holistically conceived, made up of insight, beliefs, values, attitudes, emotions and behavioral dispositions that informs and is informed by ordinary experience. It has cognitive content best described as a framework of ideals, beliefs and values about oneself, one's relationships with others as well as with reality.

Logically intrinsic to this framework and rooted in an idea of what is real and of ultimate concern, is a concept of what makes life good. According to Mott-Thorton, a concept of the good life may be related to concepts for God, and God's will for our lives, or it may not. An idea of the good life informs human actions but doesn't determine them: we may act inconsistently with our idea of the good life and still maintain that the ideal is good. We choose to act according to spiritual values or we violate them. An idea of the good life influences behavior (when it does) through a network of unexamined assumptions, prejudices, or rational explanations. Our ideal is idiosyncratic; it is an organizing principle for ordinary life in terms of values, attitudes and emotions that we deploy daily.

While helpful, I suggest Mott-Thorton's definition of spirituality is a description of the worldview that a spiritual process produces in every individual rather than of spirituality itself. Worldviews are formed though biological, cultural, sociological, psychological, neurological dimensions of human experiences, as outlined in chapter one, where spirituality was defined as *a sense of felt connection* that individuals have from birth. In short, a spiritual process results in a worldview that every one has by the time they are eleven or twelve. This worldview is a system that shapes our perception of the world and it is formed through personal experience. This distinction is important to what follows, as I distinguish spirituality from other related terms.

THE SPIRITUAL VERSUS THE EXISTENTIAL

Mott-Thorton's idea of spirituality is useful but how do spiritual concerns differ from existential ones? The word existential refers to existence. All of us have existential problems simply because we are human. Existential problems arise through our need for other people and make us vulnerable to them. Unlike animals, people are dependent on others for a long time during childhood. While the term existential refers to ordinary experience, it is related to a view made popular in the philosophical perspective of Existentialism, which introduced atheism and materialism as a dominant influence on Western culture.

Existentialism has a number of roots, some of which grew in Christian soil, some that did not. Blaise Pascal, Soren Kierkegaard, Emmanuel Mounier and Jean-Paul Sartre are four people that contributed to the development of Existentialism. There are others, notably Simone de Beauvoir, Sartre's lifelong companion. The first three thinkers married existential sentiments to Christianity; the latter two vigorously opposed Christian faith. Whether Christian or not, Existentialists emphasize the radical individual responsibility that they believe makes life authentic. In living one's own life, each day we become painfully aware of absurd twists and turns in ordinary events. An Existentialist criticizes the order of things, the status quo, insisting that human freedom is linked to the roots of being a solitary individual. Existentialism requires us to practice freedom as responsible human agents. In Existentialism our responsibility is to ourselves. We are not to be constrained by fixed ideas or systems, values or tenets of belief. Our system or way of life must be personal. Existentialism calls us to project ourselves toward an open future: by acting responsibly we redefine our future by taking action. Our responsibility is extreme. Creativity, unpredictability, liberty and responsibility are principles of Existentialism.

While atheistic philosophers who contributed to Existentialism specifically criticize Christianity *per se*, Christian contributors criticize the way the practice of faith can settle into mundane living that does not make us think about ourselves. They investigated what they considered to be a perversion of Christianity, not authentic faith. They criticized what can become merely conventional in Christianity, or we might say, they criticized the conservatism that can turn radical faith into mere passivity and boredom. Existentialism paid attention to the conditions of ordinary life. As a philosophy, it was concerned with problems that arise in ordinary daily living. We distinguish existential problems from neurotic or psychotic problems, for example, by noting that all human beings have existential problems with reality but not everyone has neurotic or psychotic problems with it. Existentialism emphasizes human responsibility to think about what we are thinking about, to attend to human consciousness, rather than letting ourselves float inattentively along the conventional main stream. Being consciously aware of ourselves, living intentionally, is ceaselessly maintained as an exercise of a rich and full humanity.

Existentialism wakes us up from materialism, as does the concept of spirituality. Both ideas compel us to answer questions such as: Why should I respect other people, or myself, rather than practice harm? Why love rather than hate? What is my future? Why am I alive? Is there purpose to life? What is my work? Existentialism and spirituality mark our fragile and precious longing to make a difference in the world. We can choose to be cynical or hopeful in the face of that human longing. Existentialism and spirituality oppose living life passively.

Philosophical Existentialism asks whether or not someone is living life authentically according to a standard set by Existentialism itself. Spirituality asks whether or not someone is living authentically according to a standard implicit and explicit in his or her conception of the good life. Mott-Thorton's idea of spirituality assumes that every person must live life on his or her own terms in light of a worldview that indicates to them what makes life good. His concept of spirituality assumes everyone develops (consciously or not) an idea of the good life that shapes action and reaction. We may get our idea of the good life from the religious tradition we choose or we may get our standards elsewhere. Atheism is one source for those standards and values, and there are others.

While spirituality and Existentialism both require us to address life in a context of other people, i.e., to relate authenticity to sociality, there is a distinction between the two in that only one assumes that a spiritual world exists in addition to the material world. An atheistic Existentialist lives in a material world—even though the Existentialist thrust is to resist the pervasive influence of that materialism. Spirituality assumes that the world is both spiritual and material.

Like Existentialism, spiritually shapes thought. In particular, I wish to add to Mott-Thorton's view of spirituality an insight Rizzuto (1979) derived from Freud's analysis of human experience: she asserts that everyone has a God concept whether or not that concept is favorable. Spirituality makes more of spiritual realities than Mott-Thorton allows. From a spiritual perspective, atheists operate with a concept for God—they believe that God is not interesting or does not exist. Atheists and believers share existential problems. Both groups tell themselves stories about reality to explain how the world works. What stories do atheists tell? As one example, Sartre summed up his play, *No Exit* with the cryptic line: Hell is other people. That is his story and he seemed to stick to it. It's a story line that supports his judgment about authenticity and sociality, by asking what we can make of ourselves given the burdensome presence of other people.

In summary, spirituality and Existentialism have an experiential and narrative core. Experientially, we engage in practices that support our values and beliefs and accept responsibility for all of our actions. We tell stories to keep our framework vital.

Christianity and Existentialism are ways of life. We are shaped by the way of life we adopt. Our perception of reality is informed in its light. Our stories and actions are the answer to our questions. The human mind needs stories to provide structures for thinking about its questions. From a Christian existential perspective, authenticity is possible to the extent that we negotiate a relationship with religious standards and stories to remain free and responsible within that tradition. Religion does not enslave us if we intentionally work out our relationship with ritual, idea and story. We are not necessarily enslaved by a tradition, if we do our own appropriate spiritual work.

Spiritual work is the self-observation we engage in to help us grow up. It allows us to make sufficient sense of life so that we can go on living. Our spiritual work is to make sense of ourselves in the context of other people, according to an idea of what makes life good. Religion adds community and history to the individual work of being spiritual. Very simply, religion is 'an institution consisting of culturally patterned interactions with culturally postulated superhuman beings.'[5] Religion is spiritual work done collectively, over time, and in response to what we understand God is doing. Our society is comfortable with spirituality, but religion responds to a deep human longing for community—the longing not to be alone. Religion provides us with comfort, human and divine, but has its flaws and funny parts as well. The aim of faith education in the context of a religious tradition is to live healthy, personally directed communal lives so that our fatih can grow up.

HOW DOES FAITH WORK?

Faith is the confidence, trust, reliance or conviction that we place in someone or something. It is an attitude of the heart. Faith becomes a way of life so that other people can count on the faithful to act and respond in predictable ways. This is precisely what we mean when we say that someone is faithful. It is as much about acting as it is about thinking. Further, it is a perspectival concept: it is a way of seeing or perceiving the world. The activity of faith is to perceive the world in a particular way. Faith education develops human capacities so that people learn about faith and learn to exercise faith. When they understand what faith is, people begin to observe how they exercise faith. This seems to have been Jesus' point in focusing on faith; he drew people's attention to their own exercise of faith, so that it could grow. During faith education we learn to notice how we exercise faith generally. Faith is steadfast, firm and reliable and is lived out in the company of others. Exercising faith alters the one who practices it so that a person becomes faithful; ideally the faithful shape Christian community so that it becomes God-infused in a way that is compellingly attractive.

We learn about faith at home and at church. Our education begins in infancy and is acquired bodily, by the ways we are held, look upon, spoken to and treated in general. Faith also comes by thinking, by the use of reason that each human being has as a consequence of being a rational person. In addition, faith is acquired and understood through reading scripture and seeing how faith operated in the lives of those whose narratives are recorded in the First and Second Testaments. Scripture declares that there is only one utterly safe object to anchor human faith—God and God alone.

When people asked Jesus what they must do to do the works God requires, he replied, "The work of God is this: to believe in the one he has sent."[6] Scripture does not say that God is the only object of faith, God anchors faith and must have no rivals. In scripture, the faithful learn to rest their deepest dependence in God. In placing ultimate dependence in God and what God says, their humanity is profoundly affected. In exercising faith they enjoy relationship with God. Faith in God influences humanity, just as a game of peek-a-boo affects an infant's relation to the world beyond his vision of it. Because of these effects, all of us are well advised to pay attention to the objects we put faith in. Suppose we choose to put our faith in God. This act implies that the relationship we would be lost without is our relationship with God. We are deeply saddened by other losses, or seriously injured by them, but we are not utterly lost due to losing them.

Being faithful means remaining faithful to God as the foundation of our faith. God is the groundwork. When we put faith in other things, or when we learn to observe what things we tend to put our faith in, Christians ask themselves whether this or that object is in competition with our reliance on God. If other objects—money, position, knowledge, work, sex, play, certain people—are in competition with our reliance on God, we are making these other objects into idols. For example, if we worship other people, rather than showing them the ordinary love and respect that is appropriate to human beings, we turn them into things, into idols. In the process, their loss of humanity is profound. True believers learn how to put faith in God and in other things as well, without making those other objects equal to God's importance as the foundation for faith. God said: "You shall have no other gods before me." God had to give us this commandment after Eden. After we made the wrong move with faith in the Garden, God had to spell things out.

God has to spell things out for people because faith is wild. Faith is wild because human beings, by themselves, are incomplete. Adam was incomplete. Incompleteness compels us to attach faith to something. (I think it is only when we believe all else has failed that we make an idol out of our own image.) If conditions for attachment are *unfavorable* faith adheres to strange objects; as a consequence people go astray and may remain lost. As we will see, Eve and Adam ate fruit from the wrong tree in Eden. People do pick substitutes for God. Despite the dangers, the aim of faith education is not to domesticate faith, forcing it to be tame rather than wild. Tame faith is too timid to fully engage the adventure of living faithfully. The educational task is to enable faith to grow up. Faith must grow up if we would be well. Faith does not lose its wildness entirely when it grows up. Faith is vital. It is potent with energy. How often have we seen people, late on in their years with God, attach faith to a strange object? Maturing faith learns to recognize the right objects and learns to value them in the right way. We must learn through living because, in Eden, we failed to take God's word at face value.

In adhering to the right objects, maturing faith increases our capacity for making sense of the world. A strong, positive bond forms between learning to put faith in the right objects, in the right way, and being able to make sense of the world. Taken together, these two aspects of faith education teach us how to grow up. Choosing appropriate faith objects and regarding them in the right way is part of learning to make sufficient sense of the world. In Eden the world made sense. We lost Eden. After Eden, we have to work at making sense of the world. We have to work at growing up. Growing up is the core problem in the Christian life.

The Limits of Faith

Faith education is the activity of faith learning to grow up. Faith education is lifelong learning. I want to explore further the assertion that faith is wild and never entirely loses its wildness in growing up. If we expect mature faith to protect us from all uncertainty and suffering we will be dismayed. If we expect mature faith to bring us to the place where we no longer need it, we misunderstand the human condition. Faith cannot make perfect sense of the world. If the world made complete sense, faith would be superfluous. Its inadequacy in leading us to make perfect sense of life is faith's main attribute. Faith falls short of entirely making sense of human experience because it is both friend and stranger to human comfort. We come to faith, sometimes slowly, and choose to remain faithful often in the absence of comfort. Faith does bring comfort but also calls for adventure if we get too comfortable. Yet faith is not cavalier. We are not called away from comfortable resting places merely because faith admires adventure. There is nothing wrong with rest.

We are called to adventure because staying comfortable is not our main occupation as believers. Faith is comforting in the same way that a faithful friend brings comfort. From God's perspective, as revealed in Genesis, the aim of human life is intimacy with God. The metaphor of intimacy with God is expressed in terms of walking with God. Adam, Eve and other people walked with God. In scripture, God shows us how to walk with Him and each other; God shows us by walking with us, whatever life brings—including suffering. In our intimacy with God, we still have questions; faith cannot make complete sense of life, even when we are walking closely with God. Though they may complain and argue, the faithful talk to God even if life does not satisfy them with the sense they can make of it at a given point in time.

There is another reason why faith cannot make complete sense of the world. Evil inhabits the world; evil is irrational. When faith tries to succeed at making sense of life, evil aims to frustrate the effort by showing the greatest skill imaginable for making non-sense. Evil is the enemy of our efforts to make sufficient sense of ourselves, other people and life in general. Very often people will come to accept physical suffering and even emotional suffering through realizing that all of us are flawed and sinful. But intellectual suffering, the suffering of not being able to make sufficient sense of an event, or someone else's action, is like a sliver in the mind.

Deep suffering comes of not being able to make sense of something. We feel alone and ask: Why does he humiliate people? Why does she hurt me? Why did this devastation happen? In mental suffering we find no complete answer to our questions. Evil is irrational. When children ask us why, why, and why again, we often tire of their probing. But our parental and grandparental duty is to remain with them. We console them as they ask. Consolation means to be with the lonely one.[7] The question why alarms us if our reason hoard is empty. Whether or not we can give a satisfactory answer, it is adult work to wait with children while they ask. They must ask. To ask why is the key to unlock mental suffering? Children must learn to ask why questions and wait for a response. We are all compelled to ask why. Yet mature faith realizes its need for a friend more than an answer. We need a response more than a reason. Our deepest

170

need is for the consolation of Presence; human faith relies on more than mere rationality. Mature faith waits on its relationship between a human agent exercising faith, and faith's object, God. Mature faith walks alongside God questioningly, and patiently learns to regain its composure over the inevitable anxiety of being human.

Growing Faithful

Our spiritual work is to make sufficient sense of life according to a model or standard that we accept as a way of explaining the purposes for living. It is hard work. If spiritual work is to make sufficient sense of ourselves, other people and life in general, mental suffering bars the way to getting satisfaction—to feeling entirely healthy and whole. Trust comes into play when making sense fails. Trusting God at this point is difficult. But trust is not a way to dispense with anxiety; it is a way to live with uncertainty. Suffering is intensified by evil's ability to keep life from making sufficient sense. Yet this fatal trick is evil's own undoing. If we give ourselves permission, we bring our non-sense into the Presence of God. Faith lives with the uncertainty that non-sense causes. In God's Presence faith finds consolation and protection from the anxiety that fear breeds. After all, trust is employed only if we are unsure of ourselves. When we come, God tells us stories.

When we cannot make rational sense of life, it is best to tell stories. Stories satisfy. They provide a homeland where we garner meaning. As adults, if all is well, our stories convey and reinforce our idea of what makes life good. We offer our stories to the questioning child. Stories take time to share. In telling a child the right story, at the right time, in the right way, for the right reason we accomplish two goals simultaneously. We practice making sense of life by responding to a simple human need and we offer our gift of time. In recounting our stories, we do as God does. When we are older, and our own questions dog our heels, our stories continue to bless us with their usefulness, as food for thought. The Garden of Eden is one such story; it is as good for those who are three as for those who are ninety-three. It is a true story. We know it is true because, as we listen, we partake in the Story—we recognize ourselves. Eden does not give us precise reasons why evil is in the world: it shows us evil and reveals its characteristic drive to distract faith. What is it that enables some people to bring their uncertainty into God's Presence and ask for a story? It is faith growing up.

Faith education aims at learning how to grow up by facing problems that are typical of human life. Faith education is conservative and transformational. Education is conservative due to two of its duties. Education's first duty is to conserve tradition so as to pass itself on to each generation. Education also has a duty to a variety of learners: its means of expression must appeal to the young, the old, the simple, as well as intellectuals. As a consequence, Christian educators focus on the essential narrative of the faith. We attentively read scripture from beginning to end and expect the Story to hang together. This is a humble task that, oddly, is hard to keep simple. Faith educators do not themselves play at the borders of ordinary intellectual interest by toying with scholarly critical approaches to biblical text. We leave that inquiry for those intrigued by the questions that draw them there. We make use of their insight but that quest is not our work. What we aim at in faith education is intelligent reading as a source for spiritual growth. We awaken people to their own authentic questions and provide opportunities for an inquiry that follows the path of these questions.

Faith education leads to authentic inquiry but aims to conserve the faith as well. Yet, in being conservative, in an ecological sense, it does not promote conservatism. Conservatism closes its eyes to ordinary life, by cementing faith ideas and by building a place to stop and stay. The walls around this resting place can reify. The adventure of the faithful is not lived from a fortress, by those who refuse to move out into the light of day. Education, properly understood, does not build faith fortresses. It equips us for adventure. It gives truth and method to carry in a backpack. Faith education is life long learning. It is not mere conservatism, which refuses to attend to the way things are in the world, closes its eyes to reality and keeps a death grip on tradition. With our eyes closed, reality cannot teach us how to grow up. Christians learn about faith from reality. God invented reality. In Eden, reality makes faith possible and necessary.

172

Reality moves faith forward and away from conservatism. Faith education has conservative duties and also transforms the learner. When we are learning, we not only receive a tradition from those before us, we reflect on that tradition from our current circumstances, i.e., our history, culture and social location, with help from the Holy Spirit. The Holy Spirit is alive. In addition to receiving a tradition, God speaks with us personally.

In conservatism, people grab a piece of a tradition and ignore parts that do not conform to aspects they prize. The tendency to hang on to what is convenient is especially strong in those who remain inside fortresses—who think of faith as a noun only and not a verb. Christianity is The Way. The Christian tradition is large and expansive. There is room for diversity and difference. While there are borders to what we believe, the field is big enough to accommodate excursions. Christians have always had to live with tension between essentials and non-essentials of the faith. In mature faith, while constant in Being, God moves with us. God with us, Immanuel!

The Gift of Faith and the Loss of Eden

One aim of faith education is to comprehend (as fully as we are able) what it means to be a spiritual human being. If we read Genesis attentively we see that faith and humanity are entwined. To begin with, God created the world in such a way that faith is possible. God brought order, established boundaries and assigned work to every living thing that came forth as God spoke. The earth was formless and empty. God established borders around the elements, putting the waters and land in place. God called for Light. He separated light from dark. God grew plants that produced their own kind and animals that produced their own kind. We continue to count for our very existence upon Creation's orderliness.

All things created consist in God. As one example, formlessness and emptiness would not beget science. Meticulous investigations by modern science are possible only because the universe is orderly and predictable. The academic disciples that flourished in the twentieth century emerged out of the certainty that creation was orderly and predictable: that we could surmise what happened thousands of years ago because of what we observe each day. Scientific investigation is grounded on faith. The Sun, Moon and stars move in their ordered paths. Day is separated from night. Miraculously, a newborn baby begins to sleep during the dark of night and stay awake during the light of day. Orderliness established through God's activity as Creator grounds human faith. If earth was unpredictable, we could not make sense of it. Faith is our reasonable response to the order of things. Creation inspires more than academic disciplines. In addition to an orderly and predictable creation, God made the world lavishly beautiful. God is Artist. Creation demonstrates creativity. Eden was designed to provide the greatest advantage for faith to flourish and permits us to make sense of how the world works. We experience a reality created by God.

Faith is built into reality. Reality confirms the wisdom of putting faith in the predictable length of days and seasons, in rain falling to water the earth and sun shining to warm it. At its simplest, faith education is a reasonable response to the way things were in Eden. It is not so much that Eden was paradise, particularly if we think of paradise as a place without dangers, but Eden made sense. God made a sensible world. God created an orderly world in which faith could grow. God saw that it was good. We were made for Eden. We were meant to walk with God and work with creation. But even in Eden human beings were originally incomplete. Adam was incomplete. God did not make us on a model of self-sufficiency. Outside of Eden our original incompleteness shows up as insecurity. After Eden, reality teaches us to have faith but also tests our faith to the breaking point. Outside Eden, humanity is helpless against Nature. Our bodies can betray us to disease. Other people may fail to meet our most basic needs while we are dependent upon them. Ruthlessness in the workplace can destroy a career. Children who rebel render useless a life spent nurturing them. Genesis shows that human helplessness lasts a lifetime because we are essentially incomplete. But incompleteness is ambiguous. There is more than one side to human helplessness.

God made a descriptive statement about Adam. After the first man was created, God said: It is not good for man to be alone. This is the only time during creation that God said something was not good. Human beings, in our original condition, are incomplete: even though we can enjoy ourselves, we need God and we need other people. The possibility for human intimacy depends upon our original condition of incompleteness. Being incomplete is not the same as being flawed. It means we are human. On one hand, incompleteness is a human strength when we accept our condition as a gift from God. Incompleteness necessitates human solidarity. In their original solidarity, Adam and Eve were naked and unashamed. Solidarity is a positive outcome of original incompleteness. Our incompleteness is real and no delusion—we are too helpless to look after our own interests by ourselves. We do not come into the world or grow up without an investment by other people.

Because the first person was incomplete, God made another person as his companion. It is not merely that Eve was designed as Adam's helper in Garden work. Rather, Adam is essentially incomplete without another human being. She also was incomplete, though both are fully human. As evidence, Eve demonstrated her humanity by acting as a moral agent in conversations with the serpent. Out of the condition of her incompleteness, she made a choice, as all human beings do; she chose not to take God's word on faith.

Incompleteness opens us up to anxiety. Inside and outside of Eden, while it is not a sin itself, anxiety readies us for sin. Our deficiency is not the result of the Fall; it is our essential condition before the Fall. We are incomplete by design. Incompleteness is not a mistake. Incompleteness is the risk of being human. Incompleteness reveals itself as dangerous and humiliating helplessness before the power of Nature, the frailty of our own bodies, or misuse by other people. While we were in Eden, being incomplete made us human: we were vulnerable yet safe.

But even in Eden incompleteness intensified anxiety. Eve desired wisdom presumably because she felt its lack. Sin is the choice to get rid of anxiety through our own efforts. It is the refusal to take our uncertainty to God. Coupled with the loss of Eden, incompleteness leaves us vulnerable and unsafe. Intimacy became one of the dangers of living. In Eden, intimacy was the freedom to be known at a deep level—to be vulnerable yet feel safe. After Eden, like our original parents, sensing that they were naked, now we are ashamed. If we wish to learn intimacy, we must remember Eden. Learning to be an intimate human being is the spiritual work of faith.

Faith and Moral Constraint

In Eden intimacy was related to morality. Moral responsibility began in Eden. Morality refers to the way we treat other people and the way we treat ourselves. Morality is not a curse but keeps us human. Adam and Eve's incompleteness grounds their moral responsibility. They had choices to make from the beginning and there were dangers. They were free to satisfy their need for food but freedom had limits. God said: "You are free to eat from any tree in the garden; but you must not eat from the tree of the knowledge of good and evil, for when you eat of it you will surely die" (Gen.16b-17). What did our original parents lose as they tasted fruit from the tree of the knowledge of good and evil?

It is interesting to note that Eve exaggerated the limits placed upon them by God. In her conversations with the serpent, Eve added a limit to God's instructions. Was Eve compelled to conceive of God as unreasonable before she could go against God's Word? God said not to eat of the fruit and gave Adam a reason. Eve said they could neither eat the fruit *nor touch it*. She hesitated over the reason for not eating this particular fruit. God had said: "You will surely die" but the serpent altered God's Word and said "You will not die...You will be like God" (Gen.3:1-5). Eve came to believe she would receive wisdom if she ate the fruit. She took a bite. Is there anything wrong with wisdom? Adam bit as well. Then wisdom let them see that they were naked. They no longer wanted God to gaze upon them.

When God came to walk with them in the cool of the evening, they hid. Their choice revealed itself in the act of hiding. No one had to tell God what happened. Sin expressed itself in their being. God asked questions. Adam and Eve got to blaming God and each other. When Adam and Eve blamed each other, it was the demon of shame speaking. I imagine it was no longer possible for them to gaze into each other's eyes. There were consequences for everyone. The world is no longer Eden. God sent them out of the Garden so they could not make an utterly fatal mistake. The Story of Eden shows us that our original parents were incomplete in themselves, limited by the requirements of moral responsibility and were expelled. What loss! They were out in a world they did not create and could not control. But on their way out, God gave them clothing, to ease the anxiety of being human—and ashamed.

If we learn this much about being human from Eve and Adam what do we learn from their offspring? In addition to the lives of Adam and Eve, Genesis tells us about three of their children: Cain, Abel and Seth. Abel kept flocks. Cain worked the soil. Seth came later. Cain and Abel brought an offering from their labor to the Lord. Genesis tells us that: "The Lord looked with favor on Abel and his offering, but on Cain and his offering he did not look with favor. So Cain was very angry, and his face was downcast" (Gen. 4:4-5). What do we learn from the story of these two boys? What do we learn about faith from them? What do they reveal about being human? Cain's downcast face is so completely credible. We can imagine him. We do not ask whether the story is true. We all know why he was angry. We recognize that feeling. It has a name.

But what happens next is surprising. God approached Cain and spoke to him. Whenever I read this story I am astonished that God sought out Cain and asked "Why are you angry? Why is your face downcast? If you do what is right, will you not be accepted? But if you do not do what is right, sin is crouching at your door; it desires to have you, but you must master it." God took Cain's moral responsibility seriously.

I am compelled to wonder what you sense as you read the conversation between God and Cain. What is the tone of God's voice? What is the look on God's face? Our own conception of God is caught in our answer to these questions. Do you know the rest of the story? Cain killed his brother Abel—in cold blood, as we say. The first murder! God was not done speaking with Cain and said: "Where is your brother Abel?" The story continues. Woeful consequences followed Cain's action. He is sentenced to be a restless wanderer. What is it that actually disturbs Cain about this punishment? This is what he said: "My punishment is more than I can bear. Today you are driving me from the land, and I will be hidden from your presence; I will be a restless wanderer on the earth, and whoever finds me will kill me." God put a mark on Cain so no one would kill him. While Cain's punishment remained, God relieved the crushing pressure of these consequences so that Cain could bear the anxiety of being human—and alone.

Cain's offspring followed the murderer's pattern. One of his descendents named Lamech bragged to his wives. He said to them: "I have killed a man for wounding me and a young man for injuring me. If Cain is avenged seven times, then Lamech is avenged seventy-seven times." (Gen. 4:23-24) The outcome of Adam's and Eve's action in the Garden opened up the full range of human harm that continues to hurt us, but they also had a third son. When Eve gave birth to Seth she said: "God has granted me another child in the place of Abel, since Cain killed him." Seth had a son, and named the boy Enosh. When Enosh was born, we are told, people began to call on the name of the Lord. With the birth of Seth, the possibility of walking with God was again clear to people. Cain, Abel and Seth show that humanity has two options: we can follow the murderous path Cain blazed or we can walk with God.

If we reflect on what we learn about faith and humanity from these passages in Genesis, we see a pattern that plays out in the First Testament and makes Christ's coming into the world the necessary outcome of Eden. Human beings exercise faith and unfaith. God draws close to us and we draw close to God. This relation between us works both ways. Suppose we begin in faith. Then for one reason or another, we turn our gaze away from God. We try faith out on other objects. We lose intimacy. We get lost and find ourselves in grave difficulty. We suffer. As a consequence of suffering, some people have a change of heart and allow faith to lead them back into God's Presence, even with uncertainty clinging to their heels. As a result of suffering, other people find substitutes for God and remain in the wild—as restless wanderers. It is compelling to notice how the pattern of faith revealed in humanity is met by God's absolute refusal to diminish our need for Him. God never relieves the requirement that people must live by faith. But God does relieve anxiety. God shows compassion. He covers Adam and Eve with clothing. God places his mark on Cain. His grace operates in concert with faith. In faith there is tension. On our side, we exercise faith and unfaith. God is resolute about our need for Him and responds when we call. God is love. To grow up faithfully is to learn to live well with the tension inherent in having faith and experiencing unfaith.

FAITH EDUCATION FOR LIFELONG LEARNING

Very simply, lifelong learning begins at birth and ends at death. Spirituality is our human longing for a Voice to speak to us—to convey our value. We long for conversation and consolation. If faith is to be healthy lifelong, children must converse about spiritual concerns. Do children typically have this opportunity? In a society that spends so little time listening to children, it is unlikely. Without the freedom and encouragement to hear our own thoughts about God in the context of an attentive other person, it is hard to grow up with a healthy faith. Children depend on adults who listen to their thoughts so they can learn to make sense of themselves and other people. Faith education embraces childhood experience as a source of insight for growing up. Its approach relies on making connections between the child and adult. Childhood longings mature as our concept of God is transformed by experience. Maturity implies allowing our concept of God to grow up without denying a basic human limitation, our need for consolation. Faith education offers a model of growth that prizes childhood religious experience without leaving us childish.

If we want to educate the young we must take seriously the way they understand God as our starting point. I agree with Ana Maria Rizzuto (1979, 1998) who asserted that some people cannot be faithful because they are terrified by the concept they hold for God. Others replace God with substitutes that pre-occupy them. This was Freud's pattern. He distanced himself from a God he praised when he was a small boy; later in life he substituted other satisfactions for his early belief in a consoling God.[8] There are people who do not believe in God because they are afraid of their own regressive wishes. While still others have a concept of God that is compatible with consolation—with seeing God as love.[9] If we were fortunate children, someone provided the healthy consolation and protection that permits a concept of God to grow up. Those who are unfortunate cannot find consolation and are left alone, perhaps with a sense of duty that drives them (to their detriment) addictively to tend the very people whose parental duty it was to nurture them. After reflecting on Freud, I am more, rather than less, sure of our need for a God who consoles. Unmet human need leaves us clinging to longings we are compelled to address—one way or another. Faith education helps us clarify and address the concept of God we carry with us from our earliest years.

The Natural History of God

The purpose of faith education is to help believers grow up faithfully. Unless we state our assumptions, we cannot evaluate whether our educational practices are effective and focus us in the right direction. The following assumptions ground the educational aim of helping a concept of God to grow up:

- The central aim of faith education is to help people grow up in the fullness of God
- All human beings have an image of God built out of their experiences from birth
- An image of God, feeling for God, and an idea of God equals a concept of God
- At birth, infants have a sense of self that enables them to negotiate relationships
- As we age, we face essentially the same problem as infants do: we must be ourselves in the presence of others and work out the tension between inner and outer worlds
- Our concept of God needs to be recreated throughout life and particularly during crises if it is to be found relevant for lasting belief, as we work out the tension of being ourselves in the company of others

Taken together, these assumptions suggest that we need to help children work out their feelings and thoughts about God in a way that enables them to be authentic, i.e., be themselves, yet be collaborative with others. Yet I do not suggest that the aim of faith education is to form well-adjusted adults, or to prevent suffering. We are not trying to help Christians conform to the world or ignore its harsh realities. Faith education is grounded on spiritual benefits and blessings of belief in God. Yet we want the roots of faith in the inner life to grow and flourish into a healthy relationship with a religious tradition and the world. In order to establish the relationship between these assumptions, I outline a view of the inner life of children. The young must integrate images, feelings, and ideas of God into a concept that provides them with adequate means to go on living. Children must reconcile their personalized concepts of God with formal concepts presented in church if they would be part of the religious tradition.

Let us begin with the assumption that every child, every human being, has an image of God built out of the initial experiences of their first few years of life. By the time a child is five years old, through "the busy factory of the child's imagery," which is a matrix of "facts and fantasies, wishes, hopes, and fears" and through exchanges with parents, the child concocts an image of God.[11] Throughout life, images of God may undergo revision, repression, recovery and reconciliation. As adults we never finish with the ways that God came into being personally when we were children. However it came into being, and the process of forming an image of God is complex and mysterious, the God a child creates will emerge from memory whenever the puzzles of life, death, and birth—with all their unfathomable realities—are staring the adult in the face. We never leave behind the image of God that we acquired in childhood but, as adults, we may not be able to say what it is; that is, we may not have consciously considered our image of God.

Children get their image of God through encountering parents, siblings and significant others in their early years. For example, direct encounters between mother and child—the eye contact between them—is a source for the first elaborations of an image of God.[12] Power is exercised in the gaze behavior between mother and child. On the one hand, infants negotiate these encounters by

181

regulating the level and amount of social stimulation to which they are subjected. They can avert their gaze, shut their eyes, stare past and become glassy-eyed in refusing to engage. Through the decisive use of gaze behaviors they can reject, distance themselves from, or defend themselves against their mothers. They also reinitiate engagement. They can reconnect when they wish by gazing, smiling and vocalizing. Autonomy or independence is operating in all social behaviors that regulate the quality or quantity of engagement.[13] Infants are not powerless. They have a sense of self from birth.

On the other hand, mothers exercise social power. The effects of power influence not only the relationship between mother and child but also the child's images of God. The mother acts like a mirror for the child. Initially, infants need to see their own reflection in their mother's eyes.[14] There are two mistakes during this gaze behavior that adults might make: parents exalt a child or are unresponsive. That is, the child may be under-valued or over-valued. Both of these misdirections of the child's sense of personal value have serious consequences for the child's image of God. These misadventures are related to the use of power in personal relationships.

In discussing the role of power and magic in childhood, the previous chapter contains a description of mother-child encounters that I want to elaborate. To begin with, a mother's face is present to an infant to provide a perspective on his or her own being. This insight reminds us of creation: God created human beings "in his own image." A child that does not experience responsiveness comes to see the mother's face as a surface, as "a thing to be looked at but not into;" as a result, the child's freedom and confidence to go beyond or into the mirror is limited.[15] The child cannot move into the mirror to see the real mother or to get a clear reflection of his or her own real self. On the other hand, if adults exalt the child, the child acquires a bloated and unreasonable estimate of his or her personal worth. The child attributes excessive powers to the self. In the gaze behavior between infant and parent, a child depends on appropriate responses from adults. Children may be exalted to the point that they lose an accurate mirroring of themselves or they may be deprived of responses that give them emotional sustenance.

If encounters continually go wrong, a child may develop a false self: self-esteem and self-concepts suffer, as does a child's God concept.

The effects of social power, between infants and parents, come to be associated with the child's image of God and self-image.[16] The development of empathy in children is encouraged or discouraged through the exercise of social power during gaze behavior between adult and child. Ultimately, an image of God is invested with feelings that arise out of these encounters. When faith educators approach children these images are already present. We work with them sensitively if we wish to encourage a healthy concept of God. This analysis of parent/child relations is not meant to intensify the guilt that parents may feel due to an extreme responsibility that modernity placed on the nuclear family. Rather, I wish to identify ways that the church can take up its communal duty to assist parents in educating children so that each unfolding concept of God grows toward maturity.

A concept for God is not only constructed out of direct physical encounters. Children build God concepts in the borderlands, i.e., the imaginative spaces between their inner experience and the direct physical encounters with other people, as already mentioned. If you reflect for a moment, you see that thought-life flourishes in the borderlands of imagination. Recall the game of peek-a-boo the infant plays with his father. An infant is capable of sensing Presence, even when alone. Here lies the strength of spiritual experience. Here lies a potential problem: we may merely imagine God and therefore prevent God from being God in our lives. God must be allowed to speak *personally* in order for us to know God. But first we must sense the role that imagination plays in forming our thought-life and the way we think about God. Thinking is powerful.

Letting God Grow Up

Children get their image of God from other sources in addition to their own families. In conversation, art, architecture, social events and the media, God "is presented as invisible but none the less real."[17] In particular, the 'house of God' conveys God's Presence, rules and rituals, whether or not a child enters the building or spends much time there. When children come to church, each one has a pet image of God tucked under an arm, like a teddy bear. 'Teddy bear' images of God are significant. In order to be fully human we must have transitional objects that enable us to move on in maturity. When our transitional objects are age appropriate, it is a sign of health and well-being.

Our transitional objects help us grow up. We know "that teddy bears are not toys for spoiled children but [are] part of the illusory substance of growing up."[18] Human beings cannot be human without illusion. Illusion and reality are not contradictory terms. Psychological reality cannot occur without relying on a specifically human transitional space for play and illusion. The "type of illusion we select—science, religion, or something else—reveals our personal history and the transitional space each of us has created between [our] objects and [ourselves]...our illusions, in this sense, provide the space to find "a resting place" to live in.[19] God is a unique transitional object.

Recall that every human being has a concept of God (including feelings and thoughts about God), whether favorable or unfavorable, and whether or not he or she puts faith in God. This is because God is a special transitional object, unlike other transitional objects we use to signal we are growing up. All transitional objects have a life inside and outside the individual as well as a life in the space between inner and outer experience. For example, a teddy bear is a real object in the nursery as well as an object in the inner world of the child. The teddy bear means something specific to a child—it means comfort and portable permanence perhaps. Children eventually leave teddy on the shelf when they outgrow its usefulness as an image of safety. They move on to other objects that provide security, friends perhaps. Leaving teddy on the shelf is a sign that the child is moving on and growing up. Unlike teddy, however, the image of God is permanent.

The image of God does not leave nor is God left on the shelf. It is no more possible to lose our image of God than it is to lose our image of father and mother. The image of God is not forgotten. Instead of losing meaning over time, God gains in meaning. God resurfaces at crucial moments. While it may appear that God is rejected or neglected, our image may be repressed—God is always potentially available for further acceptance or rejection. The atheist prays as he rushes to the hospital after hearing his wife was in a car accident. A dying woman accepts Jesus as Saviour and Lord. But faith educators are not satisfied with emergency room concepts for God. The authentic, thoughtful life examines its images and ideas and builds its concepts intentionally. If our image of God is fit to help us grow up, it unites with ideas of God in such a way that our concept carries us toward maturity. While we never lose its history, it is through persistent spiritual work that our concept of God becomes a resting place for our soul's joy.

Let us be clear that an internal God concept is not the God of the bible. God concepts are constructed out of experience and are personalized representations of God. Even those who have not read the Bible have a personal image for God. There is no such thing as a person without an image of God.[20] Suppose a two-year sits beside you in church and asks: Where is God? I see pastor Bob. I see mommy in the choir. But where is God? That child is beginning to articulate the conscious construction of a concept for God. The task of creating and finding God is never completed in the course of human life. It is a lifelong process that moves with us from birth to death. As we face death, we come to final terms with our God concept.

God is unique as a transitional object in another sense as well, i.e., in addition to gaining rather than losing meaning over time. God sees the heart: God is the only transitional object that has complete knowledge of the self: one cannot escape the searching eye of God.[21] God's all-seeing knowledge of us means that our images, feelings and ideas of God are entwined with our images and ideas of ourselves. We see ourselves in part as God sees us. It is essential to our sense of self that we consider our concept of God. As one example, Psalm 139 conveys confidence the psalmist feels as God looks into his heart: past, present and future. The psalmist finds God's omniscience and omnipresence comforting. In the safety of God's omnipotent care, the psalmist celebrates his soul's well-being. The psalmist sees himself as a person of inestimable value due to God's constant watch-care. Do we?

FORMING A CONCEPT OF GOD

As educators, we are aware of two aspects of experience that influence childhood. There is the concept the child is putting together personally and there is the official concept within a religious tradition presented in a formal way. Both the personal and the formal concepts for God are conveyed to the young child experientially. The educational activity implied in helping a concept of God grow up aims at engaging the personal and formal in dialogue with one another. But we must be clear that dialogue is experiential for pre-school children. That is, it matters very much how we touch and talk to children. It matters to the formation of their concept of God how we look at them. Whether at home or at church, every time a child is physically, emotionally or sexually abused, God's reputation suffers. In addition to being vigilant about abuse, we must ask whether our educational programs put a stumbling block in the way of a developing concept of God.

Educationally, parents, grandparents, teachers and pastors must concern themselves with a child's personal image so that formal ideas of God will encourage the child to grow towards faith maturity. The relationship between the personal and the formal is complex. Educators must be aware of the existence of personal images and realize that personal concepts change over time. Endless processes of reshaping, rethinking, ruminating, fantasizing and defending come to a child's aid as the God concept unfolds. During a lifetime, the formal God of religion and the personal God of the child face one another. Hopefully dialogue between them is possible, productive and healthy.

Earlier I said that images, feelings and ideas of God equal a concept for God. I make this equation simply to clarify the educational process I wish to elaborate. I do not suggest that the formation of a concept of God is as neat as my mathematics imply. First of all, what is the content of an image of God? Positive images of God convey God loves me, holds me gently, safely, smiles at me and speaks kindly to me. Each image carries a feeling. An image of God is based upon experience, is emotionally laden, is connected to the primary objects of the child's environment and supports all

186

subsequent development in an unfolding concept of God. This is the content, the basic set of assumptions that Wittgenstein uncovers as the bedrock of ordinary experience—a layer of solid rock that seldom shifts, although personal earthquakes do occur. Through the use of reason we may come to question whether we want to continue deploying assumptions that have structured our perspectives on the world. A healthy relationship between experience and reason is ongoing in the formation of our concepts of God. Ideas of God are formed as a secondary process and are the result of conscious thinking.

For example, there is the idea that God is the creator and the maker of everything beautiful and good. Ideas are statements about God that satisfy the questions we ask: Where is God? What is God like? While our ideas of God may meet intellectual needs they leave us cold emotionally. We do not put trust in an idea of God alone. In order to trust God, we must feel something in relation to our idea of God. Our feelings are generated by experience. Ideas of God originate in inferential thinking about cause and effect. When children are out walking in a field and want to know how a large boulder came to be there, it may satisfy them intellectually to say that God put it there. If an image of God as One who holds them in almighty, kind and generous arms unites with the idea of God as One who keeps everything in its place, the concept of God as omnipotent begins to form in an emotionally and intellectually satisfying manner. God's power and knowledge include a capacity to care for the child as well as to care for and control the earth.

It is important that educators have a store of ideas about God to draw on when addressing a child's questions. Yet teachers must also know that even those who believe intellectually that there must be a God may feel no inclination to accept him unless their images of previous interpersonal experience have fleshed out the concept with multiple images that coalesce in a concept that is acceptable emotionally.[22] A concept of God must provide for us intellectually and emotionally in order to help us grow up. The integration of ideas of God with images of God requires persistent self-observation. Our concept of God is formed slowly through the inner spiritual work of uniting image, feeling and idea. Bringing them together is precisely the work of growing up spiritually.

Religious faith is a powerful regulatory structure of organized social life. We need systems of belief to organize our understanding of the world in order to make sufficient sense of it—otherwise we go mad. Without systems, we are confused and lost. Spiritual work carried to maturity reconciles personal images, thoughts and feelings about God with formal ideas. If our private God does not coincide with the official God we have endless difficulty: the potential for individual illness and family tragedies is very high. Since our personalized concept cannot be made to disappear, it can only be repressed, transformed or used,[23] the church is called to assist in the reconciliation between private and official views of God, if it is seriously committed to Christian faith maturity.

Part of the task of reconciliation between private and official concepts is to recall four possible God concepts that people tend to form: there are those who trust God completely; those who are unsure; those who believe God does not exist or is uninteresting, and those who are terrified of a God they wish they could eradicate from their minds. We respond educationally to people with each one of these four concepts of God very differently if we want to help their concepts of God grow up. Relying on the effective power of the Holy Spirit, our hope is to help children transform their personalized concept into the foundation of a hopeful, faithful life.

If personal and formal concepts of God are effectively integrated, Christian faith is a lasting source of self-respect and spiritual nourishment that meets human need from birth to death. When we know we are securely held in the unconditional, accepting, loving arms of God, who gives wisdom to those who ask and gives generously and ungrudgingly, we can offer support, love and service to others—living a life that is *filled to the measure of all the fullness of God.* Faith educators attend educationally to personalized concepts of God before they try to give children formal concepts. When working with adults, faith educators attend to the current concept of God that learners bring to the encounter. The approach of intentionally working with concepts of God that are already there enables us to realize the purpose of faith education, which is to help people grow up faithfully in community with other believers and to live peacefully and productively in the public world, as purveyors of God's image. As ideas of God form in a healthy environment, faith maturity enables us to equip ourselves for the world's demands. Well-formed faith encourages us to be trustful and trustworthy. In terms of faith education, the twentieth century witnessed a decline in social trust and trustworthiness.[24] To educate people effectively during the twenty-first century, we reclaim the role faith and trust play in civic life. But first let us try to understand how we went off the rails with faith and trust. A central figure in faith's mis-direction is Sigmund Freud. He promoted the idea that trust in God is infantile; all trust is suspect and reality itself requires relentless skepticism if we would not be caught out as fools. His politics of disappointment fundamentally shaped education and particularly religious education. We need to understand him better. In the chapter that follows, I examine faith education as an approach to help believers allow their concepts of God grow up, by situating maturity in our current cultural context.

THE PROBLEM OF GROWING UP

The thing we desperately need is to face the way it is.[1]

Perhaps when the modern age began to question whether
God was dead a spark of breath was extinguished from our
lives. Rituals are about the right to fiery beliefs, whether they
are pagan or deeply religious ones, and they open the vocal
instrument in ways most of us would deny is possible.[2]

THE APPROACH OF FAITH EDUCATION

If faith is personal, universal and global, what sort of education
does it require? Faith education depends on personal learning.
It also takes the social context seriously, as signified in the last
chapter by examining Existentialism, spirituality and faith. Until
we see that religious education was intentionally dismissed from
the public sphere and understand that its demise was unwarranted
and ill-advised, it is hard to be confident as we teach believers to
know God and Jesus Christ. Without confidence, we are defensive
and embarrassed about being people of faith. Recovering religious
education grounded on spiritual education is a positive response to
the prejudices of the last century. In this chapter, I address one of

those prejudices, the idea that reality is only material. The practice of excluding the spiritual from descriptions of reality was used to get rid of religious education. But to disregard the spiritual is to deny human experience. To disdain the spiritual is to disadvantage the way we know anything at all. Christian religious education has the goal of knowing God personally and is influenced by the means we use as we teach toward that goal. But if our methods instill passivity and boredom because they are essentially defensive, we do not produce followers of Jesus.

What is a model for learning that helps achieve best practice regarding the purpose of helping people grow into the fullness of God? Faith education relies on teaching implied in life long learning. Learning faith is necessarily personal. Even best practices do not create God concepts; concepts come with learners as they walk in the door. Faith education helps a childhood God concept unite with formal concepts to enhance a believer's worldview so that it can change over time and satisfy human need at each stage of life and during crises. In faith education, teachers find out what learners know, believe, think and feel before they teach and before they pass on the rituals of the faith to them.

In this chapter, I argue for a relationship between ritual and meaning-making. By ritual, I refer to Christian practices of prayer, Baptism and Communion, as a few examples, but I discuss ritual in a much broader sense. When Freud's criticism of religion took aim at ritual, it weakened our capacity to make meaning in a way that he failed to anticipate. His hypocrisy is inexcusable, especially since he continued to rely on rituals to make life meaningful to the end of his days.

I also propose that faith education encourages learners to make meaning by learning to allow the realities of ordinary living to challenge the God concepts they currently hold or that currently hold them. Yet I reject a secular interpretation of reality that excludes spirituality from its purview. Teaching in faith education takes its direction from the learners' learning and from dimensions of the human condition that include a need to make meaning, which is the engine of personal formation. To reclaim a positive attitude towards religious education, I examine the dual possibility of growing up as a person of faith, particularly in North America but also elsewhere, in terms of influences that compel us to decide whether to grow up as faithful or grow up as Freudian. My purpose is to show that growing up in Christian faith is a better pathway than following a trajectory proposed by Freud, and accepted as gospel in secular twentieth century society. Especially in North America, Freud's influence is ubiquitous. On the positive side, he spelled out how people learn on their own, as well as with help of someone who listens attentively. Faith education relies on personal learning, built up through ritual and a particular use of reason. Personal learning is the primary approach used in faith education, but it has a relationship with other approaches that unfortunately lost value in the twentieth century.

GROWING UP FAITHFULLY

Education in the twentieth century had three main approaches that structured a learner's experience: memory work, lecture listening and personal learning. Memory work got a bad reputation in the twentieth century because it became little more than memorizing. Memorizing was thought of as a hindrance to creativity. Yet memorizing is only a small piece of earlier approaches based on a medieval concept of memory.[3] Memory is foundational to learning. If all learning is organizing experience, what we hold in memory is the material we organize and elaborate through further learning. Kant, as one example, had a rich and creative process in mind when he used the term memory.

Due to conditions associated with mass schooling, memory work degenerated into mere rote repetition. But having a solid foundation for memory is essential to a life of faith. The strength of memory is its capacity to bond together learners and teacher so as to initiate the young into oral communal knowledge. Knowing and speaking shared knowledge builds community among those who repeat their cultural story. This form of incorporating youth into community generates empathy and solidarity among members of a collective oral and text tradition; tradition is passed from older to younger and eventually is owned by all members. The young are successful when they demonstrate their knowledge of what is held up as culturally important and when they can behave appropriately as insiders to that culture and tradition.

The second approach, lecture listening, exposes students to the finished products of an educated mind: the teacher teaches, the professor professes. Lecturing assumes that students do not know what the teacher knows; learners listen and come to acquire teacher or professor knowledge in whole or in part by sitting through the lecture. Students attend to what the teacher has in mind. The evidence of successful learning is demonstrated if students reproduce the teacher's knowledge. Good students get some distance from the lecture by asking critical questions, using their power to reason by noticing the pattern of a lecture, its organizing principles, as well as gaps or omissions that leave a teacher's knowledge open to critique.

While memory work is found in oral cultures primarily (although every culture depends on a foundation in memory to some extent), lecturing relies on the development of text-based literate culture. To learn to be reasonable in the context of a lecture, students must get inside the lecture and also get outside of it, so to speak. The best student is one who can accurately summarize the lecture and also speak from outside of it to critique its strengths and weaknesses. Lecturing relies on the development of an organizing principle and has a structure that provides a framework for thought.

Each approach to teaching and learning has advantages and disadvantages. The danger with memory work is that learners do not think for themselves. Solidarity can suffocate learners' potential to get sufficient critical distance from communal knowledge to ask questions and think authentically. Further, initially at least, memory work coheres around an authority structure that prepares learners to accept and follow those in charge. Do we want learners to follow any authority that happens to present itself, or do we want the young to reflect critically on the culture they find themselves in? The willingness and ability to gain critical distance from our surroundings is an essential feature of the mature Christian mind.

Lecture listening provides an educational setting for getting critical distance but has disadvantages as well. What if students have neither interest in the teacher's knowledge nor a foothold into what is being said? What if there is nothing in the student's mind to connect with the lecture so that listeners cannot sense the importance of this knowledge *for them*? Lecturing can be self-serving. The interests of teachers may have no relationship to the interests of learners. Lecturing is effective when a teacher is providing a framework for thinking about something, if teachers want to give learners the big picture of a subject. It is also effective when introducing new ideas. Lecturing is an efficient use of time. But learners are easily frustrated and get angry when required to sit and listen to lectures that interest the teacher but not them. As I have been saying, faith education takes the learner's own learning as its starting point, but uses these other two methods as appropriate.

GROWING UP FREUDIAN

In addition to needing to reflect on its methods, faith education has a twentieth century cultural problem. It is hard to grow up in the faith and express belief in the Almighty if one feels it is childish to trust God. I do not refer to feeling that longing for God is child-like, and hence attractive. Child-like trust is winsome—in a child. Rather I refer to a common belief that putting trust in the protection and consolation of God is infantile—it is regressive and essentially reveals our failure to take up adult life manfully. On one view, these sentiments, that child-like trust is attractive and that it is infantile, are rooted in the helpless naiveté of children, which we outgrow as adults. On a second view, the need for consolation and protection is consistent with our original condition in Eden, that is, with the human condition itself. In the Garden we were made for community with God and other people. We were incomplete and limited. People were not designed on a model of self-sufficiency. Feeling helpless is inevitable, and lasts a lifetime. As a consequence, our appropriate response to helplessness is to enter the Presence of God to receive strength and wisdom to do the spiritual and moral labor of building human community in concert with doing personal spiritual work as well.

The prevalent belief, that trust in God is infantile, implies that if we want to grow up we do so by turning away from an infantile state. All helplessness is seen as infantile. Grownups trust their own resources. They stand on their own two feet. As Kant put it: have the courage to use your own understanding.[4] Helplessness is immaturity that can be eradicated. The evidence that people are grown up is autonomy; they are self-governing, i.e., they inculcate appropriate rules for living and direct their own lives accordingly—from the inside. The second belief, that we are incomplete in ourselves as part of the design of humanity, is in contradiction to the first belief. Which view should orient our interpretation of what it means to grow up? An answer to this question will ground our understanding of what growing up should be like and will assist our effort at self-observation. Perhaps we need these views to inform one another; maybe they are not mutually exclusive.

The idea that faith is infantile is the position taken by Sigmund Freud (1856-1939) and others who follow his wake. I want to consider his view on modern maturity so as to position faith maturity within the context of this century. Freud misled the twentieth century about maturity, but he also shaped the 1900s, perhaps more than any other single person. In the last few years it has become popular to dethrone Freud by pointing to multiple errors in his work and mistakes in his life. I do not wish to remove Freud from the mainstream of modern thought and toss him away, even if that were possible. I want to understand and reflect on his perspective in light of scriptural insights on humanity. His theories are flawed and his life disappointing at critical junctures. Are we surprised? Faith education requires that we converse with cultural figures such as Freud. It is a common human pattern to worship influential people by straining out every aspect of their lives in our thirst for direction and then to discard them when we think we have had our fill, as if by turning our backs, we remove their influence from our cultural history. In contrast, faith education aims at a point between hero worship on one hand and demonization, on the other. Freud cared deeply about human suffering. He dedicated his life to trying to make other people happier than they were when he first met them. His misdirection for modernity arises from personal history that calls for compassion. Compassion is better for the mind than hero worship or demonization.

Freud established his own idea of the relationship between maturity and religion. He described religion as the result of the infantile illusion of being protected by a kindly father. He proposed that mature adults must free themselves from childhood longings for such a man. In maturity, according to him, we renounce infantile wishes and embrace down-to-earth realism hence a mature response to adult life rejects God. But the presence of God in adult life is more than mere wish fulfillment for consolation from a kindly human father. God has no active role in Freud's system. He also omits the active role that mothers play in forming ideas of God. This omission clarifies Freud's rejection of God. He repressed the role his own mother played in the formation of his picture of God—and he was incorrect to do so. Concepts acquired in childhood do not lose their force simply because we age (which is his own theory of object relations). Freud's general focus on regression does not show us how to grow up, given that all of us inevitably have a concept of God built into the mythology of our mental life. An idea of God (the way God is represented in our thinking and experience) forms part of the story we tell ourselves about reality. Our concept of God cannot die but remains to affect the way we live. Freud's view of regressive infantile longing denigrates childhood religious experience as well, and fails to acknowledge the permanence of our need for consolation throughout adult life—a need evidenced in his own life.

In response to Freud, faith education embraces childhood experience as a source of insight for growing up. Faith education relies on making connections between child and adult. Childhood longings mature as our concept of God is transformed by experience. Maturity implies allowing our concept of God to grow up without denying a basic human limitation, our need for consolation. In faith education, growth follows a model explained by the term experiencing. In experiencing we do not so much lose our early conceptions of God as we allow them to fold into emerging insight. This is a model for growth that prizes childhood religious experience without leaving us childish.

Suppose we take Freud's advice and turn away from our wish for protection and consolation, what happens to childhood longings? The question itself intimates that all is not well if we close our eyes to what we wanted as children. Let me be clear that faith education would not teach us to remain precisely as we were when we were young. Faith education calls for a second naiveté, as Paul Ricoeur puts it. Second naiveté is a useful term, as is post-critical faith, or second orality. These terms are attempts to describe the purpose of faith education, which is that people can grow up faithfully and move from basic trust (if they are fortunate as children) through a critical phase and return to trustfulness and trustworthiness that is based on an accurate reading of the real world—a second naiveté that is schooled by spiritual reality and critical realism. This third period comes after we have learned to speak our first spiritual language fluently and have begun to question its personal application. Second naiveté rejoins human helplessness with adult experience in a way that Freud would not accept; at least I assume he could not accept this possibility. His life is now a closed book.

Why bother with Freud at beginning of the twenty-first century, particularly when establishing faith education? There are many reasons. His genius shaped our current understanding of humanity. But why did he reject God? What form of salvation is offered in psychoanalysis? Freud did not dismiss the human need for salvation. He felt each person must find his or her own way of being saved— but salvation was a personal quest only. It is essential for faith educators to observe the paths to salvation that Freud charted. Freud's rejection of religion as a way of finding salvation and healing mirrors much of the twentieth century movement away from God, in the West at least. Why did God's influence on intellectual life die in the twentieth century in western liberal tradition? What can we learn about faith by examining God's death in the lives of men such as Freud? Why did Freud kill God? Is a picture of Freud as a satisfied, self-sufficient materialist correct? Can humanity live on the material alone?

Freud rigorously promoted the exclusion of religion from the education of children. Why? He dismissed religion *per se.* He specifically promoted the exclusion of Judaism and Christianity but dismissed other religions as well. What is learned about faith by regarding those who turn away from God? Also, what can we learn from Freud about education? Psychoanalysis is an educational method and is instructive for transformational learning. But our deepest inquiry has to do with how we are to understand human helplessness, particularly if we are adult believers who stay within the tradition of our childhoods. To Freud, the evidence that we have grown up is that we turn away from a childhood need for consolation. I agree that in growing up we must move away from many things, but as I examine Freud's inestimable contribution to modernity, it becomes clear that he was never able to renounce a need for consolation. He misled modernity, in this way at least. Growing up and remaining faithful is not a sign of immaturity. Understanding maturity from a Christian faith perspective is enlivened by another look at human helplessness. Freud compels us to take that second look. He also contributes to the way Christians consider the problem of growing up.

Freud invented a mythology of connection, to ground an interpretation of the world—his relation between a patient and a psychoanalyst. Along with Marx and Nietzsche, he operated according to a hermeneutics of suspicion, what I would call a hermeneutics of disappointment. The psychoanalytic relation is essentially an interpretive talking cure—to redress the absence and loss Freud uncovered in the dynamics of family life. He produced a praxis of healing (psychoanalysis) as a way of speaking with the suffering due to disappointment and harm endured in the inevitable helplessness and dependency of childhood. In psychoanalysis, the analyst stands in for the offending person. The psychoanalyst is present to the sufferer while, when a child, his mother was absent. The psychoanalyst is kind whereas, when a child, her father was cruel.

Freud offered healing to the sufferer without God's help. He put his faith in science. He said: we have science. If belief in science is an illusion, then we are in the same position as religious believers, but science is no illusion. Give science more time. No, science is no illusion. But an illusion it would be to suppose that what science cannot give us we can get elsewhere.[5] In the all-encompassing face of science, religious rituals and religious ideas were to be discarded. To Freud, nothing could withstand reason and experience. Religious ideas could not escape the fate of being thrown out so long as they try to preserve anything of the consolation of religion. Freud thought that if religion watered itself down, so to speak, and confined itself to believing in a higher spiritual being whose qualities are indefinable and whose purposes cannot be discerned, a diluted religion would be proof against the challenge of science. But he also thought that in diluting religion, faith lost its hold on human interest.

Freud implied that what makes religion attractive—its offer of consolation—is precisely what makes it infantile. He asserted that whenever religion *abandons* its claim to provide safety and comfort, it is rendered useless. In this I think he is correct. The strength of Christian faith is its power to heal, forgive and restore. Freud went on to say that if religion retains its offer of consolation and protection, it fails in the face of science, of reality, i.e., bare necessity. Was he right in his second assertion? To him, religion makes an offer it cannot fulfill. The object of religion, faith in God, is an object that does not respond. For Freud, God is absent. God's silence has no positive value. Silence signals God's inability to show up, to rescue or protect. To Freud, God does not protect us from Nature, our own bodies or other people. God is incapable. God is not there, whether or not you need help. In contrast, people can depend on psychoanalysts. Psychoanalysis attends to profound absence. In those who come for help, parents and siblings were either absent or else the direct cause of trauma. His method addresses traumatic experience, i.e., events that make too many demands on the personality. Trauma produces loss. Traumas occur when no one is present to help. God does not show up. The psychoanalytic relation focuses on the absent, lost or substitute object. Absence is not a secondary aspect of behavior but the very place in which psychoanalysis dwells. Speaking of absence is the essence of the analytic dialogue between analyst and patient.[6]

Loss produces suffering. Freud was overwhelmed by suffering—his own and other people's. He expressed frustration at the weakness of his intellect to provide a cure. But he tried. The core of suffering is loss—unmediated loss. In his own youth, he felt inescapably responsible for his siblings and himself—a family his parents did

200

not adequately provision—a child neither protected nor consoled. He felt compelled to be the family provider.[7] One story recounts a dinner invitation Freud received. During the meal he was barely able to put meat in his mouth because he knew his sisters were at home and hungry.

In trying to comprehend the effects of family on neurosis, Freud analyzed the idea of a king from primitive [sic] cultures.[8] He freely associated the king with the father image, and nature with the mother image. In examining their relationship, he pointed out the ambiguity that subjects feel towards the king: they both love and fear him; they respect and resent him; they feel tenderness and hostility toward him. Freud asserted that the king's life was only valuable so long as he discharged the duties of his position by ordering the course of nature for his people's benefit. If he failed, homage turned to hatred. Worshipped one day, he is killed the next. He noted there was nothing inconsistent in the behavior of subjects who kill the king when he does not protect them. If he will not preserve them, they will make room for one who will. Along with an excess of freedom that kings enjoy, there is an excess of restriction. Through ceremony and taboo the king's life is elevated to a double value but is also a tortuous unbearable burden to him. He can use his power to benefit his people, but they distrust and suspect him of its abuse. They watch him always.

Fathers too should protect and consol. Freud's analysis of family power puts the failure of care on a par with abuse. The failure to care is abusive. He had this insight first hand. Freud generalized from his own experience and applied these insights to other people. His family of origin held extremely high expectations for him and offered astonishingly low support. Throughout his life, his mother in particular placed many demands on her 'golden Sigi'. His father provided no escape from these demands except as a young boy when they used to run away together for long walks in the woods. His father was a disappointment, but was not to be challenged. By himself, Freud was unable to stand up to his mother, an inability that lasted until her funeral—which he did not attend. In many ways he could not leave home until she died. If families set a steep challenge without offering support appropriate to meet that challenge, a child's well being is adversely affected.[9] Children who are unprotected by adults feel profound rage.[10]

Freud turned his anger towards God. Like a modern-day Job he raged at God's silence. Unlike Job he cursed God and his religious faith died. Despite his father's plea that he should return to the faith of his forebears (Judaism) and his childhood, Freud turned to science. To him, it was science not religion that had the power to make things show up. In articulating his rage against God, he was partially effective. But he did not leave behind the magical world of myth and ritual. He found ways to console himself. His severe sense of absolute responsibility was not softened by reliance on God. He chose control as a way of addressing the sense of responsibility that he felt for those he wanted to cure.

As one of many modern reformers, he humiliated religion. Its rituals and ideas lost favor. The twentieth century repressed God. The faithful lost the art of speaking Christianly in quiet confidence in the pubic square. Many times, believers remain at a loss to speak of God in public, except for some who work themselves into a frenzy to do so. In one way, the word spirituality has emerged to allow us to speak about God without saying the word religion. Does religion deserve its bad reputation?

REALITY AND RITUAL

What is religion really? Religion is the collective response of the corporate experiences of God—of God's action with humanity, as a particular faith tradition understands it. Godly action in the world grounds religion: In the beginning, God created the heavens and earth. God so loved the world that he gave his only Son. Jesus bore our sin in his only body on the tree. Religions are both repositories of spiritual experience as well as agencies that shape experience. Religion shapes identity—both personally and collectively. Identity is formed through being in the presence of people who hold beliefs about the world they express in action and social interaction. Religion begins in action and is sustained through action. When it is human action we call it ritual.

202

Religious ideas are grounded in the rituals that compose a tradition's view of the world, of humanity and of God. We learn to be religious by engaging in the rituals of religious communities. That pattern of action shaping idea applies to all of life. Take as one example learning what the concept book means. A child is not invited to his mother's lap and told: Son, a book is a square or rectangular object that contains pages on which are written words that tell a story. This is a book. No, the child is invited to his mother's lap and she reads him a story. She holds a book in her hands, she reads the words, turns pages, answers questions and points to pictures. He listens, rests in her lap, looks at pictures, asks questions, turns pages and makes comments. Their interactions compose the experience of what a book is about. Later, he picks the book up and brings it to her and asks for a story. He performs this ritual because he believes this is what a book signifies. He learns about the idea book through their actions.[11]

Maybe she points to a book and he brings it to her. His response draws them into a three-way encounter—mother, book, child. Her action is ritual when she performs it repeatedly. Behavior is linked to ritual. Through play, invention and games, mother and son establish a pattern: the boy notices that behavior patterns he generates get a signal in return. He brings the book to his mother. She sits down on the couch. He climbs up on her lap. He sends forth messages and receives messages in return. The play of ritual is formed in acting something out and discovering that it works. Such probing, sending out, and playing in the world to see what will answer, is basic to ritual, to language and to culture.[12] In the context of repetition, the child senses what books mean. If she only performed these actions once it would be hard for him to distinguish books from other toys. It is not only laden with meaning at the outset—the mother already had a meaning for books—ritual constructs and sustains the meaning that conveys the meaning she attaches to books. Rituals teach us to know the world in a particular way, i.e., ritual shapes reality. Ritual is work done playfully.[13]

The work of ritual is to ground us in reality. We do that work by experiencing particular rituals that operate within the system of other people's ways of acting. At the start, these other people are parents or people committed to looking after us. Children learn to believe a host of things, and learn to act according to these beliefs. The personal system of inner thought is built up bit by bit, made up of what is believed. In that system, some things stand unshakably fast and some are more or less liable to shift. As mentioned earlier, what stands fast does so, not because it is intrinsically obvious or convincing by itself, but rather because of what lies around it.[14] Reason applies itself to the mythology of mental life, challenging, refreshing and reconstructing its elements over a life time.

To say that children construct and organize a mental system is not to say the perspective they acquire is systematic or tidy. It may be messy, full of odd bits that contradict one another. It is a system in the sense that it provides the context in which the child thinks about the world. It is a communicative system. Whether or not people hold these elements consciously, the elements of a mental system (and its framework) communicate to the person and to other people about how the world works. The system fits together because it was experienced holistically. A system is coherent not because it is logically consistent or even accurate. It is coherent through use. The child uses it to make the world cohere to the system the child has in place: the world is seen it its light. The world as experienced fits the picture the child holds.

An opportunity for growth appears when something happens that does not fit the system we have for the world. All such growth causes pain. The world spins out of control momentarily. Concepts change due to tensions between personal systems for reality and reality that comes from outside a system and refuses to fit within it. Imagine two teenage boys trying to talk to each other about books. One of them is the child in our example. The other is an orphan, shunted from house to house, who never met his mother nor sat on anyone's lap to hear stories told lovingly. These two boys have different systems. The meaning of a book is not the same for them, though they both may value books. In conversing, reason alone will not convey the differences in their conceptions of what a book is about.

Rituals shape spiritual life. Suppose we are shipwrecked on a desert island. Several of us survive. The island is a jungle. We find water in a particular place. We walk to this place each day because our thirst is daily. In doing so, we make paths along the jungle floor. As we repeat these actions, paths are established. Bending down to drink from the stream with trees overhead we find that our well-worn pathways create a shelter. Rituals enfold us in safety. Safety and satisfaction are built through repetition. Rituals are shelter in the storm of life. In them we find the means to go on living. Thirst drives ritual. We go to the water expectantly and drink. Each of us must go. No one else can drink water on our behalf to our benefit. We must be present at the stream; water must be there to satisfy our thirst. Rituals are like that. They satisfy a need for meaning. Ritual action makes sense within a particular universe of meaning, a particular island.

Suppose the stream dries up. It no longer sustains life for us. We are distressed but we can change our ritual. We start a different path to another stream. The water is the same, just in a different location. The point of ritual is the satisfaction that it brings: water for thirst. If we choose the safety of habit over the satisfaction of thirst, we are in trouble. If we keep going down the same path to a stream that has dried up, merely because it is the only path we know, we die of thirst. Our community perishes. The point of the ritual is to get the water. We create rituals to make and sustain meaning—they build a defense against the hazards of Fate or Nature, our own bodies and other people. But if safety becomes our only concern it can distract from satisfying our thirst. The aim of ritual is connection, relationship, communion with God and other people. We cannot domesticate God. When we love safety more than what is Wholly Other, when we fear leaving a particular path even though the streambed is dry, superstition takes over ritual meaning-making. The ritual traps us. We mistake the path for the point of going. We are afraid not to perform the ritual because something bad may happen if we fail to take the precautions that characterized our actions in the past. Obsessive-compulsive behavior follows superstition; it is its partner. Ritual has the power to ground us in reality but is always in tension with reality that does not fit our pattern. Ritual must continue to connect us with a reality that is greater than our pet systems if we want to grow up faithfully.

The point of faithful ritual is to encounter God. By itself, attending church will not save us, if we do not meet God there. Only God can save us. Ritual is a time-honored method for accomplishing something real in the world. We show up in prayer; God shows up when we pray. Draw near to God and God will draw near to you. In prayer we make ourselves emphatically present to God, by offering up our full attention. God demonstrates perpetual Presence by responding—the still small voice or the event that answers a need. The relation between God and us sustains and is sustained by faith. To warn and comfort, the book of Timothy says that: "If we died with him, we will also live with him; if we endure, we will also reign with him. If we disown him, he will also disown us; if we are faithless, he will remain faithful, for he cannot disown himself"(2Tim. 2:11-13). Our faithlessness (the neglect of ritual) cannot destroy the faith relation. Thirst is not quenched by ritual alone. Yet in ritual we come to the Stream that flows from the throne of God and the Lamb; a Stream that nourishes and heals everywhere it touches. In faithful ritual, we dip cupped hands into that Stream and drink. This aspect of ritual, meeting God who responds in return, is one that Freud failed to appreciate. He focused on ritual but missed the relation.

Ritual also establishes moral life through practicing actions that are appropriate to particular things and relationships. Once you know what a book is for, you are constrained to treat books in certain ways and not in other ways. Rituals establish appropriate methods and boundaries for relating to things, other people and ourselves. Rituals do not come from nothing. Ritual knowledge builds up from birth and elaborates upon simpler behaviors already known. Our ideas for encountering God are learned on our mothers' laps and in our fathers' arms. We learn what is possible with God whom we cannot see by exercising faith with those we can see. This is the principle that Freud discovered between a child's experience with people, objects in the world and images of God. His discovery is insightful for faith educators. The discovery implies that whenever we engage with a child educationally, ideas are already there in the child, formed by the ritual experiences of their lives.[15]

Rituals create possibilities and constraints by setting up specific boundaries. In the moral domain we cannot assume that people are reading from the same moral script. Learners come with ideas of what constitutes the good life and we are obliged to work with those ideas. In morality, there is ritual conflict. But also there are common moral themes. Most of us know clearly when someone trespasses across our moral boundaries, even if we refuse to accept that our actions constitute a moral trespass for someone else. Hence we have the daily need to pray: Forgive us our trespasses, as we forgive those who trespass against us.

A ritual is moral territory that has been staked out.[16] Rituals mark moral boundaries. Sin is a trespass of those boundaries. When we are trespassed against, the world spins out of control. When we trespass, the world spins crazily for someone else. Worldwide transgressions like the Holocaust, Hiroshima and 911 spin the moral world out of control. For a time, with vast transgressions, moral life collapses, as it does during historical periods when any and all behavior appears to be permitted. If anything is possible, no one can flourish. The need for ritual is most acute when people feel a prolonged or acute absence of moral guidance. The chief desires of human beings that are most in need of ritual constraint, because we are most lax in our boundary-setting, are sex, food, violence and the power to dominate.[17] The strength of ritual is the sense of obligation that is incorporated into action. To feel obligated to the right people, in the right way, for the right reasons, for the right length of time— grounds moral life. If paths that guide moral behavior grow over and cannot be found, individuals and groups grope along in a condition known to psychologists and sociologists as *anomie*, the absence of law or norm. Under the conditions of *anomie*, life loses value.

If we compare the role of ritual in constructing moral boundaries on one hand, and satisfying spiritual needs on the other, we glimpse a dilemma. The tension in ritual that the faithful learn to master is the freedom to let ritual guide us to God and to moral consistency, without allowing ritual to become an end in itself. How much is too much obligation? How can we be religious without getting caught in a trap Freud detected? He said that religious ritual is nothing more than neurotic obsession? Freud's hermeneutic of suspicion, when applied to religious ritual, marks off faithful from false trust.

Faithful trust is placed in God not in our means to God. If the streams dry up, or we are faithless, we are not abandoned by God.

Everywhere, at all times, and in all places, God's gaze scans the earth, searching for signs of faith. God is like a woman who turns her house upside down and scours it, looking for one lost coin of faithful response. She scours the house until she finds what was lost. God is like a shepherd ranging far and wide over the hillsides, looking for one lost lamb. He calls its name until he hears it answer. He returns to the fold with the lamb in his arms. Jesus told stories revealing the heart of God. The Holy Spirit seeks those who will put faith in God. This is what the scriptures show us about God's character. But talk of faithful trust is easy to say. What of a desperate soul? Freud knew what desperation felt like. For him, religious rituals offered no help. The purpose of faith education is to help us grow up faithfully. Growing up requires that we face a tension between ritual and reality that Freud identified as the source of religious neuroses. If we wish to be mature people of faith we must come to the place where our rituals are meaningful, on one hand, and where reality is not ignored, on the other.

Ritual Meaning Making

Baptism and Holy Communion are Christian rituals that express faith. Prayer is a ritual. So is going to church. Through ritual, religions tell us what the world is like, what we are like, what God is like. Religions describe reality in a particular way. These views of reality build a framework for thought and action. They tell and show us how to treat other people and ourselves. They tell and show us how to relate to God. They instruct us in life's purpose and prepare us for what to expect in this life and the next. Religions assume there is life after we die, but they differ in their interpretation of what the afterlife is like. The connection between a framework for reality and rituals that structure reality is beneath the level of our conscious reflection most of the time. We do not think about rituals and reality so much as we make use of them as we think, judge and act. When we ask whether religion deserves a bad name, we notice that ritual in particular lost favor in the twentieth century. Ritual came to mean empty ritual only.

Anthropologist Mary Douglas was interested in ritual.[18] She asked why some people stop using ritual or become anti-ritualistic. They do so, she said, because they interpret ritual as an outward form that is empty of internal meaning. The term ritual came to be seen as empty during the 1960s and 1970s. Yet rituals are necessary as we construct social experience. Our social experience enables us to know God and to know how God is to be known. Why were so many people against the forms of worship that characterized the 1950s? Douglas posits that anti-ritualism is essentially an authority struggle. People who refuse to use the current rituals cannot sense their meaning or they disagree with the meaning that inheres in these rituals. They want a different meaning for their experience: "Symbols are declared to be meaningless when there is a conflict about authority: somebody means to say something and somebody else quite simply does not accept that meaning; though they may yield to superior power, the symbols have not persuaded them. Symbols can be rejected, they can be changed, but we cannot do without symbols. Anyone [who challenges] authority should challenge its particular symbols and find new symbols so as to pit against one discarded form of expression another at least as coherent."[19] Freud did precisely that: he invented a mythology to replace religious ritual for those who suffer traumatic loss. He established a new narrative and symbol system to replace religion. His affect on religious ritual was profound.

Douglas pointed out a role for ritual that focuses the duties of religious education. She noted that rituals are transmitters of culture and constrain social behaviour. Rituals create solidarity and hierarchy among the group that uses them. They are systems of control as well as communication. She wondered if all rituals are restricted codes since their meaning is largely implicit.[20] What did she mean? Suppose you and I go to a movie and then go for coffee afterwards with someone who has not seen the same show. We talk about the movie. Because you and I saw it, you do not elaborate your interpretation of certain scenes of the movie. You say: "That scene with the horse. I didn't think she would ever stop screaming. What he did was stupid." A third party can make no sense of these sentences. You are speaking to me in the shorthand of a restricted code. Ritual can be a restricted code. Restricted codes are efficient, powerful, simple and beautiful among people who have seen the same show. But for those outside that experience, they make little sense. Douglas concluded that anti-ritualism in the mid-twentieth century was the result of a generation of children that grew up without internalising patterns that prepared them for the religious rituals in church. Rituals in church did not command their obedience; they could not attribute authority to them. Symbols of solidarity and hierarchy were not understood. Consequently a form of aesthetic experience was closed to them. They did not see in religious ritual the means to go on living. These rituals were nothing that they needed. Church did not quench their thirst for meaning.

The first task, then, for faith education is to ground children in memory-making rituals. A second task builds reason upon that foundation. The union of memory and reason produces a second naiveté, which is the third aspect of growing up faithfully. Healthy identity forms through connection and individuality: we are grounded in ritual, followed by a period of crisis in which other alternatives are explored, followed by a third phase characterized by commitment or the making of firm decisions.[21] Faith education attends to the limits of ritual, but plays ritually as well. Douglas surmised that in the mid-twentieth century there was scant memory in children on which to build a secure and reasonable faith. They looked elsewhere.

Memory is the play between ritual, story and experience. Faithful ritual and narrative are foundations for growth. Empty ritual, of course, cannot ground memory. We cannot build reason on a vacant lot. Memory is formed through interactions with God and other people who converse with us. Rituals call for an answering voice. Rituals are a plea for response. Rituals are relational.

The Loss of God and the Need for Repetition

Freud only observed the human side of ritual. He went farther than saying religious ritual was empty; he said they were a neurotic obsession. He posited that the only reasons we are religious are the following: our fathers were religious, they passed the faith on to us and transmitted faith cannot be questioned because our fathers disallow challenge. That is, children are religious due to cultural imperialism. Religion is passed on to us against our will when we are young and we are never allowed to debate or refute its tenets. That was a part of Freud's experience; it does not explain everyone's experience. He made other claims about religion. He tried to show that religion and its practices are infantile and that, as such, they prevent thinking. The free range of thought is corralled; ideas cannot go where they wish, due to the fences of faith. He assumed that, in order for people to be free, thinking must be unfettered, it must have no limits. This is the outcome that Kant predicted might happen to the idea of pure reason, a move he thought that would destroy reason itself. Freud believed that science liberates us, not religion. He was not wrong to value science, but he was wrong to think that human thinking has no limits.

He rejected the idea of rational limitation, *per se*. He believed intellectual freedom was seriously limited by any attempt to teach religion to children: he said that religious rituals and ideas bind a child's head and enfeeble the intellectual powers of an average adult. He asked: Can we be quite certain that it is not precisely religious education which bears a large share of the blame for the relative atrophy of average intellect? He thought it would be a very long time before a child who was not influenced began to trouble himself about God and things in another world.[22] In short, religious education threatens intelligence. As far as Freud was concerned, by the time the child's intellect awakens, the doctrines of religion were unassailable. His opinions echoed throughout the twentieth century as support for the exclusion of religion from primary education. But these very opinions did not describe his own life story.

Freud identified a problem between the average person and civilization that up to his era made religion necessary but in time he thought would disappear. The problem was that religion controlled (what he called) human instinctual nature, if reason failed. His psychological ideal privileged the intellect but he thought the masses had access to reason that was insufficient to control their passions.

211

His perspective on the need for religion and the ordinary human dislike of civilization focuses an aspect of his view of reality. Freud posited that:

- The masses are ignorant and lazy
- They are hostile toward civilization
- Civilization is a burden to all of us
- Educated people understand why we must have civilization and are rational
- Therefore educated people don't need God
- The masses need God to enforce their acceptance of civilization
- Cultural demands cannot all be given rational human explanation to justify them
- Some can and rational justification will suffice for those demands
- We must separate rational cultural demands from God
- Then we are compelled by rational cultural demands only
- Other cultural demands are susceptible to change
- Under the right conditions people would understand why cultural demands are necessary and would become friendly towards them
- The reason for the constraints of civilization is social necessity
- Due to their understanding and acceptance of social necessity eventually the masses would lose their hostility towards civilization and would no longer need religion.[23]

There are weak spots in Freud's perspective. Do people dislike civilization? Is this an empirical claim? What is meant by civilization? Is it civilization people dislike, if they do, or do they hate the way some people freely exercise power abusively over others? Are there any well educated people who know they need God?

Freud would say there are no educated people who know they need God, but he would do so on the strength of a circular argument. He defined being educated and rational in terms of not needing God? If you need God, you must not be educated. Being educated equals not needing God. How does this circular argument countenance experience that is contrary to it? What would he accept as evidence that he might be wrong? If he refused to accept any evidence to the

212

contrary, his circular argument is closed to reason. And further, consider his general ridicule of the masses. Who are the masses? Surely not you and I! In reading his works, we recognize Freud's views in the prejudice that religion faced during the last century. His disdain for religion was not a result of prejudice only however. There is a deeper, more compelling and troublesome motive for Freud's rejection of God. He could not find God in his own experience or locate a need for God in his inner being. His incapacity is neither trivial nor easily dismissed.

Freud would agree that human beings are inevitably anxious, as proposed in the previous chapter. He focused on anxiety's role in describing human development. He thought that as children grow up, not everything that causes anxiety is suppressed by rational operations of the intellect. Children have infantile neuroses (e.g., fear of the dark) some of which they outgrow, some that are overcome only through psychoanalytic treatment later on. As a time intensive talking cure, psychoanalysis shows up as necessary in Freud's system to enable people to grow up by healing the neuroses that will not go away by themselves. In his view, society as a whole has neuroses: religion is the universal obsessional neurosis of humanity. Like the obsessional neuroses of childhood, it arose out of the Oedipus complex, out of the child's ambivalent feelings for the father/king.

The Oedipus complex is Freud's fundamental tenet of faith.[24] His mythology of loss hangs on an original wrong that humankind committed against a primal father. To him, the murder of a primal father was an actual historical event, the memory of which passes from one generation to the next. To him, turning away from religion will occur with the inevitability of a process of growth. He thought that his own era was the juncture of that critical phase in the historical development of humanity. Like many in the nineteenth century, he thought individual growth was modeled on the growth of humanity as a whole. Humanity as a whole was growing away from its primitive origins; his era made a central contribution to that movement. To him, religion was an amentia: a state of blissful hallucinatory confusion[25] that hindered the prospect of growing up. His view did not anticipate, and cannot account for, the resurgence of religion on the world stage that occurred at the end of the 1980s.

But he conceded that religious folk have one advantage, if we would call it that: since religion is a universal neurosis, the religious are spared the task of building personal neuroses. Further, history helps us view religion itself as a neurosis—its teachings show up as religious relics—an opinion he eventually built his personal world around. To grow up, religion must give way to reason. The movement from faith to reason would rid us of many cultural prohibitions: in this way the task of reconciling people to civilization (see his argument above) would to a great extent be achieved. Like Kant, Freud held that reason led the way to maturity; unlike Kant he would not ground reason on religious memory.

Freud was very clear. He believed the truth contained in religious doctrines is so distorted and systematically disguised that the mass of humanity cannot recognize it as true. Religion is symbolic of truth but its symbols mislead, just as the symbol of the stork misdirects children who ask where babies come from. The symbol deceives. So it is better to avoid disguising the truth we tell children and not withhold from them knowledge of the true state of affairs, commensurate with their intellectual level.

When Freud said that religion is symbolically true he was only allowing that religion itself supported his Oedipus complex. He traced a fantastic line from a time before Moses to the life of Jesus and showed, to his satisfaction alone, that Judaism and Christianity give evidence of the truth of his Oedipus premises. All, he thought, one has to do is tweak the scriptures just a little to make them fit his fabulous plan.

EDUCATING REALITY

In texts in which he ridicules religion, it is not clear that Freud was comfortable with his position. Leaders of his own Jewish community begged him not to publish *Moses and Monotheism*. He referred to himself as a Jew all his life—a godless Jew. The book *An Outline of Psychoanalysis* was written after his anti-religious books, at the end of his life, and it has nothing of the mental fluctuation that is found in the texts that dismiss religion. I do not believe Freud was anymore comfortable with killing God than is the child who kills her father for raping her. The murder is a double wound. We need the people we trust to love us, even when they fail to provide the care we cannot be entirely human without. Harm goes deep. Freud experimented with eradicating God as a way to find out what would happen without religious narratives that misdirect intellectual life and trap us in neurotic ritual. He thought he was justified in holding out hope for the future, if we followed the path of his irreligious education. He said that if his experiment proved unsatisfactory he was ready to give up the reform and return to his purely descriptive judgment that human beings are creatures of weak intelligence, ruled by instinctual wishes. He did not offer humanity much of a choice. The masses are either ignorant or on drugs.

In contrast to religion, which is a delusion, Freud counted on what he called an education to reality.[26] His sole purpose in writing books on religion and culture was to point out the necessity to move from religion to reality. His prescription: Let reality enable you to grow up. The infantile state is schooled by reality: we must all leave home. With science we will face Fate: by withdrawing any expectation of an afterlife and concentrating all our liberated energies on life on earth, we might succeed in achieving a state of things in which life would be tolerable for everyone and civilization no longer oppressive to anyone.[27] Along with Kant, he thought it was at least advantageous to be thrown upon our own resources; as a result, he said, one learns to make a proper use of them. His advice: Endure fate with resignation.

In promoting the demise of religion, Freud argued against himself. Coming from his own religious background he was able to argue both sides, from faith and unfaith. He was aware that some system was necessary to ground human experience during childhood. He also knew that human need itself is a piece of reality, an important piece. Religion responds to human need. He toyed with the idea that perhaps religion has its advantages. What if it allowed for a refinement and sublimation of ideas that permit it to be divested of traces of primitive and infantile thinking? What remained would be a body of ideas science could not contradict or disprove. His solution from the side of faith: dilute religion so it is no longer offensive to science. But from the side of unfaith, he had already dismissed this possibility earlier on.[28] From the side of faith, rejecting religion comes down to an attempt to replace a proved and emotionally valuable illusion (science) by another one, which is unproved and without emotional value (religion). Freud sent home his final blow to the argument he had with himself. He admitted that it is hard to avoid illusion—but he held fast to one distinction: his illusions were not like religious ones, i.e., incapable of correction. They did not have the character of delusion. He believed that religious values are both illusions and delusions. Science is an illusion. He volunteered that if experience showed those who would follow him that he was mistaken, he would give up his expectations for science as a way out. But he would give science more time. His god was reason.

Freud admitted that his personal system to explain suffering might be an illusion. An illusion is humanity's defense against the weakness and helplessness made evident by Fate, the source of anxiety. We console ourselves with illusions. We compensate unsatisfied frustration in civilized life by storing up ideas that help us tolerate helplessness. Illusions are built up from childhood and the childhood of the human race. They offer protection. An illusion is not necessarily false. An illusion is not the same as an error. Illusions are derived from human wishes and sometimes approach psychiatric delusions. The difference between them is that delusions are essentially in contradiction with reality. But even illusions set no store by verification; they are impervious to proof.

Freud thought of science as the only road that leads to a reality outside ourselves.[29] He did not so much claim that his system for making sense of suffering was correct, though he believed it; he felt that this system hung together as a way of life. Elements of Freud's system were dismissed by others as insupportable, e.g., his Oedipus complex itself, but he continued to use them to build a frame of reference to explain suffering. He invented a mythology to explain why a child might want to kill his or her parents. Freud discovered child abuse. The illusion he devised permitted adults abused as children to talk about their suffering for the first time and be believed. He listened mostly to women talk of being raped by their fathers; he witnessed the hysteria that disordered their adult lives. He believed their stories. As a result of these interviews, he presented his theory to the Vienna medical elite in 1896. He thought his theory would make him famous.

He did not predict the outcome. For his insight, he suffered Vienna's rage. Crushed under the fury of hell that swept over him, a year later he was desperately poor and exhausted. He made a move that is hard to phrase in terms of the horror he unleashed on those whose stories he had honored by listening to them. He decided his theory of child abuse must be wrong. After all, if he were right the sheer number of child abusers in Vienna and throughout the world would be enormous. He decided that children, women in particular, wanted sexual attention from their fathers so they fancied the rape encounter. The diabolical idea that women do not mind being hurt was fostered by his new sexual theory.

Publicly at least, he asserted that children have ambivalent feelings towards their parents. They love and hate their fathers, for example. Freud reduced the complexity of a child's need for parental love to sexual desire. He maintained that mothers are the first to seduce their sons. He mistook a child's natural need for family love as an expression of sexual desire. The medical model that structured his inquiry focused his mind on looking for the one demonstrable cause of complex phenomena. As he said: our need for cause and effect is satisfied when each process has one demonstrable cause.[30]

He thought he had located the germ for the wide spread disease of female hysteria. He hoped the insight would make him famous. How appalling: he recanted his discovery and strengthened the trap for another century of abused children; further, he tried to persuade them they wanted what happened. Yet the opposition he faced must have been a tidal wave of relentless, hot fury. Those who have experienced the rage of only one man accused of sexual abuse might imagine the groundswell of hatred Vienna directed at Freud and his family. His new and public illusion of childhood sexuality was an attempt to protect his reputation and family from ruin. Once again, he was at the center of a storm (his family of origin being the first) in which he felt unprotected. In a way, discovering child abuse did make him famous though even those closest to him persisted in saying that he had been wrong the first time. His mythology of loss makes sense as a narrative of the abused. There are indications that privately he did not reject his original interpretation.[31]

At the beginning of the twenty-first century we could tell Freud that his illusion about children wanting sexual attention from parents is a delusion. He was right the first time. Science is no protection against the manufacture of delusions. But Christianity failed to practice its own preaching. Timothy says: "Anyone who does not provide for relatives, and especially for immediate family members, has denied the faith and is worse than an unbeliever" (1Timothy 5:8). Jesus was very clear: "But if any of you causes one of these little ones who believe in me to sin, it would be better for you to have a large millstone hung around your neck and to be drowned in the depths of the sea....See that you do not look down on one of these little ones. For I tell you that their angels in heaven always see the face of my Father in heaven" (Matthew 18:6; 10-11). If Christians had followed God's Word in the twentieth century, we might have provided a positive witness for Freud! How can reality help us grow up if its images are under pressure from social circumstances in which children are unhappily born and reared?

In Freud's fury against God, religious folk were robbed of the integrity of religious ritual, particularly Holy Communion, and lost an art of voice that goes along with telling our stories in a social climate of respect. If believers had steadfastly retained reverence for the efficacy of religious ritual and idea, and practiced the faith, Freud and his followers would have had less success in silencing us. And we had our own internal skepticisms to contend with. How did we lose the power of faith? Let us not forget that the victory of unfaith over faith in the twentieth century was due in some measure to the accuracy of Freudian analyses of the human condition. Bad faith is a delusion. After Freud, how do we converse with a world that sees only too well the weaknesses of people who call themselves Christian? How do we learn to speak in good faith? To begin, we have to understand where we have been.

MECHANICAL MATERIALISM AND
THE REALITY OF SCIENCE

We lost confidence to speak about faith in ordinary public life in the twentieth century partly due to a modern emphasis that shaped Freud's rejection of God. Freud began his academic life in a milieu of scientific mechanistic materialism that specifically renounced any place for the spiritual in human being. The growth of the natural sciences, technology and industrialization during the early period of his academic life seemed to confirm materialism as the best description of reality. Scientific investigations undermined the plausibility of the presence of a soul in the human person. In the war between religion and science, as it was waged among Freud's contemporaries, "materialism won the battle...religious persuasions had no place in questions of natural science or medicine."[32]

In the materialistism of the era (c1855) the "interconnections of mechanical-natural laws had to be investigated to the very end without philosophical or theological reservations;" as an outcome of scientific research, it came to be believed that "there was no activity of consciousness without cerebral activity, no soul existing independently of the body; religion had nothing to do with science and—if it counted at all—was a private affair."[33] Within a materialistic, mechanistic worldview, "the world as a whole, and also the human mind, [were] explained by the combined activity of materials and their forces. God is superfluous."[34] The materialistic mainstream that Freud negotiated was moved by a notion of energy or force. The world was held together by energy. In taking up medicine, Freud adopted a medical mechanism that was inherently atheistic. He turned away from the faith of his Jewish family and his positive encounters with Christianity as a small child, under the tutelage of his first nanny.

His reliance on science eventually took the form of what we call scientism. He took as his organizing principle for understanding the world a view of material life driven by force or forces; psychoanalysis itself is an economy of energy or force. Combining scientific laws (e.g., the first law of thermodynamics[35] and the law of entropy[36]) his intellectual cohort produced a mechanistic theory of the human body, which was understood as the interplay and transformation of physico-chemical forces. With the demise of the spiritual and the rise of scientific explanation, unity and connection within human life were thought to exist between the energy forces of the material world alone. Prior to privileging the material world, unity and connection were thought to exist in the spiritual world. In one way, religious perspectives are essentially mythologies, or grand narratives, of connection. Religion tells us how we are linked to each other, to God, the earth and a universe that God provided.

The consequences of mechanical materialism are severe. To snuff out the spiritual is to lose our connection to a way out, beyond human frailty. Human helplessness remains. Rejecting God did not alleviate Freud's longing for consolation and protection. Rather he found a substitute, the compulsive, repetitive pattern of buying antiquities—relics of religion modeled on images from the very pages of the Phillipson Bible that engrossed his childhood. After his father's death, less than a month afterwards, he began collecting antiques and artifacts that peopled his office and which he was careful to take with him to England for his office there—where he died. These antiquities cheered him up, consoled and protected him—as he noted himself.[37]

Freud substituted art for God. His general theory of substitution implies deep personal loss as the core experience of those who make these substitutions. Substitution asserts that repression drives human energy to focus on one thing (a substitute) when something else is actually causing a disturbance. Substitution is a symptom that crops up due to unachieved instinctual gratification, which drives repression. Through repression, the ego excludes from consciousness the idea or association that was the carrier of an unwelcome impulse. In repression, energy is expended so as not to think about an event, relationship or idea. Suppose a man feels anxiety. Substitution comes to his aid by redirecting his attention to something different from the origin of the anxiety-producing idea. According to Freud, the substitute satisfaction is achieved, but pleasure is not experienced, i.e., the release of tension, because the satisfaction provided by the substitution is greatly crippled, displaced or inhibited. Substitution does not satisfy. Rather than providing pleasure, substitute satisfactions acquire the character of compulsion. That is, in repression we reject something in our consciousness. We look elsewhere. But looking elsewhere cannot satisfy; attending to substitute objects does not relieve tension. Instead, substitution drives a person to keep on substituting, just as drinking alcohol to forget problems compels a person to keep drinking alcohol, while personal and social problems pile up.

Substitution defines an addictive cycle. Once established as a pattern, symptoms ceaselessly reiterate their demand for gratification and compel the ego to put itself on guard, but the substitute cannot gratify the original loss. The symptom can look like a ritual, for example, ritualistic and compulsive hand washing. The ritual takes on the quality of compulsion. Since the ego loves peace and abhors anxiety, it tries to reduce tense energy by engaging in the ritual. The ego engages in ritual as a way to reduce the mounting tension caused by the original disturbance, a trauma that put too great a burden on the personality. Substitution is born of, and produces, anxiety. It is a vicious circle. Substitution is always a distraction and always compels repetition.

The definition of substitute gratification explains what Freud observed in religious ritual and intimates how a love for safety gained supremacy over authentic satisfaction, for him. As the ego tries to incorporate the symptom, the compulsion for gratification becomes a more potent force. The ego seeks gratification in the symptom, the empty ritual, which will never provide satisfaction. In performing the substitution, two symptom-producing activities result:

- Undoing or blowing away the originial loss
- Isolating, a period of time in which nothing is allowed to happen

Isolation can look like concentration or focus but it is not. Isolation is more like paralysis. The mind isolates what has just occurred (the substitution) to keep the substitution from being associated with other disturbing thoughts. Blowing away the event can come across as cavalier, it may appear as comfortable indifference. But it is not; blowing away is a method of defense that should not deceive those who observe it. These two activities are characteristics of neurotic behavior. Uncontrollable anxiety is at the core of neurotic substitution.

Freud looked for a demonstrable cause of anxiety and made some suggestions.[38] The faithful believe that demonstrable causes are to be found in Eden. Everyone suffers anxiety. But neurotic and psychotic patterns are not universal. Not everyone has suffered the enormous losses that abuse causes, even if the numbers who suffer trauma are immense. We minimize trauma if we claim that we have all suffered to the same extent. Yet aspects of Freud's mythology provide a way to think about learning that can apply to all of us, because they address the existential aspect of human life and describe it aptly. The following chapter is an elaboration of this point. But Freud's inherent dilemma is unresolved: how do we live faithfully beside those for whom God has not shown up? What art of voice will let God show up to them? If he were alive now, I wonder what Freud would think of his experiment? Like much of our human effort, his contribution is a mixed blessing. What parts of his experiment might nurture faith maturity, given our social and historical circumstances?

Spiritual Exhaustion

In response to what he saw of modernity, Alexander Solzhenitsyn described the West as spiritually exhausted.[39] We are weak, he observed. The source of our weakness can be found in our excesses. The source of spiritual depletion in the West is the role we have given to science—but let us rather say, to an excess of science. As Freud himself said: "every excess carries the seeds of its own surcease."[40] Science entered the seventeenth century West as a "new way of knowing, one that promised to augment human power and proceeded to deliver on that promise dramatically. But the power it delivered proved to be over nature only; it has not increased our power over ourselves (to become better people), or over our superiors (God, angels). How could it have? Power can be wielded only over one's inferiors or at the most one's equals."[41] In their passion to find the means for social salvation, modern reformers did not see that the scientific method has limitation built into it: It is restricted *in principle* to telling us about parts of reality only, those parts that are beneath us in freedom and awareness. Science was celebrated by Freud as an improved way of knowing that he thought had no limits.

What modern reformers did not comprehend was that science originated in a particular form of power, the power to devise controlled, repeatable experiments. Scientific knowledge, pure or applied, emerges only in regions where scientists exercise control— that is, have power over the materials they work with. Science came to be seen as an unrestricted way of knowing and the most reliable way of knowing the real world. Science came to define reality. Medical materialism searched for the one demonstrable cause of complex phenomena so as to unpack the truth about reality. But the so-called real world of medical materialism excludes everything that is greater than human beings in freedom, intelligence and purpose. As scripture says, human beings were created a little lower than the angels.

Science excluded spirituality and the consequences for human life are serious. Scientific inquiry tends to value what it can control and devalue what it cannot. Science models the idea of causation on an upward flow from the less developed of living things to the more developed. Human value survives, if it does, in the face of enormous odds. Evolution—the only creative agency science allows—is prodigal. Human value is reduced from slightly lower than the angels to naked apes. In the end time conquers all.[42] It helps to see what is wrong with ideas when we have a century to see where they led. Rooting out spirituality moved modern reformers to put all their trust in science as a way of understanding the world. As one of them, Freud traded science for religion.

Science failed Freud. His theories are now persuasively criticized from the perspectives of philosophy, ethnography and theology. He relied on views that were incorrect. Psychoanalysis itself does not satisfy the most elementary requirements of a scientific theory.[43] But I do not intend to denigrate psychoanalysis. The point is that psychoanalysis is something other than a scientific theory—it is a mythology of loss and at its best—a practice of radical kindness. It does pick out a fatal flaw in religion. What do we say to those for whom God does not show up? And what of bad religion, of religion lived for the safety of ritual alone? A careful reading of Freud reveals that human beings are as capable of neuroses as they are of religion, and vice versa.[44] Religion can become nothing more than neurotic ceremonials. Freud's genius was to uncover the semantics of desire in which demands are made but not met. The analyst not a pastor fills in gaps left by silence.

The psychoanalytic relation is a dialogue that places itself between the patient and the analyst. In this dialogue someone shows up who will speak and listen—and interpret, so as to console. The patient comes for healing because she suffers repetitive behavior that disables her, as one example. She begins to observe herself with an analyst's help. Her repetitive behavior becomes, through psychoanalytic interpretation, a pathway to remembering the past and recovering self-knowledge. Through healing, she regains her self. She re-establishes conduct that is consciously chosen and healthy. Freud wrote clearly at the end of his life to show that medical power cannot be misused without destroying the analytic relation itself.[45] Once understood, Freud revealed that repetitive behavior is a doorway to self-knowledge. While many of us have never experienced psychoanalysis first-hand, myself included, its insight can be useful to those engaged in life-long learning.

The psychoanalytic relation, as an interpretative talking cure, addresses trauma caused by the pathology of touching. A trespass of touching produces harm. Harm is expressed in repetitive behavior that on its own cannot secure healing for an original hurt. Freud's attention to repetition is a refusal to hope for the transformation or conversion of desire and fear. He was not a person of hope. His refusal to admit other paths to healing does not seem to be based on analysis itself but comes from Freud's personal unbelief.[46] While belief may distract us from reality, we must never underestimate the power of unbelief to be just as distracting.

In making his interpretation of religion, Freud ignored Text as an authoritative source for meeting God. He denigrated the need for consolation. But as Plato said in the *Phaedo* there remains in each of us an infant [waiting] to be consoled.[47] Freud's own wife remained persuaded by the vitality of religious ritual. While he refused to allow household observances during his lifetime, after his death Martha

Freud returned to the Friday evening Jewish rituals that formed her childhood. But if he was one-sided with respect to ritual, Freud was right to focus on suffering in the project of growing up. To become mature, all of us must face suffering and evil and fit these realities into our personal understanding of the way the world works, the nature of God and the tendencies of other people. Evil is no delusion. The twentieth century gave abundant empirical evidence of the reality of evil. Evil needs an antidote. In response, 'God loves me' describes, but does not argue. The assurance of answering faith comes through the play of Presence, Text and Action.

CHRISTIAN REALITY

We are indebted to Freud for revealing how bad religion operates. But what of good religion, how does it work? As Freud well saw, religion is an art of bearing the hardships of life. His analysis of the function of consolation moved religion from its pre-occupation with fearing God to the realm of desire.[48] The heart of faith is not that we fear God but that we long for God. Freud asked whether there was anyone there to hear our cry for help and satisfy that longing. He decided there was not; people should stop asking. We should grow up. But is consolation infantile or does it serve adult life in an essential way? When we investigate them in later chapters, the problems of opposition and empathy reveal that our need for consolation is the groundwork for being humane with other people and kind to ourselves. Receiving and giving consolation is the art of growing up—it is the very means through which we mature.

How does Jesus demonstrate good faith? In response to Freud's proposal of an education to reality, what is Christian spiritual reality? How does reality operate to move us forward? How does Christian spiritual reality help God concepts grow up? These are central questions. As we close this consideration of consolation and ritual, we realize that the scriptures do not give us a treatise on growing up, rather, Jesus shows us what God intends for us to know about ourselves. Jesus came so we could grasp what God is like.

In Matthew 9:35-36 we read: *Jesus went through all the towns and villages, teaching in their synagogues, preaching the good news of the kingdom and healing every disease and sickness. When he saw the crowds, he had compassion on them, because they were harassed and helpless, like sheep without a shepherd.* In Matthew 18:1-4 we read: *At that time the disciples came to Jesus and asked, "Who is the greatest in the kingdom of heaven?" He called a little child whom he placed among them. And he said: "I tell you the truth, unless you change and become like little children, you will never enter the kingdom of heaven. Therefore, those who humble themselves like this child are the greatest in the kingdom of heaven."* Jesus focused on the child and compelled his disciples to look at what the child could teach them. He went on to say in verse 5: *And whoever welcomes a little child like this in my name welcomes me.* Can we hear Jesus? North American society does not love its children. We do not even love the child that each one of us once was, although we may be enslaved to its petulance.

What do children understand that links them with heaven? I suggest that the child Jesus calls as our example of faith connects childhood with being adult. In Luke 9:46-48 we read: *An argument started among the disciples as to which of them would be the greatest. Jesus, knowing their thoughts, took a little child and made him stand beside him. Then he said to them, "Whoever welcomes this little child in my name welcomes me; and whoever welcomes me welcomes the one who sent me. For whoever is least among you all is the greatest.* Mark recorded the same event with different details included. In Mark 9:33-37 we read: *They came to Capernaum. When he was in the house, he asked them, "What were you arguing about on the road?" But they kept quiet because on the way they had argued about who was the greatest. Sitting down, Jesus called the Twelve and said, "Anyone who wants to be first must be the very last, and the servant of all." He took a child whom he had placed among them. Taking the child in his arms, he said to them, "Whoever welcomes one of these little children in my name welcomes me; and whoever welcomes me does not welcome me but the one who sent me."* The gospel of John does not record this story. Rather, John records Jesus referring to the disciples as children. If we want to know what children have to teach us, observe this child in your mind's imagination.

Watch the child. Jesus calls the child and sets the little one in their midst. Is it a boy? Is it a girl? The child is called into their midst and comes. We already know these disciples. They do not like to make room for children. They have more important people to consider. But Jesus invites them to consider the child. Jesus sets the child in their midst, draws the child closer to stand beside him, and gathers the child into his arms. What is the child doing while all this is taking place? Observe the child. The child did not wait to understand Christ's call. Jesus called and the child came. The child came, first in the middle, then next to Jesus, then the child was gathered up into open and welcoming arms. As the child is sitting on Jesus' lap, I can see the head lean back on Jesus' shoulder, eyes searching the faces of the disciples, but all wariness is gone. One foot dangles over Jesus' leg. The arms hang loosely at the child's side—the muscles relax. The child rests in the arms of God. The child makes no move toward self-protection. All is well. This is the consolation of God. Come into the Presence of One whose lap is ready for you. You are not too heavy for God. See the child. Be the child. Notice what Jesus is doing. Observe what God is doing through Jesus. In prayer we come and climb up onto God's lap.

FREUD AND PERSONAL FAITH SYSTEMS

Freud's great intellectual strength was in building thought systems. He was a mythmaker. Dismissing religion and killing God fitted his personal system. As he showed, the ego itself is a system builder—an organizer of perception and experience. All learning is organizing. Neurotic behavior arises from the ego's inability to organize perception and experience into a coherent picture to accord with reality. It is a personal faith system gone mad. The ego, from Freud's perspective, is compelled to make sense of the world, to incorporate and systematize. Freud's contributions, which are many, help us see what happens when experience become so intensely frustrating that it refuses to make sense. Suffering which is not explicitly physical, but is emotional or epistemological, is the outcome of experience and perception that cannot be made to fit into the organization of the ego. What lingers outside the ego's capacity to organize thought and feeling creates suffering. Not to be able to make sense of the world is to suffer the world. One outcome of feeling the effects of emotional, epistemological (lies, deception) abuse comes from the deep injustice of being with others who "do not get it" who do not perceive what they have done to us or are still doing. This form of suffering goes very deep into the soul. Christ on the cross prayed: *"Father forgive them. They do not know what they do."* We might say: "Father forgive them. They just don't get it."

Freud's personal faith system was neither rational nor neat. It had strange and inexplicable bits and pieces that he used to weave together an interpretation of the meaning of loss. Personal faith systems are not neat rational systems. They have loose ends and contradictions. If we were to build a perfect system it would be because we could not afford faith. Reality is messy. It is not only what Freud says about religion that helps people of faith, it is the system itself that he constructed to replace religion that allows us to witness the inherent messiness in every human system. I am not, for a moment, suggesting that Christianity is nothing more than a human system. I am referring to personal faith systems that we make out of Christianity. I refer to the bit of Christianity that we live by and made our own, when we are young.

As scripture says: *We see through a glass darkly.* We do not see the whole picture. We do not need the whole picture as a reference point for making sense of the world from a Christian perspective. As we read in Ecclesiastes 3. 9-14. *What do workers gain from their toil? I have seen the burden God has laid on the human race. He has made everything beautiful in its time. He has also set eternity in the human heart; yet people cannot fathom what God has done from beginning to end. I know that there is nothing better for people than to be happy and do good while they live. That each of them may eat and drink, and find satisfaction in all their toil—this is the gift of God. I know that everything God does will endure forever; nothing can be added to it and nothing taken from it. God does it so that people will revere him.*

What do we need? We need to know we are God's children/ friends, no matter what happens. We need to commit ourselves to being God's children, no matter what happens. We need to offer

God faith. We allow God to shape an unfolding of faith in our being. The courage to face suffering is an unenviable but inevitable motor drive for growing up. We have two options: we can suffer with God; we can suffer without God. What will you choose?

Freud's unconsoled suffering left him with the need to organize experience into a system that held together and stayed in place, without God. He was trapped in his own repetition. Christianity is a personal faith system that holds together in the context of other people and the Presence of God. It demands the courage of faith and trust, without apology. At its best, Christianity is a balm for soul suffering—a way of life that ministers healing rather than mental tidiness. It is precisely in the context of a world gone mad that we need faith—we need the consolation of Presence. We need to know that we are heard, forgiven, valued and loved. We are helpless to give ourselves this assurance. Human beings cannot stop needing consolation despite the difficulties we face in letting ourselves rest in the satisfactions of faith in God.

Freud reminds us to take healing more seriously than has been the recent tendency in religious education. Healing is for mind, body and soul. As to their intellectual health, we confidently educate children in the pathways of faith, knowing that it is the concept for God that they inevitably have in their being that we address. It is up to learners to let incomplete concepts of God shift in shape. Teachers trust that Deep calls to deep. As to body and soul, educational practices that focus on rituals of healing help restore and demonstrate the tender care God shows to those who will listen and attend. While educators and learners walk together through these practices, God is the One responsible for the efficacy of the ways we offer healing.

In the following chapter I reassess what it means to grow up in faith and focus primarily on the mental liveliness of living faithfully.

7

THE PROBLEM OF THINKING FAITHFULLY AND REASONING CRITICALLY

"Science sets in only after we have realized
that we do not know the world
and that we must therefore seek the
means of getting to know it".[1]

"Suddenly there is a point where religion
becomes laughable," Thomas Merton wrote.
"Then you decide that you are nevertheless
religious." Suddenly![2]

THE PROCESS OF FAITH EDUCATION

A main concern of faith educators is the mental liveliness that enables people to be mature. Faith education encourages the personal faith systems (worldviews) of believers to accumulate new meaning. There are three aspects of faith education that encourage people to let their worldviews accommodate new experience, and hence to grow up into the fullness of God. The first

memory *reason*
insight

aspect is memory, the second is reason, and the third is insight. Faith education provides insight through the marriage of memory and reason. Insight is their offspring. This chapter investigates educational relationships between memory and reason, and the effects of their union on the growth of personal understanding. The next two chapters consider the way insight develops over a lifetime as we face two problems that typify human experience: the problems of opposition and empathy. The point of this chapter is to say that memory and reason require one another. They are not at odds. But we need to understand how they work together so that insight is born. My purpose is to show that personal faith systems or worldviews are founded on memory, which is reviewed through self-observation (the second aim of faith education). Maturity proceeds by using reason on memory to produce insight. I explain relationships between faith and reason to point to the limits of reason in its union with memory. In addition, I provide an example of two ways of life that help clarify the process of growing to maturity through gaining insight into the way we hope to live.

A FOUNDATION IN MEMORY

The first task of faith education is to secure and establish memory-making experience. Children and new believers hold stories from scripture and encounters with Christians in their hearts as a first step in perceiving what it means to be people of faith eventually. A second task builds reason upon the foundation memory provides. In saying that reason comes second, I do not imply that memory making experience alone establishes the foundation for thinking that comes later. Memory and reason are connected all the way along since the human brain does not separate feeling and thinking. I separate memory and reason in order to understand how they work.

Establishing memory and building reason are two early tasks of faith education. Insight is not one of the tasks teachers set up for, as they do with memory and reason. Insight is an outcome of personal, spirit-filled work. As we learn together, we share these insights. Yet educators help create conditions that encourage insight to be born and increase. They are midwives of insight. This then, is the process of faith education: establish memory, build reason and nurture insight. Before we can enjoy the benefits of maturity however, we must ask a prior question. *Why Grow Up?* Although maturity is attractive, it does not *demand* attention. Where do we see the measure for maturity in the culture of the twenty-first century? What is our context for understanding maturity?

I suggest present circumstances celebrate *immaturity*. Educators are as compelled to consider the media effects of modern media for the same reasons Plato used to criticize the poets of his day. Educators believe that the stories a society tells, and its manner of telling them, shape human character. The ideal of maturity is central to understanding how we view human character. As an example of our stories and their media, North America is peopled by television personalities who have turned immaturity into an art form. Popular characters have an inexhaustible capacity for doing what mature people would neither say nor do. Since the *modus operandi* of the television industry is to get and keep people focused on a small screen, it does not provide distracting images of maturity that can turn our hearts in compassion to the world outside our television rooms, though we may be incited to give money to people far away by efforts made on the screen.

TV does not aim to make people think or hope as they watch. Traditional images of maturity appear trite and uncomplicated when set beside the dazzle of people who specialize in soul shocking insult games, betrayal and violence. On TV, when friends insult, betray or mock each other, the targeted person returns next week without reference to being hurt and plays the part again—*sit com* amnesia. Real people do not forget harm done to them. The laugh track draws us into its mockery when TV folk trespass humane boundaries. We laugh at pain rather than seek forgiveness. TV cannot afford forgiveness. We watch alone. TV is required to create and sustain dependencies that fuel the industries that stand behind them. Television is a substitute for real life—and appears to cost so little. It is increasingly effective at drawing us into its tiny world. Yet TV images we watch can act back on us to create reality after their own kind—maturity suffers in this relation, if we all try to talk like TV.

EDUCATING FAITH

In a media blitzed world how can maturity express itself
meaningfully? While maturity is attractive, it does not create the
conditions of dependence that drive television. Maturity does
not dazzle. It does not flicker or fade. Television must sell itself.
Maturity is relaxed. TV people must be slim, beautiful and have
perpetually perfect hair. Maturity accepts itself with love and good
humor. Television must intensify and sustain anxiety in viewers to
succeed for advertising. The medium continuously presents us with
impending disasters that never actually happen, in order to keep us
locked on. TV watchers tire easily but stay put. Maturity commits
itself to a way of life that compels us to take life seriously but not
fatalistically. TV continuously flashes images that cause us to hold
our breath. Will the next image push us over an edge? What will we
see next? As we watch, we do not observe and think about what a
character could or should say or do. We watch waiting, with baited
breath.

Maturity is not a voyeur. It breathes freely. The Jesus prayer, *Lord
Jesus Christ, Son of God, have mercy on me*, is called the breath
prayer.[3] The truth of this prayer keeps us breathing in the breath
of God until we find rest. The willingness and ability of maturity
to relax releases the simple human enjoyment of everyday life.
Does maturity ever watch television? *Yes!* Maturity does not abhor
or neglect its own culture. Yet it is not looking for a substitute for
real life. Maturity realizes that as each new day dawns it once again
becomes possible for human society to turn to God and tell each
other good stories, true stories of what it means to be human—
through the medium of television as much as through any of the
marvelous inventions of humankind.

Maturity does not envy the world's apparent dazzle. Maturity
thinks for itself. It loves the world but is not addicted to worldly
ways. It is discerning. In the world, it does not assume the form of
the world. Maturity regards the world, looking for opportunities
to offer healing where it is broken and communion where it is apt.
Christian maturity relies on a standard that loves the world but is
not its virtual copy. Our standard came from outside the world's
system, entered the world and lived among us for thirty-three years.
Jesus lived a mature life that included others but was not dominated

234

by them. Maturity is neither radical individualism nor absorption into communal life.

Faith education aims to help people mature as they work out commitments and relationships between authenticity and the Christian standard. Maturity must learn to be itself in the context of being faithful. Faithfulness implies the presence and influence of other people. The question of how to live personally as well as faithfully is one this chapter investigates. The relationship is defined through links we forge between memory and reason.

But a question tugs at our sleeve. Why grow up? Well, if we do not, we are empty: we cannot sustain our own inner life and we have nothing in our hearts to offer others. The immature cannot be trusted. They do not practice self-observation. They do not see themselves as others see them. Practising self-observation helps us realize what we are doing. Through self-observation, faith education enables us to develop a personal life of faith: establish memory, build reason, nurture insight. Before we learn to observe ourselves, however, we must first attend to the foundation of human thought.

All thought is formed from experience shaped memory. What we describe as character is based on memory recorded in the heart. We think with and act on what we have been given from infancy onward. Under favorable conditions, we converse with others, building up the certainty inherent in trust and dependability. This is memory work; children learn the language of life and acquire a heart of faith. They learn to converse and question by hearing other people talk and inquire. Learning is caught, in context. The movement of faith is typified by putting trust in others who show themselves to be trustworthy. During the early years, faith is transmitted to the heart: it is taken in; learning as organizing equips us with a framework for living, thinking, accepting, and believing—children drink in a universe of meaning that enables them to make sense of the world. An at-home inner world is confirmed within the language and experience of memory-based, memory-transmitting community. What do the young hold in memory that forms their first faith system or picture of the world? We must remember that we do not get our pictures of the world by satisfying ourselves that they are correct, or because we are satisfied that they are correct. Modern critiques argued this point effectively. Faith systems are inherited backgrounds against which we later distinguish between what is true and what is false.[4] Personal faith systems are a mythology of the heart. Images and ideas that compose them are learned practically, for example, in how children learn what a book signifies.

Several images for memory help clarify its nature. These images are intended to work together to express what is meant by memory informed during childhood. In the first image, memory is like a river, recalling Wittgenstein."[5] Experience flows over the riverbed of our personal faith system, like river water; some of the materials that make up the riverbed can and do change with time. Sand shifts easily, rocks move more slowly, when exposed to reality that exists outside our original world picture. But in order to have a world picture at all, at some point we must begin with assumptions and decisions. As children our assumptions and decisions belong to those who look after us. Parents do not violate the freedom of childhood by passing adult assumptions and decisions on to their offspring; it is the nature of human thought that we must begin somewhere. These hardened ideas, our riverbed of thought, are those we use to think with; children learn by believing adults. Doubt comes after belief.[6]

A second image suggests that some of our thoughts are like the scaffolding of a building. The framework determines its shape and must be present in order for the building to proceed.[7] We need secure ideas to support the personal work we do later. A third image suggests that some of our ideas or thoughts, that we hold to be true, are like hinges on a door. A door cannot open without the use of its hinges. We do not think about hinges when opening a door, we use them. The very possibility of doubt depends upon the fact that some of our ideas are exempt from doubt; just as opening a door depends upon the hinges on which it turns.[8]

As a result, it is wrong to assert that an irreligious education is intellectually superior to a religious one, as Freud asserted and the twentieth century believed. Science is not better than religion as the singular originating assumption for a way of life. An irreligious education is only one particular world picture complete with its own riverbed, scaffolding and hinges. Something must be taught as a foundation.[9] All thinking, not just religious thinking, directs future thought. Atheistic thought is no exception. Human hearts are limited in this way. Freud and other modern reformers prized the free play of the mind and unhindered inquiry more than many other tenets of the modern perspective. Science was assumed to be capable of investigating everything. But "it is not that we cannot investigate everything and for that reason we are forced to rest content with assumptions; rather, if we want the door to turn and open, the hinges must stay put."[10]

All human beings have hinges on the doors in the rooms of their mythology-laden hearts. To know something from a Christian perspective is to express comfortable certainty—certainty that is no longer struggling. Comfortable certainty is not hastiness or superficiality, it is a form of life.[11] Freud did understand the need for a foundation for the heart, though he did not refer to the heart *per se*, but underestimated the inevitable formation of concepts for God whether or not children grow up in homes that teach religion. He did not take his own discoveries of the human condition seriously enough to realize that every human foundation would have a concept of God in its framework. This is true for those who grow up among believers and for those who do not. If we give children an irreligious education, how will they mature in their conception of God? How will they mature spiritually?

The educational question is whether children can learn to think inside and outside their original mythology eventually. Is it possible for children to become mature through honest doubt? If faith is a system, so is doubt. Doubt itself rests on what is beyond doubt. You can only tentatively test the ground you stand upon if it remains fairly stable while you examine it. We need a solid place to stand while we make mental experiments. Doubt that doubts everything is not doubt; it is nihilism or madness. With such doubt there is no ground on which to stand. A way of life is only possible if an individual trusts something. Christianity is a way of life. Growing up will take us through the dark valley of doubt and the dark night of the soul during which we feel our concepts shift and change, while nothing yet gives them a new shape. But doubt is not sufficiently relational as a way of life. There are people who marry doubt instead of reason. It is pointless to try dialogue with them. As my grandmother used to say, "Save your breath for hot soup". While we accept that it is necessary and good to inquire, the process of faith education assures us that doubt is not the only companion we bring on our journey.

Making Memory Good Enough

There is more than doubt to concern the faithful. People of faith can be too certain that they have a grasp on reality. Being too sure of ourselves may be a reaction to the anxiety inherent in being human. We are sometimes too sure of ourselves as a way to eradicate anxiety. Freud was particularly helpful in describing the way unconquerable anxiety can keep us from growing up. Unconquerable anxiety derails maturity. The two names Freud gave to the complete derailment of maturity are neuroses and psychoses. For present purposes, the main difference between them is the role that reality plays. In neurosis, reality is weakened but still able to get through to inform and shape the neurotic system. In psychosis, reality is unavailable to the patient. Psychoanalysis is more helpful to neurotic than psychotic derailment because the success of a talking cure depends upon a patient's ability to allow reality to guide a reinterpretation of internal perceptions about the world in healthy ways. Neuroses have some access to reality. If a talking cure relies upon the successful use that it can make of reality, *so does every educational endeavor.*

Being too sure of ourselves is sometimes expressed as political fundamentalism. In its various forms, it is a refusal of transformation. Transformational learning depends upon a healthy relationship between reality and the personal faith system of people who want to grow up. In life-long learning, we need firm ground for understanding real people and real life but our goal is comfortable certainty, assurance that no longer struggles, but remains attentive to what it observes.

Learning maturity is lifelong. In lifelong learning, personal faith systems either remain the same because we choose to keep them or change in concert with reality. Personal systems must become 'scientific' if we use that term in its best sense. Science and reason come into play when we realize we cannot comprehend the world as we have conceived it so far. Reason and reality work together. But the reality that leads us forward is more than merely materialistic and empirical. It is also spiritual. We test the validity of personal systems against other systems to know how good they are, or to see what to keep and what to renew. We also discern what to contextualize for our own time and place and what to leave as riverbed and therefore immoveable—true for all times, all places and all peoples.

But, while it must hold itself accountable to reality, memory is partial. A human heart is a finite space. No religious tradition, vast and diverse as it is, attends to all there is to say about God. A personal faith system is not equivalent to the religious tradition that generates it. Limitation characterizes personal world pictures. Personal systems remain partial until, as Christians believe, we see God face to face and finally know as we are fully known. What changes in the growth of a personal faith system from birth to death is its partiality—its inadequate capture of what God wants to convey to us through Scripture and the life of Christ. Faith education uses scripture to edit personal faith systems in light of what the text says to us personally and communally. We name and release our inadequacies and partialities. Over a lifetime we unlearn and learn many things. In lifelong learning, we approximate God's Word and will.

Growing up implies a willingness and ability to learn from a faith tradition and from reality. The work of maturity is grounded on relationships between the personal, the traditional and the real. We see how our faith tradition differs from our personal system by attending to what is going on in the world. At some point on the road to growing up, we must decide whether to keep the faith, to change it for good reasons, to convert to a different tradition or to another way of life. We must choose. Certainty must stop struggling. The fear for educators at this point is that the young will choose not to follow the faith of their mothers and fathers. That fear is potent. But a new level of maturity is not possible without a decision to purchase the bedrock on which one's life of faith has been built. If children decide not to buy the foundation of faith, it should not be because adults refused to let them think for themselves or neglected their education. The work of elders is to live faith realities in all their beauty, fullness, healing and hope. It is hard for the young to grow up well if adults are immature. The freedom to keep the faith and loosen our grip on some of its aspects *so as to grow in maturity* depends upon the condition of a personal faith system itself. Only healthy systems grow.

It is for God alone to say how healthy we have to be in order for Grace to move us toward maturity. And God is full of surprises. Yet it is essential to establish conditions, from a point of view of human responsibility at least, under which a personal system is or is not good enough to grow up. We continually witness the outcome of immature faith and practice in our churches. Our collective immaturity makes this analysis critical to our spiritual health. How does a personal faith system operate? What can go wrong in its movement toward maturity?

Memory Gone Awry

In our personal histories, our first encounter with every object in the world was introduced to us initially in a particular context, in an individual way, at a unique time by specific people who were poised at one moment in the flow of their own lives. We live through life amid echoes of our first encounters and successive experiences with these objects in the world. For example, we met our first mother/ woman and our first father/man in this way. All other ideas we form about men and women come from an original point of intimate contact. Even brothers and sisters do not experience parents in exactly the same way. All of these first encounters constitute an interior personal world of experience.

Personal faith systems are made from these encounters and subsequent thought and feeling elaborates them into a story about life's meaning. Personal systems explore phenomena in the world (a unique man or woman) and interpret the totality of the world from one point of view, as continuity, and generalize to the way that all human beings behave. Recall that earlier I said that the personal faith system is not so much coherent in the sense that it is absent of contradiction and conflict; rather it coheres through use—as we try to make sense of the world. Coherence and continuity are constructed from the materials of an individual heart, socially constructed. Social construction does not imply that people can only think the thoughts they were immersed in at birth. We can think for ourselves and think outside the system. But the context in which we learn to make meaning strongly influences the manner and content of the meaning we make.

Remember that I am using the word faith in a broad cultural way as well as in a specific Christian sense. In personal faith systems as they form, putting trust in something is an absolute need—it is necessary for all peoples, times and places. We develop a view of the world from the perspective of an inner thought system built from its starting point. We project our thought life, with all its definitions and descriptions, on the external world much like a movie projector shows a movie on a large white screen. Admittedly the screen for our perceptions is not blank like a movie screen; it is the world. It is an ability the real world has to show up underneath the perceptions we project onto it that eventually moves us to maturity if we allow reality to instruct us.

While we are immature, inner perceptions form our conception of the outer world. There is nothing new in what I am saying by describing human learning in this way. All learning is organizing experience. The organization so formed acts back on the outer world so that our understanding of the world looks similar to the inner workings of a socially constructed individual heart. When we are young and need to form a foundation for thought, it is inevitable and good that we operate in this manner. Further, a personal faith system is not just the result of an intellectual process; it is the accumulation of all events that occur to us—bodily, mentally, emotionally, economically, socially, racially and culturally, as well as in terms of gender. The heart's thought is holistic. Throughout life there remains a tendency, which may be universal, to think that all other people are really just like we are and to transfer to them all the qualities, attitudes, and perspectives with which we are familiarly acquainted and intimately conscious.[12]

When a personal faith system goes off the rails it does so by refusing to link up to reality that is larger than its at-home world of experience. It refuses to link up with the reality of other people and God. The internal system refuses to budge from its initial world of perception and certainty. Reality is barred from entering the personal faith system so as to interact with what is already there. Neurosis is one example of derailment. Essentially a neurotic system refuses to let go of the certainty it feels about its interpretation of the world regardless of costs to the individual. As Freud said, the real world that neurotics shun is dominated by the society of human beings and institutions created by them; estrangement from reality is at the same time a withdrawal from human companionship.[13] What is going on?

According to Freud, in every neurosis it is not the reality of experience but the reality of thought (the power of thinking) that controls the personal faith system. He pointed out that an "intellectual function in us demands the unification, coherence and comprehensibility of everything perceived and thought of, and does not hesitate to construct a false [link] if, as a result of special circumstances, it cannot grasp the right one."[14] If the individual will not consult reality, the sovereignty of an inner reality is established over the reality of the outer world. The way to insanity is paved. Grasping false connections does not always produce madness but it does produce harm. The failure to take the perspectives of other people seriously into account through stubborn, egoistical certitude damages human community. Freud gathered his description of the tendency people have to falsify what is really going on by preserving the sovereignty of their own train of thought from his knowledge of dreams, phobias, compulsive thinking and delusions.

The aim of mental systems he described is to make sense of experience. Even though harmed by child abuse, war or rape, experience is still forced into making sense. Suffering can cause the most stable train of thought to jump the rails. If suffering results in illness, a personal faith system has derailed: the neurotic person tells the one story that still appears to make sense to try to hold the world together. Neurosis is based on the belief that there is only one movie ever playing—it is the interpretation the neurotic person projects on the world to make sense of it. Only that interpretation is correct. When personal faith systems derail, their owners come to think of everyone else as stupid. Nothing dissuades them from the certitude of their perceptions until they are well. Being well means paying the cost of dealing with reality. While ill, neurotic individuals live in a special world in which only the neurotic standard of currency counts. Only ideas intensively thought and affectively conceived from an internal point of view have value, regardless of whether they harmonize with outer reality.[15] But what is reality like?

This is where believers have the greatest difficulty with Freud. We believe the world is made of material and spiritual realities that are inseparable despite the prejudice of modern reformers. God abides with us. This is a reality we know. If materialistic world-views force us to choose, we would rather seem crazy than be lonely for God. It is reasonable for Christians to allow the Spirit to move them. It is precisely the art of hearing spiritual and material truth that inspires us toward God. We call out to God. God hears the cry of the heart.

Christians believe they must wrestle with the spiritual as well as the material and that both are sources of human suffering. Human suffering produces common patterns that can create neuroses and lead to bad religion. Unlike modern reformers such as Freud, Christians do not believe we can eradicate suffering from the world. But have we underestimated the educational significance of suffering? Our personal faith systems can only be good enough if we grasp the role suffering plays in the struggle to stay faithful. Suffering is real. As appalling as suffering is, lifelong learning must find a way for suffering to be one of the foremost teachers in our attempt to grow up. To mature, we must face suffering. In pre-modern Christian faith systems, suffering was expected. Facing suffering was one of the primary ways Christians came to understand and experience the fullness of faith. But suffering can also produce unconquerable anxiety.

For Freud, and modernity generally, suffering was to be avoided and prevented, at all costs. He made major contributions to our understanding of how we get sick and how to get well. Many Christians use and provide psychoanalytic practice as a framework for restoring mental health, but we have not been clear enough about concepts of the soul that Christianity and psychoanalysis share. Faith education is not a substitute for psychoanalysis. It is not about psychological health *per se*. It is about having a healthy heart over a lifetime. Without an articulate concept of the human heart and its relationship to the body and mind, without a spiritual psychology of the heart, without articulating the relationship between faith and reason, an education for spiritual growth is directionless. Faith education helps to understand humanity so that we can be fully human and entirely faithful. What are the heart issues that direct faith education?

While I realize Christians make mistakes and leave the faith, comfortable certainty is our faith ideal. We move ahead in its light. Blessing follows the life of faith. Those of us who do not adhere to a prosperity gospel tend to neglect telling each other about spiritual benefits of faith and how they are achieved. *Can we say what makes Christianity attractive?* Could we tell others? What is the context in which faith's appeal expresses itself? We are reluctant to state the benefits of trusting God because we are self-conscious about making statements that seem like promises if we are not sure we can support them with reality. But faith education is care for a heart that rests on the promises of God. After the lofty aspirations of the nineteenth century, the twentieth century was typified by broken promises and failed hopes. Promises make us anxious. How can we have comfortable certainty in the promises of God? Only through faith: "In [Jesus] and through faith in him we may approach God with freedom and confidence" (Ephesians 3:12). Christians in the past were not as shy as we are to talk of the spiritual benefits of being faithful.

What follows is a summary of two models for extreme living. Each way of life furnishes the heart. These models shape personal faith systems. I compare the inner monk and the unconformed artist. They have similarities and differences but a core difference is in what each rejects as it assesses reality. Both prize the inner life and depict this internal living space as the site for fulfillment. Both emphasize existential responsibility for the growth of character. Both delineate common human patterns. Each holds up an ideal for human fulfillment. The first view upholds an ideal based on the inner monk. It is a pre-modern ideal. Its hero and model is Jesus. I will spend more time on this view because it is less familiar. The

244

second prizes the ideal of an unconformed artist. It is a modern ideal. Its hero and model is Socrates. Neither view is materialistic. In each, the inner life is of its essence more than material. The first view privileges spirituality, the second prizes an aesthetic dimension of human life. In comparing these two ways of life, we can pick out direction for the spiritual art of growing up that is able to address human spiritual needs in the twenty-first century.

The Inner Monk

Christianity as a way of life is not monolithic: there are many currents within the mainstream. In an earlier chapter, I outlined four ways of expressing what really matters to people so that some people organize the way they try to make the world a better place through the use of head, heart, mystic and kingdom spiritualities. One of these ways is a central aspect of the Orthodox Christian tradition. This tradition focuses on the inner life of believers—the heart of faith. Its source is an ancient mystical school of prayer that emphasized inner spiritual work referred to as guarding the heart, stillness, attentiveness, self-observation or watchfulness. All these terms cluster around essential aspects of the soul's spiritual work.

The instruction of the Niptic Fathers, early spiritual masters of the Orthodox tradition, is found in a collection of writings originally written in Greek and gathered in *The Philokalia;*[16] the texts date from the fourth through the fifteenth centuries. *The Philokalia* constitutes a psychology of the heart that has some of the elements of modern psychoanalysis but is far removed from a modern cosmology. The word Niptic refers to the practice of watchfulness. What unifies this current of Christianity, although it was clearly not uniform, is its emphasis on watchfulness and the use of the Jesus Prayer, *Lord Jesus Christ, Son of God, have mercy on me.*

The individual writings, most of which are aphorisms, "show the way to awaken and develop attention and consciousness, to attain that state of watchfulness which is the hallmark of sanctity."[17] *The Philokalia* writings are not philosophical propositions or doctrine, although they presuppose and rely on Christian doctrine. Rather they offer direction for an education in contemplation.

Contemplative practice is a type of self-observation called guarding the heart. The outcome of guarding the heart is that knowledge lying within the soul is uncovered, delusion is dismissed and believers become receptive to the Holy Spirit who teaches all things and brings all things to mind. This is part of the work of the Spirit: "But the Counsellor, the Holy Spirit, whom the Father will send in my name, will teach you all things and will remind you of everything I have said to you" (John 14:26).

The practices of *The Philokalia* centre on soul work in which believers learn to attend to their thought life. The benefits of faithful practice are made clear: it is "learning which is not a matter of information or agility of mind but of a radical change of will and heart leading [people] towards the highest possibilities open to [them], shaping and nourishing the unseen part of [their] being, and helping [them] to spiritual fulfillment and union with God."[18] The purpose of watchfulness is to become an undivided heart, the site of God's enduring Presence. The self, or heart, becomes a place where God delights to dwell. Self-observation has a relationship with moral virtue. To know oneself is the goal for practicing virtue. Self-observation is a method of self-knowledge. Conforming to moral virtues and keeping God's commandments, attending church and participating in public worship are all pre-requisites for the inner work of the heart. They are interdependent. The inner life and the outer life operate in concert. But daily effort is spent guarding the heart. The inner life is the source of spiritual strength. If the inner self is watchful, it can protect the outer self—the way we act before others. The aim of guarding the heart is to work with the Spirit to allow our interior living space to be furnished as God's home.

The unity of this tradition is brought about through a focus on guarding the heart through attending to the Jesus Prayer, which invokes the name of Jesus, but is neither a technique nor a Christian mantra. It is prayer addressed to the Person of Jesus Christ that expresses our living faith in him as Son of God and Saviour. In prayer, one holds up a mirror to the heart and finds both good and evil. The art of prayer cleanses the heart through God's activity and human cooperation. The Jesus prayer is single-phrased, it is simple;

it is prayed often through the day and night as need arises. It must be free of all images and thoughts. Why is this the case?

From the perspective of fourth century Christianity, thought most often referred not to the ordinary sense we use now, but to evil thought provoked by demons. Thought could also refer to conceptual images or divinely inspired thought, but guarding the heart implies building a defence against evil thoughts in particular. Therefore, the Jesus prayer and one's attentiveness to thoughts as they enter the mind, are weapons that inexperienced monks, who wish to follow this way of renunciation, deploy against the demons. In this view of the inner life, the Jesus prayer and breathing with the Holy Spirit are armour used against the wiles of demons whose master is Satan. Believers were to hate Satan and his demons and all that these enemies might sow in their souls, but they were not to hate other people.

The Jesus prayer, said in the depths of the heart (with body, soul and spirit) and practised by the intellect, produces sweetness in one's inner life, intensifying watchfulness and humility. Humility is attentive forgetfulness of what one has accomplished. Attending to what is within is both a remembering and a forgetting that directs the intellect towards holiness. In prayer, one learns to have an exact knowledge of inner thoughts and learns to recognize thoughts that defile the intellect and make it lazy. Self-observation is a process of discernment. According to the ancient view, unless the faithful hate the world they cannot worship God. What then is the worship of God? To worship God in the inner life is to have nothing extraneous in the intellect during prayer: not sensual pleasure as we bless God, not malice as we sing His praises, not hatred (of other people) as we exalt God, not jealousy to hinder us as we speak to God and call Him to mind. The sentiments that we aim to root out of the heart are those that harm us; they prevent the intellect's communion with God. Through spiritual knowledge the intellect learns to uproot these destructive aspects of evil effects on the intellect.[19]

The intellect (*nous*) is the highest human faculty. When purified, it is the instrument for apprehending God; it is the spiritual centre of human life. Prayer of the heart is not just of the emotions, but of the whole person, the body as well. Heartfelt prayer is passionate and often draws one to tears. The practice of prayer can be true or counterfeit but the benefits of inner stillness come only to true practitioners. Stillness is not the same as silence but signifies the absence of evil's effects and the absence of discursive thinking. Discursive thinking, according to *The Philokalia*, refers to reason, (*dianoia*) which is not disdained so much as it is required to accept its proper role.

The heart makes use of reason after self-observation has done its work. No personal use can be made of reason in the absence of self-observation. Reason does not work as a stand-alone. Reason needs material to work upon. Reason is a discursive, conceptualising, logical faculty in humankind. Its function is to draw conclusions or formulate concepts derived from data provided by revelation, spiritual knowledge or sense-observation. To the Niptic Fathers, knowledge produced by reason is lower than spiritual knowledge since it does not imply any direct apprehension or perception of the form of created beings, still less of divine truth itself. Intuiting, which is the activity of the intellect, is beyond the scope of reason; it is capable of perceiving the essential form (principle) of every created being, just as Adam was able to name each creature.

Spiritual knowledge (*gnosis*), which comes through the intellect, is distinct from the knowledge that comes through the use of reason. Spiritual knowledge is inspired by God and linked both to contemplation and to immediate spiritual perception. It is in this sense that intuiting is greater than reasoning; intuiting is a form of reception, whereas reasoning involves the human agent much more fully in the construction of knowledge. The doctrine of the Fall operates here. Knowledge that does not come directly from God has less value because it more clearly involves fallen human beings. The spiritual work of the one who is receiving knowledge from God is to be as open and clean a receiver as possible.[20]

The spiritual model is the male experience of the inner monk. There is a significant difference between experienced and inexperienced monks. The focus of inexperienced monks is to learn how to catch thoughts as they first enter consciousness. Inexperienced monks must learn to observe each thought and attend to it. As thought enters, it is identified. Evil thoughts are rebutted. The task of rebuttal is to recognize, counter, expose and destroy evil thoughts as they enter the intellect. Evil thoughts infiltrate the intellect in the form of images of material things. The Jesus prayer is invoked as the means for rebuttal since only an activity of Grace is effective in destroying evil, not human striving. The person strives to be attentive; victory belongs to God. Inexperienced people must be willing to learn to attend to consciousness so that rebuttal is possible.

St Isaiah the Solitary, a Desert Father from the fourth or fifth century who reflects the spirituality of that era in Egypt and Palestine, portrays a poignant expression of the battle of the inexperienced monk. His description deserves a full reading:

> So long as the contest continues, a man is full of fear and trembling, wondering whether he will win today or be defeated, whether he will win tomorrow or be defeated: the struggle and stress constrict his heart. But when he has attained dispassion, the contest comes to an end; he receives the prize of victory and has no further anxiety about the three that were divided, for now through God they have made peace with one another. These three are the soul, the body and the spirit. When they become one through the energy of the Holy Spirit, they cannot again be separated. Do not think, then, that you have died to sin, so long as you suffer violence, whether waking or sleeping, at the hands of your opponents....while a man is still competing in the arena, he cannot be sure of victory.[21]

The spiritual struggle of the faithful is to achieve unity of heart. Dispassion, in St Isaiah's work at least, does not regard passion negatively. Rather, dispassion is purity of heart. It is a state of reintegration and spiritual freedom.

The spiritual work of the inexperienced monk is to be attentive so as to overcome the enemy of the soul's joy, the demons. It may seem odd to hear of demons in the twenty-first century. Yet the Niptic Fathers were determined to see in the opposition to spiritual growth the effort of one enemy only. Satan alone was blamed for spiritual hardship. Monks were to attend to their own sins and practice repentance rather than dwelling on the sins of others. Watchfulness is spiritual work in which one minds one's own spiritual business.

They were not to blame other people for their suffering and inner struggle. As scriptures say, our struggle is not against flesh and blood. The demons were the only enemies of a believer: they had as their unremitting purpose to prevent the heart from being attentive. In this view, the demons know how greatly such attentiveness enriched the soul so its evil members worked energetically against its fulfilment.

Spiritual work counters the provocations of the Enemy of the human heart. The work of the inner monk enables one to mark murderous and predatory thoughts as they approach the heart and note what they say and do. The descent toward sin was articulated for the inner monk. As an evil thought enters, provoked by the demons, our own thought chases after it and enters into impassioned discourse with it. An inexperienced monk attends to shunning these thoughts at the soul's gate. An experienced monk, on the other hand, can admit them because he has learned to censure them. The pattern for temptation is as follows: Provocation, then coupling, then assent, then concrete action, then the sin itself.[22] The sin itself is characterized as a form of captivity in which engagement with evil thought grows habitual and continuous: unswerving passion aims at attainment of the thing desired. In the sin itself, passion is negative.

As a thought experiment, to explain how this system operated, suppose someone humiliates an inner monk. Immediately he thinks of revenge—the thought presents itself unbidden. He is *provoked* to think of revenge. The thought of revenge enters consciousness. Yet in provocation, a thought is still free from passion if an image entering the heart is glimpsed by the intellect. So the monk might realize: I want revenge. He has an opportunity to consider revenge fully. But if the monk *couples* with the thought, he communes with it in an impassioned or dispassionate way. The monk considers revenge. He pictures himself humiliating the one who injured him. At this point he has several options, but if he moves to concrete action, however slight, he has moved toward assent. With *assent*, which is the pleasurable acceptance by the soul of the thing seen, he focuses on the image of revenging himself on another; he imagines the other person's discomfort. If he becomes captive to his desire for revenge, the image of humiliating the other fills his mind—nothing else enters; he can think of little else. *Captivity* is the forcible and enforced abduction of the heart, it is engagement with the object, disrupting even the best inner state. Passion in the strict sense is engagement that lurks in the soul over a long period—desire for revenge is hoarded in the heart. It is essential to note that the monk is not guilty for considering revenge—revenge springs upon him when he feels humiliated. He is only guilty if he marries the desire for it.

Regarding these stages of temptation the first (provocation) is sinless; the second (coupling) is not altogether free from sin; taking concrete action is dangerous; the sinfulness of the next stage (assent) depends upon the inner state; and the struggle (captivity) itself brings either punishment or victory.

Suppose he takes revenge and experiences the outcomes of doing so. Observing the outcomes leads to repentance or chastisement. Repentance and chastisement are able to educate the monk, giving him an arsenal of reasons the next time temptation beckons. Niptic Fathers did not make it a great mistake to reflect on revenge if they were humiliated. Certainly the psalmist reflected on revenge. As we reflect on revenge and bring reason to bear on our reflection, we consider the outcomes of seeking revenge. In reflecting on revenge, we consider all the costs involved in carrying it out and the costs involved in not carrying it out; reason shows us that the cost of getting revenge is greater than the pleasure it may provide.

The monk who rebuffs the initial provocation or regards it dispassionately has at one stroke cut off all the sinful stages that follow.[23] We could say that the experienced monk cannot be fooled by the attraction of seeking revenge. He knows its havoc too well. It is not that he simply obeys: rather, he weighs the full consequences, one of which is obedience[24] and decides how he will act to influence the world. With reflection from the heart, thoughts of revenge are always dangerous but they are not necessarily fatal. The inner monk, when experienced in spiritual warfare, is able to recognize and defuse the power of thinking evil thoughts so that the intellect, free from all images, enjoys complete quietude. The Niptic Fathers are clear that it is not only evil thoughts that can lead us astray. Good thoughts can lead to disaster if taken to excess.

Experienced monks do battle with thought; allowing thoughts to enter they discern those that are from the enemy—whether they appear good or evil at the outset. By reflecting on the reasons in his heart, the monk is better able to learn appropriate self-regard. But is watchfulness nothing more than the repression of thought? It is not. It is the regulation of thought.[25]

Reason flourishes on groundwork that is properly prepared. Preparing the ground for reason implies that thought is not driven by the omnipotence of thinking. Disciplining the heart aims to control the excesses and deficiencies of thought; it does not aim at empty-heartedness. It protects against hard-heartedness. It is not afraid of thinking. Unless a monk learns to sense the nature of thought as it enters, discernment never grows. Therefore, to begin, he practices control over thought so that later he can observe how each thought tends to operate within him as it enters consciousness. He can only provide himself with reasons for entertaining or dismissing thought if he senses what it does in his heart once inside. Employing reason depends on educating the heart to refuse thought so that an inner space is created in which discernment becomes possible. Guarding the heart aims at discernment.

Reason assists the experienced monk. Recall the three questions of self-observation. These questions are implicit rather than explicit in the Niptic tradition. They are: What is God doing? What do human beings tend to do? What am I doing? During self-observation these questions enable us to consider how to live life faithfully. Without censure, discernment does not grow. Self-observation reveals patterns that characterize sin as well as godliness. Reason persuades our will when we see how these patterns affect the heart. The Spirit reminds us of what God is doing and tends to do. Reason, under the authority of the Spirit, enables us to blend self-knowledge and knowledge of God with knowledge of other people. Self-observation opens the heart's gate to reason only if it first learns to operate the gate by choice. Reason is not useful unless the heart has practiced opening and closing the gate. Reason, on its own, cannot be counted on to produce goodness. Self-observation is necessary so that the heart has time to marshal resources of Spirit and reason.

Self-observation gives us time to consider how to live well and is not unrelated to the advice of existential psychologist Rollo May. He said, "Freedom is the pause between stimulus and response and in that pause choose."[26] To pause is to catch a moment between the stimulus of sensing a thought that degrades the self as it flits across consciousness and the act of engaging with it. Into that moment we are free to invite Jesus: *Lord Jesus Christ, Son of God, have mercy on me.* But first we have to learn to sense what is passing before consciousness. We have to be awake. Next, we learn to sense the moment between sighting an evil thought and linking it to other thoughts so that it breeds evil. In self-observation we continually fix and halt thought at the entrance to the heart. It is only in stillness that we can attend to consciousness.

Halting thought at the gate of the heart is practised by the inexperienced monk before he learns to be discerning over his inner life. According to *The Philokalia*, an intellect that does not neglect its inner struggle will find that—along with other blessings that come from always keeping a guard on the heart—the five bodily senses, too, are freed from all external evil influences, through the heart's stillness, unprovoked by any thought. Self-observation is a spiritual method that if practiced over a long period, frees us with God's help from impassioned thoughts, impassioned words and evil actions. The Niptic tradition believes that watchfulness leads to a sure knowledge of God, helps us penetrate divine and hidden mysteries, enables us to fulfil every commandment in the Old and New Testaments and bestows every blessing of the age to come. Watchfulness leads to purity and of heart and unity among the hearts three aspects: body, soul and spirit.[27] A modern heart trembles in the presence of such promises—not simply because we know about the excesses of Gnosticism.

The Unconformed Artist

The pre-modern heart was intimately connected to the heart of a community. Unity of the heart is framed by an outer life of obligation. An inner monk may be solitary but not isolated if he wants to be well. The practices of self-observation were not meant to exist separately from the Church. Within community even experienced monks obeyed the Abbot. Obedience was one way to ensure health in the inner life. Spiritual masters of this tradition knew that excesses of the inner life could lead to madness if left undisciplined by prayer and unconstrained by community. While an emphasis on soul work secured unity within the heart, goodness was dependent on the heart's relationship to God and other people. There existed outside the monk a framework for goodness that constrained the inner life. External constraint on inner life constitutes the main difference between an inner monk and an unconformed artist. And further, the experienced monk was guarding his heart not promoting an image of himself.

One prominent modern model for the good human life is that of the artist—life as art. Life modeled on art comes in three varieties or genres.[28] All of these ways of living artfully have the life of Socrates as their model. The first two genres depend directly upon Socrates, while the last one is indirectly influenced by his life. Socrates demonstrated the first variety. Plato provided us with the record of Socrates' life. Socrates would hail people in the streets to question them about what they knew—to help uncover what was not known. The inquiry he practiced, on himself and others, was a way of life. Socrates had no arguments to persuade people that his mode of life was right for all. He understood clearly that his authenticity, as Socrates, depended upon its exercise. If his interlocutors abandoned a conversation he began with them, he had no arguments to offer as to why the life he followed was best for all. He believed the examined life was inherently worth living.

If Socrates lived the first model for an art of living, Plato authored the second model. Plato wrote about the second variety of an art of living by describing Socrates. He believed Socrates' life was best for everyone—good for all. Those who could should imitate it; those who could not imitate must try to approximate it. Plato provided a series of controversial arguments to support his universal claim about the good life of Socrates. Both Plato and Aristotle tried to show that a single type of life is best for every human being: they argued for an art of living a good life that is universal—good for everyone, everywhere, for all times.

The third variety of living artfully is the least universal. In this view, human life takes many forms and no single life is best for all. Freud fits with this third model, along with others, such as

Montaigne, Nietzsche and Michel Foucault. The third way celebrates a life that only its author and few others can follow. If an inner monk is notorious for 'hating the world,' an artist is infamous for 'hating the masses'. Artists are elite. Like great artists, those who follow this third way must avoid imitation. They cannot imitate others. Those who imitate are no longer originals; they become derivative and forgettable, leaving the field to others. Further, few others may imitate an artist. Artists do not want their life to stand as a model for the world at large. They do not want to be mass-produced. The whole point is to stand out from the crowd.

Those who follow them must develop an individual art of living. If the life of an artist gains many followers, he or she becomes standard; the work ceases to be remembered; it appears as the normal way of doing things—a fact of nature rather than an individual achievement. Artists of this third way put their life on exhibit but not so that others can imitate them directly. Hence life must be lived in the extreme. One becomes oneself by being different from all others. The only adequate model for an aesthetic life is Socrates and this is due to his silence—we know almost nothing about how he came to be what he was. We have his life, but no instructions. The third model for an art of living offers no rules to live by.[29]

It there are no rules, life is not often lived in the service of morality yet those who admire this way of living assert that it enriches and improves human life generally. This is a point at which artists differ most from inner monks. Both seek unity of an inner self, but as Freud said: "[Psycho]analysis makes for *unity*, but not necessarily for goodness....too heavy a burden is laid on [psycho]analysis when one asks of it that it should be able to realize every precious ideal."[30] The careful reader will recall that Freud's analysis of civilization carried the accusation that the masses are ignorant and lazy—the masses were the problem. In making his claim about unity and goodness Freud is well inside an art of living. For the artist, an individual holds the prominent place. The artist is radically personal. The pressure to be an original ensures conflict with moral frameworks. To be moral is to be mundane. As Nietzsche said, morality draws the individual towards the herd. Freud took up the third way in an art of living when he asserted that each of us must find our own salvation. But he did express concern about the radically personal because he showed how the excesses of the heart could lead to mental disorder.

There are similarities between psychoanalysis and an art of living. The unfettered freedom of speech typifies both a talking cure and an art of living. In a talking cure, one must say everything. An art of living is focused on telling the truth; frequently, truth that makes ordinary people uncomfortable. This is similar to Socrates' method of philosophy, but not the same. He told the truth to his society and suffered for it. His practice aimed to change people's lives on an individual level by confronting them with discomfiting thoughts. The primary truth he told through conversation with others revealed their deep ignorance about ideas people previously thought they understood. Socrates told the truth to uncover ignorance. His questions probed thought until ignorance revealed itself.

It is essential to note that Socrates' method aimed to help people think clearly about they way they were currently living—not simply to make people squirm. His was an invitation to reflection. He was inviting people to copy his practice of conversation but not to copy his life; he didn't place his own value at the centre of life. In saying everything, Socrates invited reason to make a new order out of what was merely conventional and habituated thought. What is the aim of the life of an artist in saying everything? Are there inherent limits to freedom of expression?

For the extreme artist, freedom of speech is inviolate. Everything can, must, be said; censure sickens society. All experience, every idea, is fodder for learning. Images proliferate: unlike monks, artists disdain external order. Experience "is a passing show of discrete, disconnected images lacking in coherence, depth and substance" that culture reflects and intensifies but does not attempt to order.[31] Order is suspect. Life happens.

Therefore, there is tension in the life of an artist between the freedom to say everything and a compulsion to do so; excesses of the heart can bring us to the brink of madness. How is the heart to find its own healthy way forward? Why do we worship the extremists in our culture the way that we do?

REASON AS EXPERIENCING

A personal life of faith has radical qualities. Like an inner monk and an unconformed artist, the faithful read their own hearts as text and comprehend the relationships between desire and action. Personal faith must read culture and balance itself on the margins of mass experience. Loving the world is possible if we are not addicted to its ways. The faithful blend discernment and commitment. Yet tension for the faithful is felt between the inner world of personal faith systems and the communal world of faith traditions that have a history and style of their own. The faithful require an education in reason that is personally grounded and socially inclusive. Reason helps to negotiate a path between a life of doubt on the one hand, and sovereign certitude on the other. Reason is personal and social. Reality moves reason forward. What do I mean by reason? What do I mean by reality? How do they conspire to form faith in the heart?

Modernity defined and categorized language and concepts with endless precision. Order was supreme. This in part was due to the birth of modern nations that depended on a national language to unify its disparate citizenry, e.g., France and Germany. The German language produced linguistic precision that reversed reason and intuition (Kant is central here). The Niptic tradition followed Greek inspired distinctions about reason and intuition that placed the direct apprehension of the essences and principles of beings, and of God, as the highest human faculty. Modern reformers gave reason primacy over intuition. Human reason became the highest human faculty. The effects of this reversal weakened reliance on faith alone. Reason was deployed to curb the excesses of faith that were thought to be common in pre-modern experience. But one view of reason emerged that fits with self-observation as we are exploring it. Hegel (1770-1831) placed reason within the activity of observing self-consciousness in what he termed 'experiencing'.

To understand experiencing, consider the difference in two types of conversation. In the first, we are speaking with those who do not look at us, do not seem to hear anything we say, categorize us in ways we find objectionable and misinterpret who we are, even though we are standing in front of them, trying to let them see us as we are. In this type of conversation we are misrecognized: others neither see us nor hear what we are saying, so that they cannot sense what we are in our uniqueness. In the second type of conversation, we are engrossed with someone who really looks at us, without making us feel the need to hide, who hears what we are saying and senses what we are doing even when we cannot be articulate about the complex feelings we have. As we converse, one or the other of us is able to put into words what we recognize as that which we really are. Through conversation, we see ourselves in a new way and the other person is central to this self-recognition. The conversation is effective. We sense that we are different from, but able to understand each other. Both participants change as they talk together; the trajectory of change in thinking and feeling is drawn by contributions each one makes. Conversing is a dialogue, not a battle. Neither voice is silenced. Neither voice is victorious.

As an example, suppose a father and small son sit in an ice cream shop. The father drinks his cappuccino while the little boy eats ice cream. It is a favourite place. As the father is reading, the little boy stops eating ice cream and begins to ease off his chair. The father notices. He looks at the boy and quietly says, smiling: "If you don't stay on your chair we will have to go home." The little boy stays on the edge of his chair. The father gets up and goes to the boy. Kneeling down, he says quietly: "If you don't stay on your chair we will have to go home." He gently puts the boy back securely in his chair. Returning to his own chair, he picks up the paper. After a few moments, the little boy moves to the edge of his chair. The father notices. He comes over to the little boy and says: "I said that we would have to go home if you don't stay in your chair." He gets the boy's jacket. The little boy replies: "Daddy, I want to go home." The father laughs and hugs his son. They put on their coats and leave hand-in-hand.

Hegel's philosophy of consciousness is similar to this second type of conversation. *Experiencing,* or dialectical movement,[32] is a dialogue within ourselves that comes into being due to the lively, interactive voice of others. The reality that moves experiencing is caught in the possibility of hearing the voice of the other speak for itself, including the Voice of God. Experiencing is a process of paying attention to our own consciousness in the presence of others, whether the other (the object of our gaze) is from the natural world, from the world of other people, or from our own personal world,[33] i.e., our sensations, thoughts, opinions, interpretations and religious experience. Reality, i.e., the objects or phenomena from the natural, relational and personal aspects of our consciousness, present themselves to consciousness and a dialogue takes place.

Consciousness grows through the dialogue it has within itself. It is a dialogue between what Hegel refers to as natural knowledge and real knowledge. To him, natural knowledge provides us with thought that appears without any effort on our part. As soon as we sense the other, our knowledge of the other shows up as natural knowledge. To use our example, the father looked at his son in the ice cream parlour and assumed the little boy wanted to stay there as much as he did. We might say that natural knowledge is our taken-for-granted idea of objects (images, thoughts) in consciousness. Seeing them is effortless. There is no work involved in our gaze because we assume we know the object of our glance in advance of really looking. The father had to look a second time. Real knowledge is the real being of the object that consciousness is concerned to explore. Real knowledge lives behind the back of what we take for granted. Real knowledge refers to the way phenomena essentially and really are in themselves, as they exist apart from our incomplete or unfinished view of them. It is the difference between looking at the moon while lying on our backs on a summer evening, and walking on its surface.

In the dialogue between natural and real knowledge, natural knowledge shows up as unfinished. Sensing that there is incompleteness in natural knowledge is made possible through *skepsis*, which is the seeing, watching, scrutinizing to see what and how beings are as beings.[34] There is a constant tension within consciousness between natural knowledge and real knowledge. The tension is natural knowledge's resistance to real knowledge and to *skepsis*. Dialogue is not scepticism. The sceptic does not believe in transformation and fosters sovereign certitude as a defence against dialogue. The sceptic dismisses the other, turning its back on the object.

Dialogue is not a method or approach; it is open to the lively being of the other; its aim is simply to follow the movement of its object of study.[35] Yet real knowledge typically makes natural knowledge uncomfortable. In order for growth to occur, Hegel thinks there is even a kind of violence between the two ways of viewing phenomena in which natural knowledge tries to refuse real knowledge and the movement of conceptual shapes that he believes characterizes the growth of consciousness. Both real and natural knowledge play an important and enduring role in dialogue, but natural (taken-for-granted) knowledge must release its grip on sovereign certitude.

As mentioned earlier, Hegel's concept of experience is grounded on the idea of *conscientia*, which "refers to the gathering into presence of the kind in which that is present which is represented."[36] In the second type of conversation, consciousness literally means being conscious of, intentionally conscious of what presents itself to us—the phenomena we experience as the voice or presence of another. To Hegel, experience has three senses. Firstly, experience refers to receiving raw sensory material. Secondly, it refers to receiving sensory material that undergoes some conceptual processing. Experience goes beyond mere sense perception and, I suggest, is eventually organized into a personal faith system. Thirdly, experience refers to a process and a product in which our attentiveness to phenomena results in a change in the shape of the object of consciousness. It is at this point that a personal faith system has the opportunity to grow.

The third sense results in a sublation of consciousness so that our idea of an object moves forward in a way that is closer to its actual being—the way it really is apart from our incomplete conception of it. The third sense produces tension in dialogue between natural knowledge as it moves through *skepsis* to real knowledge. The movement of consciousness that results, requires that some of what we understood about the object will shrivel and die, and some of what we understood takes a new shape—a process that conveys the meaning of the term sublate. In the growth of consciousness, the new shape annihilates the old shape but the new bears a necessary relationship to the old, since the old shape is part of the particular configuration of the growth of the new one.[37] Ordinary people are capable of experiencing the growth of consciousness. A neurotic system hinders experiencing and a psychotic system prevents it. For Hegel and Freud the process of consciousness is remarkably similar. In faith education, experiencing produces growth in our concept of God. All transformational learning takes *conscientia* as its model.

The growth of consciousness is always grounded on experience in the first sense in which I used the term, i.e., on raw sensory data. In experience we catch sight of something, a person or a thing, for example, the way that someone's mouth is turned up at the corners. In observing that object, our sighting of it brings the phenomenon into view. In being attentive to the turning up of this particular person's mouth, we do not just see the person's mouth, we sense what the person really is, or at least we observe more of what that person is: we perceive in a new way. Now it is the other's presence that directs our gaze, not our own thoughts or notions about the phenomenon. Our contribution is precisely *not* to contribute our notions and thoughts about the phenomenon but to let the other person's mouth speak for itself.

On Hegel's view, experiencing differs from doubting as understood by Descartes. In doubt we have a thought X (my friend is worthy of my trust) and in our activity of doubting we fully consider not X (my friend is not worthy of my trust) to be the case. After we reflect on not X, we doubt our doubt (we mistrust our mistrust of our friend) and return to X (my friend is worthy of my trust). That is, when doubting ends, things are much the same as they were in the beginning. In experiencing, as conceived by Hegel, as we are engrossed with X, we become attentive to X in such a way that our consciousness of X shifts and changes shape. The direction of the change arises from the nature of the concept, as it really is, rather than from our need to return to what is comfortable. The new shape for X annihilates the old shape of X so that the old X dies for us and a new shape takes its place. We now have a new shape for consciousness to consider.

It may be that our first awareness of the movement of shapes in consciousness is the recognition that an old shape for a concept has died. This realization can cause us pain. That is, I may think my friend is trustworthy because she always meets me at the precise time we agree upon. I trust her because she never fails to show up.

The shape of my concept for trust rests on never having been let down. If she does not come one day, I become attentive to her not coming and to the relationship between the conceptual shape I have for trust and her being. In dialogue I may come to see that she has a complex life, so do I. Trusting her does not mean never being let down; trust means something more, it signifies confidence that has hope and some certainty in it. The freedom to hope makes certainty comfortable. But I risk pain and loss in the process and cannot look forward to a comfortable place to which I may return. I cannot go home to my old concept of trust, but neither is the new one entirely strange and without any trace of the old one.

To Hegel, the process of annihilation changes the shape of our idea of the object we are observing. If we reflect upon our current shape for an object, *and we allow the other to be itself,* what dies is our inadequate notion about the object, our idea of trust, as an example, in the strong light of new observation. What draws experiencing forward is the relationship between current concepts and reality. The role that reality plays is central to the possibility of the growth of consciousness. The engine that drives the movement of shapes for a concept is the contradiction that lies at the core of experience.

The engine that drives the movement of shapes for our idea of something is the contradiction that, to Hegel, lies at the heart of all our experience with phenomena, and indeed, lies within ourselves.[38] Contradiction makes concepts move and change.[39] This is why educative events disturb us. Sometimes we must be let down in order to see how trust operates? Disappointment makes trust wise. In addressing contradictions, Hegel insists that it is clear conceptual work (reason) that moves us forward in dialectical inquiry: Reason begins to reconcile what is in contradiction within the each concept, within each person.[40] But the object must first show up before reason is of any use. Becoming conscious of the concept of trust stored in memory comes first. Reason plays a central role in the dialogue that discusses the contradictions between trust and mistrust. Reason reconciles opposites, yet the identity of each part is preserved in some way in the shape of the new concept.[41] That is, the prodigal can go home, but home is reconceived.

Silencing the Skeptic so Faith Can Flourish

I suggested earlier that we learn about learning from Freud. In lifelong learning, the ego (Freud's term for a personality's organizing system) systematizes or organizes perception and experience. The ego must work with the id and the superego as it moves toward a psychically healthy way of engaging reality. The ego's work is complicated by the id (everything inherited at birth) and superego (a precipitate of parental influence). The superego is a new agency that emerges around five years of age and leads to the formation of an inner world of object representations in which those who surround the child, and are important, become the inner population of a personal faith system. Internalizing the outer world regulates the child from within.

Freud believed that an ego wants to establish harmony among its parts and works toward this end if it gets the right help. (The heart also longs for this harmony.) The ego tries to incorporate suffering by interpreting the meaning of suffering in a narrative it tells about the world. In response to suffering, psychoanalysis offers an interpretation of experience that may re-direct the ego toward harmony and health. What does psychoanalysis have to do with the Christian faith? Can we make good educational use of what Freud discovered about the human health, without dismissing religion?

In some ways psychoanalysis replaced practices of spiritual healing in twentieth century Western society. We stopped speaking of souls and started talking of psyches. But if we closely examine what Freud proposed was possible for a normal ego, his descriptions resemble pre-modern Christian beliefs and practices about how to be spiritually well. The point of contact between Freud and the Niptic Fathers is the practice of self-observation. In the *Philokalia* there is very little detail given about how to observe ourselves. It was not necessary to describe a practice on paper that was primarily passed on by apprenticeship.

Freud connected psychological insights to self-observation. He thought that a pathological idea could be traced back to the elements in the patient's mental life from which it originated, and would simultaneously crumble away, freeing the patient from it. His prescription for health: Tell me everything.[42] In order for patients to get well, they must learn to observe their own thinking. There were two aspects to self-observation in his view. The patient prepared for the practice by paying increased attention to psychical perceptions and by eliminating the criticism that normally sifted through thoughts as they occurred. Resting on a couch with eyes closed was pre-requisite for the concentration needed to give full attention to self-observation.

So, suppose a man is trying to observe himself. The doctor insists that he renounce all criticism of his thought, as it is being perceived. Freud described his practice in the following way, which is particularly useful to consider in full:

> We therefore tell him that the success of the psychoanalysis depends upon his noticing and reporting whatever comes into his head and not being misled, for instance, into suppressing an idea because it seems to him meaningless. He must adopt a completely impartial attitude to what occurs to him, since it is precisely his critical attitude which is responsible for his being unable, in the ordinary course of things, to achieve the desired unraveling of his dream or obsessional idea or whatever it may be. I have noticed in my psychological work that the whole frame of mind of a man who is reflecting is totally different from that of a man who is observing his own psychical processes. In reflection, there is one more psychical activity at work than in the most attentive self-observation, and this is shown amongst other things by the tense looks and wrinkled forehead of a person pursuing his reflections as compared with the restful expression of the self-observer. In both cases, attention must be concentrated, but the man who is reflecting is also exercising his critical faculty; this leads him to reject some of the ideas that occur to him after perceiving them, to cut short others without following the train of thought which they would open up for him, and to behave in such a way towards others that they never become conscious at all and are accordingly suppressed before being perceived. The self-observer on the other hand need only take the trouble to suppress his critical faculty. If he succeeds in doing that, innumerable ideas come into his consciousness of which he could otherwise never have got hold. The mate-

rial which is in this way freshly obtained for his self-perception makes it possible to interpret both his pathological ideas and his dream-structures."[43]

In self-observation, attention is paid to the pathway of thought. Health is not produced by censuring thought but by allowing a psychoanalyst to interpret it. Health follows a new interpretation of thought that re-organizes one's personal faith system (my term, not Freud's). It is as if the psychoanalyst must do the work of reason that the heart cannot accomplish on its own, due to its distress. Yet, if reason is deployed too soon in self-observation, it forecloses on insights that may emerge.

There is a common theme between monks and patients: reason must wait. To those who could not be successful at self-observation, Freud proposed the following:

> The ground for your complaint seems to lie in the constraint imposed by your reason upon your imagination. It seems a bad thing and detrimental to the creative work of the mind if Reason makes too close an examination of the ideas as they come pouring in—at the very gateway, as it were. Looked at in isolation, a thought may seem very trivial or very fantastic; but it may be made important by another thought that comes after it, and, in conjunction with other thoughts that may seem equally absurd, it may turn out to form a most effective link. Reason cannot form any opinion upon all of this unless it retains the thought long enough to look at it in connection with the others. On the other hand, where there is a creative mind, Reason—so it seems to me—relaxes its watch upon the gates, and the ideas rush in pell-mell, and only then does it look them through and examine them in a mass. You critics...are ashamed or frightened of the momentary and transient extravagances that are to be found in all truly creative minds and whose longer or shorter duration distinguishes the thinking artist from the dreamer. You complain of your unfruitfulness because you reject too soon and discriminate too severely. Nevertheless...relaxation of the watch upon the gates of Reason, the adoption of an attitude of uncritical self-observation, is by no means difficult to achieve.... [and many] patients succeed after their first instructions.[44]

That is, in psychoanalysis the patient practiced telling everything in order to eventually learn to guard the heart and master himself—success that was impossible to achieve without an analyst. Freud would not agree with an inner monk's interpretation that demons are responsible for illness in the inner life. He ridiculed the idea of a spiritual world inhabited by demons. But the inner monk and the psychoanalytic patient must learn to let reason wait. Reason itself can sicken. If we are unwell, we must learn to re-interpret the narratives we tell ourselves so we can grow up to face reality.

For unconformed artists, growing up means leaving home and never returning: there are no prodigal sons. Artists abandon their connection to the society in which they live and push moral limits as a studied way of life. The evidence of being grown up is a life radically different from the lives of those around. The artist must be free. Is transgressing moral boundaries necessary to an art of living? The refusal to admit limitations carries its own constraint, often in the form of social disintegration and sometimes in the form of madness. Who else suffers when one artist collapses from within?

What does Christianity offer to an art of living? Certainly Jesus lived with style. According to an art of living, artists cannot afford communities that apply constraint. But is the idea that we can live as radical individuals true to human reality? The answer to this question comes more from a mythology of being than it does through empirical fact. The question of legitimate and illegitimate forms of social constraint within Christian community is an issue I pick up in the following chapter.

With respect to the dialogue between faith and reason, for both the inner monk and the unconformed artist, reason cannot be deployed too soon in the process of self-observation, if this process is to accomplish its work in the human heart. How might reason operate more effectively in an inner life to provide for the possibilities of personal growth? How can reason work with reality?

FAITH EDUCATION AS LIFELONG LEARNING

Lifelong learning is the activity of reaching forward and arriving somewhere new.[45] In *experiencing*, we allow reality to influence the shape of our concepts. Being reasonable implies a developing willingness and ability for the social[46] and personal growth of consciousness as opposed to sovereign certitude—the dogmatic attachment to a settled shape for ideas that we hold to be the end of the matter. Reality moves the process. In faith education we are confident of God's Presence in reality, which leads us to a deeper appreciation of human experience. In lifelong learning we anticipate that our concepts will change over time. Insight grows in a healthy inner life—aimed neither at prurience nor prudery. In faith education we regularly practice disengagement from culture in order to sense what is happening in our hearts. For example, we fast from cultural products that inhibit our efforts to guard the heart. As we fast, we observe ourselves. Self-observation regulates our inner living space so that memory and reason cohabit—a necessary condition for the birth and growth of insight.

Perhaps we began life in a censured environment. Perhaps as children there were no censoring adults. Most educators from Socrates and Plato onward prized the importance of censorship because they believed it allows the best elements of character to flourish in the young. But we have not all been protected. We live in a culture that frowns on censorship, promoting free expression that amounts to letting the loudest voices shout whatever they want. Over a lifetime, faithful people practice withdrawing from society and then return to it. On returning, they are not dazzled by culture or abhorrent of it. Upon returning, they invite the world into their inner homes. After a time away, they are able to discern whether or not some of their guests are wrecking the furniture. Fasting from culture, refusing fundamentalism, guarding the heart are means for becoming mature. But a faithful life is not a life of ease. On the contrary, maturity requires that we learn the lessons that the problems of opposition and empathy teach us. In the following chapters, we will see how opposition works with empathy to produce the insight that moves the faithful to live fully in the Presence of God.

8

THE PROBLEM OF OPPOSITION

Were it to depend upon rulers, their own education will
first have to be improved, for this has for a long time
suffered, owing to the great mistake that they have been
allowed to meet with no opposition in their youth.[1]

In the ideal detective story the reader is given all the clues
yet fails to spot the criminal. He may avert to each clue as
it arises. He needs no further clues to solve the mystery.
Yet he can remain in the dark for the simple reason that
reaching the solution is not the mere apprehension of
any clue, not the mere memory of all, but a quite distinct
activity of organizing intelligence that places the full set
of clues in a unique explanatory perspective. By insight,
then is meant not any act of attention or advertence or
memory but the supervening act of understanding[2].

THE PERSPECTIVE OF FAITH EDUCATION

Faith education involves ancient Christian practices aimed at
inner wholeness. The Niptic tradition offers a perspective
on Christian living in which believers, by reflecting on the
heart, in cooperation with God, move forward into maturity. An
idea implicit in that tradition, invites us to believe that we can gain

mastery over our hearts, in the company of other believers who are engaged in similar disciplines. I suggest that victory over the heart is learned in a field of social interactions best described by the problem of opposition. To master our hearts, we need to understand how power works. Exercising power over ourselves in a healthy way is related to learning how to use power when we are with other people. The problem of opposition is ultimately provided to us by God and played out in the world, as well as in our faith communities. Wise Christians are no longer destabilized by power's exercise—wherever they find it. Instead of being caught off balance, they shift from playing power games to understanding the spiritual structures that underlie the problem of opposition. They learn to see in opposition an opportunity for knowing God more intimately and they perceive a new openness to live out the freedom Christianity offers through Christ's resurrection. Through mastering opposition, Christians learn how to manage the dynamics of legitimate versus illegitimate social constraints. In this chapter, I outline the problem of opposition by using examples from King David's life and Christ's example. My purpose is to show that opposition exposes us to intense anxiety but by learning how to address its underlying patterns, we allow it to teach about God and we gain freedom to be God's friends.

Gaining mastery over the heart is about understanding freedom. As we guard or govern our hearts, we recognize two aspects of freedom: the liberation God secures for us through salvation and practices of freedom we acquire as we grow up faithfully. This chapter distinguishes between these two aspects of freedom—one-time events and daily practices. We find the distinction in scripture. After we are liberated or saved as a one-time event, practicing freedom daily produces insight. Freedom is not an open invitation to do whatever we like. In faith, we are free not to be the slaves of other people. The problem of opposition presents us with opportunities to practise freedom versus remaining enslaved. We are enslaved if we are living out purposes that others have for us rather than living out plans we choose for ourselves, with God's help. We are enslaved if we are living without the self-mastery God expects from humanity

(Genesis 4). Without self-mastery, we come to believe our behaviour (even if it hurts us and other people) is beyond our control.

In learning to mature in freedom, we face opposition that inheres in a life of faith and eventually come to see how power operates to enslave or liberate us. The problem of opposition is an opportunity to enjoy freedom in Christ. With the first form of slavery, following plans others have for us rather than those we find for ourselves, it is too hard to discern God's voice amidst powerful voices of other people. With the second form of slavery, the absence of self-mastery, it is too easy to believe we are powerless, even though we have God as our helper. If we are trapped in the conditions of slavery, the problem of opposition is a way out. Opposition presents us with the opportunity of identifying appropriate boundaries between ourselves and other people as we learn to put our faith in God. In practising freedom, we learn to do our own spiritual work in collaboration with other people who are similar to us and different from us. Part of the work of enjoying freedom is figuring out how the many differences and similarities among believers should affect the way each one of us lives out our faith.

We cannot understand the problem of opposition and the practices of freedom without asking the following questions: Who is the self who is liberated as a follower of Jesus? How am I related to others? What are the boundaries around personal freedom? What are legitimate constraints communities place on choices I make? These questions are not asked independently of the culture in which we find ourselves or separately from the standards that inhere in Christianity as a way of life. Christian freedom is not the myth of radical freedom of western liberalism in which each individual is autonomously free to pursue personal happiness regardless of others (this is actually a way of being out of control); but neither is it the domination inherent in a communal way of life that forecloses on the possibility of living authentic personal lives. It is in the way we work at the problem of opposition, and how we understand opposition, that freedom is understood and practised.

The problem of opposition is larger than the issue of conflict. When conflict breaks out, it is because the problem of opposition was not addressed effectively enough to let differing ideas, rituals, beliefs and practices be exercised with personal and communal integrity. If the problem of opposition is effectively addressed integrity remains intact. There is a difference between the game of opposition (opposing others to preserve ourselves) and the problem of opposition, as I am using the expression. The game begins at birth and ends at death. Without opposition we do not grow up. From birth we are endowed with a capacity to govern the actions of other people and to resist their governance of us. Government in this sense applies to all social relations. Every human being exercises power in the sense of governing the behavior of other people. Every human being is governed by the exercise of other people's power. Freedom is learned in the presence of power. The game becomes the problem when we begin to sense that winning and losing is not all that is involved in living life faithfully. The problem of opposition helps the faithful become adept at exegeting the powers that affect their lives.

GOVERNING THE HEART

To see how to guard or govern our own hearts maturely, we must learn to detect the way power works legitimately in social relations and distinguish it from domination. Social power operates among individuals, in families, schools, churches and communities, as well as throughout economic and political life. It is evident in all social relations. Power is a human good that can be misused. An infant exercises social power to bring a parent to her side when she is hungry. If you observe a group of adults in a room with a four-month old baby, you sense an effective use of social power. Ordinarily staid adults make odd sounds and ridiculous gestures and do so even in the presence of other equally posh grownups. The baby has them in her grip. The effective use of social power secures her nurture. Power is good when it is exercised within reasonable social boundaries. Outside those boundaries, it can deteriorate into domination.

As noted, exercising social power permits us to govern others, ourselves, and to be governed by other people. When it is exercised justly, it is characterized by fair measures of give and take. In order to describe social power as governance, we must distinguish

272

between power and domination. Domination stymies the free use of power. Domination can be subtle and systemic and is always negative: it subtracts power from some people so others get more than their fair share.

In bureaucratic organizations, for example, the negative use of power "is incapable of doing anything; except to render what it dominates incapable of doing anything either, except for what this power allows it to do," so that all its modes of expression reduce [people] to [blind] obedience:[3] Domination refers to a static state in which one person (or small group) blocks a field of social relations so effectively that every other person included in that field is rendered passive in the face of their maneuvers. The movements of those kept passive by the aggression of the leader(s) are extremely confined and limited. While resistance to domination is possible, it is very costly. Under the conditions of domination, each passive person's opportunity to speak or act is cut off. Resistance is possible, but dangerous.[4] Dominating leaders are well situated within the group. They are able to organize political dynamics so personal interests are secured at the expense of other people. Frequently, the dominating leader will harm someone (fire, insult, treat unjustly) as a warning to all others that they will be hurt if they get out of line.

An organization led by domination may succeed in some ways but does not support the well-being of all its members. A dominating leader is typically superb at spotting resistance and equally skilled at snuffing it out as a way of perpetuating passivity and propping up the structures of domination. In a state of domination, the leader controls a group of people who passively adopt practices they count on to keep them out of trouble—although nothing is guaranteed. They may still suffer, no matter how agreeable they try to be. Passivity in followers is maintained through fear—the real or imagined fear of losses they sense that they could not endure. They are over-controlled; boundaries around them are suffocatingly close. In domination, there is an interplay between the two forms of slavery mentioned earlier. Some people are enslaved because they follow the leader's purposes passively, while others are enslaved because they exercise no self-mastery. Dominating leaders themselves are enslaved in the second sense: they are capricious and unrestrained.

No one, no system, holds them accountable. They are out of control. They behave as if there are no boundaries.

If we consider dominating systems from the perspective of those held passive, these people neglect their social duty to resist and hold dominators accountable. They tell themselves a story in which the cost of resistance is extremely high. In making this point I do not blame the victims, but liberation comes about through telling ourselves a new story. Those in the position of a dominator justify their excesses by telling themselves a story that legitimates their double value; their easy access to harming other people is an expressive of their excess value. They justify the absence of accountability in multifarious ways. They may even blame victims for their own feeling of being out of control. The narratives of dominance characterize the heart of these folks but they also get support from the social world at large for their excesses. The social world fails to help them achieve a reasonable opinion of their personal value.

Unlike the ordinary exercise of social power, domination is unjust. It is an offence against humanity. Domination eliminates the healthy opposition that tries to resist injustice. Opposition is resistance that confronts domination. As a prime example, Moses resisted Pharaoh in order to initiate freedom for the Hebrew slaves in Egypt. Under the conditions of domination, opposition initiates liberation. Resistance propels people out of the cycle of passivity. Someone acts to set boundaries. The Hebrew people came to see God as liberator—the Living Lord who loved them. Moses' opposition to Pharaoh was carefully structured. Playing the game of opposition with integrity limits domination. Under the conditions of ordinary daily life, opposition maintains the practices of freedom. Release from Egypt did not end the struggle with opposition. It took a long time for Israel to realize that opposition is part of God's plan for helping his children to grow up faithfully.

In summary, while liberation set the people free from Egypt, the practices of freedom were learned in the wilderness and in the Promised Land. While liberation is a one-time event, the practices of freedom arise through daily, lifelong learning. With the healthy exercise of social power, people learn to be free to govern each other, to resist the governance of others, or choose to cooperate. They are free to exercise power and resist effects of its exercise when these effects threaten to stymie them. Social power is exercised through words, gestures, glances, gaze and silence along with many other bodily expressions acquired in cultural scripts that direct the game of opposition. Since slavery is embodied, liberation and freedom are as well. The game of opposition transforms into the problem of opposition when players intentionally reflect on what they are doing and consider carefully how they wish to live their lives and practice freedom daily. Opposition reveals appropriate boundaries between people and helps us learn how to act accountably with others.

When we effectively address opposition, we work out social relationships based on the healthy exercise of power and avoid the state of domination. Before we can resist the illegitimate effects of social power and free ourselves from domination, we have to learn to recognize power's negative effects. Conflict is not always resistance to domination. Conflict may break out because people who say they are arguing over issues or ideas are actually participating in unsavory ways of playing the game of opposition. The game of opposition can be played with or without integrity. Integrity refers to engaging the problem of opposition and resisting slavery. But it is not always easy to interpret the signs that we are enslaved.

Liberation and the practices of freedom are revealed in scripture. In scripture we find examples of people who lived with the problem of opposition in a spiritually healthy way, given their cultural context. First I consider what is meant by liberation and practices of freedom and then I investigate the lives of King David in the Old Testament and Jesus in the New Testament, to uncover patterns for living well with the problem of opposition.

LIBERATION AND PRACTICES OF FREEDOM

The Old and New Testaments each convey a core narrative of liberation. In the Old Testament, the Hebrew people were freed from slavery in Egypt. Moses led the people out of bondage into the Promised Land, almost. That is, he nearly got there. Before he died, he climbed Mount Nebo and looked across at land the Lord promised on oath to the descendents of Abraham, Isaac and Jacob. Moses' heir, Joshua, took the people into the land to call it their own. Both Moses and the first generation of those who were rescued miraculously from slavery in Egypt failed to make it to the new land. They did not survive the desert. We tend to describe the liberation from Egypt as an act of God's Grace followed by forty years of futility. Why was going on?

For one thing, former slaves did not know how to live with freedom once they found it. They knew how to respond to being set free, over night; they followed those instructions precisely. Yet they were not sure how to live with freedom on a daily basis while on the move in the desert. Once they experienced privation, they yearned for the ease of Egypt. They mis-remembered their experience. Why did this new life have to be hard? Once freed, the hardships of migrating seemed worse than slaving for Egyptians. Desert life was demanding. It was difficult in a different way than living in slavery had been. The skills of slavery were not the attributes of freedom. Once in the Promised Land their problems were not over. They had other people to contend with and the persistent problem of idolatry. They worshipped the gods of their neighbors and betrayed the Living Lord who had shown them love by setting them free. God set them free but also intended to guide them through the daily practices of freedom. The basic rule of daily freedom was: Put your faith in the One who rescued you from Egypt and formed you as a people.

The people of Israel did not always read the signs of the times appropriately. They turned away from following Yahweh if other options opened up. When offered a choice, they often made the wrong one. If other groups challenged their loyalty to God, they gave in. They saw opposition itself as a sign that something was wrong. They did not see that practices of freedom are at peace with the problem of opposition. Opposition is precisely the pathway to the heart of God. We follow God by getting the problem of opposition right. But human beings are understandably confused. We want freedom to be easy, immediate and inexpensive. Once we are out of Egypt, freedom hardly ever happens that quickly again. We must learn to live freely.

King David handled opposition more wholesomely than the migrating children of Israel, though he is not the only victorious one among the kings, priests and prophets of the Old Testament. He is interesting though because we glimpse his heart through reading the Psalms. The prophet Samuel who anointed Saul and David as kings over Israel, referred to David as a man after God's own heart. David wrote and inspired the Psalms. From an Old Testament perspective, his life exemplified the struggle to live for God in an agonistic culture. Through working out the problem of opposition, David learned the heart of God and freed his own heart to a great extent. Insight comes from struggling through the suffering associated with opposition that threatens to undo us, but does not succeed. The faithful learn slowly that sometimes what is won is only the insight gained through struggle: to the world, it may look as though the fight is lost. But like Job, insight allows believers to see God's face. The practices of freedom help us mature as we make use of insights produced by the problem of opposition that aim to free us from slavery.

In the New Testament, slavery is spiritual and tends to use the word salvation rather than liberation. Salvation frees us from bondage to sin. Our salvation was secured through the life, death and resurrection of Jesus Christ—who is wholly God and wholly human. Jesus took upon himself the sin of us all. Through his dying and rising again, human beings are set free to live godly lives and become God's friends. If Jesus had not paid the penalty for sin, we could not please God. This is what Christians believe. Just as with the release from Egypt, God saved us from sin miraculously and suddenly. In liberation and salvation, a human being took action and cooperated with God's plan for redemption: in the first case it was Moses, in the second it was Jesus. But human beings could not accomplish the event itself—it was supernatural. God alone is Liberator and Savior. With the practices of freedom in daily life, the dynamics are different. While God remains the primary agent of freedom, and our guide, in order to learn freedom, people participate in redemption by working with God over a lifetime. The mystery of growing up faithfully unfolds as we learn to rely on God in concert with relying on the human capacity to resist slavery.

The practices of freedom link liberation and salvation to daily life. Practicing freedom requires us to face enemies that are social, cultural, racial, gendered and economic as well as spiritual. There is no isolationism in practices of freedom. We do not get full spiritual freedom if we turn a blind eye to cultural conditions of slavery and focus entirely on spiritual or religious concerns. If we are dominated by materialism we will be hindered spiritually. Liberation and salvation initiate the practices of freedom; the problem of opposition sustains them.

From the perspective of faith education, the problem of opposition is necessary for our growth. Opposition from the external world and from our own hearts establishes and perpetuates the practices of freedom that produce insight to make us wise. Insight moves wisdom. Wisdom is more about what we do than what we think. We can see how to live well with the problem of opposition by examining two lives: David and Jesus. If the faithful need to establish memory and build reason, as the previous chapter implies, it is during a third intellectual and emotional activity that insight is produced by facing opposition. Opposition is a means to insight. To call opposition a problem is not to say that it is an irritant to be eradicated. It is an emotional/intellectual opportunity that is spiritual as well.[5]

Opposition and Spiritual Intelligence

Life brings problems. Problems are not the same as puzzles. A puzzle has a finite number of predictable solutions. A rubics cube is a puzzle with a limited number of solutions, each one essentially as good as any other. No matter who picks up a rubics cube, solving the puzzle is accomplished in essentially the same way. When a solution is reached we put the puzzle on the shelf. When we finish, we can move to other unrelated puzzles if we wish, or rest from playing. A puzzle is a game that is hardly ever serious. In contrast, problems are extremely serious. A human problem does not have a few clear solutions; it has many potentially satisfying (or disastrous) outcomes. Any particular solution we choose has as much to do with human agency and creativity, as it has to do with the problem itself. Resolving a problem depends on an agent's perspective on it. When a problem is resolved, or adequately addressed, the result often opens out into other issues that were not obvious at the start. Related problems may emerge with the resolution of the first one. The work of addressing problems is never over. The choices we make as we face problems are significant in a way that is different from playing at puzzles. As an example, getting to the Promised Land was a problem that, once solved, meant learning how to take possession of the land and make it home. Having the Promised Land as home meant attending to political, religious, economic, hygienic and legal aspects of life in the emerging community.

Problems are always situated within a variety of holistic contexts. If liberation and salvation require our willingness and ability to cooperate with God's rescue, the practices of freedom require us to develop spiritual intelligence over a lifetime, effectively addressing the problems life brings. What do I mean? Intelligence is the ability to solve problems, or create products, that are valued within one or more cultural settings.[6] A human intellectual competence entails a set of skills that help with problem solving and enables a person to resolve genuine difficulties that are encountered in a particular field of endeavour. Intelligent people create effective products or solutions in response to problems. Intelligence refers to a potential for finding and formulating problems—thereby laying the groundwork for the acquisition of new knowledge.[7]

Intelligent people identify the types of problems that characterize a field of interest and address these problems satisfactorily. A human intelligence must be genuinely useful and important, at least in certain cultural settings.[8] In this way of looking at intelligence, there is not one type that some people have lots of and others have in limited amounts, there are many ways to be intelligent. This approach includes a description of intelligences that address a variety of core abilities, two of which are pertinent to the practices of freedom in the field of faith education.

The first set of skills needed to solve spiritual problems is interpersonal. Interpersonal intelligence is the ability to make sense of other people. In learning and practising the skills involved in comprehending others, we build on a core capacity to notice differences among people; in particular, contrasts in their moods, temperaments, motivations and intentions. In advanced forms, this intelligence permits a skilled adult to read the intentions and desires of others, even when these have been hidden. As one example, Anne Sullivan was able to help Helen Keller speak, even though the young girl could not see or hear. Interpersonal intelligence allows people to address problems that arise in trying to understand and work with others. In its simplest state, it is the ability of infants to discriminate among the individuals around them to detect their various moods. It begins with competencies required for affect attunement. In its advanced form, interpersonal intelligence allows someone to read others and act on that knowledge. Moses had interpersonal intelligence. Most religious leaders have it, or need to develop it, if they wish to be effective.

A second set of skills necessary to solve spiritual problems is intrapersonal intelligence, in which we effectively make sense of our own hearts. Intrapersonal intelligence is grounded on a developing sensitivity to internal aspects within us—our feelings, wishes, interpretations, dreams, intentions and plans. Intrapersonal intelligence enables people to have a viable and effective model for their own life and includes knowing what they consider to be essential to a good life. An experienced inner monk is good at intrapersonal intelligence. As a private form of knowledge, it requires some public expression, e.g., as songs, poetry, essays or utterances to gain social value. Intrapersonal intelligence does not merely remain private but shapes our activities. It allows us to solve the problem of trying to understand and work with ourselves. Its core capacity is access to one's feeling and thought life. This knowledge involves the capacity to distinguish between feelings, e.g., I am feeling embarrassed not discouraged; and thoughts, e.g., I want to resolve this problem but not lose my integrity doing it. Further, self-knowledge permits us to label feelings and thoughts, use symbols to convey them (words, pictures), and draw upon them as a means of understanding and guiding our behaviour. Spiritual intelligence utilizes interpersonal and intrapersonal intelligences. In addition, in spiritual intelligence we are learning to make sense of God and God's action in the world, his revealed truth and the life of faith. In the growth of spiritual intelligence, we learn through the problem of opposition to find and feel at home with the heart of God.

An outcome of all education is the flourishing of intelligence. The outcome of Christian maturity is a willingness and ability to address spiritual problems by seeking action that pleases God. This competency is spiritual intelligence. Spiritual intelligence comes to our aid and increases as we engage with the problem of opposition.

The purpose of faith education is to help people grow up. Faith requires collaboration between the inner life, the material world and other people. There are tensions among these worlds. Those who mature learn to live well with tension. Achieving balance in the midst of tension is an art and discipline. In response to the tension in maturity, faith education outlines elements of living faithfully from the inside that include the following:

> An articulate heart that is owned by a self and that
> Conveys the values of its inner life in the presence of others
> Makes and keeps its commitments
> Has an idea of a good life that upholds biblical standards
> Interprets culture in light of its commitments

The problems of opposition create situations that try our patience and push the limits of what we believe we can handle. And yet they are precisely the means through which we mature.

THE PROBLEM ITSELF

The problem of opposition is a contest that decides between healthy and unhealthy human development. Opposition is more than conflict. Opposition establishes the relationship between a self, a community and the world at large. Opposition is the playground of morality; it is the context that teaches us what to expect from life, from other people and from ourselves. If the problem of opposition goes well, our concepts of God grow up as we resolve tensions among the three worlds of faithful living: the cultural/material, personal (inner), and relational (outer) worlds. Opposition is fundamental to human existence. Our idea of what makes life good is challenged by and produced through the problem of opposition. What do I mean?

First of all, what underlies any conception of the good life? An idea of the good life, which every person has, focuses on personal happiness. In the following dialogue, Kant introduced a struggle between ideas of the good life and moral constraint in order to situate the fundamental role of our desire to be happy.

Teacher: What is your greatest, in fact your whole, desire in life?
Pupil: (is silent)
Teacher: That everything should always go the way you would like it to.
Teacher: What is such a condition called?
Pupil: (is silent)
Teacher: It is called happiness (continuous well-being, enjoyment of life, complete satisfaction with one's condition).[9]

Many of us are like the pupil. We are unaware that personal happiness drives our conception of the good life. But personal happiness is a human good. The problem of opposition arises when personal happiness is challenged and it pivots around a central concern we have: we want to maintain our personal happiness when other people appear to, and do, threaten it. Opposition compels us to work out appropriate boundaries around the pursuit of personal happiness in the presence of other people and things. Every culture provides a script for the problem of opposition. Social life is so directly affected by the particular boundaries human beings establish and maintain around themselves that cultures inevitably provide pre-arranged patterns to reduce the harm one person may inflict on others. (Domination violates these taken-for-granted boundaries in shocking ways so that ordinary people are thrown off balance—giving the dominating leader the advantage of surprise.) As we mature, we need to identify the particular cultural script that constitutes the problem of opposition and compare it with Christian principles.

We do not grow up without the help of other people. Opposition arises at birth as we try to work out the power relations that invest family life, school culture and friendship. The problem of opposition is relational and educational. It is relational because it reveals how much difficulty we have when we try to comprehend life from the perspective of other people. It is educational in that we accumulate knowledge personally: through the presence of opposition, we gain self and social knowledge. We learn our lessons by being with others.

Let us focus on the teacher-learner relationship. Following Kant, Jean Piaget emphasized a teaching-learning relation that privileged individual knowledge. For Piaget, genuine intellectual accomplishments could be measured only on the basis of what a learner was able to do *unassisted* by any other person. That is, intelligence is indicated by the work learners do independently of others. L.S. Vygotsky, who corresponded with Piaget over these issues, disagreed with him. Vygotsky understood intelligence to include the capacity to learn from instruction in what he referred to as 'the zone of proximal development'.[10] For Piaget, human development is essentially individualistic and solitary. To Vygotsky, human development is essentially social. To Vygotsky, learning meant working alongside other people who know more than the learner. Learning and intelligence imply more than what learners can do by themselves: learning is collaborative. In Piaget's system individuals acquire cultural capital as a personal possession and as a statement of their individual merit. In Vygotsky's system cultural capital is collectively owned. The collective ownership of cultural capital characterizes agonistic societies in general. The individualistic ownership of cultural capital characterizes literate, text-based societies influenced by modern western values of individualism, progress and materialism.

Western educational systems tend to follow Piaget. Learning can be measured only if it produces individual intellectual property that can be assessed as such. Individuals are ranked according to the acquisition of their private stock of knowledge. On this view, intelligence is a common quality: some people have a great deal and some have almost none. In part, Piaget and Vygotsky disagreed because they were thinking of education and culture differently. I suggest that their cultural scripts and expectations led them to different conclusions about education. They understood the problem of opposition differently. Vygotsky gave apprenticeship and mentoring a higher educational profile than Piaget allowed.

To Vygotsky, a community plays learning games together without violating essential rules. In Vygotsky's view, a group of collaborators accomplishes learning. In Piaget's system every learner is essentially in competition with every other learner.

I want to make several observations based on disagreements between Piaget and Vygotsky. Firstly, the problem of opposition exists within a particular cultural setting that influences how we establish and maintain social boundaries and pursue personal happiness. Personal happiness is modelled either on individualistic or on collectivist assumptions—we are either individuals or members of a group. Secondly, broad cultural themes affect people differently: issues of race and gender are examples of the complexities that face us as we try to secure our personal happiness. Thirdly, the problem of opposition is held accountable by the standards of a way of life that is intentionally taken on and typically differs from one's cultural script. Suppose we consider the way of life of an inner monk and an unconformed artist that both are African Americans. Being African American is common to them but their identities are informed by two very different ways of life. They will not be similar but will have common experiences under certain conditions, e.g., institutional racism. In the problem of opposition, we intentionally engage with cultural scripts and with standards of a way of life so that the pursuit of personal happiness brings a diverse set of challenges when we try to secure personal happiness. In the midst of attending to scripts, diversity and standards, we are also called on to attend to particular people.

In summary, the problem of opposition is a locus for numerous demands. In order to make clear the dynamics of opposition and its role in helping us grow up, I outline aspects of the lives of David and Jesus. In them, we see the problem of opposition played out. If we learn from their examples, the positive outcomes of struggling with opposition are conveyed in personal growth and intimacy with God.

DAVID AND OPPOSITION

After wandering in the desert for forty years and finally becoming established in the Promised Land, God's people developed a religious culture through Moses' leadership. God made them a people through the institution and culture of the Law. God was their Sovereign and Shepherd, but eventually they asked for a king to rule over them. They told Samuel the prophet they wanted a king in order to be like the peoples around them. Samuel was angry. He inquired of the Lord. The Lord responded: "Listen to all that the people are saying to you; it is not you they have rejected, but they have rejected me as their king" (1Sam. 8:7). God instructed Samuel to give them a king but also to inform them of the inevitable hazards: taxation, conscription, war. Samuel told them a king is a leader who may abuse power. In asking for a king, they opened up the possibility of being dominated. They moved from the practices of freedom back to the potential for slavery. With Samuel's warning from God, the people hesitated due to the sobering possibility of power's misuse, but then they pursued their request.

The context for Israel's desire for a king is significant. God granted their request. But through Samuel, God clearly held both the people and the king responsible for the practices of freedom. Samuel said to the people: "Now here is the king you have chosen, the one you asked for; see, the Lord has set a king over you. If you fear the Lord and serve and obey him and do not rebel against his commands, *and if both you and the king who reigns over you follow the Lord your God—good!* But if you do not obey the Lord, and if you rebel against his commands, his hand will be against you, as it was with your ancestors" (Sam.12: 13-15). God formed the Israelites into a people through the Law; following the Law constituted their freedom. For them, liberation and the practices of freedom are in the Torah—Genesis to Deuteronomy. Since God is Creator of humanity, God knows how freedom is maintained. Obedience to God and human freedom are not mutually exclusive. The message of the Old Testament is consistent, persistent! God says: Put your faith in Me alone.

Saul was chosen king. He was a head taller than others and handsome. Physically, he was the sort of man other nations chose as king. He became spiritually fit to be king suddenly and miraculously. Samuel anointed him and prophesied: "The Spirit of the Lord will come upon you in power, and you will prophesy [with a procession of prophets]; and you will be changed into a different person." After being anointed, God transformed Saul's heart. All these signs were fulfilled in one day (1Sam.10: 6-9). Saul was dramatically prepared for kingship but unable to exercise God's call upon his heart. When Samuel tried to introduce him publicly, Saul hid himself among the baggage and could not be found. From the start, troublemakers surrounded him. He was plagued by self-doubt. Saul was immersed into the game of opposition, not for the first time in his life but with greater intensity. He did not play the game well from God's perspective, although he may have played it according to the cultural expectations of his day.

The people's request for a king was a failure to live out practices of freedom. They still did not know how to live with freedom once they found it. God eased the sin of their request by saying that if the king was a man after God's own heart, all might go well. Being king is not inherently evil. Saul failed to follow the Lord and his commands. David succeeded. Yet both men sinned. What was the nature of David's success? How are Saul and David different?

Saul failed and was rejected, just as Cain failed to offer an acceptable sacrifice. David entered the leadership race while Saul was still king but was working without God's favor. From the beginning David was caught in a dense net of opposition. David was a shepherd. In his first public act of bravery and loyalty to God, he slew Goliath, the Philistine enemy of his people. But he was drawn into the problem of opposition as he did so. Three of his older brothers were in Saul's army. He had come to bring them food. When he arrived he saw Goliath and sensed terror in the Israelite camp. He asked the men why they feared the enemies of the Living God. His oldest brother heard his questions and burned with anger: "Why have you come down here? And with whom did you leave those few sheep in the desert? I know how conceited you are and how wicked your heart is; you came down only to watch the battle." David replied, revealing a long history: "Now what have I done? Can't I even speak?" 1Sam.17:28-29 David continued to question the men until Saul heard of him and reluctantly asked him to help with Goliath. This event initiated David's public acclaim and immersed him in conflict with Saul. After several victories, everyone knew the song: Saul has slain his thousands and David his tens of thousands.

David was a man after God's own heart precisely because he learned to bring problems of opposition before the Lord and allowed God (sometimes) to participate in their solution. He was the youngest of his brothers, with few of the physical advantages for leadership that Saul had. Yet God chose him as king. While men look at outward appearance God looks at the heart. It was in David's heart where his victories were won. His kingship was plagued by opposition. The games of opposition did not always go well—sometimes despite his innocence, sometimes due to his sin. The agonistic culture of David's day had certain rules about how to play the game of opposition. At times he followed those rules and other times he did not. When he addressed the problem of opposition in a way that pleased God, he listened to God first as well as to other people like Abigail or Nathan. In order to understand the growth of David's heart for God, we can identify cultural cues that David followed sometimes and rejected at other times. I suggest that the difference between Saul and David is that David was more than merely a member of his culture. He transcended his cultural script at times in order to follow God's heart. God's heart always transcends a particular culture.

Agonistic Cultures[11]

For David and Jesus, the problem of opposition was situated within an agonistic culture. To differing degrees both of our exemplars resisted the general cultural script of their era. To sense their resistance, we have to understand the dynamics of agonistic culture itself.

David was anointed king. He was the top man in an agonistic hierarchy in which, if he chose, he could pursue his personal happiness at the expense of all other interests. He had double value as king. He also had to protect his honour; that was part of the game. Games of social honour directed the cultural script for David and their influence is with us still. Communal relations in agonistic cultures are based upon exchanges of honour. These exchanges constitute, and are ordered by, a system of honour and shame. The term agonistic comes from the Greek word *agon* or warrior. Honour refers to self and social respect. It is the value people have in their own eyes and in the eyes of the social group. Honour is a claim to positive worth and social recognition that goes with personal value. It is public. People are ranked according to its distribution.

An agonistic culture is a social web worked out through exchanges of honour between warriors: winners and losers. In general, honour and shame systems structure traditional, stable, agrarian, hierarchical societies. Honour and shame systems typify the Mediterranean world of antiquity, specifically the cultural world of scripture but may also describe many cultures today. Honour indicates a person's social standing and rightful place in society and is assessed on the basis of one's power, gender and position on the social scale. In traditional cultures, social precedence has less to do with wealth than honour. Once he was king, David had the most honour, and had the most to lose. The honour of his people was tied to his honour and the ways he managed it. Before he was king, while Saul remained in the position, Saul perceived all of David's actions as a threat. Even though he had opportunity, David did not dishonour Saul while he was alive, or at his death, eventhough Saul tried to kill David. Caught unreflectively in the game of opposition, Saul lost the honour of being king.

Honour is an abstract concept. It becomes concrete in a particular society. Social honour orders every culture, at every historical period, but what brings honour varies from culture to culture and from time to time. Exchanges of honour influence family systems, cultural roles and public values. Honour is distributed and personal identity is formed through membership in face-to-face family groups. Social interaction is structured by kinship, patronage, slavery, the separation between public and domestic space, and gender. The division of labour in agonistic cultures is based on gender and social location. Honour and shame systems also characterized medieval France. The French court was central to political relations in Europe. As a result, honour and shame systems shaped the elaborate modern power structure that emanated from rulers and extended *via* a bureaucracy to the local level in western culture.

Greco-Roman societies were agonistic cultures. In the Roman Empire honour had its source in Rome. Those outside the city had less honour and therefore less power. Honour meant honour for the nation, i.e., the Roman people or empire. To have honour was to be related in some way to the emperor and the aristocracy. The focus of honour in Rome signalled a shift from family honour (in which knowing the family name meant knowing the person's value) to national honour, that is, from a Hellenistic to Roman perspective. During the twentieth century in the West, we dropped the Roman model for social honour: people were no longer willing to fight and die for their country's honour. For example in North America, social honour came to be represented primarily by material wealth, expressed in the belief that people with money must also be good, upstanding citizens.

Gender is socially constructed in agonistic cultures and has a religious model. In the monotheism of Judaism, Christianity and Islam there is an idea of a male creator god and the corresponding idea of the male whose role is primary. The female role is subsidiary—a role most clearly expressed through procreation. Paternity refers to a life-giving role and associates men with the power of God. Women who lack this power are constitutionally inferior, which causes an appropriate and prescribed feeling of shame in women (within an agonistic context). Shame is a woman's proper and admirable response to the social conditions of inferiority. The contrast is striking: good men avoid shame; good women express shame. A dishonoured man is shameful; a dishonourable woman is shameless. In systems of honour and shame it is important to uphold divisions between the sexes. Men must maintain control over women to preserve their honour. The defence of male honour is paramount. The loss of family honour has social, political, religious and economic ramifications. Men compete among each other to defend their masculinity and must be able to defend the chastity of women under their control. The loss of a woman's chastity brings (male) shame on the household; as a consequence, all women are regarded as potential sources of shame. A loss of honour for the male head is a loss for the whole household. Outside the household a shameless woman has no safety.

Shame for women refers to modesty, shyness and deference. Female chastity is a source of male honour. The virtues of agonistic cultures compel a woman to be modest and obey men. To be shameless is to lack concern for one's own honour and to be insensitive to the opinions of others. The appropriate attitude for women is silence; they are not to teach men or claim authority over their husbands or other men. In the Old Testament, Sarah was a perfect model of modesty. Modesty is expressed though a woman's appearance and the deference and obedience she shows her husband. Young women are to show self-control, chastity and good housekeeping skills. This view of a good woman is also based on a Hellenistic ideal of proper women in contrast to prostitutes. Women can be assertive among other women. In agonistic cultures, powerful women frequently do battle over social position: one powerful, proper woman will attempt to shame other women who are her competitors. These contests are frequently carried out over who has (sexual) access to and influence with the dominant male. If women show assertiveness outside the circle of other women they are perceived as posing a challenge to men within a challenge-riposte system. A challenge to men leaves women vulnerable to punishment. Agonistic cultures assume that women consciously play the challenge-riposte game and that there is only one legitimate game going on.

Honour is expressed through recognizing and maintaining one's boundaries around property, a household and one's own body. The boundaries that people assimilate in honour and shame systems provide them with a socially shared map of the way things are, of the placement of people, things and events. The social map is generally condensed in a symbolic form in the physical body of each person. Each body is a personalized map of the social order. The head has a prominent role in honour and dishonour, as does the face, which is the focus of awareness, especially the nose. The expression, 'his nose is out of joint' conveys that someone feels resentment. If someone must ask permission to speak or act, this submission signals less social honour than the one who gives permission. In general, to enter spaces owned by one's equals without permission is considered an act of aggression. To gain access without permission to an inferior person does not engage the perpetrator in the game of opposition because the game is only played among equals. Personal boundaries of inferior people are inconsequential in games of honour.

To preserve personal honour one must maintain one's boundaries according to the social map. Boundary lines around a person include all that is worthwhile and worthy and all that is held sacred, e.g., family, patrons, kings and God. Between equals, trespassing a person's boundaries without permission causes resentment. Resentment is the psychological state of feeling distressed and anxious because personal expectations and demands are not acknowledged by the actual treatment received at the hands of others. It is a sense of moral indignation at the perceived injustice of the behaviour of others toward oneself. It is a reaction to behaviour not in keeping with one's power, sexual status and social role. Those who have no honour cannot afford the luxury of resentment. Honour systems assume that some people have it, some do not, and that the distribution, though unequal, is legitimate.

Honour is ascribed or acquired. If it is ascribed, it is endowed or bestowed through inheritance or grants of honour. Honour is acquired through challenge-riposte. If honour is ascribed, it comes passively through birth, family and endowment (like inherited wealth). If it is acquired, it is achieved at the expense of someone else's honour (like acquired wealth). People with social honour remain dependent on family and kin to affirm their self-worth. In this sense, honour is a dependency because we need others for grants of honour. The worst fate is to be called a Fool. In order to maintain a father's honour in his position as head of the household, his children must obey him and affirm his power over them. Children who disobey shame their father publicly; he loses honour, reputation and respect. The value of the father is absolute. In the social web, posts, positions, offices and functions are sacred. Public opinion is sovereign. In addition, social honour converts to ethical honour or implicit goodness. The king/father can do no wrong and is the arbiter of right and wrong.

In a culture of honour and shame, a person receives status from the group. Recognition from others is central to personal identity.

Honour depends on valuations made by significant others and social interaction is a competition for recognition. Contests for recognition take the form of exchanges based on challenge and riposte. The challenge and riposte metaphor comes from fencing. Contests of honour are carried out through the use of words, gestures or force. It is a game that one person wins and one person loses because honour is a finite substance. In these social games, one defends one's own honour. An exchange of honour permits people to express esteem for another person, or its lack. Those who observe the contest record wins and losses of face and pass the outcomes among the social group: a loss of honour is not merely a personal or private disaster.

Challenge and Riposte

In fencing, riposte refers to the action of giving a quick thrust after parrying a lunge. A riposte is a return thrust, a counter-stroke, which may be expressed through an effective reply by word or action. To parry is to ward off a blow or turn aside a weapon; it means to stop, ward off or evade a challenge. Challenge-riposte is a type of social interaction in which people hassle each other according to socially defined rules in order to gain the finite quantity of honour that the other brings to the match. Honour is neither created nor destroyed; it is passed around or kept. In agonistic cultures, almost every social interaction outside the household is perceived as a challenge. Challenge-riposte describes a constant social tug-of-war, a game of social push and shove. It is a type of social communication. It is a zero-sum game in which winner takes all. As a form of communication, the pattern is as follows: a challenger sends a message to a receiver in public. There are strict rules between challengers and receivers: only equals can play and they must be recognized and recognize each other as such. An inferior person does not have sufficient honour to play the game. A superior person's honour is not engaged by an inferior's affront, although the superior has the power to punish impudence. A man is answerable for his honour only to social equals. What he does to inferior people does not result necessarily in a loss of honour. In an agonistic culture for example, what a man does to his wife does not impact his honour, even if he is physically abusive of her.

Three phases of challenge-riposte reveal relationships among challengers, receivers and the audience. There is a challenge: some word and/or deed signals an action from a challenger; the perception of a message is sent to the receiver and the public; reactions arise from the receiver of the challenge and the public. In challenge-riposte there must be a claim: challengers claim to enter the space of receivers. The challenge may be positive (space sharing) or negative (space dislodging). A challenge threatens to usurp the reputation of the receiver. The social perception of a challenge depends on the social status of the sender in both the recipient's and the audience's view. Finally there is a riposte, a reaction to the message. The riposte may be a positive refusal (contempt, scorn, disdain), an acceptance of the message and offer of counter-challenge or a negative refusal that would amount to a non-response. Non-response represents a failure for the challenger. Neglecting a challenge constitutes a loss of honour for the recipient of the challenge, if it signals an inability to play the game. Dishonour is communicated by trespassing someone's space. Actions are more important than words, as is tone of voice or gesture. How one speaks matters more than what one says. Trying to withdraw a challenge by saying 'I didn't mean it' is not acceptable and does not erase the challenge. Withdrawing a challenge requires the indulgence of the receiver (if the receiver is seen as an equal).

In cultures based on honour and shame, social space is established through opposition. I suggest that individualistic North American cultures are still constituted through opposition based on honour and shame but we do not play these games in the same way that David did. In both contexts, opposition is conveyed through endless win-tie-or-lose games in which reputation and honour are on the line. In agonistic cultures, the capacity to maintain one's good name derives from dominating people rather than possessing things. A man's reputation is maintained through his ability to dominate his household, control inferiors outside his household and win contests of honour with equals in public. This was David's social context. He was not playing as an individual according to modern cultural scripts. He was a member of a group and its highest member. The rules for kings were different. We need to understand the difference between individuals and members if we wish to understand David.

Dyadic Membership

In agonistic cultures personal identity is not modeled on individualism. If the basic unit of social analysis in western culture is a solitary individual, the basic unit of social analysis in agonistic cultures is a dyadic member. In these cultures[12] the basic human unit is more than one. Dyadic members are connected with a social unit that forms personal identity within the context of others who are essential to that identity, primarily the family. As members, the dyadic person is embedded in "an undifferentiated family ego mass."[13] This relation among significant others is caught in the expression, "You are because we are" and "It takes a village to raise a child". As a result, dyadic members continuously need others to know who they are— which is not a form of identity weakness, although it may seem so to individuals. Dyadic members are persons, single beings and unique in that singularity, yet aware that "I" always implies a "We" that is inclusive of the "I". They know that their singular communications and interactions always involve that "We". Identity is formed through internalizing the family view and making it personal, a project that they hold to be necessary to being fully human. For dyadic members, to be human is to live out group expectations personally. A member's loss of honour shames the entire group.[14]

For members, the focus for identity is not on personal ego but is directed towards the demands and expectations of those that bestow or withhold social honour. The group perception of a dyadic member is central to that person's ability to live well in society. For example, educational systems provide for the intellectual accomplishment of the group rather than an individual. Without their group, dyadic members would cease to be. To compare them, an individual asks himself, Who Am I? to locate and form personal identity. In contrast, the dyadic member asks the group, Who do you say that I am? to cooperate with a corporate identity and live up to it. Dyadic identity is linked to other people. Dyadic people make sense of others by thinking collectively. Individuals make sense of others by beginning with inner reflection on the self. Identity for dyadic members is formed sociologically while individuals are constituted psychologically, roughly speaking.

Conscience itself is constructed differently within individuals and members. For dyadic members the group bestows personal value. For dyadic members, Kant's instruction that each individual must use his own understanding as a guide to ethical behaviour would not make sense. Dyadic personality "involves [a] general lack of personal inhibition in favour of strong social inhibition."[15] Other members are witness and judge of each member's social and moral success. Conscience literally refers to a dyadic member's sensitive attention to the public image of the group. To members, conscience implies relatedness; they are bound to live up to the full awareness of the perception others have of them. Conscience has the purpose of aligning personal behaviour and self-assessment with that image. Dyadic conscience internalises what other members say, do and think.

Conscience is formed differently in individuals. Individual conscience is a psychological construct that is *inside* as a personal voice, moved by autonomy and self-control. The formation of personal identity requires listening sensitively to one's own voice in the midst of many other voices and separating out alien voices while attending to one's own as guide to moral aims and conduct. The individualist's moral point is to distinguish an inner authentic voice from the talk of other people. Others are understood as foreign voices that may distract from the personal freedom to attend to the inner voice. According to Kant, conscience is grounded on internalizing rules that individuals choose to take on. Autonomy is central to moral agency. Individuals are connected to the world of other people through those rules but the duty of the moral life is inherently internal. Individuals have a self-imposed duty to follow and continually assess whether their inner voice is reflected in outward actions. The individual is witness and judge of his own moral success. Self-esteem is established individually. Hence the individual has a self-image and a sense of self-esteem that he places on that picture. An individual could feel justified in taking a particular course of action, regardless of community values; a dyadic person could not.

Individuals and dyadic members have a different relationship to the social body. For members, the group shuns those who do not conform to ways of talking, walking, or speaking that are deemed appropriate. For the dyadic member, there is nothing *inside* that does not register outside. Emotional language is expressed bodily; for example, anger is a gesture witnessed by others who know precisely what it means. Individuals live within themselves by keeping their feelings and thoughts to themselves. Dyadic members live in common with others. Individual identity is private. Personal moral identity in dyadic members is experienced through bonds of attachment that link members to a relationally generous interdependent world. Personal moral identity in an individual is formed *inside*. In order for moral success to be secured, what is within the individual must be contiguous with outward actions carried out in a materially scarce, hostile and competitive world.

David was not an individual. He was a member of an agonistic culture in which games of opposition were continuously, relentlessly played. His response to a threat to his honour can be understood according to the rules of his culture. Yet he was also a man after God's own heart. David acted reflectively when called on to consider the social constraints others set before him. He was transformed, as a mere member, by inviting Yahweh into the social games of opposition he could not avoid. Often, David played them with spiritual maturity.

THE PSALMS OF OPPOSITION

In what I call the Psalms of opposition, we sense David's struggle to find and follow God's heart. I assume David wrote or inspired these particular Psalms,[16] which reveal either his or his culture's understanding of the personal world of those who suffer opposition. My interest in gathering thirty Psalms of opposition is the evidence they provide of David's struggles with other people that still apply to us. I chose these Psalms to reveal the range of hope and frustration, failure and success the poet experienced as he put his faith in God.

A pattern forms in those who understand yet transcend cultural scripts in order to follow God's heart. To lay out the pattern, I make use of Walter Brueggemann's organization of the Psalms.[17] At no point does he refer to opposition the way I do, but he is helpful to the project because he marries text criticism and pastoral, devotional insight. Along with him, I intend the organizing principle of Psalms of opposition to open a small window on spiritual experience "to help us see things we might not have seen otherwise."[18] Believers examine these poems, an anatomy of a desperate soul, because they reveal life as we experience it ourselves; they speak about social power and how it goes wrong in human society. They teach us to rely on the governance of God as we learn to govern our own hearts.

The Psalms of opposition are songs of lament. They cry for help and express complaint. The Psalmist calls out to the Lord because he is disoriented by the troubles of opposition that press him personally. These are not Psalms that name and abhor Israel's enemies or disdain the enemies of Yahweh. In these songs, the Psalmist longs to escape or repay a human enemy. He shouts to Yahweh who is typified as his source of his rest and refuge. Yahweh listens attentively. The Psalmist does not imagine God's absence, but God has not shown up as yet.

Overall the Psalms convey that the relationship between Yahweh and author is not in question—although Yahweh may not have fulfilled the Psalmist's request. The nature of help the Psalmist longs for is one of the central issues in Psalms of opposition. Outlining a range of poetic requests points out some ways in which the Psalmist grows up. We lose out emotionally if these Psalms are not used in worship. They provide a way of naming the patterns and hot points of suffering. We could understand much more about the human condition if we were familiar with them. Our own suffering is relieved when we realize how opposition operates and when we read complaints that God attentively listens to, from the heart of one who is deeply hurt.

In Psalms of opposition Yahweh is perceived as one who can act to ameliorate the harm suffered when honour is lost or threatened. The Psalmist chooses to seek heavenly help for earthly battles. He pleads to the Lord: *Vindicate me. Rescue me. Let me hide my self in You. Be my refuge, my strength and my rock. Hear me. Have mercy.* Whatever difficulties the Psalmist has with Yahweh, the presence of the Lord is background to a foreground of trauma that compels the poet to rely on God. The Lord's presence is not in question, even if the Lord's apparent inaction is confusing or frustrating to the suffering Psalmist.

The Psalms of opposition are personal. In these Psalms, the poet has an enemy he hates or fears. They record the common human response of fight or flight in the face of adversity. In Psalm 54 the poet says that strangers are attacking him. Psalm 109 rages against someone who returned friendship by attacking the poet with lies and hatred, without cause. He reflects on this friend who has become an enemy: the chilling dismemberment from community, family and the future conveys anger he does not hide from God— violent feelings are vented before the Lord. In Psalm 140, passion drives him to want "the heads of those who surround me [to] be covered with the trouble their own lips have caused. Let burning coals fall upon them; may they be thrown into the fire, into miry pits, never to rise." The Psalm implores Yahweh to rectify his loss of honour and address the threat to his person. In Psalms 35 and 109, deep rage is expressed without restraint. There is no hint that his intensity is inappropriate or that Yahweh might reject his fierce desires. Yet, while rage is expressed, it is also submitted to Yahweh and relinquished to him so that the speaker is moved to practice the freedom of putting faith in the Lord. Further, the community is saved from a bloodletting that can never be satiated.[19] The Psalmist pours out his heart to Yahweh instead of visiting violence on his enemy. Vetting violent feelings before God is a practice of freedom.

In Psalm 55, on the other hand, the Psalmist is afraid of one who was a friend. He is beset by fear and trembling. He can think only of flight: "Oh, that I had the wings of a dove! I would fly away and be at rest—I would flee far away and stay in the desert; I would hurry to my place of shelter, far from the tempest and the storm." At times the Psalm expresses anguish more than rage. The Psalmist laments: "If an enemy were insulting me, I could endure it; if a foe were rising against me, I could hide. But it is you, one like myself, my companion, my close friend, with whom I enjoyed sweet fellowship as we walked with the throng at the house of God." The desire to flee or fight is sometimes triggered when he is innocent, sometimes when he recognizes he is guilty, and at other times when, as in Psalm

69, he cries out that he is forced to restore what he did not steal. The Psalms of opposition track a pattern in which suffering is not neatly measured on the basis of what he justly deserves due to what he has done. Our freedom begins when we realize that there is no measure for measure: we do not suffer in neat mathematical calculations based on what we do or do not deserve. This recognition grounds the practice of freedom.

Shame is a perpetual trouble in Psalms of opposition. Sometimes the Psalmist wishes that God would put to shame all those who seek his life, as in Psalm 40. In some poems, he begs God not to let others be put to shame because of the way he is publicly treated. In Psalm 69 he cries out for the sake of the community and says: "May those who hope in you not be disgraced because of me....For I endure scorn for your sake, and shame covers my face....people make sport of me." But he also realizes in Psalm 62 that his salvation and honour depend on God. Learning to notice the patterns and effects of shame, on us and other people—including their reactions to us, provides relief from the shame that inevitably sticks to us when games of opposition produce personal harm. Gaining sufficient distance from our own shame is a practice of freedom. Seeing how shame affects people in general and drives them to do the evil things they do, is one outcome of courageously facing our own shame.

The poet senses the effects of opposition in his body and feels deeply threatened. In Psalm 69 he laments: "the waters have come up to my neck. I sink in the miry depths, where there is no foothold. I have come into the deep waters; the floods engulf me. I am worn out calling for help; my throat is parched. My eyes fail looking for my God. Those who hate me without reason outnumber the hairs on my head." Acknowledging our terror before God so as to weigh its effects on the way we treat other people is a practice of freedom.

Psalm 143 conveys the desperation of being pursued by enemies that crush the Psalmist to the ground and make him dwell in darkness so that his spirit grows faint and his heart is dismayed. Psalm 142 points out: "Look to my right and see; no-one is concerned for me. I have no refuge; no-one cares for my life." In Psalm 56, he pleads with God: "Record my lament; list my tears on your scroll—are they not in your record?" In Psalm 57 he is terrified: "I am in the midst of lions; I lie among ravenous beasts—people whose teeth are spears and arrows, whose tongues are sharp swords." Accepting that God values us despite the way others treat us is a practice of freedom. He knows he is not worthless to God. Psalm 56 affirms his faith: "In God, whose word I praise...in God I trust; I will not be afraid. What can human beings do to me?" In Psalm 37 the poet understands that resting in God enables him to resist the sins that beset the games of opposition. He advises himself and others: "do not fret because of those who do evil. Do not fret—it only leads to evil. The insight that God limits the danger others create for us relieves the pressure of opposition. Learning to curb the tendency to fret is a practice of freedom.

The nature of one's enemies is a striking feature of these Psalms. Enemies may be emotionally distant or may be friends, emotionally close or next of kin. The Psalmist laments because strangers are attacking him (Psalm 54) and friends or those he cared for like family are betraying him (Psalms 35, 41, 55). Psalm 64 describes enemies who practice evil. The wicked are noisy conspirators. They shoot their words like deadly arrows from ambush. They are cunning and devise plans to hurt, trap and betray. Their evil is intentional, planned in advance. In Psalm 140 the wicked are violent. It is their tongues that do evil. They plot against the Psalmist, planning to set a net to catch him in. David frequently perceived that the wicked set traps for him. Those who do evil believe Yahweh will not see what they are doing nor hold them accountable. Foolishly, they set traps without fear of being caught. The Psalmist comes to see that those who do evil eventually fall into the traps they have set for others. Taking a long view on the problem of evil is a practice of freedom. When we let go of our understandable desire for revenge and allow God to repay, we practise freedom.

The notion of traps being set, of plots being planned, of danger on every side and behind one's back, is pervasive through the Psalms of opposition. The twentieth century taught us to call these claims paranoia. If we applied the psychopathology of everyday life to David, we would see him as a paranoid individual and turn up our noses, or turn our backs, on his perception of the threatening games going on around him. In doing so, we miss the point of suffering that characterizes opposition. To be blunt, if we have the flu, we vomit. We do not choose to disgorge our inards; it is part of being ill. The Psalms of opposition purge the suffering soul. The suffering associated with the problem of opposition does not produce what we call paranoia. We attach a paranoid label to sufferers because we do not sense the social role that fear, shame and loss are playing in these games. The fears the poet names are inevitable in opposition: they are personal and pervasive but not paranoid. They accurately represent the real dangers faced and felt by all who suffer from the problem of opposition.

Uniquely and wisely, the Psalmist invites Yahweh to calm these fears and provide shelter. The Psalmist seeks rest in God alone. God is his refuge and his strength, a very present help in times of trouble. In handing fear over to Yahweh, the Psalmist eases the tension of opposition and transforms frightening games into problems to solve with God's help. In handing his fear over to God, he acknowledges its power over him and his incapacity to ease it in his own strength. Resting in God is not a substitute for taking action in the world; it is the preamble to doing so. Treating fear, shame and loss with compassion (even our own) constitutes the daily practise of freedom.

Opposition that produces suffering is eminently personal: it is directed against honour and reputation, as well as against the body. An attack that generates fear may be carried out privately or publicly, yet the one who is targeted understands and feels its full intent. Its effectiveness is to isolate; being personal is its potency. It took David a long time to convince Jonathan that Saul was trying to kill him, though Saul carried out acts of aggression in full view. If we do not comprehend the pattern of personal suffering, we will not see the inevitable role that fear, shame and loss play and we fail to sense their effects on the human condition. We will refuse hospitality to those in our community who are weakened by them, but not crazy. Without recognition from the social world, the pattern of existential suffering due to the problem of opposition, is seldom identified for what it is. Its pattern goes unrecognized. Without frameworks to organize experience we cannot learn from it. Jesus is our perfect model for practices of freedom and the problem of opposition.

301

JESUS AND OPPOSITION

It is because he was innocent that Jesus reveals the games of opposition so clearly. At times during his ministry he echoed phrases from Psalms of opposition: *My God, my God. Why have you forsaken me?* Jesus' ministry is an art of opposition. He was pitted against the religious rulers of his era due to emphases he chose to place on the life of faith. The connections with the Old Testament are unmistakeable. Once again people, especially the religious elite, failed to accept God as their king. "Shall I crucify your king?" Pilate asked them. "We have no king but Caesar," the chief priests answered." (John 19.15) God's leadership in a life of faith is its fundamental characteristic; God allows no equals in the contest for our hearts. Our love is to be for God and God alone. The difficulty people had in the New Testament was one of recognition. Many could not recognize Jesus as the Messiah. Of course many others did. The inability to acknowledge Messiah is partly due to the social context of agonistic culture that made recognizing him so hard. It was too difficult to separate cultural expectations of honour and shame from the manner of God's loving ways. People chose religious culture over God, even though Jesus consistently referred to his own actions in the light of the Old Testament witnesses to the way God acts in the world.

While Jesus made it clear that he came to fulfil the Law, he opposed the culture of honour and shame. He spoke to women and acknowledged them as friends. He honoured children and described entrance to the kingdom of God as a path to be travelled by those who were willing to be God's children. He honoured a younger son in preference to an elder son, because the younger actually carried out the will of God (even though he first shamed his earthly father by refusing to do what he asked of him). He ate with tax collectors and sinners. He conversed with Samaritans—and was even alone at a well talking with one of their women. He reminded Jews that the Old Testament gifts of God's grace, healing for the sick and food for the hungry, were given to folk outside the Hebrew fold. In reaction to Jesus' inclusiveness, those who initially "spoke well of him and were amazed at the gracious words that came from his lips," (before he reminded them that God fed the widow of Zarepath and healed Naaman the Syrian) turned adoration to fury. They admired him one moment and tried to kill him the next. (Luke 4. 14-30) Jesus did not fit their expectations for the Messiah. Even John the Baptist came to wonder if Jesus was the One sent by God. When Jesus eventually spoke of his body and blood as food for the faithful, many fell away from his teaching. His disciples remained. Peter confessed that they had nowhere else to go; only Jesus had the words of life—he was the One sent by God.

Jesus' identity is the central struggle in the problem of opposition that played out over the three years of his earthly ministry. What is amazing is the persistence of his efforts to persuade those who doubted that he was who he claimed to be, while maintaining his intellect and integrity. Jesus performed miracles to feed the hungry, cured the lame, gave sight to the blind, raised the dead. He made brilliant arguments to counter sceptical minds. He told stories to hold in memory—slow release capsules of truth and insight. His passion erupted in drastic acts: he overturned profiteering in the Temple to uncover schemes that kept the oppressed from worshipping God freely. Jesus renamed the religious order: My father's House is a house of prayer and you have made it a den of thieves. He did not stop trying to convey his identity, never cheapening himself in the attempt.

While the pattern in John's gospel is different, all four gospels recount the complexities of opposition that Jesus faced. In addition to his miracles, stories and actions, locating several events will outline tension between Jesus' identity claims and the difficulty of his generation to recognize him. In the first three gospels the pattern is as follows after he is initially introduced:

- Peter's confession that Jesus is the Messiah
- Transfiguration (a supernatural testimony to Jesus' identity)
- Triumphal entry into Jerusalem (affirming Jesus as the One sent from God)
- His arrest (a betrayal and apparent victory of opposing forces)

303

- His dying and rising again to unveil the liberation offered to all who are crushed by a broken relationship with God

Unlike the pattern in the other three, from beginning to end, John's gospel is the sustained and systematic articulation of Jesus' identity as Son of God and records reactions from the social world sparked by his claims about himself.[20]

One of the most striking features of Jesus' view of opposition in contrast with David's is the role assigned to Satan. For David, enemies are other people. They may be strangers, friends or family members. The contest is over losing or gaining social honour: someone wins, someone loses. David wanted to win. But he came to value following the heart of God over success in the social world. Instead of carrying out actions against enemies in an agonistic culture, he listened to Abigail, who later became his wife. In response to Nathan's narrative, he humbly sought forgiveness for failing to remember that even the king must follow God's laws. He loved Absalom his son more than he valued defeating the rebellious attack Absalom led against him. He had to be reminded of his role as king though his heart moved him to isolate himself in lament over Absalom's death. Through the practices of freedom, David learned to address human enemies. Wars against enemies were won or lost in the ordinary material, everyday world. Wins and losses brought visible consequences.

Jesus announced a spiritual role in the problem of opposition played by Satan. The devil was not new to the Hebrew mind; people seemed to know what he was talking about, but the emphasis redesigns our relationship to other people. Matthew, Mark and Luke record Jesus' temptation in the wilderness. Satan visited him and tried to dissuade Jesus from the plan he choose to follow. The issue is whether he would follow the plan or be enslaved by Satan's purposes. Jesus resisted. The devil left him for a time. In this context, Satan is one who is interested in gaining converts to his own purposes, which are opposed to the Word and ways of God. John's gospel does not refer to the wilderness experience but introduces the role of Satan in opposition Jesus encountered from religious authorities.

In John 8:44, Jesus described those who follow God and those who follow Satan and includes religious leaders who opposed him in the latter category. He described the devil and his ways. The devil is a murderer and liar—the father of lies. In him there is no truth. Jesus is pointing out that the conspiracy to kill him were clear indications of their heritage. The devil is identified as the one who tempts Judas to betray Jesus—that is, to hand Jesus over to suffering.

It is as if John reached back into the book of Job and opened the curtains of heaven to uncover a source of human suffering in Satan's plot to put the faithful to the test. Job suffered not because he failed God, but because of Satan's challenge; he suffered, not because he was inadequate at following God, but because he was so good at it. But even his goodness needed God's touch. The consequence of his suffering is a new and vital vision of God.

In Luke 8:12, Satan is credited with removing seed sown in the hearts of people who hear the message about the kingdom but do not understand it. In Luke 10: 18, he is depicted as falling from heaven like a flash of lightning after the disciples have success in ministering the gospel. Satan is described as having his own kingdom in Luke 11: 18 and as binding in suffering the woman who had been hemorrhaging for eighteen years, Luke 13:16. In Matthew 13: 39, he is credited with sowing weeds in a wheat field. Satan is an enemy in God's kingdom and actively seeks its demise. In Mark 8:33, Jesus identified the devil's influence when Peter tried to turn Jesus aside from the plan he had set for himself, under God. Satan aims to set our minds on human rather than divine things. Later, Jesus told Simon Peter that Satan had asked to sift them all like wheat, but assured Simon that he had already prayed for their recovery.

Satan's role in the problem of opposition is complex. In letters that follow the gospels, Satan's role is elaborated more fully. The devil is a player in games of opposition. While clearly not equal to God, Satan is not to be treated lightly. Evil is no illusion. Yet James 4:7-8 is practical and clear: "Submit yourselves therefore to God. Resist the devil, and he will flee from you. Come near to God and he will come near to you." Spiritual intelligence and the practices of freedom require us to become discerning and courageous about evil and Satan's role in mis-directing the faithful. The most liberating aspect of Satan's role in tempting people is that our enemies are no longer human: other people are not the enemy. We do betray each other and hand others over to suffering, as Judas did to Jesus. But we can be redeemed. We must calculate the devil's damage in our account of how and why others have wronged us and be cautious about making (even apparently good) plans that are not first laid before God.

OPPOSITION AND A MIDDLE GROUND

The problem of opposition can confound our faith and constrain its development, or it can instigate the process of growing us that is central to Christian faith. Empathy is a middle path between the extremes we often go to when we are caught up in opposition. The greatest opportunity, when spiritual intelligence is pitted against the problem of opposition, is the growth of empathy. It is a difference that makes all the difference. Opposition tempts us to hide ourselves in arrogance and pride. Spiritual pride is essentially a failure of empathy. Success at games of opposition may lead to the accumulation of social privilege in the form of wealth and honour. This imbalance can seduce us into inflating individual, family, racial or national value at the expense of other people. In the Christian life, money itself is not our main temptation, although materialism is seductive. Failing in empathy breeds arrogance and hardens the heart. On the other hand, success in the problem of opposition can lead to confidence and trust in God as well as faithfulness to the plans we set for ourselves under God's direction, as it did for David and Jesus. The aim of faith education is to live a life of integrity. The growth of empathy is its central feature. A wealth of respect or material resources may come to us, or may not. We cannot live on money alone. Spiritual pride and empathy cannot grow together in the same human heart. They are mutually exclusive. If we allow pride to flourish we will not see the need for empathy. In order to remain faithful, we need God's empathetic understanding of the human condition. God empathizes with us.

The Psalms of opposition show us that God listens to our complaints, without complaining. Those who keep silent do not enjoy intimacy with God. David revealed himself to God. He came clean and gained victory over fear and hatred, at least some of the time. The same offer of intimacy was extended to Cain but he did not entrust his anger to God's safe keeping. In the Kingdom, anger is not wrong in itself; anger is often named as an attribute of God. *In your anger do not sin.* But we are diminished when anger overwhelms our capacity to empathize with an enemy so that our action breaks out in revenge. Empathy gives us time to allow our fear of other people to relax. It is only Satan—evil itself because it is irrational, that we should fear.

The wisdom of the inner monk prevails. This is the move that Jesus introduces into the problem of opposition. Satan tempts us to hate and fear each other. Jesus came to break down the dividing walls and make us into one new humanity. The practices of freedom have at their core a developing capacity to let fear and hatred flow into the safe keeping of the Almighty and remain there despite our suffering. Maturity is made good by practising freedom. Maturity flourishes through learning to make the problem of opposition a site for learning to be mature followers of Jesus.

In the next chapter, I unpack the concept of empathy in order to position its value in the life of faith.

9

THE PROBLEM
OF EMPATHY

I will sprinkle clean water on you, and you will be
clean; I will cleanse you of all impurities and from all
your idols. I will give you a new heart and put a new
spirit in you; I will remove your heart of stone
and give you a heart of flesh (Ezekiel 36:25-26).

For out of the overflow of the heart the
mouth speaks (Matthew 12:34b).

THE FRUIT OF FAITH EDUCATION

The fruit of faith education is empathy because it is the outcome of the wise practice of freedom. The fruit of the Spirit is love, joy, peace, patience, kindness, goodness, faithfulness, gentleness and self-control (Galatians 5:22) and flows through life experiences as we learn self and other regard. Kindness to ourselves is as essential to empathy as is kindness to others. There is a relationship between the condition of our hearts and the capacity for empathy; faith education aims to strengthen that relationship. It is through empathy, as it is understood and practised, that those who love God more than any other love grow up to live faithfully. The four aims of faith education, to comprehend what it means to be

309

human, to practise faith through self-observation, to reflect on our God concepts and to become personal members of a faith tradition, take their unity and motivation from empathy. Empathy integrates these aims by showing us how to make sense of life and ourselves. Empathy is the outcome of the spiritual work of faith.

This chapter situates empathy in the context of opposition, the problem addressed in the previous chapter. Empathy comes into play as a way of responding to opposition. Opposition is characterized by anxiety, which flares up when other people or circumstances appear to threaten our personal happiness. When anxiety rises within us, an empathetic response to that feeling of panic calms us down and helps us perceive and interpret what is going on—both in our own hearts and in the life experience of someone else. Empathy permits two parties to discover and name truthfully what is going on.

Empathy is grounded on telling the truth. The kindness of empathy is expressed by compassionately telling the truth. Telling the truth makes us anxious because truth seldom lives up to ideals we create of a good Christian—those imaginary people who manage to move from birth to death without ever doing anything wrong. The ideals of the faith are offered to inspire not stultify us. We are meant to take what we are and what we are not and allow God to cleanse our consciences so that we are free of the grip of guilt. Scripture is less anxious than we are about the real conditions of human living and tells the truth about people, even though biblical standards are high.

While scripture tells the truth about people, honesty never degenerates into ridicule or abuse. In 1Corin. 6:9ff we read: *Do you not know that the wicked will not inherit the kingdom of God? Do not be deceived: Neither the sexually immoral nor idolaters nor adulterers nor male prostitutes nor homosexual offenders nor thieves nor the greedy nor drunkards nor slanderers nor swindlers will inherit the kingdom of God. And that is what some of you were. But you were washed, you were sanctified, you were justified in the name of the Lord Jesus Christ and by the Spirit of God.*

And in Hebrews 10: 19-23 we read: *Therefore, brothers and sisters, since we have confidence to enter the Most Holy Place by the blood of Jesus, by a new and living way opened up for us through the curtain, that is, his body, and since we have a great high priest over the house of God, let us draw near to God with a sincere heart in full assurance of faith, having our hearts sprinkled to cleanse us from a guilty conscience and having our bodies washed with pure water. Let us hold unswervingly to the hope we profess, for he who promised is faithful.* Empathy plays a foundational role in the possibility of being renewed spiritually. Empathy allows us to come near to God. My purpose is to clarify the relationship between empathy and renewal by addressing the issues of anxiety and guilt.

EMPATHY AND ANXIETY

Empathy is one of the primary spiritual, intellectual and practical virtues. It may very well be the least understood and the most ineffectively practiced. I suggest that if we could be empathetic, we would be different people: our relationship with God, ourselves and other people would improve. Christians have a unique opportunity to learn empathy. Christ came as God/Man. In the Incarnation we have the only complete model for empathy since it is full participation in two worlds of experience at the same time. Christians believe that Jesus is both God and human, one who came to show us what God is like and to show us what we can be like if we let God shepherd our anxiety and speak to our sin.

There is a relationship between human anxiety, sin and the failure to empathize. Ted Peters in a book titled, *Sin: Radical Evil in Soul and Society* asserts that human anxiety is at the core of our tendency to sin. To him, anxiety itself is not sin but it readies us for sin. This point is very close to the Niptic tradition's insistence that temptation and sin are not synonymous. In fact, anxiety is inevitable in human experience. If we refuse to give anxiety over to God, we shift into sinfulness as a way to try to calm down. Of course, sinning does not help quiet our souls. Things only get worse. To Peters, the core problem of sin is spiritual pride but the fault in pride is found not in selfishness, as we have been told throughout modernity; pride is most clearly characterized by the absence of empathy.

311

In pride, and without empathy, we disdain others—those who are foreign are dismissed from the Table. We focus on our own pretended goodness (which rightly belongs to God alone) until we feel justified in being cruel to others and free to harm them spiritually, intellectually, emotionally and physically. The good news is that God came among us to ease our anxiety and forgive our sin. One of the ways we realize and practice God's goodness occurs when we learn to be empathetic and allow our anxiety to relax into compassion. Empathy is a sign of our readiness to be effective witnesses of God's Grace.

When empathy is engaged, everything changes. Empathy is an act of perceiving and an art of imagining that relies on self-understanding. When I exercise empathy, I convey compassion in two directions—toward myself and toward the other. I attend to my own inner state, listening kindly to my own thoughts, feelings, needs and desires. I practise the art of the inner monk by guarding my heart. When I speak, out of the depth of my own heart, I ask the other person questions that help both of us articulate the inner state of that other person. Empathy is proactive and relies on a developing capacity to realize what other people are going through.

Empathy occurs in a given moment. It does not concern itself with judging whether an incident is in the past or present of another person's experience. Whatever it is, if it is alive for them, it is because it is remains in the present for them—their feelings about the incident are current. To be empathetic is to realize that anxiety does not distinguish between past, present and future. Feelings are either resolved or unresolved. A person is either anxious or at rest.

An empathetic person recognizes anxiety in another person, even though anxiety wears many disguises, such as arrogance, indifference, busyness or lust. Empathy offers to listen to the inner state of the other person by sensing what is presented by another and also *what is behind* what is presented as someone else's experience. In sensing what lies behind the presentation of self in ordinary life, empathy uses intuition, imagination and its own experience. But empathy is always attending to experience that is not its own; i.e., empathy attends to foreign experience.

312

THE PROBLEM OF EMPATHY

Suppose I see a friend who looks sad. He tells me his brother died. I become aware of his pain. What kind of awareness is it that I have of my friend? My brother has not died. I am not in pain. That is, nothing is happening to me to produce pain. But as I look at my friend's face, which is pale and disturbed, and listen to his voice, which is toneless and strained, I am in pain of a particular kind. My pain comes as I gaze at my friend's face. If I do not turn away from my friend, my pain continues. Anxiety is both painful and contagious. My pain does not come from outside me (from something that has happened *to me)* and yet it does: it comes from gazing at a friend's face and from a sense of what it might mean to have a brother die. Empathy is in the gaze. It is not yet knowledge, since gazing at my friend's face will not yet let me know what the death of his brother means to him. As I gaze (without staring) empathy asks questions or poses possibilities that my friend is free to accept as true or to reject as failing to describe his experience.

Empathy gazes at someone's experience but does not stare. Empathy is not rude. It is not an intruder. Its aim is to relieve anxiety not to intensify it. The aim of empathy is to establish a meaning for the inner state of the other person. In addition, the empathetic person may also try to convey his or her feeling state eventually in order to expand the self-understanding that unfolds during the encounter—if both people listen and hear what is going on. For instance, Marshall Rosenberg[1] tells a story that happened to him when another man got into a taxi with him. Rosenberg is Jewish.

After the man was settled, a message came over the cab's loudspeaker to ask the driver to pick up someone with a Jewish sounding name at a local synagogue. The man sitting in the back seat with Rosenberg said: "These k..... get up early in the morning so they can screw everybody out of their money."[2] Rosenberg felt enraged. He sat quietly, mulling over the extent of his fury. Then he followed his own first principle for empathy: stay conscious of the violent thoughts that arise in your mind without judging them: use empathy on yourself. First, gaze at your own heart. A few minutes passed as he pondered his feelings and then he began a non-violent conversation with the gentleman that eventually enabled him to convey his initial feelings, without anger, and only after helping the other man identify feelings that lay behind his comment on Jewish people. So what is empathy?

DEFINING EMPATHY

As a concept, empathy is ambiguous; it has more than one meaning. But the concept also divides into two camps or perspectives that are important to understand. My aim is to sort through its ambiguity to offer a working hypothesis for the term. To begin, empathy is often thought of as having one of the following meanings:

- The power of projecting one's personality into (and thereby fully comprehending) an object of contemplation.[3]
- The power of identifying oneself mentally with (and thereby fully comprehending) a person or an object of contemplation.[4]
- An act in which I 'feel with' another person. I do not 'put myself in the other's shoes.' I do not say, 'How would I feel if this happened to me'? I set aside my temptation to analyze and to plan. I do not project; I receive the other into myself, and I see and feel with the other. This sort of empathy does not first penetrate the other but receives the other....I receive, communicate with, I work with the other. Feeling is not all that is involved, but it is essentially involved.[5]
- The capacity to conceptualize the impact—on ourselves and on other people—of what we do and to feel appropriate and genuine sorrow and regret without thinking of ourselves as irredeemably bad. Empathy gives us the necessary mental and emotional climate to guide our behavior in a moral and self-enhancing manner without being harsh and mean-spirited to ourselves or to other people.[6]
- An act in which foreign experience is grasped; in which we sense what is presented, and what is behind what is presented as someone else's experience.[7]
- A response when someone attacks or criticizes you, in which you can be *sad* (flee, hide, avoid) or you can be *mad* (fight, protect yourself from criticism, re-establish your ground) or you can be

glad (empathize, ask questions until you understand, attend to what the other person is trying to say).[8]

• Knowing and being able to express what someone else is going through.[9]

According to these definitions, empathy between two people is defined as an act, a feeling, a response, a capacity or as power. In gathering up threads to use as a working hypothesis for the term, we might say that empathy is an insightful act focused on feeling, in which complete attention is paid to another person's experience in a way that allows the other to realize that the one who empathizes understands the essential quality of that experience. Empathy is a safe haven for the experience of another person and releases other people (and ourselves) from feeling alone and strange.

There are several types of empathy. For example, there is aesthetic empathy in which we approach a text or object of art and try to make sense of its meaning. As one example, how did you read the scripture text from 1 Corinthians 6, verses 9 and following? Aesthetic or literate empathy attempts to get at the meaning of a text. What questions came to you as you read the list of those who will not inherit the kingdom of God? In aesthetic empathy, we attend to the text and realize there is more to its meaning than the words on the page. Secondly, there is relational empathy, which is a cognitive, affective and *potentially* sympathetic encounter with foreign experience, i.e., the experience of another person.

Thirdly, there is ethical empathy, which is the ability to visualize the consequences, good and bad, of our behavior. It is the capacity to conceptualize the impact—on ourselves and other people—of what we do and to feel appropriate and genuine sorrow and regret without thinking of ourselves as irredeemably bad. Empathy gives us the necessary mental and emotional climate to guide our behavior in a moral and self-enhancing manner without being harsh and mean-spirited to ourselves or others.

Fourthly, we can add spiritual empathy, which, from Christian perspectives, enables us to relate to God who is intimately made known to us historically and biblically in Jesus Christ, through the power of the Holy Spirit. God exercises empathy. In empathy, a believer grasps the love, hope and commands of God. In response, God grasps the believer's life empathetically. Unlike us, as the possessor of complete knowledge, God is not mistaken about us, while we are often mistaken about each other's experiences.[10]

In all types of empathy there is an affective as well as a cognitive aspect. One of the difficult issues is to distinguish feeling from thinking and also show how they work together. In all types of empathy we face what is foreign. In considering the nature of empathy, I focus on relational empathy and use that discussion to understand spiritual empathy. The fundamental problem in trying to be relationally empathetic is to perceive foreign subjects (other people) and their experiences (as well as ways they experience us). Empathy raises a question: what is essential to an act of perceiving what is foreign if we want to be empathetic? If empathy involves an imaginative act—we imagine the other person's experience to some extent—what keeps empathy truthful? What is the relationship between perception, imagination and truth-telling if the experience of another person is foreign? By foreign, I simply mean experience that is not ours because it is not happening directly to us.

Relational empathy has to do with the implied assumption that foreign subjects (other people) and their experiences are given to us in a certain way and we can understand them eventhough their experience is not ours. Questions about empathy hinge on whether and to what extent we can enter into or come along side other people's experience in a way they recognize and acknowledge as getting it right. Empathetic people seem to be able to enter into or come along side experience that is foreign and narrate that experience in a way that the other person sees as accurate. I will describe relational empathy as fully as possible and mark out the boundaries around the essence of empathy as well as what I call full empathetic participation (i.e., empathy plus sympathy), which is also a model for spiritual empathy.

Two Camps

In the general discussion of empathy there are two verbs that predominate when people try to explain how empathy works. The first verb defines empathy in terms of *projecting* oneself or one's personality into someone else's experience. As an example, this is how it is defined in the Oxford English Dictionary: Empathy is the power of projecting one's personality into (and thereby fully comprehending) an object of contemplation. The second verb defines empathy in terms of *receiving* another person's experience and tends to emphasize that full comprehension of the other is very difficult. For example, empathy is an act in which I 'feel with' another person. I do not 'put myself in the other's shoes.' I do not say, How would I feel if this happened to me? I set aside my temptation to analyze and plan. I do not project; I receive the other into myself. I see and feel with the other. The sort of empathy we are discussing does not first penetrate the other but receives the other. I receive, communicate with, I work with the other. In this second view of empathy, feeling is not all that is involved, but it is essentially involved. Receptivity is often expressly contrasted with projection. As an example, I do not project in the empathetic relation, I receive the other into myself, and I see and feel with the other. From the perspective of receptivity, projecting is a mistaken way of talking about empathy.

I suggest we engage the verbs from each camp to describe empathy fully but that we acknowledge a harmful aspect in both ways of speaking. If I consider empathy to be about *projecting* my experience into someone else's experience, I must realize that those who describe empathy as receptivity hear the language of projection in terms of invasion or intrusion into their space. If we make use of *projecting* to describe empathy we must come to see that, from this perspective at least, *projecting* is an act of valuing that can be understood as an act of caring for another person. That is, I enter the experience of those I value and love; entering is intended to convey their value to me. Those who think of empathy in terms of projecting must stop short of invading, i.e., an aggressive, unlawful, illegitimate or forceful entry. Our projections may be misguided. Those who use the metaphor of projection need to realize how this way of speaking affects others

317

who cannot be comfortable using it as a model for empathy. People have to be free to refuse our attempts to project ourselves into their experience.

Those who use the language of receptivity have a difficulty of similar proportions. They typically use synonyms for empathy that imply 'coming along side' another rather than entering. This group rejects the idea of 'getting inside' as a metaphor for empathy and uses language that conveys 'getting with' rather than 'getting in' someone else's experience. From this perspective, receptivity or *receiving* is perceived as an act of caring that conveys the value of the other person. The empathetic person is engrossed with the other as a way of giving full attention to an experience that is being shared but is not assumed to be the same as the empathetic person's own experience. That is, I come alongside others and attend fully to the experience that is being conveyed. My complete and sustained attention is meant to convey their significance and credibility to me. But, just as with projecting, receiving may be thought of as having a dangerous tendency—in this case the tendency to trap the other in attentiveness by paying too much or too close attention to them. Empathy on the model of receiving must stop short of entrapment, i.e., the aggressive holding on to someone who wants to be released from my gaze. Those who use the metaphor of receptivity must become aware of how this way of speaking affects those who are not comfortable using it as a model for the empathetic act. People have to be able to escape our attentive gaze, if they wish to do so.

In summary, empathy refers to acts in which foreign experience is grasped. In being empathetic, we sense what is presented and what is behind what is presented as someone else's experience. Suppose I wish to be empathetic to the friend referred to earlier, the one whose brother has just died. I offer him my non-anxious presence and attend to his experience of loss. He needs a look from me that is not a stare, that is not intrusive. He needs my time. He needs me to suspend my judgments about what he is experiencing and to wait quietly until he is able to let me know what is happening within him, if he wishes to do so. He may need to hear my questions but may not need to hear my prescriptions. But I still must ask whether or not I will be able to understand his experience?

318

When we try to understand how empathy works, an assumption gets in our way. It is this: *What we know is really only what happens to us personally.* Further, we believe all knowledge is situated. What happens to someone else is outside of our experience. Suppose we see someone hit by a car. We feel *something*, but not a car hitting our own bodies. We do not sense how the event fits into the injured person's life history. We do not know what that other person is experiencing. How can we be empathetic? What does it mean to be empathetic? In short, what does another person need to sense in us to enable that person to believe we are empathetic? Empathy is not an activity that we accomplish singly. An empathetic act takes place between at least two people and is effective only if both parties want to remain engaged with each other. How do we learn empathy? More precisely, what does every human being already know that can be used as a foundation for learning to exercise empathy effectively? Before we can focus on the groundwork for building successful empathetic encounters we must address limitations within our own experience. We need to sense how personal experience can fly in the face of any attempt at empathy.

Empathy and Guilt

Empathy allows us to re-frame experience. Rosenberg describes the effects of empathy and says that when someone really hears us without passing judgment, when someone listens without trying to take responsibility for us, without trying to alter or mould us, then elements of our experience that seemed insoluble become soluble and confusions become clear.[11] Effects of empathy can be immediate and are always deep. It is healing. But the freedom to be a haven for other people depends upon the condition of our own hearts. Unresolved guilt forecloses on empathy. Empathy has a strong connection to guilt.

Empathy is not simply hearing another person's experience; it is not focused on our assumptions about that experience. Empathy requires us to do two things simultaneously: to be present to the other and to be aware of ourselves without getting trapped there. Let me spell this out. Empathy requires us to be with two worlds of

319

experience simultaneously—our model is the incarnation of Christ. We are able to be with two worlds because attending to our own heart is not the same as being trapped there. How might our hearts trap us? What is, and is not, empathy?

Empathy is not association, imitation, memory or mere fancy[12] (even though I say it is an act of imagining—imagining must be truthful to be empathetic). The primary reason empathy differs from all these other perceptions is that, in empathy, there is no continuity between the life experiences of one who is empathetic and the one whose experience is the object of empathetic attentiveness. It is difficult to tell the truth about experiences that are not our own.

Take for example, memory. Empathy is different from memory because memory reflects back on something that happened to me at one time in my past. Suppose I recall an embarrassing event, such as the time I was dancing with my husband and suddenly fell down on the dance floor in the middle of the dance. My friends saw me fall. Now I remember the event and think it is funny. I remember it completely. I recall the feeling of hitting the hard dance floor. I feel no pain but recall the shock of finding myself on the floor without knowing how I got there. I remember the event, the surprised looks on the faces of those around, words of concern they expressed, but as I write this, I'm laughing. My experience of remembering the event is not the same as the event itself. Memory is different than direct experience. At the time, I did not laugh, nor did I think it was funny—I was too stunned.

If I see someone else fall on a dance floor, I may have some idea of what is going on, or I may be entirely wrong. Suppose I see a woman fall who has a cruel partner. Suppose she has a weak back. Suppose she fell at another dance and something disastrous followed that fall. If I am empathetic I set aside my own experience and try to discover what the event means to her. Unlike empathy, in association, imitation, memory or fancy I am using my own actual experience as a guide for understanding and interpreting what is going on. In empathy, I do not have access to another person's past, present or future and cannot adequately situate her fall in the flow of a foreign life story. Empathy attends to the narrative someone tells about his or her experience that holds a place in a life story that I do not know. Empathy requires us to be fully present to the other without turning away or turning to our own experience, as a distraction. But how does my personal history and the condition of my own heart influence empathy? How does my experience help me attend empathetically to someone else?

A Poetry of Presence

Empathy has rhythm and rhyme. Empathetic encounters have a beauty of gesture and experience that nourishes and heals all those they touch. Empathetic experience has four aspects, in that we:

- Experience events directly—these we call 'our own experience'
- Experience our assumptions, thoughts, feelings and judgments about our own experience
- Observe someone going though an event—this we call foreign experience since it is not happening to us directly
- Experience assumptions, thoughts, feelings and judgments about the other person's experience

All four of these aspects play a part in empathy. What part does each aspect play?

In terms of the first and third aspects of experience, our own versus someone else's, one is direct, the other is indirect.[13] Attending to another person empathetically requires us to note assumptions, thoughts, feelings and judgments that leap to mind, and then suspend them all—waiting as the other guides us through the experience and tells us about it. It is in this sense that we first attend to our own hearts, then release ourselves from being trapped there. Using the language provided by the four aspects of experience, empathy is a direct encounter with indirect experience in which we suspend our interpretation of what is going on until we hear enough about a foreign experience to give an interpretation of it that clearly satisfies its owner. In exercising empathy, we ask questions of the other person. We cannot ask effective questions of another person while we are trapped in our own heart's business.

Empathy is something like reading poetry. The poet conveys in a few dense lines the essence of something seen, felt or heard—something experienced. As we read the poem, we are not reading about our own experience, we are reading something foreign. With poetry, we realize that there is a vast horizon behind the words on the page that situates them in an experience or experiences. As we read, we are trying to grasp or sense that horizon—one we have not seen ourselves even though we may have seen one very much like it. Yet reading poetry is a direct experience in itself—it is our own experience of reading that offers insight into what the poet wishes to convey. In plumbing the depths of the poem, we emerge as we sight the horizon that frames the words. One obvious difference between relational empathy and poetry reading is that the poet is seldom present while we read it. In relational empathy, the other person is like a text to be read when its author is present.

Empathy is no less complicated than reading a poem. Having the author stand before us is an advantage and disadvantage, depending on how we like to read what is foreign. If all we really want is to get into the poem quickly and get out again, without engaging our original perceptions, if we come with a barrage of words or ideas that we wish to impose on it, then having the poet present is a nuisance. Authors have a nasty way of disagreeing with our assumptions, thoughts, feelings and judgments about their work. Poets are particularly annoying if we are in a hurry to decide on our interpretation of their experience. If, on the other hand, we want to understand the poem or person, we wait patiently until we get enough words or clues to grasp the text in its context. The metaphor of poetry reminds us that, in empathy, we do not get to read the novel of another person's experience, that is, the past, present and future of a life. We get words, gestures, hints, facial expressions, all of which are condensed signs that require our full attention if we want to weave them into a meaningful, whole experience.

As I try to be empathetic, I observe the other person for clues as to the effectiveness of my understanding. Suppose the other person gets angry, falls silent or changes the subject? Something is wrong. Empathy has become invasion or entrapment, from the perspective of the other. I must stay attentive to the whole person as I try to be empathetic. As one example, I had an opportunity to learn about empathy while participating in a research project in public schools. My professor asked me to visit a grade two class in which there were twenty-four students: eight who spoke English, eight who spoke a second language other than English and eight who spoke both English and a second language. I observed a girl who was learning English. As I sat beside her, I asked if I might look at her work. I noticed that sometimes she would speak about her work and sometimes she would fall silent. Then I noticed that if I looked at her work and not at her face, she would speak at length about what her drawings meant to her. As soon as I looked at her face, she stopped talking. I carefully avoided looking into her face and we talked for twenty minutes. At the end of the lesson, the classroom teacher asked how I managed to have such a long conversation with this little girl. I recounted to her what I learned. She then said that it was the longest period of time the little girl had spoken all year. Usually she was entirely silent.

If we use the metaphor of reading poetry, different readers will arrive at different versions of a poem's meaning. Empathy is art and method. Our own experience and self-understanding influence us as we attend empathetically to foreign experience. So, we attend to our own hearts first. Then we wait patiently and suspend our assumptions, thoughts, feelings and judgments until we have a chance to hear the other, but in making meaning we also work with our own material as well as with the words and gestures of the other person. It is at this point that we recall Jesus' directive to do to others, as we would have them do to us. The Golden Rule is complex in its application and does not guarantee our relationships will work out easily. We are limited by our own experience as well as informed by it. Sometimes we cannot understand another person, even though we try, until we get fresh insight. The following is my own story.

As a professor in a seminary I have opportunities to relate to students in many ways. I see them learn, I hear them preach, I lead them through life-changing theories and practices and I perceive the changes in their growth. I have taught in Education Faculties in other universities and know that seminaries provide a unique opportunity for multi-layered teaching/learning to develop. But sometimes a relationship can go very wrong, as it did with a student I will call Jane.

Jane was an outgoing, confident, popular student who told me enough of her story for me to appreciate that her well-being was hard won. We enjoyed each other and occasionally went for coffee. I assumed we had a good teacher/learner relationship and still believe we did, but I stepped over a line that led to a deep breach between teacher and student. I said something that conveyed to Jane that I disrespected her. I cannot say exactly what I did, for two reasons: it happened to her not to me, and, she forgave me. Forgiveness has the power to rewrite the past, under certain conditions. The issue for empathy has to do with the conditions in which forgiveness becomes possible and is effective.

The event occurred, something I said, immediately Jane was angry. She expressed her fury to me personally, and in no uncertain terms. Her rage puzzled me. I was extremely uncomfortable but I trusted her as a person even though I could not grasp the meaning she attributed to the event. We tried for over a year to reconcile but could not, at least not sufficiently. I desperately wanted to understand what had gone wrong but no insight came. I fasted and prayed because it seemed something very significant had occurred and all my teaching—my neat theories about social relations—were in jeopardy if I could not resolve the guilt I felt. I was angry with Jane. Why did she have to be so angry? Couldn't she just get over it, whatever it was; after all, I said I was sorry. We went to a chaplain/counsellor together and met several times. Nothing helped. While I had clearly apologized, it was evident to us both that I did not understand the significance to Jane of the comments I had made that hurt her. We held to an uneasy truce.

And then, by God's grace, I had my own disastrous experience—which I slowly came to see produced in me similar feelings to those Jane expressed. What was going on? I felt humiliation and rage similar to the anger she had directed toward me. As I was nursing my wounds, I realized what had to be done. I invited Jane to my office and was finally able to say that the problem between us was 100% my fault. She had done nothing wrong. The fault was entirely mine. Up to that point, I had been trying to see things essentially from my own perspective, though I thought I was trying to be fair, by showing how both of us were to blame. It was not until I was in a situation that was sufficiently similar to hers (though it was not the same) that I could make sense of her rage. Rage follows on the heels of injustice and the abuse of power. To make her suffering worse, I had no excuse. I knew better. At least, I had made it sound as though I knew better when I was teaching about these topics.

I will not forget the moment in my office when she turned to me and thanked me for confessing. She had begun to forgive me, she said, and could see me without feeling furious; but now, it was as though it never happened. I did not dwell on my own experience but relayed to her an insight God was bringing me: Sometimes an event is entirely my fault. Sometimes I am entirely innocent. Sometimes blame is more evenly divided. But when someone who has a good relationship with me suddenly gets very angry and threatens my personal happiness, I must take that rage seriously and try to discover its meaning. If we refuse the opportunities empathy offers us, hearts are hardened by guilt. The problem intensifies over time: unresolved guilt continues to harden the heart, making empathy more remote. We are so busy building and defending our inner fortresses, we do not pause to receive the insight that would help us understand.

METHODS FOR EMPATHY

My insights with Jane were informed by my understanding of the Psalms of opposition and convey the complexity engendered by the problem of opposition. Jane's anger opposed my personal happiness. Human frailty leads to conflict if we refuse the work of empathy—of trying to understand our critics from their point of view. Unresolved guilt gets in the way of empathetic listening because we turn away from someone who is expressing negative feelings toward us. Guilt drives us into a cover up operation. We want to close our ears to any and all criticism. We cannot bear to be in the wrong because we feel horrid and alone. In loneliness, we are trapped in the troubles of our own isolated hearts. This is why unresolved guilt is counter-productive to empathy. Unresolved guilt keeps us from asking questions because anything we might discover seems too costly to learn. But if we finally muster the courage to ask specific questions, we minimize the cost, lessening the possibility that a critic will reject us completely. In empathy, even if we believe the criticism to be unjustified, we attempt to ask specific questions to find out:

- What the criticism means in general
- More information, no matter how hot the topic
- What is the specific accusation?
- How our critic is offended and by what
- What you did or didn't do
- When you did it
- How often you did or said it
- What else the person dislikes about you

Overall, in empathy, we try to see the world through another person's eyes. Asking these questions of someone who is hostile usually calms a situation down because the other person feels heard. Further, we gain specific information about what it is like to be in our presence. But empathy does not leave us at the mercy of our critic's perspective, even if there is much truth in what we learn, we also ask ourselves some questions after we have heard from the other person. We ask:

- How do I understand what I am accused of doing?
- Did I do this wilfully?
- Am I expecting myself to be perfect?
- How do I understand what it means to be human?
- How do I feel about what I did?
- How am I labelling myself now?
- Is the label accurate? Is it fair? Is this label all there is to me? And what else is true about me?

- Is my regret based on a fair assessment of the negative effects of my action?
- Is the length and intensity of my reaction to myself appropriate to what I did?
- Am I learning from my error and developing a strategy for change?
- Am I being destructive to myself?[14]

These questions often need to be asked in the presence of a witness. Empathy is expensive. We cannot always be the one who offers empathy. Sometimes we need a haven for our hearts to find repentance and rest. We need someone whose kind, non-anxious presence allows honesty to flourish, who does not let us drown in self-punishment and negativity. Yet even with such a witness, there comes a moment when we must attend empathetically to ourselves, regardless of the severity of what we did wrong, to let our hearts rest in the repentance God will always accept from a heart committed to loving the Lord more than any other love.

Empathetic people realize they are (at various times) the sinner and the sinned against. Empathy helps us not recoil from faces of those we have hurt; empathy helps us not withdraw from those who have hurt us. Empathy teaches us to pray: *Father, forgive us our trespasses as we forgive those who trespass against us.* Forgiveness, under the conditions of empathy, cleanses the conscience and renews the heart. In empathy, we are born again.

EMPATHY AND CHILDREN

Healthy encounters parents have with their infants provide good models for empathy that is neither invasion nor entrapment in the senses referred to earlier. In a healthy relational encounter, parents and infants attend to each other and can escape or resist each other's gaze. I describe the healthy encounters between parents and infants to build the groundwork for empathy. Recall that in empathy we are posing a complex question: *What does the other need to sense in order to believe that I am attending empathetically with them?*

One aspect of a fully engaged empathetic act is that those who empathize come to sense what the other person requires in order to feel understood. Our basic human capacity for empathy shows up if we examine some of the research on infants' ability to engage in interpersonal relationships. This research helps to see how the empathetic relationship works in practice.

In the first seven to nine months of life, there emerges the first deliberate sharing of interpersonal space with those who care for an infant.[15] Exchanges between caregiver (in the research it is typically mothers) and infant take place through *shared attention* to a third object. During this time the child is developing a subjective self. This period is also described as the foundation for the development of the soul, i.e., the seat of emotion, intuition, and receptivity to God, as well as receptivity to other people. The following example explains how shared attention to a third object works.

Suppose an infant's mother turns her head and looks out of the room to gaze at something distressing. (See Figure 4) Immediately the infant follows her gaze with attentive anxiousness. Neither says anything because the infant cannot yet talk. But pre-linguistic expressions of *shared attention* and *shared feeling* are communicated from infant to mother and back again. In these exchanges, non-verbal intimacy becomes a real possibility: gestures, postures, facial expressions and sounds work together to provide shared meaning as infant and mother gaze at a third object. Infants at this age are capable of initiating an encounter of this kind by gazing at a third object that the mother then looks toward. Babies are capable of initiating shared attention (gazing with another person at a third object), shared intention (persistently signalling that an intent is to be understood by the other) and shared affect (shared feeling) even though infants have no oral language. Affect attunement—the experience of shared attention, shared intention and shared affect—is similar to the empathetic act, although if falls short of empathy.

When infant and mother attune themselves to one another with respect to a third object, the mother responds to the infant in a particular way. Affect attunement is the recognition and restatement by the parent of the child's affective state. It is a complex operation involving several important factors:

Figure 4: Affect Attunement

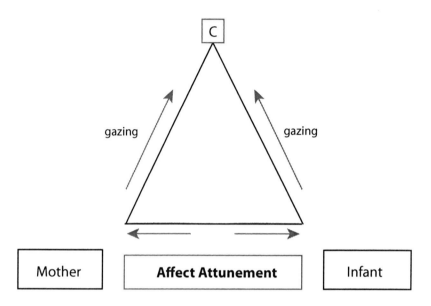

The Third Object = C

- An accurate reading of the baby's behaviour
- An intimate history of the child's feelings, giving rise to the ability to participate in those feelings
- The ability to respond with different, non-imitative, but accurate behaviours that signal to the infant that his or her affective states are understood, such as "I am reading you, and I'm responding in rhythm, in pattern, in resonance, in synchronicity with your feelings"
- For emotional attunement to occur, the infant must be able to read and understand that response.[16]

As with Figure 4, a primary way we indicate to children we are resonating, or feeling with, is by matching the intensity of our responses to the intensity of their actions. Mothers match the beat, rhythm or shape of an infant's gesture or sound but do not imitate it exactly. Imitation does not contribute to affect attunement. Affect attunement builds mutuality between mother and child. Imitation is distressing. We may recall a family member or friend who copied our words exactly and repeatedly, as a way to annoy us. It worked.

Attunement is a dynamic ongoing process. In these rituals between mother and child, there emerge pre-verbal, pre-symbolic and proto-symbolic activities (patterns for later use), accomplished without spoken language. The development of spoken language is a mixed blessing.[17] While spoken language helps us relate ourselves to other people in a new way, it is also a problem for the integration of self-experience and self-other experience. The interdependency of meaning-making in preverbal infants is remarkable. Mothers read their infants. Babies inform their mothers. In constructing meaning together, infants and mothers take turns leading and following to accomplish this essential communicative task. When children begin to talk, they narrate their own lives and can change how they perceive themselves. Narrating one's life is not like other forms of thought. Narrative structure may prove to be a universal human phenomenon reflecting the design of the human mind,[18] but there is a problem with using spoken language in empathetic relationships.

A new level of relatedness is possible when children begin to talk. But while this shift does not eclipse pre-verbal experience, language recasts and transforms some of the intersubjective experiences that infants and mothers were so good at, so that words and pre-verbal experience lead two lives. There is an ongoing non-verbal experience and there is a verbalized version of that experience. These two types of experience are not always in harmony.

Spoken language grabs hold of a piece of the conglomerate of sensing, thinking, feeling, wanting and doing that constitutes non-verbal experience. Words selected may not convey the wholeness of that experience. That is, we have *world knowledge* (experience) and *word knowledge* (spoken language); the two do not always match. With spoken language something is gained and something is lost. The child "gains entrance into a wider cultural membership, but at the risk of losing the force and wholeness of original experience."[19]

Empathy relies upon *world knowledge* and *word knowledge* for its effectiveness, but *world knowledge* is extremely important, perhaps more so than most of us realize. In empathy, we have the opportunity to attend to another person *bodily* in a way that does not require spoken language, although spoken language can be used. If empathy is effective, we make use of *world* knowledge and *word* knowledge. When someone is hurt, we may fail to draw near because we are afraid of saying the wrong thing, so we stay away from those who suffer. But empathy does not have to speak at all. Of course it may. A fully participatory act of empathy conveys bountifully that we are understood and safe because our experience makes sense to at least one other person. Empathy lets us know that we are neither crazy nor alone. Surely, to be understood at this level is the deepest longing of the human heart. When we are suffering, or when we overflow with joy, we want others to catch sight of what is going on from our perspective.

Perspective-taking

Children can take another person's perspective and imaginatively put themselves in that person's place. Perspective-taking is related to empathy and offers another way to understand how it does or does not develop in the lives of many people. As we have seen, infants are capable of affect attunement with significant other people. Johannes van der Ven (1998) organizes his understanding of the potential for empathy, by relying on research to identify how young children catch sight of something from another person's perspective. Perspective-taking behaviour indicates potential for the growth of empathy. The following is a summary of five levels of perspective-taking that form the groundwork for empathy, at least potentially.[20]

Level One: Infants cry when they hear other people cry. Through mimicry, an infant is able to demonstrate a similar emotion expressed by another person. By this language, a child is able to take another's perspective. The activity of putting oneself in someone else's place falls short of empathy and takes two forms. The first form is self-focused: a child, let's call him John, puts himself in another child's place, let's call her Jill, by imagining what it would mean if the situation happening to Jill was to impinge on him. Suppose John sees and hears Jill cry. First he thinks of himself, he is self-focused. The second form of the first level of perspective-taking is other-focused. John comes to imagine how Jill feels in this situation rather than to be concerned about whether what is happening to her might happen to him. Even eleven-month-old children are able to function at this level. The first level contains some cognitive aspects.

Level Two: The second level is explicitly cognitive and consists of two other-focused dimensions. The first dimension of the cognitive aspect of the second level is signalled by John's awareness that Jill has internal states that are independent of what John is experiencing internally. John sees that something is going on in Jill; it is different from what is going on inside him. The second dimension goes further than the immediate presentation of emotion: John takes account of Jill's personal history, and/or tries to imagine it.

Level Three: This level is primarily affective, with two important dimensions. First, John realizes that Jill is experiencing and going through her own emotions rather than emotions he might have in a similar situation. The second dimension goes beyond 'the here and now' so that Jill's emotions are understood as emerging from her personal history. This empathetic understanding can be found among two to three year olds. van der Ven describes this process as though the cognitive and affective aspects are separate (one in level two and other in level three) but the important point is that John focuses on Jill's feeling and has a feeling and a thinking response to her tears. He realizes his feelings are different from Jill and what she is feeling. He sees the emotion from her perspective rather than his own, to some extent at least.

Level Four: At this level, perspective-taking transforms into partial sympathy. This happens when John experiences a feeling of compassion for Jill as he experiences her suffering from feelings such as sadness, grief, worry or hopelessness. Sympathy goes along with a desire to help the other—John feels sorry for Jill. It is important to note that he has moved his focus from what might happen to him and is paying attention to what is happening within her. It is hard to know how the transformation from perspective-taking to sympathy is accomplished and what stimulates it. It may be that parental modelling is central.

Level Five: At this level trouble may be introduced into the relation between John and Jill because this level involves asking who is to blame for her distress. Three options emerge:

- No one can be found to blame for causing her pain. The absence of someone to blame reinforces sympathetic distress. John feels worse for Jill if no one can be found to blame.

- Someone is identified as causing her distress. This move may lead to anger in John as he observes her pain. When someone is found to blame, his feelings may alternate between sympathetic distress and sympathetic anger. John may feel anger and sorrow for Jill. He may alternate between feeling distressed and feeling angry. This roller coaster may intensify his anxiety.

- If Jill can be blamed for her own distress, sympathy decreases and the potential for empathy dissolves. Perhaps victim-blaming is a strategy people use to relieve their own distress when they see someone suffer. John may blame himself for Jill's distress because of something he did or did not do. Shame and guilt surface if he blames himself. As already mentioned, self-punitive feelings of shame and guilt hinder the development of empathy.

These levels identify perspective-taking but also show how progress towards empathy can run off the rails. Instead of letting empathy relax into compassion, John may turn away from Jill, blame her for her own problem, or blame himself, and express anger toward her. That is, he may turn toward her in compassion or turn away in rejection. Turning away is a response that is open to those who encounter another person's grief, sorrow, loss or joy. The road to empathy is risky. It is not a simple human puzzle; empathy is a complex human problem.

THE PROBLEM OF EMPATHY

Figure 5 draws the problem so we see empathy as attentiveness to foreign experience. The fact that another person's experience is foreign to me is helpful and unhelpful in establishing an empathetic encounter. Suppose a man named Jim is going through something that calls for attention. He may be suffering because his wife is dying. Or he may be joyful because he has just passed an important, career focusing exam. In either case, he has a powerful experience that attracts Judy's attention.

Judy attends to Jim's experience, which we label C; let's say, he has just passed a significant exam. Judy gazes at his experience while Jim narrates the circumstances around it. Judy gives her full attention to his experience. The diagram tends to make empathy look clean and simple, which we know it is not. However, it does make it obvious that Judy's attention to C is directed by the experience Jim tells her. She is not gazing directly at Jim but at his experience. Gazing at all that is involved for him is significant because Judy must sense what

Figure 5: The Problem of Empathy

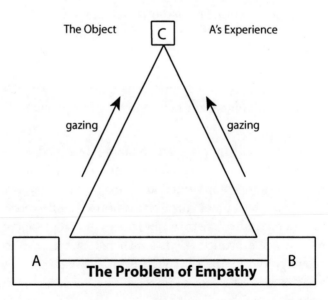

334

the story about C conveys about human experience generally, so as to grasp its common human themes, as well as how it affects Jim personally.

Let us say that Judy is effectively empathetic with Jim's experience, i.e., with his account of passing this exam. Under this condition, she gives C her full attention and does not invade or trap Jim in any way. At some point in an effective empathetic encounter, he will say or indicate that she understands his experience. Empathy is effective when he senses that she knows what is going on in C. That is, Jim is satisfied by the encounter.

But in empathy things can go wrong and often do, even among very nice people. We must keep in mind that Jim and Judy have a different relationship to C. It is with respect to these differences that empathy either satisfies or fails Jim. Remember that C is foreign to Judy. It is foreign, not because passing an exam has never happened to her, but because this particular exam, in this particular life story, has not happened to her. Differences may lie in the category of common human experience that Judy and Jim assign to C, as well as with respect to the particularities of

- The way C happened to Jim,
- The time in his life that it happened
- The personal, family or cultural circumstances Jim brings to it

Suppose for example, Jim is an African American living in Canada and Judy is a white person whose family was one of the first families to settle in the city where they now both live. What else might go wrong with empathy as Jim and Judy gaze at the experience of passing an important exam?

- Judy may claim to *know* C as well as Jim does
- She may claim to be *the* authority on common human themes associated with C
- She may rely on assumptions, values that she does not check out
- She may feel envy or resentment towards Jim

As a consequence of any of these moves, Judy may turn away from the experience Jim is relating to her. If she fails to be empathetic, turning away may:

- Be due to the pressure of the moment
- Be moved by feelings so intense she cannot gaze at C
- Come about due to preoccupations with her own future
- Come about because of judgments she is unable to suspend
- Come about due to hindering aspects of her personality, e.g., unresolved guilt or unconquerable anxiety

When she asks herself if she is empathetic, she asks herself:

- Am I attending appropriately to C
- Which she realizes is foreign to her,
- So that she might arrive at full participation in C
- Am I staying with C
- Without engaging in imperialism or entrapment
- Have I allowed the experience to remain foreign (i.e., not hers)
- She does not turn away due to pressure or personality

Under all these conditions, empathy is full participation in foreign experience if she also has a similar feeling to the inner state that Jim expresses; that is, if she experiences empathy plus sympathy.

A person may be empathetic whether or not he or she feels sympathy with a foreign experience; but without sympathy it is not a fully engaged participatory empathetic act. If we cannot share the feeling, we remain to some extent an observer rather than a participant. Since we cannot and would not want to be obliged to share all the feelings we choose to empathize with, it is essential to understand the difference between gazing upon someone's experience and remaining steadfast in our gaze, without turning away, and actually being able to join in the experience. If we cannot remain steadfast, if we turn away, empathy fails. But I cannot be obliged to be in sympathy with everyone in every instance of an empathetic encounter.

I recall a man I met who came to our church with a friend who was a prison chaplain. The man was a notorious sex offender who had served his time and was released from prison. He came to our church to find sanctuary from the crowds surrounding his residence that came every week like clockwork to march in front of the house to protest his presence in the community.

I remember the day someone in our church cast a suspicious glance at him. I recollect sensing his pain in the sanctuary; I felt it physically, though I was across the room from him. I went to him and he sobbed as soon as he saw me. He told me what happened. We cried together. He decided that day to return to prison even though his sentence was complete. He could not bear the pressure of censure any longer. He turned to me and said: *What do they want me to do? Lie under a truck and let it run over me?* He spoke quietly. I cannot claim to understand the sorrow he felt; nor do I understand how anyone could bring himself to harm others as he had done—his victims will wrestle for the rest of their lives with what he did to them. I was not in sympathy with his feelings (I did not feel them) but I could attend to his pain while their tumult rolled over him, so that he did not have to be alone or feel crazy.

Empathy requires balance. Figure 6 outlines an Aristotelian model for deliberation. If we use this model and consider empathy from the perspective of its excess and its deficiency, we can achieve balance more ably. In deliberating on empathy we come to see how to draw empathetic responses into our way of living.

If you refer to Aristotle's *Ethics* first-hand, you will note that he did not distinguish culture as an element in deliberation. He did not consider cultures other than his own. Elements of deliberation include the concept of empathy, cultural messages about empathy, personal tendencies with respect to empathy, the excess of empathy, its deficiency and the mean between them. The point of deliberating is to get a sense for exercising empathy in the right way, with the right person, for the right reasons, at the right time and the right duration, so that character is formed by the reflection and action that follow appropriately from the process. Through deliberating upon empathy, a path opens up between the excess and the deficiency that we aim to follow; the path is called the mean. The mean is not in the middle

Figure 6: Deliberating on Empathy

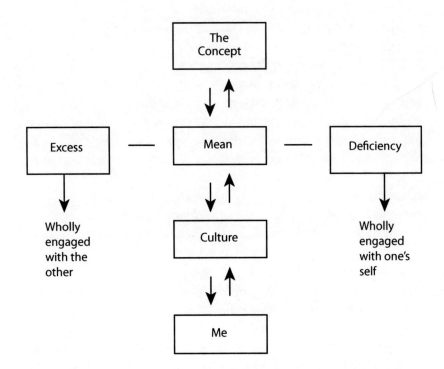

between the two extreme ends necessarily. The mean may be closer to one side than the other; its position is identified once all elements are adequately understood.

If we garner aspects of empathy presented so far, it is a proactive virtue that enables one person to attend to two worlds of experience. Relational empathy allows other people to feel sure their experience makes sense; they relax and realize they are neither alone nor strange. Empathy is an act of perceiving and an art of imagining that helps someone who is empathetic to narrate a foreign experience in a way that its author feels is accurate. Empathy tells the truth but may or may not require us to speak. Empathy relies on insight informed by our own experience, but is not trapped in that experience. Empathy calms anxiety and cleanses guilt, through God's grace. In empathy, I learn to be kind to myself at the same time that I am kind to others.

It is a way of perceiving, of seeing the world; it is a gaze that gets its object right. If the object of our gaze is a text, person, our own hearts or a moral act, empathy is essentially the attentiveness of our gaze: the focused and informed observation of what is going on. This then, is the concept of empathy that will guide our deliberation.

If I wish to deliberate on empathy, I must come to understand what my culture conveys about it, as well as my own pre-dispositions toward it. Teachers engage students with empathy by encouraging them to gather cultural materials (e.g., magazines, images, songs, stories, movies) that convey current interpretations. They ask learners to record an experience of conflict and personally reflect upon their reactions to it by using empathy. Personal reflections should remain private, but learners contribute general insights to a class discussion based upon their personal experience. The process of deliberation situates the concept of empathy within a framework built from cultural and personal perspectives on what empathy is and how it can be exercised.

The mean that is mapped out through deliberation is positioned between the extremes of excess and deficiency. In order to assess the extremes we must decide what empathy essentially is, as we understand it. In general, empathy is attentiveness to foreign experience. We acknowledge that it is possible to have too much attentiveness, so that empathy becomes entrapment and it is possible to have too little, so that empathy invades someone else's experience.

As the diagram indicates, an excess of empathy is expressed through being wholly engrossed with another person's experience at my own expense. When I am exercising too much attentiveness, I lose touch with myself, my needs, feelings, aspirations and goals. I essentially lose myself. Losing myself does not help the other person. Generally the other person feels suffocated by excessive concern. Suppose the mother of an adult daughter learns the young woman has cancer. The mother loves her daughter and becomes so entirely focused on her daughter's health that she loses touch with her own well-being. In all likelihood, the daughter will express anger, fall silent or try to slip away from her mother's gaze in some fashion. Empathy fails due to the mother's refusal to attend to her own life as well as her daughter's life.

In its deficiency, empathy is wholly engrossed with one's own experience at the expense of another person. Deficiencies of empathy result in inattentiveness, neglect of foreign experience and can be described as judgmentalism. In judgmentalism, the one who is gazing at a foreign experience underestimates differences of degree and/or of kind that play out in the object of his or her gaze. The foreign quality of the experience is dismissed. Suppose a father learns that his son wants to be an artist. The father is sure that an artist's life will lead to perpetual poverty and grief. The father loves his son and becomes so focused on his certainty that an artistic life is unsustainable that he loses touch with the aspirations of the young man. In all likelihood, the son will express anger, fall silent or try to slip away from his father's gaze in some fashion. Empathy fails due to the father's refusal to attend to the boy's gifts as well as to his own fears.

What then is the path empathy takes between its two extremes? The first aspect of appropriate empathy is that two worlds of experience must not conflate into one, as they do in the extremes of excess and deficiency. In excess, the two worlds of a daughter and mother collapse into the daughter's illness. In deficiency, the two worlds of the son and the father collapse into the father's certainty that he alone is right about the future. The appropriate path for empathy encourages calm; anxiety relaxes. For this reason, the mother and the father will not locate the mean for empathy in exactly the same spot on the diagram. Deliberation is personal. The father will become aware that he must lean in the direction of attending to his son's life, that is, in the direction of empathy's excess. The mother will learn to lean towards the deficiency side of the model; she will lean towards valuing her own experience. In general however, we can say that empathy as a concept has more to do with attending to someone else's experience than with being pre-occupied by our own. The mean for empathy as a general model lies on the side of excess, of attending to another person's experience and away from ourselves. But how can we become effective at calming the anxiety in our own hearts long enough to allow another person's experience to show up truthfully?[21]

SPIRITUAL EMPATHY

We learn empathy from the life of Jesus. He came to show us what God is like and to reveal what we can be like when we are rooted in the love of God. If we consider the path empathy takes, it is only as we are fully engaged by the empathy of God, finding rest from our sorrow, and feeling the affirmation of God's presence in our joy, that we are able to reflect God's empathy freely to someone else. It is only as we find repentance and rest that we are able to pass on the comfort of empathy to others. It is only through God's Grace that empathy is effective.

If relational empathy is an insightful act in which we give complete attention to someone else's experience in a way that allows the other to realize we share and understand the essential quality of that experience, spiritual empathy is relational empathy mediated by God. If empathy refers to acts in which foreign experience is grasped and we sense what is presented and what is behind what is presented as someone else's experience, it is the example of Jesus that enables foreign experience to be grasped truthfully. If relational empathy involves two people attending to a third object, it is the power of God that heals our blindness as we gaze at someone else's experience. The answer to the question of what another person needs to sense in order to believe we are relating empathetically with them is realized through the activity of the Holy Spirit. Apart from God, we cannot be empathetically attentive to another person in the fullest sense. If empathy has the power to heal, it is due to God's concern for both parties in the empathetic relationship. Jesus provides our example for spiritual empathy. As we gaze at Jesus Christ, we see each other more clearly.

In Luke 7:36-50 we read a story of Jesus, a Pharisee named Simon and a woman who is alien to the social situation. Jesus was invited to dinner with Simon and his guests. A woman enters the room. She is weeping and washes Jesus' feet with her tears, wiping them with her hair. It is difficult to imagine this scene in the twenty-first century, let alone in the strong group culture of Jesus' day. By ordinary standards, Jesus is caught between Simon, his host, and the woman, who is his admirer. At no point does Jesus speak rudely to either of them, which is remarkable in itself. Though he is positioned between them, he seems not to feel trapped.

As we read through the story several times, certain aspects of the narrative emerge. What is the direction of Jesus' gaze throughout the narrative? Where is the woman? Where do you think she is looking? Where do you think she looked as she entered the room? What is Jesus' posture? Likely Simon and Jesus would assume the same posture. Where is the table placed with respect to Jesus and the woman? In verse 39, where is Simon looking? That verse says: *When the Pharisee who had invited [Jesus] saw this, he said to himself, "If this man were a prophet, he would know who is touching him and what kind of woman she is—that she is a sinner."* What are some of the possible reasons for Jesus' next comment: *Jesus answered him, "Simon, I have something to tell you."* What inquiry was Jesus answering, since Simon only thought to himself that the woman was a sinner? Was Jesus answering Simon's bodily expression of disgust, a feeling that came from the overflow of his heart that he could not hide from the Master of the human heart?

Jesus tells Simon a story that poses a question to the Pharisee. Two people owed money...One owed more than the other....Neither could pay...The money lender cancelled both debts. Now, who will love the moneylender more? Simon answered with the observation that the one who owed more would love more. Jesus affirms Simon's tentative judgment. Then he does something quite odd considering the circumstances. He invites Simon to look at the woman. As Simon is gazing at the woman, for the second time, Jesus forgives her sin, tells her that her faith has saved her, and she can go in peace.

In Figure 7, the woman in this story is alien even though she is culturally the same as Simon and his guests. She is alien because her sin is public knowledge and because she does not belong in the room with the others. Throughout the story, she says nothing. It is her action that captures everyone's eye. Simon is a member of an elite group. Jesus is invited because he is rather interesting to men such as Simon. We are not told about the relationship between Simon and Jesus, but we are told that when people begin to question Jesus' authority to forgive sin, it is Simon's guests rather than Simon himself that are murmuring. We do not need to assume that Simon

Figure 7: Spiritual Empathy

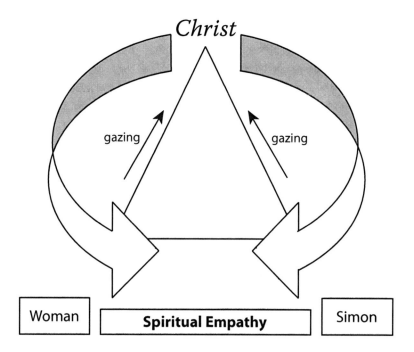

insulted Jesus by not giving him water for his feet or a kiss as he entered the room. Jesus is focused on acts of love rather than on following custom.

As our intermediary, Jesus uses his position between these two people to enable Simon to see the woman in a new way. Without anxiety or embarrassment, Jesus waits quietly while Simon looks at her a second time. He waits patiently for Simon to respond without embarrassing the Pharisee. Jesus affirms the judgment Simon makes in response to the story. Jesus does not deny that the woman is a sinner—he only points out that she loves abundantly. The narrative Jesus tells was not meant to humiliate Simon. Rather, the narrative about love nudges Simon's attention away from the woman long enough for Simon to look again and see her for the first time. The shift in Jesus' gaze is aimed at allowing Simon to see that both he and the woman are sinners. Her outrageous act is an expression of radical love. It is as if Jesus is saying: Yes, Simon, you are right she is a sinner. You were not wrong about her. She loves me. Simon, focus on love?

In summary, an empathetic Christ stretches out his arms to embrace the woman and Simon. Neither is dismissed. Spiritual empathy enables us to relate to God who is intimately made known to us through Jesus Christ as well as through the work of the Holy Spirit. Jesus opens up the possibility that Simon will be empathetic toward the woman. Empathy is an option for Simon, once he shifts his gaze from the woman's sin to her act of love.

How do you understand the empathy of God? What are the conditions of the human heart that encourage the growth of empathy? If the heart is the soil in which empathy grows, then attentiveness to our own hearts is a central feature of faith education that cannot be ignored and must be understood and practised. The effective use of empathy requires training and trying. While trying is personal, training is communal. The following chapter examines the art of theological reflection as an activity of the heart. Theological reflection is an issue of training in our churches and our seminaries if we hope to encourage faith maturity among people who claim to trust and love God.

REFLECTING THE HEART

Above all else, guard your heart, for it is the
wellspring of life. (Proverbs 4:23)

Blessed are the pure in heart, for they
will see God. (Matthew 5:8)

Whoever believes in me, as the Scripture has said,
will have streams of living water flowing
from within. (John 7:38)

The body is essentially an expressive space through which other
expressive spaces come into existence, and, so, bodily spatially...
is the very condition for coming into
being of a meaningful world.[1]

THE HEART OF FAITH EDUCATION

The heart of faith education produces the fruit of empathy. Its approach, process, perspective and all of its activities cohere in the heart of the faithful as they find rest in God. What would be the evidence that the heart has found its rest in God and is restored, through repentance, to a fruitful life of faith? This is an important question. Many are in the church but not in Christ. In Christ, we enjoy the resources of Grace, knowing that we are not

345

better than others, we are confident that God loves us. I suggest that the evidence a life is held securely in God's embrace is found in the *attempts* believers make to live faithfully. Faith is lived out in the heart's struggle to follow God rather than its own way. It is in trying to be faithful that we come to know the heart of God. God is the strength behind our feeble or effective attempts to be people of faith. Trying is personal spiritual work—trying more than succeeding. Yet a faith community is partly responsible for the effectiveness of personal struggles to know God. Christian community has a duty to educate people (leaders and congregants) in the art and discipline of being faithful. If trying is personal, education is communal. Christian communities have a duty to teach people how to reflect on God so personal effort actually produces the fruit of faithfulness.

In this chapter, I present a view of theological reflection that aims to bridge gaps between personal attempts and communal responsibility for teaching people how to know God more fully. Theological reflection is an educational process in which we invite God into our thinking about what to do and how to live personally, and invite God into our decision-making as communities of faith. I believe churches are weak in their ability and willingness to reflect on and talk together about what God wants, so they do not gain direction for ministry from their encounters with the Living God. This needs to change.

If theological reflection is so important, why am I content to say that trying matters more than succeeding? Is my faith in God so weak that I want an escape hatch when things don't work out? What does it mean to try to be faithful? Trying implies two things. First, trying means that I should not give up "though the earth give way and the mountains fall into the heart of the sea" (Psalm 46:2), since God does not give up trying to communicate with us. Second, when I say that trying is more important than succeeding, I am not saying that we merely try to understand God; rather, in trying, we come to see that it is God who brings about success. What actually happens is not due to our effort. The courage to go on trying will face and overcome the tendency to give in to fear. Scripture warns us repeatedly not to fear other people. If we fear other people and make feeble efforts in the background of an issue and then, as a result of our feebleness, fail, we miss the mark of the high calling of God.

Yet there is something I fear about success. I am afraid of the lust that drives people to succeed by eradicating all opposition to their particular plans and personal happiness. Being successful for them means silencing potential threats to the ease they have in getting their own way. I fear the idolatry that lies behind driving for success. If the highway to success takes this route, we lose all capacity and motivation to be empathetic—we no longer want to know what someone else is experiencing; we habitually turn away from them due to an insatiable desire to carry out the plans and projects we believe will continue to produce success. In our drivenness, we find no rest with God and we may even attribute our madness to God.

Despite the human tendency to mistake our own will for God's, I believe the faithful can be masterful in living godly lives. Scripture says that "His divine power has given us everything we need for life and godliness through our knowledge of him who called us by his own glory and goodness." (1Peter 1:3) Godly living is the goal, but how do we learn to be masterful at faith? Recall that faith is an activity, like others that we gain mastery over; therefore we can learn what it means to be masterful people of faith by realizing what it takes to master any skill or competence. Gaining mastery over faith is an essential activity of the heart.

Activity of the heart unites the personal and communal with the heart of God. Our attempts to be a person of faith are situated within a caring community. As a consequence, the hearts of the faithful follow after the heart of God. God's heart is One: as we turn toward God we draw closer to each other. Regardless of failure or success, at any time, place, or for any reason, the faithful turn their hearts toward God. And God, because of the very essence of what it means to be God, will turn and heal people. Scripture tells us that God's willingness is unending. God turns toward those who try and those who repent of their feebleness at trying. When we are doing our best, God is doing God's best. This chapter focuses on the embodied learning that enables the faithful to link their hearts with the heart of God. In this chapter, I outline how people achieve mastery; learning the art of being faithful alters the condition of the heart: deep calls to Deep. God hears and responds.

PUTTING FAITH INTO THE WORLD

If we are trying to master faith, what might that process look like and how will we know we are making progress? Hubert Dreyfus (2001) identified seven *stages*[2] of learning that culminate in mastery. His approach applies to the life of faith, since his notion of embodied learning is a pathway to acquiring practical wisdom. Dreyfus argues persuasively that if the body is omitted from the learning environment, people lose the ability to recognize relevance, lose their adeptness at skill acquisition, and lose a sense of the reality of people and things, all of which results in the loss of meaning. Mastery is acquired through apprenticeship. As noted in chapter one, learning to be a person of faith occurs as we acquire other skills and knowledge from dedicated, knowledgeable people who sense what is needed for faith to flourish and who are committed, passionate and dependable.

To clarify the mastery of learning, I focus on learning to drive, since it is a wide-spread skill. I referred to Dreyfus's stage one in the first chapter. In this stage, learners are inexperienced. They are given features and rules of the skill to be mastered. The teacher begins by decomposing a task environment into context-free features that beginners can recognize without the desired skill. These features are domain-independent. The beginner is given rules for determining actions on the basis of these features, like a computer following a program. This stage is furnished by features and rules. The learner must recognize the features presented and engage in drill and practice, to become familiar with them and their rules of use. For example, learning to drive is a motor skill. Learners must recognize domain-independent features such as speed, which is indicated by the speedometer. Learners already have experience with speed that can be applied to understanding speed as they learn to drive. Then they are given rules, such as, shift gears when the speedometer points to ten. They become skilled with features and rules and move on to the next stage.

In stage two, advanced beginning, learners have some experience. As the novice gains experience in coping with real situations and develops understanding of the relevant context, he or she begins to note, or an instructor points out, useful examples of additional aspects of learning how to drive. After seeing a sufficient number of examples, learners come to recognize these new aspects. Instead of rules, learners are given instructional *maxims* to apply to new situational aspects, recognized on the basis of experience, as well as to objectively-defined, non-situational features recognizable by the novice. A maxim is a principle of action that a learner takes on and tries out. Unlike a rule, a maxim requires that learners already have some understanding of the domain to which the maxim applies. Learners become discerning with respect to maxims. For example, advanced beginning drivers use situational aspects such as engine sounds as well as non-situational features such as speed to decide when to shift gears. In addition to rules acquired as a novice, they learn the maxim: shift up when the motor sounds like it's racing and down then it sounds like it's straining. Engine sounds cannot be adequately captured by a list of features. Features cannot take the place of a few choice experiences in learning the relevant distinctions by failing sometimes and succeeding at other times.

In stage three, learners are competent. They have experience and can identify the potential relevance of any incident while they are driving. But learning now begins to distress the competent driver. With more experience, the list of potentially relevant elements and procedures (road conditions, sudden actions by other drivers, finding one's way using maps) that learners are able to recognize as important, is overwhelming. Because discernment is missing, performance at this point becomes nerve-racking and exhausting. Learners may well wonder how anyone ever masters the skill or gains know-how. To cope with the overload and achieve competence, people learn, through instruction and experience, to devise a plan, or choose a perspective to determine which elements of the situation or domain must be treated as important and which can be ignored. As students learn to restrict themselves to a few of the vast number of possibly relevant features or aspects, understanding and decision-making become easier.

This stage is critical to the eventual success of the learner. As Dreyfus pointed out, to avoid mistakes, the competent performer seeks rules and reasoning procedures to decide which plan or perspective to adopt. But rules such as these are not easy to come by if the learner is expecting the ease with which features, rules, relevance and maxims were acquired at the beginning. In learning anything, there are more situations than can be named or precisely defined in advance. No one can prepare learners with a complete list of possible situations, and what to look for in each one. Learners must decide for themselves what plan or perspective to adopt, without being sure it will turn out to be appropriate.

Given the level of uncertainty inherent in becoming competent, coping is frightening as well as tiring. Prior to this stage, learners can rationalize that they were not given adequate rules for doing what they want to do. When they have someone else to blame, they feel no remorse for errors. But at this stage, results depend on learners themselves; they feel responsible for their choices and for the confusion and failure that occurs. On the other hand, choices sometimes work out well; learners experience elation unknown to the novice.

The role of emotion in becoming competent is important. Embodied human beings take success and failure very seriously. Learners at this stage are understandably scared, elated, disappointed, or discouraged by the outcome of their choices. As competent learners become more and more emotionally involved in the task, it is increasingly difficult to draw back and adopt a maxim-following stance, as advanced beginners are able to do. The strangeness of this stage is felt deeply: as learners believe they are getting better at a skill, they actually begin to feel worse about what they are doing. Involvement is disconcerting. One response to the distress may be to withdraw, but this is the wrong move. Many people on the path towards a faithful life pull back at this point because experience does not fit the idea they had for faith.

Unless learners stay emotionally involved and accept the joy of a job well done, as well as remorse for mistakes, they will not develop further in the task of becoming masterful. They will eventually burn out trying to keep track of all the features and aspects, rules and

350

maxims that the domain requires of them. In general, resistance to involvement and risk leads to stagnation and ultimately to boredom and regression.

At this point teachers matter a great deal. They influence whether students withdraw into dis-embodied minds, or become more emotionally involved in learning. A teacher's manner and embodied perspective towards driving a car (or living the life of faith) is a model for learners. Teachers may be involved or detached: either way, their learners will pick up their approach, responses, hope or despair. If teachers have the courage to be open and involved, if they take risks and continue to learn from their own failures and successes, their courage is transmitted to learners. Courage constitutes the best possible embodied perspective for learners to experience, so that they can move on in the process of becoming masterful. For example, a competent driver leaving the freeway on an off-ramp curve learns to pay attention to the speed of the car, rather than whether to shift gears. After taking speed into account, surface conditions and the criticality of timing, he may decide he is going too fast. He then has to decide whether to let up on the accelerator, remove his foot altogether, or step on the brake, and precisely when to perform any of these actions. He is relieved if he gets through the curve without mishap, and shaken if he begins to go into a skid.

In stage four, learners are proficient. That is, they are involved, see issues immediately but must decide what to do. If the detached, information-consuming stance of novices and advanced beginners is replaced by involvement, learners are set for further advancement. Under this condition, the resulting positive and negative emotional experiences strengthen successful responses and inhibit unsuccessful ones, and the learner's theory of the skill will gradually be replaced by situational discriminations, accompanied by associated responses. Proficiency seems to develop *only if* experience is assimilated in an embodied and a-theoretical way. Only then do intuitive reactions replace reasoned responses. To recap, during these stages, the learner has moved from rules, to maxims and then to principles that are applied to situations as they arise. At this point, learning is embodied.

Dreyfus asserts that the stages of learning mastery apply to any complex skill. Learning to play chess or a subject in a classroom also require this a-theoretical and embodied aspect if learners are to move toward mastery. Action becomes easier and less stressful as the learner simply sees what needs to be done rather than using a calculative procedure to select one of several possible alternatives. Students learn to act appropriately with respect to the skill in question. There is less doubt about taking the action. People at this stage learn to discriminate among options, even though they are deeply involved. It is important to note that the proficient performer still needs to decide what to do even though he or she is discriminating. This person sees goals and salient aspects of the situation at hand but acting is not immediate. Even though seeing what matters may be spontaneous, he or she must fall back at times on rules, maxims and principles.

For example, a proficient driver, approaching a curve on a rainy day, may *feel in the seat of his pants* that he is going dangerously fast. He must then decide whether to apply the brakes or merely to reduce pressure by some specific amount on the accelerator. Valuable time may be lost while he is deciding, but a proficient driver is more likely to negotiate the curve safely than the competent driver who must consider speed, angle of the bank, and felt gravitational forces, in order to decide whether the car's speed is excessive.

In contrast, at stage five, experts see immediately what needs to be done and how to achieve the goal. The ability to make more refined and subtle discriminations is what distinguishes the expert from the proficient performer. Among many situations, all seen as similar with respect to the plan or perspective the learner has chosen, the expert has learned to distinguish those situations requiring one reaction from those demanding another. That is, with enough experience in a variety of situations, all seen from the same perspective but requiring different tactical decisions, the brain of the expert gradually decomposes the class of situations into subclasses, each of which requires a specific response. The division into subclasses allows the immediate intuitive situational response that is characteristic of expertise.

In the teacher-learner relationship, particularly in professional schools, observation and imitation of an expert teacher can replace a random search for better ways to act. In general, it is an advantage to be an apprentice. Professional schools must show how theory is to be applied in the real world. One way to accomplish this aim is to simulate the surroundings that learners will face later in their careers. Case-study learning is an approach that helps make the shift from the classroom to the world. It is not sufficient however to simply work through a lot of cases; these situations must matter to students. As Dreyfus notes, flight simulators work because they create the conditions of being in an airplane and provide the stress and risk involved in flying a plane. For case studies to work, learners must become emotionally involved. Students should not be confronted with objective descriptions of a situation but should be led to identify with the experience of those in the scenario. The most reliable way to produce involvement is to require students to work in the relevant skill domain, as apprentices. By imitating a master, they learn abilities for which there are no rules, such as how long to persist when the work does not seem to be going well, and just how much precision should be sought in each different kind of situation. The role of the master is to pass to the apprentice an ability to apply theory to the real world. For this, the master and the apprentice must be immersed in the context.

Suppose someone is trying to become a masterful medical doctor. In becoming a master at diagnosis, the teacher has learned to see an already-interpreted situation where certain features and aspects spontaneously stand out as meaningful. This complex skill is similar to the way, as one becomes familiar with a strange city, it ceases to look like a jumble of buildings and streets and develops a familiar face. The intern is trying, among other things, to acquire a particular doctor's embodied understanding of how to proceed and respond. In transmitting an informed understanding of the domain, teachers cannot help demonstrating a certain approach they use that typifies the way they do things, e.g., a way of approaching patients, asking questions, learning from mistakes. As they are apprenticed, students pick up a manner and embodied perspective. In addition to content, they adopt a style. For example, an expert driver not only *feels in the seat of his pants* when speed is an issue but knows how to perform appropriate action without calculating and comparing alternatives. On the off-ramp, his foot slips off the accelerator and applies the appropriate pressure to the brake. What must be done is done simply. The expert straight away does the right action, in the right way, at the right time.

In stage six, mastery amounts to learning discernment plus acquiring a personal style (*habitus*). For passing on style, apprenticeship is the only method available. This is not to say that teachers produce clones. Working with different masters (as many musicians do) is a way of finding one's own style. Using the music example, it is not that a young musician should go to one teacher for fingering and another for phrasing. Skill components cannot be divided in this way. Rather, one master has a style and another master has an entirely different style. Working with more than one master destabilizes and confuses the apprentice so that he or she cannot copy either, but must develop her or his own style. This is what we call mastery: personal style shapes the discernment acquired over time and through experience.

The process of learning mastery is not complete at this point. In stage seven, apprentices acquire practical wisdom, which refers to discernment, authenticity and cultural style. They add to personal style, a culturally well-situated understanding of how to practice their art so as to be seen by others as masterful. Stages six and seven are strongly related to one another, just as the first five stages prepare the groundwork for effective mastery. Stage seven is primarily concerned with learning a cultural style (*hexis*).

Cultural style is invisible unless we experience a different cultural way of doing things. This is similar to learning personal style by experiencing the unique styles of various masters. Learning cultural style is like setting up house with someone who grabs the toothpaste tube and squeezes it unceremoniously from the middle, while you always thought it could only be squeezed from the end, with precision. In stage seven learning, you notice the difference and perceive how to do things. For example, if we compare child-rearing practices in England and North America or the United States and Japan, general cultural styles determine how a baby will encounter himself or herself. A Japanese baby will make sense within Japanese culture, as will an American baby in the United States but they will not at first be understood if a switch is made. Good Canadian children generally do not sit quietly in a restaurant to eat their meals on their own as proper English children tend to do.

Once we see that culture governs how personal style will show up, we notice that cultural style shapes the perception of its culture bearers. Embodied understanding is passed on from one culture member to another, without saying anything, but simply by being in each other's presence. That is, culture is transmitted as world knowledge more than as word knowledge. In being apprenticed to our parents, we learn practical wisdom, i.e., the ability to do the right thing, at the right time, in the right place, with the right people, for the right reason, for the right length of time. When we are trying to learn mastery, at a later date in our lives, we need this apprenticing relation to guide and nurture the acquisition of practical wisdom with respect to what we aim to learn. Practical wisdom requires other people who have personal style and cultural know-how. In order to become wise, the mastery of a skill must be appropriately situated within cultural know-how. This constitutes the art of learning mastery. How might we apply becoming masterful to people of faith? What does masterful faith look like?

MASTERING THEOLOGICAL REFLECTION

In responding to the question of what masterful faith is like, let's take the example of theological reflection, which is at the heart of faith maturity. The heart's struggle with faith is expressed through an art of reflecting on theological ideas, practices and patterns. The outcomes of trying to reflect (decisions, actions) matter a great deal. But outcomes by themselves can be misleading. Recall the inner monk. Outcomes are important, but we do not get the courage to live life faithfully on the strength of what actually happens—since faith is exercised *before* we can see what will come of our efforts. We use faith *to try* living faithfully. Our work is to try; God's work is to bring success, as God wills. For believers, it is in the heart that essential work is done. Outcomes are less reliable than we like to think. We are misled by appearances; God is not. Ordinary people like you and me are fooled by those who say they are Christian but whose hearts are far from God and filled with idols, lust and lies. Such hearts do not fool God. Ordinary people are fooled by those who sin dreadfully and fall very low in the world's currency, but who finally turn their hearts toward God to gain forgiveness and a future. Such hearts do not fool God.

When we consider the importance of trying to reflect from the heart, we acknowledge that Western consciousness has been shaped by two ways of thinking about human experience: Greek and Hebrew. I wish to emphasize elements of a Hebrew worldview. But first, I raise two cautions concerning the generalizations I will make: Neither way of thinking is monolithic—there is not one 'Greek way' of thinking—but rather, there is diversity in each perspective; and secondly, it is hard to distinguish the ancient views from what they have become. For example, if we take Old Testament culture, on the one hand, and fifth century Greece, on the other, as the high points of these two ways of thinking, we could observe that, since the days of Alexander the Great (356-323 B.C.) onward, "European civilization manifests only mixtures and syntheses of the two ways of thinking, in which now one and now the other prevails."[3]

Given that caveat, reflection from the heart, based on embodied learning, marries two ancient traditions: Greek and Hebrew. A Hebrew or Semitic approach to thinking emphasizes and values movement; it is dynamic, vigorous, passionate, sometimes explosive. The Greek or Indo-European way of thinking emphasizes and values rest; it is harmonious, prudent, moderate, peaceful.[4] Hebrew consciousness did not devalue rest; coming to rest is an activity. One finds rest. Reflection from the heart is an activity of an entire body: one which is active and restful, depending. If we marry these two ways of thinking, central questions the faithful must answer for themselves have to do with rest and work. What is my work? What is not my work? These questions apply to spiritual work as much as they do to daily labor.

Robert Raikes (1735-1811), the founder of Sunday schools, modeled the point about trying versus succeeding, working and resting.[5] He brought children into a classroom relation with Scripture and Christian culture, not because he had a grand idea to reform England, though his efforts had that effect. He began Sunday schools because the noisy, dirty, foul-smelling and foul-mouthed children playing outside his print shop workroom disturbed his quiet. So he decided to bring them indoors and fit them with clean clothes and clean slates. After he realized these children could learn as well as anyone, despite their poverty, he invested time and resources in their lives, homes and families. Raikes experienced opposition from all sides as he tried to educate the poor, often from well-meaning Christians. He persisted. At one point he felt whelmed by those who wanted him to quit. While reading Scripture, he saw that his calling was not to succeed, so much as it was *to try* to be faithful. He was called to try.

Theological reflection is an activity that enables faithfulness to grow up. Difficult as it sounds, theological reflection makes sufficient sense of life so that believers continue trying to be faithful. Theological reflection results in unconquerable courage. The heart is the site for its growth. Faith education enables us to develop a communal life of faith: establish memory, build reason and nurture insight. Faithfulness comes through theological reflection that unites heart, mind, soul, body. Theological reflection is embodied thought informed by interrupting ourselves in a way I want to describe. Coming from the heart, theological reflection alters the heart. We grow up by acquiring practices of the heart that help us think about God, ourselves, other people, life in general and that enable us to draw these strands together to make sense of them, so that we make sense to other people.

THE HEART OF FAITH

Scripture declares God's focus: God looks at the heart. In 1Samuel 16:7, Samuel tried to help Israel choose a king: *the Lord said to Samuel, "Do not look on* [David's] *appearance or on the height of his stature...for the Lord does not see as mortals see; they look on the outward appearance, but the Lord looks on the heart.* The heart is central to an inner life. In speaking of the heart, Jews had in view the inner life as a unity with all its willing, feeling and thinking.[6]

357

The assumption of scripture is that thinking, willing and feeling are caught up in a conceptual web that implies acting as well. There are two words in the New Testament translated as heart: the Greek words *kardia* and *tharseo*. *Kardia* refers to the actual organ in the body and has a wide range of aspects. *Tharseo*,[7] which may be translated as 'take heart,' is a summons that implies 'encourage yourself', although the New Testament implication is that Christ stands behind us providing the resources for courage. Courage motivates and sustains thinking, willing, feeling and acting. Apart from a biblical perspective, ideas as to the location of thinking and feeling have varied historically and culturally since ancient Greece.

It is perhaps as we examine aspects of the heart's meaning in earlier eras that we begin to sense what the heart signifies and can mean to us. As an example, for Homer there was a pre-philosophical physiology that located thinking and feeling, which could not be separated, with the *phrenes* or midriff of the human being. Willing tended not to be referred to in ancient Greek philosophy; the emphasis is on exercising courage. Hannah Arendt[8] argued that the will was a uniquely Christian idea introduced by the apostle Paul in Romans 7:14-25. The Greek term for thought or wisdom *(phronesis)* was derived from its association with the midsection. Greeks who associated thought with the heart related thinking and feeling to the heat carried by the blood system; they identified the soul with fire and connected heat with consciousness. Blood was associated with perception and perception with the heart. Aristotle referred to the heart as the *arche*[9] of life, movement and sensation, and though the Epicureans dispersed the soul all over the body, the rational faculty was in the breast, as it was for the Stoics.

The Pythagorean School of medicine located perception in the brain. Rather than fire or heat as a metaphor for thought, their source for perception was the air: human beings inhale air, which is the divine *arche* of all things—the source of life, soul and intelligence. The air that a person inhales travels, *via* the various senses, to the brain. If the air is dry and pure, thought takes place. Socrates appears to have adopted the brain as the site of thinking and perception. Aristotle, on the other hand, believed there was no sensation in the brain itself. [10] For Greeks generally, the soul is what gives life to the body. For Plato, the soul had a value greater than the body; the soul was the essential part of human being—what makes us who we are. The soul was the site for thinking and feeling. Soul and body interact but the soul was trapped in the body. Aristotle differed with Plato on this point. For Aristotle, the soul did not exist without a body; he appeared to place more value on the human body than did Plato. Perhaps this was because Aristotle was a man of action: for him, knowing was equated with doing.[11] Aristotle's view was widespread, but not wholly persuasive. Plotinus, for example, followed the Platonic tradition and located the *arche* of sensation in the brain.[12] In contrast, the twentieth century used the metaphor of energy as a way to understand thinking and thought. The suggestion that faith is a kind of energy that provides us with the means to go on living capitalizes on that modern metaphor.

It would seem that Western liberal tradition has its roots in a Greek controversy over bodily sites for thinking and feeling. But from an ancient Hebrew perspective it is odd to dichotomize thinking, feeling and bodily sites for these activities. To illustrate the contrast between these two perspectives, we have the model of Socrates and the praying Orthodox Jew. Socrates was renowned for his capacity to think in a manner that disregarded his body and its needs. When he "was seized by a problem he remained immobile for an interminable period of time in deep thought;" but when "Holy Scripture is read aloud in the synagogue, the Orthodox Jew moves his whole body ceaselessly in deep devotion and adoration," [13] symbolically distinguishing between Hebrew movement and Greek stillness as indicators of thought.

From the perspective of Scripture, *Kardia*[14] is the word that concerns us most directly. The heart, in this sense, is the innermost part of a human being. It has a diverse and unified set of dimensions. The heart is the seat of rational functioning, just as it is the site for understanding, far-reaching insight and knowledge. Thoughts dwell in the heart—including evil thoughts as inner monks came to stress—along with fantasies, self-invented visions and artistic sensibility. The notion that an idea was self-invented was a sign that something was wrong, since personal insight should not depart from communal wisdom. In the Old Testament (OT), heart is closest to what we call conscience. But as we have already discussed, conscience was communally formed. In addition, the heart of a true prophet was linked to the heart of God. To speak out of one's own heart is to deviate from the truth, as the false prophets did.

The heart represents life in its totality. The heart's thinking denotes action. Scripture instructs us to direct our hearts, thereby expecting us willingly to direct our attention to God. Because thinking, feeling and acting are inseparable, religious and moral conduct is rooted in the heart.[15] The equivalent term for heart in the OT represents the centre of life and the epitome of the person.[16] The heart is both an active and a concealed aspect of the human person, making it a psychological organ in which all life is concentrated. The heart is not just indispensable to life; through God's activity in the human heart, it can become the principle of a new life.[17] What a person sees and (especially) hears enters the heart. In heart impressions from the outside world we meet pain, joy or sorrow. The heart first stores these impressions then moves us to action. Memories and divine commandments make us pious and intelligent. An intelligent person has a heart while an insane person has no heart, since piety and understanding reside in the heart.

The heart is specifically human, distinguishing us from animals. From the heart comes planning and remembering. The heart does not merely record and keep impressions. The heart has a creative function and the active role of the heart is greater than its receptive role. The heart is a spring. Ways of life, ritual and tradition, have their origin there; its primary task is to guide aright ways of life chosen by the heart. A heart can be dull, slow or hardened. That is, the heart is considered to be malleable and its flexibility comes as a result of the thinking, willing, feeling and acting. The human heart is not absolutely pure; it inclines to falsehood, division and pride. Scripture refers negatively to divided or double hearts and asserts an ideal for a pure, single or undivided heart. A catastrophe of the heart is that it can become hard as stone.

Scriptural metaphors for the heart include soil, treasure, a tablet and a room. A hard heart, like hard soil, is perceived as a fundamental barrier to God and godly action. The seed of God's Presence will not grow. Hardheartedness cannot be hid. God is concerned about the heart, tests and examines it. God renews the heart. He makes it pure and firm and moves it to be one with His. But we are also responsible for the condition of our hearts. Its soil, treasures, what is written upon its surface, what finds a home on its walls, all are of concern. But the heart lives in a body that is also a gift from God.

An Embodied Heart

The heart relates to the unity and totality of the inner life represented and expressed in the variety of intellectual and spiritual functions of the human person. The New Testament concentrates on the heart as the main organ of spiritual life: in the heart dwell feelings, emotions, desires and passions. As with the Old Testament, the heart is the seat of understanding, the source of thought and reflection, the seat of the will and reason (*nous* and *dianoia*) and the source of resolves (willing, choosing). Thus the heart is the centre in human beings to which God turns, in which the religious life is rooted, which determines moral conduct. The heart has to do with living well here and now so that we will feel at home in heaven. But if we examine the uses of the term body in the New Testament, value is ascribed to *a heart within a body*, uniquely to Christianity, which modernity underplayed.

In the Old Testament, interest in the physical body has to do with healing, washing, bathing, cleansing, or with ceremonial responsibilities to a dead body. There is a reference to the social body in Judges. Also there is a metaphysical reference to the spiritual importance of the body in Ezek 36:26, for example: *A new heart I will give you, and a spirit I will put within you; and I will remove from your body the heart of stone and give you a heart of flesh.* The body is not referred to in negative terms, but rather as a problem to address when it is diseased and to be avoided by pious people if it is dead.

The concept of the body in New Testament (NT), referenced in 121 verses, differs from the OT due to the significance of Christ's body and his Incarnation. In the NT, the human body is material and spiritual. Jesus pays unique attention to the body. He implies that the body as a whole is more significant than its parts, if these parts cause us to sin. Further he says that the eye is the lamp of the body. *So, if your eye is healthy, your whole body will be full of light; but if your eye is unhealthy, your whole body will be full of darkness. If then the light in you is darkness, how great is the darkness.* (Matt 6:22-23). He advises us to attend to bodily needs without anxiety. *Therefore I tell you, do not worry about your life, what you will eat or what you will drink, or about your body, what you will wear. Is not life more than food, and the body more than clothing?* Matt 6:25. His emphasis does not degrade the body but prizes it. He says: *Do not fear those who kill the body but cannot kill the soul; rather fear him who can destroy both soul and body in hell. Mat 10:28.* Since the body is both spiritual and material, its eternal aspect will be clothed in a new body after death. Just as Christ's resurrected body is both material and spiritual (but in a new sense), we too gain a new body for eternity. The soul is understood to reside in a body, in this world and the next. It is an embodied heart's work to get us ready for life after death.

Christ's own body is model and metaphor for the spiritual community we call the Church. His body is referred to in about 25% of all references to the body in the NT. Christ gives his body to us as a sacrifice in two senses: in his death and resurrection in which he atones (or pays the price) for our sin and through the feast of communion. The holiness of Communion is sealed as a sign of continual refreshment and restoration available to believers through the body and blood of Christ. He offers his body for our bodies' sake. The ritual is a sign of union with other believers. The sharing of Christ's body is personal and communal—a sign of individual redemption, an act of corporate solidarity. The body emerges from the NT as an integrated site for spiritual vitality and renewal and the site for thinking, feeling, willing and acting. Nothing derogatory is said about the body. We are warned that severity to the body is of no value in checking self-indulgence. If punishing the body is of no use in helping us turn toward the heart of God, what does help?

Theological Reflection as a break in the flow of experience

As we attend to our hearts empathetically, theological reflection takes on rich significance. At this point, I explore theological reflection as an embodied thinking/acting/speaking, informed by an objective break with subjective experience. During the break, faith seeks to sense what we are doing/saying/being in relation to what we hope to be or become. This inquiry assumes that we are often inattentive to an embodied theological stance in the daily practice of faith. Theological reflection takes seriously the contribution embodied awareness makes to thinking. There is an effective relationship between theological reflection and human maturity, if we attend to the embodied heart—and varied ways it 'thinks'. First of all, tension in theological reflection shows up if we compare monastic practice with the scholarly discipline that currently shapes what we study in seminary education. Monastic practice, based on *oratio, meditatio, and tentatio* (prayer, meditation and testing), is an adventure in self-transformation that emphasizes engagement with text and tradition grounded on obedience to, text and tradition. Through obedience, the subjectivity of believers is altered as a consequence of their attentiveness to sacred texts and the lives of the faithful. Monastic practices of heart, mind and body preserve and conserve ritual and tradition, although obedience is not mindless. Under favourable conditions, reason moves the flow of theological reflection.

On the other hand, discipline in the scholarly sense excites the mind's inquisitiveness about the faith tradition that it investigates: It is thinking about thinking about faith. Its discipline was derived from critical inquiry and motivated by modern (Renaissance) impulses toward emancipation from pre-modern religious world views, by the desire to pursue the free play of the mind, and by the privileging of individuality over collective membership in religious communities. As mentioned in earlier chapters, the freedom to follow inquiry wherever it might lead was the hallmark of a modern mind.[18] Modern theological reflection compiled and organized reliable ideas or propositions of the faith and laid out historic conflicts among these ideas. In contrast to this modern sensibility, monastic discipline suspects intellectual practices associated with critical thinking and perceives an intellectualism that keeps its distance from tradition and the rituals of faith, e.g., the suspecion is that critical thinkers will lose their faith.

In monastic discipline, one draws near to tradition to be transformed into its likeness. In scholarly discipline one keeps one's distance in order to challenge, question and critique tradition and text, to test its capacity for satisfying the intellect (cognitively) and for allowing thought to follow its own lead without constraints from the faith tradition and other people. I propose that theological reflection could retain its critical aspect so that it satisfies the need for scholarly inquiry, while still encouraging the adventure of self-transformation that monastic practices offer. We could employ both insight and reason in the art of theological reflection, following the pattern for reason outlined in Hegel's concept of experiencing and recalling Kant's warning that reason has its natural limits. But while thinking is powerful as an influence on theological reflection, I wish to consider the body and its role in moving us to act in the ways that we do. To understand theological reflection, we attend to the entire body rather than to thinking alone.

How Modernity Went to Our Heads

In making a case for theological reflection from an embodied heart, the term *habitus*[19] is useful. Charles Wood was also concerned to marry theological inquiry to the transformational, personal effects of the monastic tradition. Following his lead, I examine the idea of *habitus* in order to point out its nature from the perspective of embodied, thoughtful, theological practice. Wood describes his view of theological education and compares it with three others that he says have been influential, namely: spiritual formation models, 'traditioning' models and professional or church leadership models. In laying out his view, he identifies *habitus* as the site for theological inquiry, as well as its product. To Wood, theological *habitus* has both personal and intellectual qualities so that it refers to an individual's disposition to be reflective as well as to the outcomes or products of that reflection. Theological *habitus* refers to one's subjectivity and to outcomes of that subjectivity. Further, there is a relationship between personal dispositions (developed capacities) and the outcomes that result. Both the disposition and its outcomes comprise the theological *habitus*.

In general, in theological reflection, learners begin with a particular subjectivity (just as a young child has a particular concept of God). This subjectivity is informed through theological reflection (one way or another) and is transformed (at least teachers hope it is). Wood describes some of the difficulties and mis-directions that frustrate educational hopes (for students and teachers). In doing so, he defines *habitus* ultimately as the disposition to bring, and the products of bringing, "to conscious scrutiny behaviour [that] might otherwise be governed by habit, or convention, or unconscious motives, or various other factors."[20] If people have a disposition to be theologically reflective, they can be counted on to bring to conscious scrutiny, the personal thought and action that supports Christian faithfulness, and distinguish among other thoughts and actions. The positive result of educationally transformed theological *habitus* is Christian discernment. If we consider what was said earlier about the experienced monk in the Niptic tradition, we can see parallels between Wood's notion of theological reflection and what ancient Christians believed was possible in the life of the faithful.

From Wood's perspective, *habitus* is vision-oriented and essentially cognitive. It refers to a way of seeing and cognising about faith. I do not intend to dismiss vision and thinking (in the cognitive sense) as organizing principles for theological reflection. But I want to extend the use of the term *habitus* to include elements that incorporate a fuller range of everyday experience by including what we do bodily as an object of conscious scrutiny. The following questions animate this inquiry: What does it mean to reflect theologically in the midst of the press and flow of ordinary life? How does religious thought operate? Do we think through our eyes? How does theological reflection work if we consider more than the head and the eyes? Have only the head and eyes been considered safe for doing theology? What does privileging the head and the eyes communicate about the body?

The inner monk did not privilege sight; the heart and body were taken seriously. Andrew J. Strathern, an anthropologist, suggests that it was Rene Descartes (1596-1650) who established a dichotomy between body and mind that strongly influences us still. Descartes proposed that the soul/mind had no physical extension (*res non extensa*) yet possessed the capacity to think (*res cogitans*); and he thought that the body had physical extension but no capacity to think. According to Strathern, by making this assertion, Descartes "set up a realm of the physical or material that could be apprehended as a thing and studied by the transcendental capacities of the soul/mind."[21] The "extreme separation of the soul from the body made it possible not only to isolate the sphere of reason and the intellect from the sphere of practical, embodied life but also [exaggerated] the male-female dichotomy that was grafted onto this dichotomy of mind and body."[22] In relation to theological reflection, Descartes proposed that intellect was the connection between God and man [sic] even though body and mind were created in God's image. In his dichotomy of mind and body, he "preserved a hierarchy of mind over matter that was essentially theocentric" [23] and gendered. His contribution continues to influence our ideas about the appropriate site for theological reflection[24] that theological reflection is done in the heads of men.

The tendency is to believe that theological reflection anticipates and privileges seeing and minding as the two acceptable activities that comprise thought. I suggest we should retain our focus on the head and the eyes but also pay attention to our bodies as they operate within the world. Scripture expects us to attend to our hearts and our bodies. What do we embody about theological truths in our everyday lives? What is the theological significance of embodiment? Further, how can I practice theological reflection bodily and what does an embodied approach tell me about theological ideas? In response to these questions, the term theological reflection will refer to a particular way of 'speaking' that takes account of the opportunity to speak in a sensitive, thoughtful, embodied manner. In putting forth this view of theological reflection, I suggest that effectiveness means sensing what I am doing as much as what I am thinking, so that the right to 'speak' theologically is well situated in the everyday world.

This point echoes earlier references to world knowledge and word knowledge that characterizes a wholistic view of human communication, which we all have access to and that we all use in ordinary living. I want to unite these two aspects of communication and situate their role in theological reflection, to say that it is only when what we say mirrors what we do that we can claim to be living theologically integrous lives. What follows, then, connects theological reflection to practical wisdom, as the outcome of learning mastery.

Faithful Living

Faithful living may come from an earnest heart but its expression finds completion in public life. Confident faith is free to speak in secular and religious contexts. My interest in describing theological reflection, as mindful embodied thought, is to improve the recognition that faithful talk receives in secular contexts. Christians should move freely between secular and religious worlds. To discuss the issue of recognition and the practice of theological reflection, I use insights from Pierre Bourdieu (1930-2001), a French sociologist. One of his first interests was the interplay between social honour and social recognition. He was fascinated by the idea that struggles for recognition are a fundamental dimension of social life and that the high stakes in these struggles have to do with gaining and losing a particular form of capital he called symbolic capital. Through his sociological investigations he came to believe that social strategies that shape the accumulation or loss of symbolic capital are neither conscious and calculated, nor mechanically determined, but are a product of what he called the 'sense of honour' or the particular feel for the game of honour.[25] He developed the view that there is a logic of practice that inheres in strategies aimed at securing social honour that are above time and the effort of individual people. That is, strategies are learned, but not consciously or formally, by being in the presence of those who play them out themselves.[26] He used language as an anology to reveal this logic of practice; it helps to keep in mind, as his view is unpacked, to think of language as a combination of world and word knowledge.

Bourdieu included the socio-historical and practical character of language as an important element of daily speech. For example, he believed that "everyday linguistic exchanges are situated encounters between agents endowed with socially structured resources and competencies, in such a way that every linguistic interaction, however personal and insignificant it may seem, bears the traces of the social structure that it both expresses and helps to reproduce."[27] In short, there is more to language than what is said. Bourdieu was not a structuralist. The structuralists, he believed, analyse language in a way that separates it from the struggles that established a particular language as the formal and dominant one and they forget that other languages have been eliminated or subordinated to it.

He was critical of linguistic structuralists because he thought they were imperialistic with their theoretical frameworks. The dominant or *victorious* language is what linguists commonly take for granted as the language of a particular people group. As examples, in the United States, struggles between standard (or white) English and Black English, or Spanish versus English are very complicated and heated. In Canada, there is tension over French and English languages. By analogy, there is a *victorious* modern site for theological reflection (the head) and a *victorious* body (white, middle-class, male). This victory marginalizes others who differ from its primary characteristics. I am fully aware this is not a new point. My concern is to provide a way of being theologically reflective that may offer healing for relationships that have been severed by gender, economic and racial conflict. It is essential to find new ways to interact with those who differ from us if we hope to strengthen our attempts to be faithful members of the diverse communities to which we belong.

If we want to face diversity, Bourdieu is useful because he is even-handed. He refused to privilege the *victorious* ideal competence in speech production (in the sense that linguists who are structuralists use the expression ideal competence), but does not make war on *victorious* languages in order to defeat and replace them with others. Rather, he wanted to understand how *victorious* languages operate so that it becomes possible to speak and be heard in the fields where they hold sway. This point is significant. I do not think we improve the practice of theological reflection by making war on those who have up to now been *victorious*. In our practice, we must affirm that we are all part of the human community of faith. We attempt, through and in Christ, to be a new humanity. Those who are disprivileged can learn how to be heard in a field that has a particular historical shape to it by finding a way to speak that does not rob them of their own voices. The primary intention for embodied theological reflection is not only to be inclusive within a faith community, but to find innovative and effective ways to speak in public. In the twenty-first century, this is an essential task for Christians voices to master. I assume that when we learn to speak more inclusively, we will communicate more effectively to those who do not believe in God. To accomplish this aim, we need to enliven modern theological reflection by exposing it to pre-modern practices and post-modern critiques,[28] without discarding the gains made during modernity.

To accomplish the aim of situating speech effectively, Bourdieu wanted to take what he called a reflexive sociological stance. What does it mean to be reflexive? In addressing the practice of situating speech effectively, Bourdieu focused attention on a practical competence that speakers have. He describes a practical sense in which people are able to produce utterances that are appropriate to the circumstances they face. In his view, this practical competence cannot be derived from the written or oral utterance of an ideal speaker. This point is crucial to easing tension between the church and the world. Competent speakers embed sentences (in terms of word and world knowledge) in practical situations that are tacitly adjusted to the relations of power between them and those who listen. Practical wisdom involves the capacity to make oneself heard, believed and respected. Those who demonstrate practical wisdom know when to speak and how to sense that those who listen reckon they are worthy of attention.

THEOLOGICAL REFLECTION AND
THE RIGHT TO SPEAK

The right to speak, in this view at least, is grounded on a speaker's competence in using the right strategies, in the right way, at the right time, with the right people and for the right reasons. But right is ambiguous: entitlement depends upon an effectively situated utterance (orally and bodily) that is the product of a culturally astute sense of the game of social honour. In trying to situate speech, two common problems arise. We may treat a linguistic exchange as an intellectual (i.e., cognitive) operation only and fail to notice the body's strategies that secure or lose the right to speak. In missing or misconstruing an opportunity, we miss the significance of associated forms of power and authority that shape all communicative situations. Secondly, we may allow one (so-called) right way of speaking to dominate theological conversation so that we never develop a capacity for spiritually sensitive, well-situated theological talk.

While those who feel excluded from the right to speak theologically should not make war on the victorious, neither should they comply with domination, by giving up their difference. To lose an authentic voice is to fail to contribute insight to the human condition. I suggest rather that they learn how the *victorious* language operates so that they can effectively situate their voices into the context it has created. I acknowledge that there is a certain injustice in this advice. If we are all God's children, why should some of us have to work so hard, while others of us enjoy the priviledges of dominance? I agree that it is not fair. This side of heaven, many things are not fair. But the contribution that differences make to the mainstream is too important to lose.

The point for theological reflection is that there is not one right way to speak theologically, so much as there needs to be competent, well-situated ways: a way that is right for a particular time, place and people. In my experience, modern theological talk does not enjoy the right to be heard in our culture; seminaries do not show students how to be competent, innovative speakers so that they can be heard in the market place once they leave. Yet this capacity is central to faithful witness. Theological reflection presently does not have a secure position in the everyday discourse of ordinary people. Its absence is remarkable and is a debilitating loss to human being.

What sort of talk is theological reflection? In coming to his views about honour, social power and speech, Bourdieu took seriously J.L. Austin's work on words.[29] Austin described performative utterances, such as christening a ship, in which the saying of the ship's name and the smashing of a bottle of champagne on its bow is a ritual that changes a state of affairs. The ship now has a name and can begin its journey. Naming, christening or baptizing children are performatives in that an infant who has no name or spiritual home, now has them. Performing a wedding ceremony is another example. Churches do well to keep these roles in society if they want to maintain a cultural voice. Funeral services provide a further example and are an important opportunity to enact and retain the cultural authority of belief.

Performative utterances are carried out by those who have authority to do so. They get this authority from the institutions that give it. An institution to Bourdieu is any durable set of social relations that endows individuals with power, status and resources of various kinds.[30] Institutions *authorize* people to secure the efficacy of what they do. In general, authorized theological talk takes place behind closed doors and has become a sub-cultural activity ordinary people do not understand; it is embarrassed about itself in public.

I want to push this point further. In discussing power and the embodied authority of someone's voice, a distinction is central to showing how Bourdieu's views relate to theological reflection. When people speak, they are always speaking in a context. Bourdieu used the term field to describe the context in which someone acts or speaks. If theological reflection is intelligent, the relationship between intelligence, domains and fields is important. Intelligence refers to the ability to solve problems, or to create products that are valued within one or more cultural settings. Intelligence can be thought of in neuro-biological terms, as did Howard Gardner (1983, 1993), although his idea of intelligence is largely cognitive.[31] To Gardner, we are born with the proclivity toward a certain way of being intelligent. An intelligence may be musical, logical rational, kinaesthetic or spatial, as some examples.

Human beings are born into cultures that house a number of domains or disciplines, crafts and other pursuits, in which people are enculturated and assessed in terms of their level of competency in them. While domains refer to people who express competence in them, domains can also be captured in books or computer programs and therefore can be detached from the people that contribute them. There is a relationship between domains and intelligences so that intelligences operate within the sphere of a domain. Domains typically require expertise in more than one type of intelligence. As an example, the domain of music includes a range of what musicians have produced in a given culture, over time. If a musically talented person plays a musical instrument well, he or she has kinaesthetic intelligence.

Once people achieve a level of competence in the exercise of intelligence within a domain, the term field takes on importance. As a sociological construct, "the field includes the people, institutions and award mechanisms and so forth that render judgments about the qualities of individual performances."[32] Those who are judged to be competent by the field are likely to become successful practitioners, that is, they are seen to demonstrate practical wisdom. If the field is not able to judge the work of a particular person, or if their work is judged to be inferior, opportunity for achievement is curtailed. On the strength of this distinction, creativity itself is shaped by the interactions between intelligence, domain and field.

The point made earlier about the dichotomy between male and female bodies is important, since the field is influenced by its perception of the body of those who are judged. At the social level, women struggle with current perceptions (often pornographic) of a female body that disprivilege them in many fields. Creativity and voice are curtailed. To Gardner, a creative individual "is one who *regularly* solves problems or fashions products in a domain, and whose work is considered both novel and acceptable by knowledgeable members of the field."[33] In fields dominated by a male body, the bodies of women are frequently found to be wanting as an authoritative site for the expression of giftedness, despite their inherent talent.

The ability to be creative depends upon one's capacity to speak and be heard in a particular field. Perhaps the most difficult issue for theological reflection, and the doubly hindering bind for women, is the failure to transport theological talk to fields other than those that are safely inside Christian sub-cultures. A central question for seminary and church educators, is how to help people learn to reflect theologically in a way that respects the internal dynamics of faithful discourse, yet can be heard in the mainstream of thought. One shift we need to make is to ensure that theological reflection pays attention to the body so that our words and our actions support a thoroughly Christian way of living.

The Body and Theological Thought

To explain the role the body has in theological reflection, we need to follow a distinction Bourdieu made between the terms objective and subjective. Subjective, in his view, referred to an embodied intellectual orientation to the social world that seeks to grasp the way the world appears to individuals who are situated within it. Subjectivity presupposes the possibility of some kind of immediate apprehension of lived experience (ours and other people's) and assumes that this apprehension is by itself a more or less adequate form of knowledge about the social world. Objectivity refers to an intellectual orientation to the social world that seeks to construct the objective relations that structure our practices in, and representations of, the social world. That is, objectivity presupposes a break with immediate (subjective) experience. The theory of the break is central for theological reflection. Objectivity, according to Bourdieu, places the primary experience of the social world in brackets and attempts to elucidate the structures and principles upon which primary experience depends but that are not directly grasped while one is caught up in subjective experience.

Bracketing is a complex term that, in general, refers to suspending judgment about the term (phenomenological object) in brackets in the sense that we suspend our current (enculturated) presuppositions about it. We suspend what we have come to take as the natural attitude to have towards what we put in brackets, so that we can reconsider what to think about it. The aim of bracketing is to permit us to purify our perception of the bracketed item so we can come to sense what is really or essentially descriptive of it, and uncover some of its general aspects,[34] a process natural to conscientia, which was described in earlier chapters. To break or pause in the midst of subjective experience allows us to consider what we are doing/saying/being in light of what we choose to be, do, or say. During the break, we attend to what we are doing or saying so that it shows up for what it actually is, rather than what we have always thought about it.

Bourdieu thought that subjectivity and objectivity are inadequate on their own as intellectual orientations. Objectivity has the advantage of breaking with immediate experience. This break is necessary for inquiry to take place. I suggest that theological reflection is one sort of inquiry that requires this break. The disadvantage of objectivity is that it cannot sense the real world of actors and therefore can incite us to turn other people's actions into mere epiphenomenona of our own constructs. That is, objectivity always retains the danger of being imperialistic. Bourdieu wanted to take account of the need to break with immediate experience while at the same time doing justice to the practical character of social life. How can objectivity link with subjectivity so as to take account of the need to break with experience (what we are doing during a given moment), yet do justice to social experience?

Bourdieu proposed the term *habitus* as a way out of the difficulty between objectivity and subjectivity. Like Wood, he identified *habitus* as a set of dispositions that incline people to act and react in certain ways. Dispositions generate practices, perceptions and attitudes that are regular without being consciously co-ordinated or governed by any rule. To Bourdieu, dispositions that constitute the *habitus* are inculcated, structured, durable, generative and transposable. Dispositions are acquired through a gradual process of inculcation in which early childhood experiences are particularly important. It is the *habitus* that provides people with a sense of how to act and speak. During the ordinary experiences of childhood, through being taught table manners, such as: Sit up straight, or, Don't talk with your mouth full, an individual acquires a set of dispositions that literally mould the body and become second nature.

These dispositions are produced and structured until they reflect the social conditions in which they were acquired: class differences are evident in the body. As an example from Bourdieu, a working class student will have difficulty knowing how to act in an elite university and, regardless of intellectual giftedness, will be literally lost for words.[35] To illustrate, he used a French example of being a big-mouthed male[36] (i.e., a working class ideal speech pattern) and being a tight-lipped male (an upper class ideal speech pattern). He pointed out that if a working class male adopts a tight-lipped style of speaking, he does so at the cost of a double negation. He is not himself in terms of his (working) class background and he is not himself in terms of (male) sexual identity, because tight-lipped practices are considered appropriate to females, not males, in a working class context.[37]

In general, there is a relationship between speaking and making meaning. The dispositions we acquire that constitute our at-home *habitus* enable us to make sense of our world of original meaning. They focus our attention on a particular way of making meaning that gives precedence to our own, over other ways of making the social world meaningful, so that other ways do not make sense to us. Practices that differ deeply from our own do not hang together or cohere for us and we have trouble reading what they mean. These practices come across as wrong or inferior, rather than merely different. This dissonance is the result of a *habitus* that gives us a feel for the particular game that our culture, religion, family or society is playing.

We learn what is and is not appropriate in the game. As an example, we grow up learning to squeeze the toothpaste tube carefully up from the bottom or to grab it unceremoniously in the middle. Similarities and differences that characterize a particular *habitus* are recognizable by other members of our group. We gain the essential currency of recognition in our own group by using the language it values most. Dispositions are ingrained in the body in such a way that they endure through the life history of an individual; they are pre-conscious and not readily amenable to conscious reflection and modification, until we are in the presence of people who behave differently. In the presence of difference, and given the momentum of our particular *habitus*, one frequently chosen option is to reject categorically and immediately what does not make sense to us. In short, the *habitus* generates inertia, or movement in a particular, steady direction. We tend to trust people who share our *habitus* and mistrust or devalue those who do not.

In providing us with a sense of how to act and respond, the *habitus* orients our actions and inclinations without strictly determining them. It is not so much a state of mind as it is a state of embodiment. It is not so much an attitude of the head by itself as it is an activity of the body in its presence to itself and with others. In acting 'dispositionally', we may be quite unaware of what we are doing as we do it. Bourdieu describes another dimension to these dispositions. Bodily *hexis* is the mythology of a particular group *habitus* that is embodied and turned into a permanent disposition, and engenders trust. *Hexis* refers to a durable way of standing, speaking, walking, thinking and feeling that is considered appropriate in a given situation and that shapes our expectations of other members of our group. The importance of bodily *hexis* can be seen in the differing ways men and women carry themselves. As examples, there is a womanly way of walking for females and a manly way of walking for males. These patterns are strongly enforced through social control of various kinds: e.g., Hey, look at him. He catches the ball like a girl! Wow, she's such a tomboy!

To experiment with this point, try walking into a familiar group in a manner that is feminine if you are male or masculine if you are female. Observe the responses. We judge the appropriateness of people's behaviour according to the bodily *hexis* of our cultural group. When individuals act, they do so in a specific setting so that their actions are not merely the result of their personal *habitus* but are the consequence of a relationship between the *habitus* on the one hand, and specific social context or field (influenced by a cultural *hexis)*, on the other. We walk differently, depending on where and who we are.

If we apply Bourdieu's point to the theological context, we note that people learn how to speak about God in a context in which Christian experience is massively real: it strikes them as the only right way to speak. For example, if seminaries use a language when speaking about God and the Bible that differs from the at-home language of students, seminary language is not only experienced as foreign, it is felt to be wrong. If learners acquire the new way of speaking theologically, they lose their original identity as believers, since personal identity is largely constructed through practises such as speaking. Further, they no longer speak like the people back home. Since communal identity is constructed through talking together in a particular, practised way, when seminarians return to the church they may have weakened their capacity to strengthen group solidarity through talking together with the people of God. The loss of a comfortable, at-home, faithful voice is not a necessary outcome of Western-based scholarly theological education, but it is common.

As mentioned, under ordinary circumstances, we speak differently depending on who and where we are. But to complicate theological education, if we have a fixed notion that there is one right way to speak about God, it is extremely painful to be called on to speak in another way. It can show up as hypocritical or sinful—i.e., as a form of betrayal. Under this condition, learners may passively reject an education that uses a foreign way of speaking. At church, congregants may seem to be attentive, but all the while they know this one way of speaking about God won't work in the world, even if people want to talk about God.

A theological community voice that does not make sense initially may be resisted for a lifetime. This unreflective resistance can leave a person with an inauthentic voice—he or she will not learn mastery by using a pulpit voice that the speaker would not use in any other context. As a result, learning is distorted. People may sit still and say nothing in order to endure church or their education. Or they may give in and carry arrogance or unease in their voices when they speak at church or encounter the world. Somehow, those who long to be masterfully faithful need to find a comfortable, natural way of speaking about God.

To summarize, the body is a site of incorporated history. The practical schemes through which the body is organized are a product of personal history and reproduce that history. Dispositions give shape to a characteristic way of being a particular cultural member are not only oral. Bodies have their own language. Theological reflection could address itself to the body, and needs to, in order to pay attention to the requirements of Christian faith in our present circumstances. Attentiveness to the body helps us sense that our bodies, not just our words, tell the truth or lie. We confer honour or insult, we harass and abuse, through the use of our bodies. Truth-telling, conferring honour and respect are aspects of Christianity that need attention if we are to live congruently with what we say we believe. On this view, theological reflection not only refers to collecting adequate ideas of the faith, it is reflection upon whether or not we are living our faith in practice. But if we take the body seriously, we will soon experience its resistance to faithful ideas.

THEOLOGICAL REFLECTION WITH INERTIA

Scripture is clear about God's attitude towards those who use their bodies as a powerful weapon in their war against others:

> Scoundrels and villains, who go about with corrupt mouths, who wink with their eyes, signal with their feet and motion with their fingers, who plot evil with deceit in their hearts—they always stir up dissension....There are six things that the Lord hates, seven that are detestable to him: haughty eyes, a lying tongue, hands that shed innocent blood, a heart that devises wicked schemes, feet that hurry to rush into evil, a false witness who pours out lies, and one who stirs up dissension among the people (Proverbs 6:12-14,16-19).

In Bourdieu's view of human experience, human actions are only rarely the outcome of conscious deliberation or calculation in which pros and cons of different strategies are carefully weighed, the costs and benefits assessed, and ethical principles are applied to specific situations. People are conceived as fundamentally inattentive to what they are doing, according to Bourdieu, unless they are being objective.

Two consequences follow from his view that influence the way theological reflection operates. The first consequence has to do with our incapacity to speak in a way that others can hear when we make pronouncements based on theological reflection, if we do not take the body seriously. The second consequence has to do with the lack of skill we typically have in paying attention to what we are actually doing bodily. Hypocrisy can be an outcome of inattentiveness. I want to unite these two consequences in the following description of problems that inhere in theological education in order to refocus on self-observation, which I identified at the outset as the second aim in faith education. The development of faithful discernment depends upon the practice of attending to what we are doing through the developed capacity to observe ourselves.

People who wish to communicate effectively must attend to what they are doing and to the situation in which they are doing it. Our practices must be understood in terms of dynamics between the *habitus* and the field in which an action takes place. The *habitus* and the field may be in varying degrees compatible or congruent with one another, or they may be incompatible. If people's *habitus* is incompatible with the field in which they find themselves, they will not know how to act, speak or be heard. If the field in which they find themselves is not congruent with their *habitus*, they may be perceived as sluggish, apathetic or stupid. Their inertia directs them in a way that is mismatched to a particular field even though their practice makes sense to them. If they do not sense the differences between *habitus* and field, they will feel incompetent and may blame themselves, without comprehending the source of their difficulty. In contrast, *victorious* language users typically do not sense the privilege that inheres in their easy access to a field through their comfort with its language. To them, it is simply the way things are supposed to be. They base their success on personal merit and mistake the effects of an easy match with their prowess for fitting in.

But Jesus did not enjoy ease of access to his culture. People reared in the particularity of a culture, race, gender and social class, move in the same direction they have always proceeded in, as Jesus noted in religious leaders of his day. But once it is perceived and understood, inertia can be altered by external force. Jesus reversed the momentum of cultural drift in his own day. If theological reflection is to encourage maturity, we must learn our culture reflectively so as to exert force upon the momentum of everyday life in a way that allows well-conceived theological ideas to influence our action and speech. To use Bourdieu's terms, and using Christ's life as model, we must learn to be objective in the midst of our subjective experience.

How does the objective break work? To this point, I have described ordinary human experience as constructed through interactions with the social world, from birth. The results of enculturated, childhood interactions form dispositions within us that set us moving in a certain direction that is difficult to alter throughout a lifetime, unless we pay special attention. Our subjective impressions about human experience are affirmed through the daily momentum of our lives. To make matters difficult, we are ignorant of the history of experience that shapes the actions and speech of other people. We misread each other. We would do well to keep this in mind as we encounter the inevitable irritations and conflicts of life, but my point here has to do with misreading ourselves as the first step in losing our capacity to make sense of other people. If we read ourselves with reasonable accuracy, we may still misread others, but if we misread ourselves, we are quite likely to mistake others.

Bourdieu is cautious about our ability to read others because he believed observation itself is limited. The observer of an action, particularly a so-called impartial observer, is excluded from the real play of social activities in which that action has meaning. In observation, there is a tendency towards cognitive intellectualism. The impartial spectator is condemned, according to Bourdieu, to see all practice as spectacle. As spectacle, the observer mistakes action that to the participant has a meaning that is invisible to the outsider's eye. In general, Bourdieu sees subjectivist viewpoints as having their centre of gravity in the beliefs, desires and judgments of agents who are endowed and empowered to make meaningful the world in which they act. Objectivist viewpoints, on the other hand, explain social thought and action in terms of material and economic conditions, social structures, or cultural logics. From an objectivist viewpoint, the latter aspects of culture are seen as more powerful than are the agents themselves.[38]

Bourdieu explores weaknesses in both perspectives: objectivism depends on understanding and orientation that it does not make explicit to itself; subjectivism neglects to explore adequately the objective social conditions (cultural themes or structures) that produce subjective orientations. He believes that neither position entirely grasps social life. He is more interested in understanding social life in terms that do justice to objective, material, social and cultural structures and to the constituting practices and experiences of individuals and groups. To actually sense what is going on in a particular situation, one needs to work with outsider perceptions and insider practical mastery in a way that does not take the latter at face value. That is, Christian discernment should permit us to get inside and outside of personal experience so as to make sense of it, to experience life more truthfully.

How does Bourdieu think this iterative relation between being outside and being inside experience is accomplished? The relation takes place through an objective break with subjective experience. The point of the break is to make what is unconscious show up to the agent who acts, speaks, and who is able to improvise. To Bourdieu, emancipation means grasping the meaning of our actions (speech is an aspect of human action). Making the objective break requires that we understand human action in terms of communal patterns and not only individually, (by learning to be sociologically as well as psychologically astute). If theological reflection implies grasping the meaning of our own actions, by operating from inside as well as outside of them, we must work from inside and outside action in a way that is directed by understanding of the principles of faith that we prize.

When we operate on the basis of a theological idea, such as neighborliness, or the Golden Rule, we take account of what we are doing in light of our understanding of what it means to be neighbourly or empathetic. The implication of Bourdieu's concepts of *habitus* and *hexis* is that we become capable of identifying common cultural themes for acting and speaking, and sense how our actions and speech compare with those themes in light of faith principles. To reflect theologically is first of all to break with our experience and to pay attention to what we are saying/doing/being, in light of our theological principles, and to ask ourselves how we want to behave as people of faith. As a second move, self-understanding based on an objective break with subjective experience enables us to recognize what other people are doing that overtly differs from the way we act or speak so as to consider whether it is nonetheless a faithful representation of biblical principles, from their perspective. I focus on the first move, but the second is also essential in a globalized cultural context.

If I were "objective," how would I change?

Loving others as we love ourselves is the golden rule of Christianity. It is found in the OT as well. God commanded that we love one another. As scripture says, "Do not seek revenge or bear a grudge against one of your people, but love your neighbour as yourself. I am the Lord" (Leviticus 19:18); and, "Love your neighbour as yourself" (Matthew 19:19). At the heart of asking us to love others, there is an invitation to be people who tell each other the truth. Bourdieu believed his idea of *habitus* is operative in the possibility of seeing and saying things more truthfully.

As already mentioned, Bourdieu treats social life as a mutually constituting interaction of structures, dispositions and actions whereby social structures and embodied (and therefore situated) knowledge of those structures produce enduring orientations to action, which, in their turn, continue to be constitutive of those social structures. Cultural themes shape and are shaped by social practice so that they are structured structures and structuring structures—they shape us, we shape them as we act in the environment they produce. Our action or practice is not automatic (people are not robots), but it results from a process of improvisation that, in turn, is structured by cultural orientations, personal trajectories, and the ability to play the game of social interaction. It is in this sense that earlier, I urged teachers to be intentional about creating a spiritual learning environment in the classroom. To Bourdieu, the *habitus* has a capacity for structured improvisation. It is a system of general, generative schemes that are durable (inscribed in the social construction of the self) and transposable (from one field to another). These schemes function on an unconscious plane and take place in a structured place of possibilities that are defined by the intersection of material conditions and fields of operation. But they can become visible to us. The point of reflection is to let what is hard to perceive in the way we act become more visible and more susceptible to innovation. How do we learn to see what we are doing?

The *habitus* is inter-subjective and the site of the person-in-action; it is a system of dispositions that is subjective and objective. It is the dynamic intersection of structure and action, society and individual.

In the *hexis* reside common cultural, racial, and gendered ways of acting. The *habitus* is the personal site of the *hexis* and is capable of innovation. The notion of *habitus* enabled Bourdieu to analyze the behaviour of individuals as objectively co-ordinated and regular without being the product of rules, on the one hand, or conscious rationality, on the other. The *habitus* is meant to capture the practical mastery people have over their social situation, while grounding that mastery itself socially, as Dreyfus outlines in learning practical wisdom.

If we gather up fragments of Bourdieu's perspective, we have several perspectives and strategies that inform theological reflection. First, attempts to speak and be heard suffer or succeed in our struggles for social honour. The strategies we learned for speaking and being heard are grounded in cultural, racial, gendered, religious and social class locations. This means that we need to sense how victorious theological discourse is played out and learn to be heard without losing our distinctive voice.

Second, we must sense how the market place talks so that theological conversation can be well situated to bring healing into the world. The process for learning to speak and be heard theologically begins by breaking with the momentum of our acquired practices so that we can sense what we currently express and ask ourselves whether this is what we want to convey. In addition, we must gather insights into common themes (*hexis*) that structure human experience and reflect on our own behaviour (*habitus*) in light of those patterns. In the first four chapters, I outlined the ways in which all human beings are spiritual and have spiritual needs. It is on the basis of these needs that we can learn to talk about God publicly. In order to respond to human needs, we must hold clear, astute, Biblically responsible interpretations of Christian principles.

If we make use of Bourdieu in theological reflection, we must learn to work from inside and outside our everyday experience without denigrating either. Working from outside provides us with common themes in human experience. Working from inside keeps us in touch with what we understand ourselves to be doing/saying/being as competent agents of our own cultural setting. Allowing the outside to inform the inside, and *vice versa*, permits us to sense what we communicate and opens up an opportunity for reflection and change. The changes that we make are informed by a critical and scholarly understanding of principles of faith.

If theological reflection were to move us in these directions, human maturity grounded on faith principles could grow and perhaps flourish. But we cannot underestimate the resistance that the inertia of experience presents to mature growth. A prayer attributed to St. Francis of Assisi captures the dilemma: Make me an instrument of God's peace. Where there is hatred, let me sow love; where there is injury, pardon. We are aware of this plea and the poverty of our responses to be people of faith when we try to follow the pattern of Christ. We are painfully *unaware* of the momentum and practices of hatred, injury, doubt, despair, darkness and sadness that shape ordinary experience. In our *inattentiveness*, we contribute to this worldly inertia. But it is possible to be more aware. The notion of critical theological reflection shaped by Bourdieu's insights would provide some of the help for which St. Francis prayed. As we invite Christ's Spirit into a pause in subjective experience, to scrutinize behaviour and thought more 'objectively', He is with us, Immanuel!

THE HEART'S PRACTISE OF FREEDOM

Jesus said, "My command is this: Love each other as I have loved you." (John 15:12) How does loving others work as I practise embodied theological reflection? To illustrate, suppose I come to sense I am in conflict with a colleague and decide I want to stop that pattern. I see that I treat my colleague in a way I would not want to be treated. I experience the compelling force of Christ's way of being with others and reflect on his way of interacting in scripture. How can I change my behaviour? Perhaps I first notice behaviour between two other people (David and John) who I sense are in conflict. As I see how they speak to each other, I notice their actions intensify anxiety for everyone. Every time David speaks in a meeting, John immediately reacts with a challenging comment that implies criticism. I observe this pattern: David speaks immediately after John; John speaks immediately after David, each time to imply weakness or inadequacy in what the other has said.

Then, during a meeting I notice I speak immediately after the colleague that I sense I am in conflict with—every time she speaks, I speak immediately after her. Even though I habitually tell myself I am only trying to be helpful and that I care about the project so I will not allow her to detract from our success, I begin to feel suspicious about my motives. As I reflect on what I say each time she speaks, I realize my comments imply inadequacies in her utterance or perspective. Further, I notice that if she speaks or suggests something I turn away, gaze somewhere else, or look down, shuffle my feet. I do not look at her when she is speaking as I do when others speak. Then I notice that I search out other faces to see how colleagues are regarding her. In doing so, I try to discover whether others support her. Sometimes I even look directly at others in the group, searching for their agreement that she is speaking nonsense. In so doing, I hope to embody the message that she does not have our corporate support. I use slight movements: lifting an eyebrow, turning the head away, frowning, being restless.

In this way, I engage in bodily practices that typify the common human pattern of undermining another person. Thoughts that lead to my behaviour come from the heart and are conveyed by the body, working as one. If I become aware of what I am doing, I conclude I am in conflict with my colleague and my behaviour is an attempt to isolate her from the group so as to weaken her position and strengthen my own. Then I ask myself whether I want to be in conflict with her and whether it is right to treat her in this way: is this how I would want to be treated? If I behave this way to her, can I claim I am trying to discover what is pleasing to God?

Of course this is only one example. To reflect on what we are doing in other situations, we must note the common human pattern that people generally treat others *in the way they have been treated in the past themselves rather than the way they want to be treated*. This is the nature of opposition and revenge. The golden rule turns revenge on its head. If we wish to treat others as we want to be treated, our behaviour must be guided by an empathetic reversal of what we currently convey bodily. Someone might object and say that I should just talk to the colleague with whom I am in conflict. But I suggest we need to change our bodily practice for a time to prepare for that conversation. If I speak to her in a climate of disrespect, the conversation may never get off the ground. If I have more or less social power than she has, the conversation will be ineffective. I may miss an opportunity for genuine empathy because my bodily presence puts the lie to my words.[39]

Conflict is eased by altering the bodily disrespect I have been showing to my colleague. Contemplating all of these thoughts and sensing what we are communicating, I decide to convey openness rather than rejection. I look at her when she speaks. I do not pick away at what she says. I do not gossip about her. I do not garner support if others oppose her. I do not try to isolate her from the group. I demonstrate respect for her in ways that do not require me to say anything about the underlying conflict, at least, not yet. This does not imply I support everything she says or does, necessarily. Rather it compels me to show respect and honour to her humanity, even if we disagree.

In all of this activity, I keep in mind that I have only one plausible interpretation of the common themes I deploy to understand her. I recall Bourdieu's caveat about being imperialistic. We are well advised to hold our interpretation of common human themes as working hypotheses and be prepared to see the situation differently, if observation and communication bring new data. We work from inside and outside our own experience. Realizing that we may misinterpret the situation (e.g., I may fail to realize how she would like to be treated) we acknowledge that we begin the process of treating others with respect by following the Biblical principle to treat others as we want to be treated ourselves. Christ's love is our example. We reflect theologically on whether we express bodily the love Christ showed us Bodily.

In this case, embodied theological reflection from the heart limits the license I previously took with my colleague. In critically reflecting on a principle's meaning (e.g., the golden rule), I apply it to my situation. In doing so, I strip the principle of its merely cultural (traditional) investment so that I can see it more clearly and apply it more aptly. In changing my behaviour, my colleague and I may never reconcile our differences entirely to my satisfaction, but I have at least freed myself from the unreflective trap of perpetually reacting to others in conflict-ridden ways. I have refused hypocrisy. In so doing, I am making some headway in sowing peace. For all of us, in sensing what we are doing/being/saying, we practice bodily our own faithful liberation. It is in the trying that we succeed, as God gives us hope. Faith education relies on the practice of theological reflection that encompasses small, permanent changes in the life of a believer, changes that come about through loving God more than any other love, and understanding that learning mastery as a person of faith is hard spiritual work.

In my view, the outcome of faith education is embodied theological reflection as described in this chapter and is the whole import of this book. Faith produces the fruit of righteousness. When we ask how we learn the heart of God, I suggest we begin in the simple ways outlined in what I say about changing our behaviour. Righteousness implies actual change in the way things are done. Making ourselves right with God is accomplished in part by making ourselves right with others. I am comfortably certain of this: when God begins a good work in us, through faith, we come to see that we can change the world, one person at a time. But we only change the world in God's way when we are willing to allow that change to renovate our own hearts first. May God show you clearly how to be a person of faith. May you know the grace of our Saviour, as you practice being faithful.

NOTES

CHAPTER 1

[1] Alister McGrath, *The Twilight of Atheism* (New York: Doubleday, 2004), 76.

[2] David Hay and Rebecca Nye, *The Spirit of the Child* (London: Fount, 1998), 104.

[3] *Spirit of the Child*, 103-104.

[4] *Spirit of the Child*, 104.

[5] The Holy Spirit, uncapitalized, is mentioned in three times in the Old Testament: Psalm 51:11; Isaiah 63:10, 11 but is emphasized throughout the entire New Testament in 338 references (NRSV).

[6] *Spirit of the Child*, 9.

[7] Richard Dawkins, *The Selfish Gene* (London: Oxford University Press, 1989), x-xiii.

[8] Stephen Shennan, *Genes, Memes and Human History* (London: Thames & Hudson, 2002), 38.

[9] *Genes, Memes*, 37.

[10] *Spirit of the Child*, 151.

[11] *Spirit of the Child*, 152.

[12] Dean Hamer, *The God Gene: How faith is hardwired into our Genes* (New York: Doubleday, 2004), 180-196.

[13] See for example, *The God Gene*.

[14] See for example, Alister McGrath *Christian Spirituality* (London: Blackwell, 1999).

[15] *Spirit of the Child*, 120.

[16]*Spirit of the Child*, 99.

[17] *The God Gene*, 141.

[18] See for example, Robert Cloninger's work on self-transcendence. He is researcher at the Sansone Family Center for Well-Being, Washington University, St. Louis Missouri.

[19] *The God Gene*, 12.

[20] Ana-Maria Rizzuto, *The Birth of the Living God* (Chicago: Chicago of University Press, 1979), 41.

[21] Josephine Klein, *Our Need for Others and its Roots in Infancy* (London: Tavistock Publications, 1987), xv.

[22] *The Living God*, 178.

[23] *The Living God*, 90.

[24] *The Living God*, 177.

[25] D.W. Winnicott, *Playing and Reality* (London: Tavistock Publications, 1971), 53.

[26] Ana Maria Rizzuto, *Why Did Freud Reject God?* (London: Yale University Press, 1998).

[27] I am indebted to Sue Phillips' presentation at the International Conference on Children's Spirituality (King Alfred's College, Winchester, 200?) for her list that started me in the direction of identifying spiritual human needs.

[28] Martin Buber, *I and Thou* (New York: Charles Scribner's Sons, 1970), 78.

[29] *Playing and Reality*, 2.

[30] John Polkinghorne, *The God of Hope and the End of the World* (London: Yale University Press, 2002), 105.

[31] See for example, the patterns for linguistic and non-linguistic representation as presented in Robert J. Marzano, et al. *Classroom instruction that works*, (Alexandria, Virginia : Association for Supervision and Curriculum Development, 2001: 72-83.

[32] *Classroom instruction that works*, 72-83.

[33] Paulo Freire, *Pedagogy of the Oppressed* (New York: Continuum, 1970), 75-118.

[34] The concept of self-transcendence is based on research by Robert Cloninger, author of *Feeling Good: The science of Well-Being.*

[35] Jeffrey Kluger, "Is God in our Genes," in *Time Magazine*, October 25, 2004, 51.

³⁶ Scoring for the spiritual questionnaire:

1 point for each true

0 for each false

14 and above: highly spiritual, a real mystic

12-13: spiritually aware, easily lost in the moment;

8-11: spiritually average; could develop more spiritual life if desired;

6-7: a practical empiricist lacking self-transcendence;

1-5: highly sceptical, resistant to developing spiritual awareness

CHAPTER 2

¹ Robert Van de Weyer, (Ed.), *Pascal* (London: Hodder and Stoughton, 1997), 53.

² *The God Gene*, 47.

³ The Promiseland Model for educating children was developed by the Willowcreek Community Church in Chicago, Illinois, beginning in 1989.

⁴ Jerome W. Berryman, *Godly Play* (Minneapolis: Augsburg 1991).

⁵ Denise Peltomaki is Children's Pastor at Portico (formerly MGT Family Church) in Mississauga, Ontario Canada.

⁶ Corinne Ware, *Discover your Spiritual Type* (Bethesda, MD: An Alban Institute Publication 2000), 10.

⁷ *Your Spiritual Type*, 12.

⁸ *Your Spiritual Type*, 19.

⁹ *Your Spiritual Type*, 13.

¹⁰ Anabel Robinson, *The Life and Work of Jane Ellen Harrison* (London: Oxford, 2002), 214.

¹¹ *The Living God*, 41.

¹² Robert Kegan, *In Over Our Heads* (London: Harvard University Press, 1997), 266-270.

¹³ Robert Kegan, *The Evolving Self* (London: Harvard University Press, 1982), 7.

¹⁴ *The Evolving Self Evolving Self*, 7.

¹⁵ *Evolving Self*, 11.

¹⁶ Kegan seemed to contradict some of his reliance on Piaget when he wrote "In Over Our Heads" a decade later.

¹⁷ *Evolving Self*, 12.

[18] *The Spirit of the Child*, 11.

[19] *Evolving Self,* 76.

[20] *Evolving Self,* 76.

[21] *Evolving Self,* 28-45; 222.

[22] Charles Derber, *The Pursuit of Attention* (London: Oxford, 2000), xxiv.

[23] *The Evolving Self,* 211.

[24] *Pursuit of Attention,* xxv.

[25] R.F. Baumeister, *Escaping the self.* New York: Basic Books, 1991), 10.

26 *Evolving Self,* 17.

[27] *Evolving Self,* 17-18.

[28] *Evolving Self,* 19.

[29] *Evolving Self,* 19.

[30] *Evolving Self,* 142.

[31] *Evolving Self,* 126.

[32] *Evolving Self,* 126.

[33] *Evolving Self,* 162.

[34] *Evolving Self,* 126.

[35] Anna Fels, *Necessary Dreams: Ambition in Women's Changing Lives* (New York: Pantheon Books, 2004), 7.

[36] Miroslav Volf, *Exclusion and Embrace* (Nashville: Abingdon Press, 1996), 29.

[37] *Exclusion and Embrace,* 29-30.

[38] *Exclusion and Embrace,* 229.

[39] *Over Our Heads,* 157.

[40] Active complicity is not victim blaming but argues that dis-privileged people participant to some extent in their abuse by telling themselves a story that to a degree at least allows another person or persons to abuse them. The importance of active or passive complicity is seen when someone attempts to escape an insufferable situation. There must be some part played by the one abused so that an exit is made available by telling a new story to one's self.

[41] Spiritual education creates environments for children to learn work, but its methods must be more than teacher talk that is met with silence. While my emphasis throughout is on the environment established through the five activities, they also hold implications for methods teachers might use. Methods matter to spiritual sensibility.

[42] Antonio Gramsci, *Prison Notebooks* (New York: International Publishers, 1987), 24.

[43] *Prison Notebooks*, 24.

[44] *Prison Notebooks*, 29.

[45] *Prison Notebooks*, 31.

[46] Pierre Bourdieu, "The Forms of Capital," in John G. Richardson, (ed.), *Handbook of Theory and Research for the Sociology of Education* (New York: Green, 1983), 242.

[47] Schools can help develop independence and responsibility in each child; eventually all children become capable of sustained inquiry, moral maturity and civil action. Independence and responsibility are not inherently friendly companions. A desire for freedom resists constraints of duty and an emphasis on one at the expense of the other marks the trajectory of educational theory and practice. Those who prize independence fear instruction as a form of indoctrination which hinders the free flight of intellectual inquiry. Those who prize responsibility disdain learner-directed approaches they think foster procrastination and impoverish intellectual habits of mind and body. In contrast to that dichotomy, Gramsci married independence to responsibility in what he called creative schools.

[48] *Prison Notebooks*, 32.

[49] Judy Harris Helm and Lilian Katz, *Young Investigators: The project approach in the early years*, New York and London: Teachers College, Columbia University, 2001. For a good example of the work children do through the Project Approach, see Karen L. Bellous, "Looking at the Trees Around Us," in Early Childhood Research and Practice (Spring) 2004 Vol. 6. No. 1 http://ecrp.uiuc.edu/v6n1/index.html

[50] Forms of Capital, 241.

[51] Forms of Capital, 248-250.

[52] *Prison Notebooks*, 34.

[53] George A. Hillery, *Communal Organizations* (Chicago: The University of Chicago Press, 1972), 226-227.

[54] *Prison Notebooks*, 29.

[55] *Prison Notebooks*, 33.

[56] *Evolving Self*, 129.

[57] *Evolving Self*, 129.

[58] *Evolving Self*, 13.

[59] *Evolving Self*, 215.

[60] *Evolving Self*, 232.

[61] *Over Our Heads*, 220.

[62] *Over Our Heads*, 221-222.

[63] *Why Did Freud Reject God*, 201.

CHAPTER 3

[1] Anthony M Coniaris, *Philokalia: the Bible of Orthodox Spirituality* (Minneapolis, MN: Light and Life Publishing Company, 1998), 37-38.

[2] An early version is published as "Faith and Social Intimacy: Learning for Life," in *Spiritual Education* Cathy Ota and Clive Erricker (Eds.) Brighton: Sussex Academic Press, 2005), 123-136.

[3] Michel Foucault, *Discipline and Punish* (New York: Vintage Books, 1979).

[4] Joyce E. Bellous, "Reclaiming EvilTalk," in *Lire Baudrillard aujourd'hui/ Reading Baudrillard Now* Association canadienne de semiotique/Canadian Semiotic Association Vol. 16, Nos 1-2, 1996:27-47.

[5] Henri Nouwen, *Intimacy* New York: Harper San Francisco, 1969: 19.

[6] John Polkinghorne, *The God of Hope and the End of the World*, (New Haven and London: Yale University Press, 2002), xxii.

[7] *The God of Hope*, xxii.

[8] *Intimacy*, 13.

[9] James B. Pratt, *The Religious Consciousness: A psychological study* (New York: MacMillan Company, 1956), 2.

[10] Pratt used this definition and others to describe religion itself. His perspective is particularly instructive when applied to faith, which to me is the more appropriate term for the psychological aspect of religion that he wished to explain. See *Religious Consciousness*, 2-3.

[11] Immanuel Kant, *Religion within the Boundaries of Mere Reason* (Cambridge: Cambridge University Press, 1998) 118.

[12] *The God of Hope*, 31.

[13] Douglas Coupland, *Life After God*, (New York: Pocket Books, 1994).

[14] *Religious Consciousness,* 1-44.

[15] Immanuel Kant, *Religion Within the Boundaries* of Mere Reason, (Cambridge: Cambridge University Press, 1998), 1-14.

[16] Wittgenstein is responding to G.E. Moore's essays, "Proof of an External World," and "A Defence of Common Sense, both of which are in Moore's *Philo-*

sophical Papers, London: George Allen and Unwin, 1959.

[17] Ludwig Wittgenstein, *On Certainty* (Oxford, England: Basil Blackwell, 1979), #94.

[18] *On Certainty, #96.*

19 On Certainty, #97.

[20] *On Certainty, #141.*

[21] *On Certainty, #144.*

[22] *On Certainty, #336.*

[23] *On Certainty, #357.*

[24] *On Certainty, #358.*

[25] *On Certainty, #378.*

[26] *On Certainty, #625.*

[27] *The Interpreter's Dictionary of the Bible* George A. Buttrick, ed., (New York: Abingdon Press, 1962), 222.

[28] *Interpreter's Dictionary,* 228.

[29] Gregory Vlastos, *Socrates: Ironist and Moral Philosophe*r (Ithaca, New York: Cornell University Press, 1991), see pages 236-242 for his demonstration of the notion of complex irony. The analysis of the term is taken from 1-44.

[30] *Socrates: Ironist,* 21.

[31] Joyce E. Bellous, "Spiritual and Ethical Orality in Children" in International Journal of Children's Spirituality, Vol. 5, No.1, 2000:12.

[32] Thorleif Boman, *HebrewThought Compared with Greek* (New York: W.W. Norton & Company, 1960).

[33] *The God of Hope,* 49.

[34] *The God of Hope,* xvii.

[35] Acts 15:24-29.

[36] *Religion within the Boundaries,* 5.

[37] Kant, "What is Enlightenment?"

[38] *Religion within the Boundaries,* 7.

[39] *Religion within the Boundaries,* 7.

[40] *Religion within the Boundaries,* 8.

[41] *Religion within the Boundaries,* 13.

[42] Religion within the Boundaries, 14.

[43] I am not suggesting that Kant is not Christian. Rather, like Hegel, Kant aimed to trim Christianity to fit the needs of the social world that was develop-

ing during his life time. He wanted morality to be based in both Christianity and secular senses of obligation to do one's duty. For Kant, true religion was do to one's duty for the sake of Duty alone.

⁴⁴ Selma H. Fraiberg, *The Magic Years* (New York: Charles Scribner's Sons, 1959), ix.

⁴⁵ *The Living God.*

⁴⁶ *The Living God*, 187.

⁴⁷ Barbara A. Misztal, *Trust in Modern Societies* (Cambridge, UK: Polity Press, 1996).

⁴⁸ *Trust*, 3.

⁴⁹ *Trust*, 5.

⁵⁰ *Trust*, 6.

⁵¹ *Trust*, 12-14.

⁵² *Trust*, 15-16.

⁵³ *Trust*, 19.

⁵⁴ *Trust*, 20.

⁵⁵ *Trust*, 20-23.

⁵⁶ *Trust*, 101.

⁵⁷ Henri JM Nouwen, *Intimacy* (New York: HarperSan Francisco, 1969), 2.

⁵⁸ *Intimacy*, 12.

⁵⁹ *Religious Consciousness*, 101.

⁶⁰ *Intimacy*, 17.

⁶¹ Harriet G. Lerner, *The Dance of Intimacy* (New York: Harper & Row, Publishers, 1989), 2.

⁶² *Dance of Intimacy*, 2. Lerner uses the word connectedness rather than closeness but I prefer closeness since I think our connections prevail despite physical distance.

⁶³ Elaine Storkey, *The Search for Intimacy* (Michigan: Eerdmans, 1995), 60.

⁶⁴ *The Dance of Intimacy*, 70.

⁶⁵ *The Dance of Intimacy*, 209.

⁶⁶ *The Search for Intimacy*, 45.

⁶⁷ Hubert L. Dreyfus, *On the Internet* (New York: Routledge, 2001), 77.

⁶⁸ *On the Internet*, 78.

⁶⁹ *On the Internet*, 81.

⁷⁰ *On the Internet*, 33-49.

[71] "The Theatre of Learning: Five techniques to develop ten aspects of universal spirituality in children," 8.

CHAPTER FOUR

[1] G.E.H. Palmer, Philip Sherrard and Kallistos Ware, *The Philokalia* Vol. 3 (London: Faber and Faber, 1984), 35.

[2] A short, earlier version appears as "Learning the Art of Self-Regard," in the *Journal of Christian Education*, Allan Harkness, (Ed.), Australian Christian Forum on Education, Vol. 46, No.1, (May, 2003), 7-19.

[3] Henri Nouwen, *The Life of the Beloved* (New York: Crossroad Publishing Company, 1992), 31.

[4] Edward Said, "Introduction," in E. Auerbach, *Mimesis* (Princeton, NJ: Princeton University Press, 2003), xxiv.

[5] *Pursuit of Attention*, xxiv.

[6] John Dewey, *Art as Experience* (New York: A Perigee Book, 1980), 3-19.

[7] Courtney Wilson, written in a paper for C M 1EO3 April, 2003, McMaster Divinity College, Hamilton Ontario, page 9. Used with written permission.

[8] *Christian Spirituality*, 12.

[9] Ellen T. Charry, *By the Renewing of Your Minds* (New York: Oxford University Press, 1997), 19.

[10] G.E.H. Palmer, Philip Sherrard and Kallistos Ware, *The Philokalia* Vol. 1 (London: Faber and Faber, 1983), 198.

[11] *Philokalia* Vol. 1, 91.

[12] *Renewing of Your Minds*, 76.

[13] *Philokalia* Vol. 3, 92.

[14] G.E.H. Palmer, Philip Sherrard and Kallistos Ware, *The Philokalia* Vol. 2 (London: Faber and Faber, 1981), 262.

[15] G.E.H. Palmer, Philip Sherrard and Kallistos Ware, *The Philokalia* Vol. 4 (London: Faber and Faber, 1995), 272.

[16] *Philokalia* Vol. 2, 92.

[17] Colin Morris, *The Discovery of the Individual* Toronto, ON: University of Toronto Press, 2000), 85-86.

[18] *Discovery of the Individual*, 86.

[19] *Discovery of the Individual*, 153.

[20] *Discovery of the Individual*, 154.

21 *Discovery of the Individual,* 155.

22 *Discovery of the Individual,* 155.

23 *Discovery of the Individual,* 155.

24 *Philokalia* Vol. 2, 92.

25 Thomas À Kempis, *Of the Imitation of Christ* (Philadelphia, PA: Henry Altemus, Pubisher. Original work published in the fifteenth century), see pages 120, 122, 127, 109, 121, 131, 128, 159, 161, 186, 193-195, 201-209, 211-213, 222-227, 231, 243, 254-256, 262, 264.

26 *Imitation of Christ,* 120.

27 *Imitation of Christ,* 131.

28 *Imitation of Christ,* 159.

29 *Imitation of Christ,* 262-263.

30 N.J.H. Dent, *A Rousseau Dictionary* (Oxford: Blackwell, 1992), 30.

31 *Rousseau Dictionary,* 30.

32 *Rousseau Dictionary* Dent 1992, 30.

33 Immanuel Kant, The Metaphysics of Morals, M. Gregor, trans. (Cambridge: Cambridge University Press, 1996), 87.

34 Metaphysics of Morals, 187.

35 Metaphysics of Morals, 184.

36 Metaphysics of Morals, 225.

37 R. F. Baumeister *The Self in Social Psychology* (New York: Basic Books, 1999), 219.

38 *Self in Social Psychology,* 219.

39 *Self in Social Psychology,* 219.

40 *Self in Social Psychology,* 220.

41 *Self in Social Psychology,* 220.

42 Pursuit of Attention, xxv.

43 *Escaping the Self,* 10.

44 *The Living God,* 105-107.

45 *The Living God,* 178.

46 *Why did Freud Reject God?*

47 *The Living God,* 177.

48 *The Living God,* 188.

49 *Playing and Reality,* 2.

[50] *Playing and Reality*, 4.

[51] *Art as Experience*, 6.

[52] *Art as Experience*, 13ff.

[53] *The Living God*, 181.

[54] *The Living God*, 91.

[55] *The Living God*, 208.

[56] *The Living God*, 211.

[57] *The Living God*, 210.

[58] *The Living God*, 179.

[59] *The Living God*, 180.

[60] *The Living God*, 199.

[61] *Philokalia* Vol. 3, 35, 39.

[62] *Philokalia* Vol. 3, 38.

[63] *Philokalia*, Vol. 4, 34.

[64] George A. Buttrick, (Ed.), *Interpreter's Dictionary of the Bible*, Vol. II (New York: Abingdon Press, 1962), 256.

[65] Gerhard Kittel and Gerhard Friedrich, *Theological Dictionary of the New Testament* Vol. IX, (Grand Rapids, Michigan: Eerdmans, 1994), 208-217.

[66] *The Living God*, 90; Marcia Bunge, *The Child in Christian Thought* (Eerdmans, 2000), 13-16.

[67] Charles Taylor, *The Ethics of Authenticity* (Cambridge, MA: Harvard University Press, 1991), 16.

[68] *Authenticity*, 16.

[69] *Authenticity*, 17.

[70] *The Child in Christian Thought*, 13-16.

[71] *Authenticity*, 16.

[72] *Authenticity*, 16.

[73] *Authenticity*, 17.

[74] *Authenticity*, 33.

[75] Howard Gardner, *Frames of Mind* (New York: Basic Books, 1983); Howard Gardner *Multiple Intelligences* (New York: Basic Books, 1993).

[76] *Frames of Mind*, 60.

CHAPTER 5

[1] David Adam, *The Rhythm of Life* (Harrisburg, PA: Morehouse Publishing, 1996), 79.

[2] Immanuel Kant, "An Answer to the Question: 'What is Enlightenment?'" in *Kant: Political Writings* Hans Reiss, ed., (Cambridge: Cambridge University Press, 1991), 54.

[3] Jose Casanova, *Public Religions in the Modern World* (Chicago, London: The University of Chicago Press, 1994).

[4] Joyce E. Bellous, "Reclaiming EvilTalk," in *Lire Baudrillard aujourd'hui/ Reading Baudrillard Now* Association canadienne de semiotique/Canadian Semiotic Association, Vol. 16, Nos. 1-2, 1996: 27-47.

[5] *Living God*, 3.

[6] John 6: 28-29.

[7] Henri J.M. Nouwen, *Bread for the Journey* (New York: Harper San Francisco, 1997), February 9.

[8] *Why Did Freud Reject God?*

[9] *Why Did Freud Reject God,* 264.

[10] A short, earlier version is printed in *Spirituality of Children: talking with children talking with God* The Third Biennial John Gilmour Lectures (Peterborough, Ontario: Murray Street Baptist Church, 2000), 1-12.

[11] *Living God*, 7.

[12] *Living God,* 187.

[13] Daniel N. Stern, *The Intersubjective World of Infants,* (New York: Basic Books, 1985), 22.

[14] *Living God*, 185.

[15] *Living God*, 187.

[16] The mother/infant relation is complex; see *Living God,* 185ff for example.

[17] *Living God,* 8.

[18] *Living God,* 209.

[19] *Living God,* 209.

[20] *Living God,* 178.

[21] *Living God,* 10.

[22] *Living God,* 48.

[23] *Living God,* 90.

[24] Robert Putnam, *Bowling Alone* (New York: Simon and Schuster, 2000), 277-284.

CHAPTER 6

[1] Annie Dillard, *For the Time Being* (Toronto, Ontario: Penguin Books Canada, 2000), 19.

[2] Patsy Rodenburg, *The Right to Speak* (New York: Routledge, 1992), 93.

[3] Mary Carruthers, *A Book of Memory* (Cambridge: Cambridge University Press, 1990).

[4] "What is Enlightenment," 54-60.

[5] Sigmund Freud, *The Future of an Illusion* (New York: W.W. Norton & Company, 1961), 55-56.

[6] Paul, Ricoeur *Freud and Philosophy: An Essay on Interpretation* (New York: Yale University Press, 1970), 369.

[7] *Why did Freud Reject God.*

[8] Sigmund Freud, *Totem and Taboo: resemblances between the psychic lives of savages [sic] and neurotics* A.A. Brill (trans.), (New York: A Vintage book, 1946), 60ff.

[9] Milaly Csikszentmihalyi, *Becoming Adult* (New York: Basic Books, 2000), 113-139.

[10] Mary Pipher, *Reviving Ophelia: Saving the selves of Adolescent Girls.* New York: Ballantine Books, 1994.

[11] Ludwig Wittgenstein, *On Certainty* (Oxford: Basil Blackwell, 1979), #110-#134.

[12] Tom Driver, *The Magic of Ritual* (New York: Harper San Francisco, 1991), 29.

[13] *Magic of Ritual,* 58.

[14] *On Certainty,* #144.

[15] *Living God.*

[16] *Magic of Ritual,* 46.

[17] *Magic of Ritual,* 39-47.

[18] Mary Douglas, *Natural Symbols.* New York: Pantheon Books, 1982.

[19] *Natural Symbols,* xxii.

[20] *Natural Symbols,* 33.

[21] *Becoming Adult,* 115.

[22] Sigmund Freud, *The Future of an Illusion* (New York: W.W. Norton & Company, 1961), 47.

[23] Sigmund Freud, *Civilisation and its Discontents* pages?

[24] *Future of Illusion*, 43.

[25] *Future of Illusion*, 43.

[26] *Future of Illusion*, 49.

[27] *Future of Illusion*, 50.

[28] *Future of Illusion*, 52.

[29] *Future of an Illusion*, 15-33.

[30] Sigmund Freud, *Moses and Monotheism* (New York: Vintage Books, 1939), 137.

[31] Jeffrey Masson, *Final Analysis: The making and unmaking of a Psychoanalyst* (New York: Addison-Wesley Publishing Company, Inc., 1990), 177.

[32] Hans Kung, *Freud and the Problem of God* (New Haven: Yale University Press, 1979), 5. According to Kung, Feuerbach is the intellectual grandfather to both Marxist and Freudian atheism.

[33] *The Problem of God*, 5.

[34] *The Problem of God*, 5.

[35] The first law of thermodynamics affirms that the sum total of energy remains constant in any isolated system, no matter what changes take place in the individual energy components (mechanical, electrical, radiant or chemical).

[36] The law of entropy affirms that heat can never be changed back completely into energy; which is the most fundamental of the laws of natural forces.

[37] Why did Freud Reject God? See for example, 1-6, 18, 131 and 260.

[38] Sigmund Freud, *The Problem of Anxiety* (New York: W.W. Norton & Company, 1936), 20-73.

[39] Meister Eckhart, *The Essential Sermons, Commentaries, Treatises, and Defense* Edmund Colledge and Bernard McGinn, (trans.), (New York: Paulist Press, 1981).

[40] *Problem of Anxiety*, 7.

[41] *Essential Sermons*, xi.

[42] *Essential Sermons*, xiii.

[43] *Freud and Philosophy*, 345.

[44] *Freud and Philosophy*, 533.

[45] Sigmund Freud, *An outline of Psychoanalysis* (New York: W.W. Norton, 1949).

⁴⁶ *Freud and Philosophy*, 534.

⁴⁷ *Freud and Philosophy*, 548.

⁴⁸ *Freud and Philosophy*, 548.

CHAPTER 7

¹ *Totem and Taboo*, 118.

² *For the Time Being*, 77.

³ *Philokalia*, Vol. 2, 385.

⁴ *On Certainty*, #94.

⁵ *On Certainty*, #99.

⁶ *On Certainty*, #160.

⁷ *On Certainty*, #211.

⁸ *On Certainty*, #341.

⁹*On Certainty*, #449.

¹⁰*On Certainty*, #343.

¹¹*On Certainty*, #357.

¹² *Totem and Taboo*, 101.

¹³ *Totem and Taboo*, 97.

¹⁴ *Totem and Taboo*, 124.

¹⁵ *Totem and Taboo* , 113.

¹⁶ The separate texts of *The Philokalia* were compiled in the eighteenth century and first published in Greek at Venice in 1782. Some of the texts were also translated into Slavonic and published at Moscow in 1793. The separate texts of *The Philokalia* were compiled in the eighteenth century and first published in Greek at Venice in 1782. Some of the texts were also translated into Slavonic and published at Moscow in 1793.

¹⁷ *Philokalia* Vol. 1, 13.

¹⁸ *Philokalia* Vol. 3, 34-35.

¹⁹ *Philokalia* Vol. I, 22-28.

²⁰ While Kant purified reason of its pre-modern taint, he also admitted its limitations. See "What is it that orients thinking" in *Religion within the Boundaries of Mere Reason*.

²¹ *Philokalia*, Vol. 1, 26.

²² *Philokalia*, Vol. 1, 171.

[23] *Philokalia* Vol. 3, 29.

[24] Dorothee Sollee, *Creative Disobedience* (Cleveland, Ohio: The Pilgrim Press, 1995).

[25] Alexander Nehamas's, *The Art of Living* (Berkeley, London: The University of California Press, 1998), 179.

[26] find quotation in Communication stuff, also is in something I've written recently.

[27] *Philokalia* Vol. 1, 161.

[28] *Art of Living*, 9-15.

[29] *Art of Living*, 184.

[30] Ernest Jones, *The Life and Work of Sigmund Freud*, edited and abridged by Lionel Trilling and Steven Marcus (Harmondsworth, Middlesex, England: Penguin Books, 1981), 433.

[31] Paul Avis, *God and the Creative Imagination* (London and New York: Routledge, 1999), 23.

[32] Martin Heidegger, *Hegel's Concept of Experience*, (New York: Harper & Row, Publishers, 1989), 23.

[33] See a description of these three modes of world in the existential psychologist, Rollo May, *The Discovery of Being* (New York: W.W. Norton & Company, 1983), 126-132.

[34] *Hegel's Concept*, 65.

[35] Charles Taylor, *Hegel and Modern Society* (New York: Cambridge University Press, 1979), 54.

[36] *Hegel's Concept*, 56.

[37] Michael Inwood, *A Hegel Dictionary* (Cambridge, Massachusetts: Basil Blackwell Inc., 1995), 96.

[38] Taylor points out that, to Hegel, the motor of dialectics is contradiction or in Taylor's own terms, ontological conflict in human experience: "Finite beings just in virtue of existing externally in space and time make a claim to independence, while the very basis of their existence is that they express a spirit which cannot brook this independence" (*Hegel and Society,* 46).

[39] *Hegel and Society*, 46.

[40] *Hegel and Society*, 48.

[41] *Hegel and Society*, 48-49.

[42] Sigmund Freud, *The Interpretation of Dreams* (London: Penguin Books, 1991), 174.

43. *Interpretation of Dreams*, 176.

44. *Interpretation of Dreams*, 177-178.

45. Martin Heidegger, *Hegel's Concept of Experience* (New York: Harper & Row, 1989), 119.

46. Growth of self-consciousness is social because consciousness has three notable features: a. it proceeds through increasingly adequate stages (i.e., it 'grows') and it is dependent on the social world for the maturation of this growth potential; b. it is essentially interpersonal and requires the reciprocal recognition of self-conscious beings (an I that is a we; a we that is an I); c. it is practical and cognitive: self-consciousness exists in a world of alien others and finds itself in those others. The other is essential to consciousness. To Hegel, this implies the establishment and operation of social institutions as well as scientific and philosophical inquiry (*Hegel Dictionary*, 62-63).

CHAPTER 8

1 Immanuel Kant, *Education* (USA: Ann Arbor Paperbacks, The University of Michigan Press, 1960), 16.

2 Bernard J.F. Lonergan, *Insight* (New York: Harper San Francisco, 1957), x.

3 Michel Foucault, *The History of Sexuality Vol. 1* (New York: Vintage Books, 1990), 85.

4 Michel Foucault, "an ethic of care for the self as a practice of freedom," in *The Final Foucault* (Cambridge: The MIT Press, 1988), 3.

5 *Frames of Mind; Multiple Intelligences.*

6 *Frames of Mind*, x.

7 *Frames of Mind*, 60.

8 *Frames of Mind*, 61.

9 *Metaphysics of Morals*, 223.

10 For a fuller discussion, see Joyce E. Bellous, "Spiritual and Ethical Orality in Children: educating an oral self," in the International Journal of Children's Spirituality, Vol. 5, No. 1, 2000: 13-16.

11 See Halvor Moxnes, "Honour and Shame," in the *Biblical Theological Bulletin*, Vol. 23 167-176; Jerome H. Neyrey, (ed.) *The Social World of Luke-Acts* (Peabody, Massachusetts: Hendrickson, 1991); Adrienne Rich, "Women and Honour: Some notes on lying (1975)," in *On Lies, Secrets and Silence, Selected Prose (1966-1978)* New York: W.W. Norton & Company, 1979, 185-194; Pilch, John J. "Beat His Ribs While He is Young," in *Biblical Theology*

Bulletin Vol. 23, No. 3 (Fall) 1993: 101-113; Aristotle, *Ethics (London: Penguin Books, 1955);* M. Strauss, "A Sociological Perspective on the Causes of Family Violence, in M.R. Green, ed., *Violence and the Family.* Boulder: Westview Press, 1980.

[12] Joyce E. Bellous, "Spiritual and Ethical Orality in Children, Educating an Oral Self," for the *International Journal of Children's Spirituality*, edited by Cathy Ota. Chichester Institute of Higher Education, Chichester, England, (June), 5.1. 2000.

[13] Bruce J. Malina and Jerome H. Neyrey, "First-Century Personality: Dyadic, not Individual," in *The Social World of Luke-Acts* J.H. Neyrey, ed., (Peabody, Massachusetts: Hendrickson, 1991), 73.

[14] "Beat His Ribs," 101-113.

[15] "First-Century Personality," 80.

[16] I have organized 27 Psalms into what I call the Psalms of opposition. The 4 common characteristics of these poems include: a problem or request, personal reference, a description of an enemy or enemies and a view of God in which God will help but has not yet done so. Psalms of Opposition are the following: 3, 7, 17, 22, 25, 26, 27, 31, 35, 36, 37, 40, 41, 54, 55, 56, 57, 59, 62, 64, 69, 70, 71, 86, 109, 140, 142.

[17] Walter Brueggemann, *The Message of the Psalms: A theological commentary* (Minneapolis: Augsburg, 1984). Brueggemann analyzes 4 of what I call the 25 Psalms of opposition.

[18] *Message of the Psalms,* 9.

[19] *Message of the Psalms*, 85.

[20] See for example, John 8: 58.

CHAPTER 9

[1] Marshall B. Rosenberg, *Non-violent Communication* (Encinitas, CA: Puddledancer Press, 2000).

[2] *Non-violent Communication,* 144.

[3] *Oxford English Dictionary.*

[4] *Canadian Oxford Dictionary.*

[5] Nel Noddings, *Caring: A Feminine Approach to Ethics and Moral Education* (Berkeley, California: University of California Press, 1984), 30-32.

[6] David Burns, *Feeling Good: The new mood therapy* (New York: Avon Books, 1992), 135.

[7] Edith Stein, *On the Problem of Empathy* Waltraut Stein trans., (The Neth-

erlands: Martinus Nijhoff, The Hague, 1964).

[8] *Feeling Good*, 135-137.

[9] Woodruff Smith, *The Circle of Acquaintance: Perception, Consciousness and Empathy*, (Boston: Kluwer Academic Publishers, 1989), 155.

[10] *Problem of Empathy*, 9-13. Edith Stein was a student of Husserl and was killed by the Nazis during WW II.

[11] *Non-Violent Communication*, 119.

[12] *Problem of Empathy*, 14.

[13] Edith Stein refers to the first and third aspects of experience as primordial and non-primordial, but I do not find her language helpful. Direct or primordial experience refers to experience in which the object is present before me here and now. Primordial experience is actual experience but she prefers the term primordial.

[14] *Feeling Good,* 137ff.

[15] Daniel N. Stern, *The Interpersonal World of Infants* (New York: Basic Books, 1985).

[16] *Interpersonal World*, 36.

[17] *Interpersonal World*, 174-182.

[18] *Interpersonal World*, 174.

[19] *Interpersonal World*, 177.

[20] Johannes A. van der Ven, *Formation of the Moral Self* (Grand Rapids, Michigan: Eerdmans, 1998), 313-315.

[21] A good test of our capacity for empathy is found by exploring the following website, http://sharemyworld.net

CHAPTER 10

[1] Andrew J Strathern, *Body Thoughts* (Ann Arbor, Michigan: The University of Michigan Press, 1996), 38.

[2] The term stage implies that later development is dependent on and grows out of earlier aspects of the process.

[3] Thorlief Boman, *Hebrew Thought Compared with Greek* (New York: W.W. Norton & Company, 1960), 12.

[4] *Hebrew Compared with Greek*, 27-73.

[5] J. Henry Harris, *Robert Raikes. The Man who founded the Sunday School* London: The Sunday School Union. This book does not provide a publishing date. From the text I assume it was published in 1854, since it celebrates the

120th Anniversary of the Sunday School. The date given for the commencement of Sunday School is 1734.

⁶ Gerhard Kittel (Ed.), *Theological Dictionary of the New Testament* Vol. III (Grand Rapids, Michigan: Eerdmans, 1968), 611.

⁷ *Theological Dictionary,* Vol. III, 25-27.

⁸ I agree with Hannah Arendt that "[t]hinking, willing, and judging are the three basic mental activities [and that] they cannot be derived from each other and though they have certain common characteristics they cannot be reduced to a common denominator." See *The Life of the Mind* Vol. 1 (New York: Harcourt Brace Jovanovich, 1978), 69. In outlining the history of the concept of the will, Hannah Arendt (1906-1975) points out that resistance to the concept may have been primarily due to its absence from ancient Greek thought, although she suggested that, in her view, Aristotle's idea of *proairesis* was a kind of forerunner of the will. *The Life of the Mind,* Section Two: Willing, 6.

⁹ *Arche* refers to a beginning, starting point, principle, ultimate underlying substance; ultimate non-demonstrable principle, see F.E. Peters *Greek Philosophical Terms: a historical lexicon* (New York: New York University Press, 1967), 23.

¹⁰ *Concise Routledge Encyclopedia of Philosophy* (London: Routledge, 2000), 851.

¹¹ Aristotle, *Ethics* (Harmondsworth: Penguin Books, 1976).

¹²*Greek Philosophical Terms*, 96-97.

¹³ *Hebrew Compared with Greek*, 205.

¹⁴ *Theological Dictionary Vol. III*, 605-614.

¹⁵ *Theological Dictionary Vol. III*, 608.

¹⁶Gerhard Kittel and Gerhard Friedrich, *Theological Dictionary of the New Testament* Vol. IX, (Grand Rapids, Michigan: Eerdmans, 1974), 626-631.

¹⁷ *Theological Dictionary Vol. IX,* 627.

¹⁸ I discuss the inherent limitations on inquiry in an essay titled, "On Thinking OtherWise." Response to Elmer Thiessen's, "Academic Freedom and Religious Colleges and Universities: Confronting the Postmodern Challenge," in *Paideusis*, 10, 1, Fall 1996.

¹⁹ Charles M. Wood, "Theological Inquiry and Theological Education," in *Theological Education* 1985 (Spring), Vol. XXI, No. 2, 73-93. Also see, Charles Wood, *Vision and Discernment* (Atlanta, Georgia: Scholars Press, 1985).

²⁰ "Theological Inquiry," 82.

²¹ *Body Thoughts*, 3.

²² *Body Thoughts,* 4.

²³ *Body Thoughts,* 5.

²⁴John Cottingham argues persuasively that Descartes' later view of a person as a union between mind and body overcame the bifurcation of mind and body that is commonly associated with his contribution to philosophy. See John Cottingham, *Descartes* (London: Phoenix, 1997).

²⁵ Pierre Bourdieu, *Outline of a Theory of Practice* (Cambridge: Cambridge University Press, 1977), 10-15.

²⁶ Pierre Bourdieu, *In Other Words: Essays towards a reflexive sociology* Matthew Adamson trans., (Cambridge, England: Polity Press, 1990), 22.

²⁷ Pierre Bourdieu, *Language and Symbolic Power* Gino Raymond and Matthew Adamson trans., (Cambridge, Massachusetts: Harvard University Press, 1991.

²⁸ In recent work titled, *The Rules of Art: The Genesis and Structure of the Literary Field,* Stanford California: Stanford University Press, 1995). Bourdieu plays out the possibilities of speaking and being heard in a given field when one is using insights that are unique and unusual to its momentum. I am indebted to my research assistant, Paul Bellows, for this insight.

²⁹ J.L. Austin, *How to Do Things with Words* Cambridge, Massachusetts: Harvard University Press, 1962.

³⁰ *Language and Symbolic Power,* 8.

³¹ Thinking and feeling are inter-related in cognition. See Renate Nummela Caine and Geoffrey Caine, *Making Connections: Teaching and the Human Brain* (New York; Addison-Wesley, 1991), 90.

³² *Frames of Mind,* xvi-xvii.

³³ *Frames of Mind,* xvii.

³⁴ See the discussion of bracketing in Irena R. Makaryk, (ed) *Encyclopedia of Contemporary Literary Terms: Approaches, Scholars, Terms* (Toronto: Toronto University Press, 1995), 511-514.

³⁵ *Language and Symbolic Power,* 17.

³⁶ This expression refers to the degree of lip movement used when pronouncing words.

³⁷ *Language and Symbolic Power,* 17.

³⁸ Craig Calhoun, Edward Li Puma and Moishe Postone, (eds) *Bourdieu, Critical Perspectives* (Great Britain: Polity Press, 1993), 3.

³⁹ I want to distinguish empathy from sympathy and support. In sympathy, I am able to feel what D feels. In support, I am able to agree with and encourage

D in the direction D is moving. In empathy, I am able to articulate D's position in a way that D would agree accurately portrays its meaning, but I may neither sympathize with nor support it.

CPSIA information can be obtained at www.ICGtesting.com
Printed in the USA
LVOW08s0607150916

504721LV00001B/2/P